THE DESTRUCTION

OF

THE GREEK EMPIRE.

The Destruction of the Greek Empire and the Story of the Capture of Constantinople by the Turks

BY

EDWIN PEARS, LL.B.

Knight of the Greek Order of the Saviour and Commander of
the Bulgarian Order of Merit

WITH MAPS AND ILLUSTRATIONS

GREENWOOD PRESS, PUBLISHERS
NEW YORK

Originally published in 1903 by Longmans, Green and Co.

First Greenwood Reprinting, 1968

Library of Congress Catalogue Card Number: 69-14032

PREFACE

MY object in writing this book is to give an account of the capture of Constantinople and the destruction of the Greek empire. In order to make the story intelligible and to explain its significance I have given a summary of the history of the empire between the Latin conquest in 1204 and the capture of the city in 1453, and have traced the progress during the same period of the race which succeeded in destroying the empire and in replacing the Greeks as the possessors of New Rome.

It may be objected that the task which I have set before me has already been accomplished by Gibbon, and that, as his chapter on the last siege of the city is carefully compiled and written with a brilliancy of style which he has nowhere surpassed, there is no need for any further study of the subject. My answer is twofold: first, that an important mass of new material is now at the disposal of any one who wishes to retell the story, and second, that Gibbon told it with a bias which makes it desirable that it should be retold.

The historian of the 'Decline and Fall' had less than half the material before him which is now available, and the story of the siege deserves telling with more accuracy and completeness than either the authorities available to him or the scope of his monumental work permitted. It is true that Professor J. B. Bury, the latest editor of Gibbon, has, by the aid of scholarly notes and of careful research, enabled the reader to become possessed of many of the details regarding the siege which have recently become known, but he would be the first to admit that there is ample room for a fuller history of the siege than that given in the 'Decline and Fall' even with the aid of his valuable notes.[1]   Gibbon himself regretted the poverty of his materials and especially that he had not been able to obtain any Turkish accounts of the siege.[2]   The only eye-witnesses whose narratives were before him were Phrantzes, Archbishop Leonard, and Cardinal Isidore.   If we add to their narratives the accounts given by Ducas and Chalcondylas together with what Gibbon himself calls 'short hints of Cantemir and Leunclavius,' we have substantially all the sources of information which were available when the 'Decline and Fall' was written.

The new sources of information regarding the siege brought to light since Gibbon's day enable us to gain a much more complete view of that event and of the character of its principal actors than was possible at the time when he wrote.   Several Continental writers have taken advantage of some at least of the new stores of information to rewrite its story,[3] but I may be allowed to claim the good fortune of being the first Englishman who has even attempted to write a narrative of that event with the whole or even with any considerable portion of the new material before him.

---

[1] *Decline and Fall of the Roman Empire*, edited by J. B. Bury, M.A. Whenever Gibbon is quoted in the text of this volume it is from Professor Bury's edition.

[2] Vol. vii. p. 163, Gibbon's note.

[3] The principal of these works are :

  1. 'Belagerung und Eroberung Constantinopels im Jahre 1453.'   Von Dr. A. D. Mordtmann (Stuttgart, 1858).

  2. 'Die Eroberungen von Constantinopel im dreizehnten und fünfzehnten Jahrhundert.'   Von Dr. Johann Heinrich Krause (Halle, 1870).

  3. 'Les Derniers Jours de Constantinople.'   Par E. A. Vlasto (Paris, 1883).

  4. Πολιορκία καὶ Ἅλωσις τῆς Κωνσταντινουπόλεως.   By A. G. Paspates (Athens, 1890).

  5. 'Constantine, the last Emperor of the Greeks.'   By Chedomil Mijatovich, formerly Servian Minister at the Court of St. James (London, 1892).

  6. Two valuable papers by Dr. A. Mordtmann (the son of Dr. A. D. Mordtmann) entitled *Die letzten Tage von Byzanz*, in the 'Mitteilungen des deutschen Exkursions-Klubs in Konstantinopel,' 1895.

Before, however, proceeding to indicate what the new
sources of information are, I must say something regarding
the second reason I have assigned why those interested in
the account of an event which marks the end of an epoch of
great traditions and of a civilisation on ancient rather than
on modern lines should not remain satisfied with Gibbon's
account of it. Though he claimed to examine the authorities
before him with philosophical impartiality, the writers known
to him belonged to the Roman Church, and he was influenced
unconsciously by their representations. These writers wrote
under the influence of the most bitter theological controversies. They are imbued with a spirit of rancour towards
those Greeks (that is, towards the great majority of the
population) who had not accepted the Union with the Church
of Rome which had been decreed at Florence. Their
testimony throughout their narratives is for the most part
that of violent partisans. But even if Gibbon, when dealing
with the disputes between the great historical Churches, had
been in possession of statements of the Greek case, his
contempt for both Churches was too great to allow him to
do justice to the questions which divided them, questions
which nevertheless, as they prevented the united action of
Europe to resist the Turkish invasion, were among the most
important of the time. His habit of thought as an
eighteenth century theist did not allow him to attach
sufficient weight to the theological aspect of the struggle
between the East and the West. Everything that smelt of
the cloister was hateful. The theological questions themselves were not worth discussion. The disputants were in
his view narrow-minded, ignorant, and superstitious. The
refinements of the definitions of the Double Procession were
useless, trivial, or ridiculous. Religious zeal or enthusiasm
was a thing to be condemned—was the mark of fanaticism
and always mischievous. In this attitude of mind Gibbon
was neither better nor worse than the majority of his

philosophical contemporaries. He differed from them in being able to bequeath to future generations a work of monumental learning, in which his and their reading of the progress of Christianity in the Eastern empire was destined to have a long and deservedly great reputation. His research and eloquence, his keen sarcasm, his judicial manner, and the powerful influence of the 'Decline and Fall' were employed to discredit Christianity rather than to try to discover amid the fierce wranglings of theologians over insoluble problems what was their signification for the history of the time of which he was treating and in the development of the human mind. He began with a period in which the emperor is worshipped as Divinity and traced the establishment of Christianity as a national faith among Pagan subjects until in a diversified form it became accepted by all; but he did this without affording us any help to see how the human mind could accept the first position or what were the movements of thought which led to the evolution of the questions which agitated men's minds in the later period.

The century in which he and his contemporaries lived was for them one of hostility to Christianity rather than of investigation, the period of Voltaire, who could only see in Byzantine history 'a worthless repertory of declamation and miracles, disgraceful to the human mind' rather than of the Continental and English writers of the modern historical school. Happily, in the twentieth century those who look upon Christianity with an independence as complete as that of Gibbon recognise that insight can only be obtained by sympathetic investigation, that for the right understanding of history it is essential to put oneself in the place of men who have attached importance to a religious controversy, to consider their environment and examine their conduct and motives from their point of view, if we would comprehend either the causes which have led such

controversy to be regarded as important or the conduct of
the controversialists themselves. The absence in Gibbon of
any sympathetic attempt to understand the controversies
which play so large a part in his great drama of human
history renders him as unsatisfactory a guide in regard to
them as a writer of English history during the period of
Charles the First would be who should merely treat with
contempt the half religious, half political questions which
divided Englishmen. While the objection I have suggested
to Gibbon's attitude would apply generally to his treatment
of religious questions, I have only to deal with it in reference
to the period of which I am treating. When writing of
this period Gibbon did not realise that the religious question
was nearly always a political one, and that union with Rome
meant subjection to Rome. But unless it be realised how
completely the citizens of Constantinople and the other
great cities of the empire were engrossed with semi-religious
and semi-political questions, no true conception of the life
of the empire can be formed ; for these questions were of
interest not merely to Churchmen but to all.

Among the documents brought to light during the last
fifty or sixty years which have contributed to our better
knowledge of the siege the most important are the ' Diary '
of Nicolo Barbaro and the ' Life of Mahomet ' by Critobulus.

Barbaro belonged to a noble Venetian family. He was
present in Constantinople throughout the siege, kept a
journal[1] of what he saw and heard, and, though full of
prejudices against Genoese, Greeks, and Turks, contrives
to tell his story in a manner which carries conviction of its
truthfulness. His narrative conveys the impression of an
independent observer who had no object in writing except
to relate what he knew about the siege. While probably
written from day to day, the diary bears internal evidence

---

[1] *Giornale dell' Assedio di Constantinopoli*, di Nicolo Barbaro, P.V., corredato
di note e documenti per Enrico Cornet (Vienna, 1856).

of having been revised after he had left the city. Its language is old-fashioned colloquial Venetian and has often puzzled Italians whom I have called in to my aid.

The original manuscript of the diary was preserved in Venice by members of the Barbaro family until 1829. After various adventures it came in 1837 into the possession of the Imperial and Royal Marciana Library in Venice. In 1854 it was entrusted to Enrico Cornet, and was published by him for the first time in 1856.

Critobulus, the author of the 'Life of Mahomet the Second,' was a man of a different type. Nothing is known of him beyond what is contained in his Life of Mahomet.[1] He describes himself as ' Critobulus the Islander.' After the capture of Constantinople, when the archons of Imbros, Lemnos, and Thasos feared that the Turkish admiral would shortly approach to annex these islands, messengers were sent to the admiral and succeeded, by offering voluntary submission and by paying him a large bribe, in avoiding the general pillage which usually followed a Turkish conquest. Shortly afterwards, Critobulus took service under the sultan and was made archon of Imbros. In this capacity he received the submission of Lemnos and other places. He continued to hold this office for at least four years. Book III. of his history contains (inter alia) an account of what he himself did as the servant of Mahomet. Probably he went to reside in Constantinople in 1460. His history covers the first seventeen years of Mahomet's reign. It is dedicated to the sultan and is followed by an apology to his fellow Greeks for having written it. While open to the charge of not allowing himself an altogether free hand in revealing the faults and cruelties of his master, Critobulus claims that he has taken great pains to know the truth of what he relates. As he wrote a few years after the siege and at leisure, his narrative does not show the signs of haste

[1] Βίος τοῦ Μωαμὲθ β'.

which mark many of the shorter narratives of that event :
such, for example, as those of Leonard, of the Podestà of
Pera, of Cardinal Isidore in the 'Lamentatio,' and of others.
As he continued to belong to the Orthodox Church and to
the Greek as opposed to the Roman party in that Church,
his history is free from the denunciations of his fellow
Christians for having refused the union agreed to at Florence.
The writer's characteristics as a Greek, but also as a servant
of the sultan, show themselves in his work. He expresses
sympathy with his own people, extols their courage, and
laments their misfortunes. But in places his biography of
the sultan reads like the report of an able and courageous
official. His training and experience in the work of government, his service under Mahomet, and perhaps something
in the nature of the man, make his narrative sober and
methodical and impress the reader with the idea that the
author felt a sense of responsibility for the truthfulness of
what he was writing. While the narratives of Phrantzes,
Chalcondylas, and Ducas recount some of the incidents of
the siege more fully than that of Critobulus, the latter gives
more details on others and supplies valuable information
which none of them have given. His Life of Mahomet is
by far the most valuable of the recently discovered documents, and, as will be seen, I have made use of it as the
nucleus of my narrative of the siege.

The manuscript of Critobulus was discovered by the late
Dr. Dethier less than forty years ago in the Seraglio Library
at Constantinople. It was transcribed by him and also by
Herr Karl Müller and was published by the latter in 1883
with valuable notes.[1]

Two other works of importance unknown to Gibbon

[1] Herr Müller's preface is dated 1869, but I am not aware that it was
published before it appeared in *Fragmenta Historicorum Graecorum*, vol. v.
The dedicatory epistle to Mahomet was published from another and a somewhat
longer version by Tischendorf in 1870 in his *Notitia Codicis Bibliorum
Sinaitici* (Leipzig).

were due respectively to Tetaldi and Pusculus. Each of these authors took part in the defence of the city. Tetaldi, who was a Florentine soldier, tells us of his escape from the slaughter immediately following the capture, and of his being picked up out of the water by a Venetian ship.[1]

Pusculus was a citizen of Brescia. Though his account of the siege is given in Latin verse, it contains many details of value of what he himself saw which are not to be found elsewhere. His poem was never altogether lost sight of, but until its publication by Ellisen,[2] in 1857, with a useful introduction, its historical value had not been recognised. The MS. from which Ellisen made his copy is dated 1470.

The late Dr. Dethier, who devoted much time and intelligent study to the topography and archæology of Constantinople, compiled four volumes of documents relating to the siege, many of which were previously unknown. Two of them were printed about 1870, but they can hardly be said to have been published, and are only to be procured with difficulty. The remaining two contain, besides Critobulus, the 'Threnos,' Hypsilantes, an Italian and a Latin version of the 'Lamentatio' by Cardinal Isidore, an Italian version of Leonard's report to the Pope, and other documents of interest to which I refer in my pages. These volumes were printed by the Buda-Pest Academy but never published. I am indebted, however, to that learned body for a copy.

I append a list of documents (other than the four prin-

---

[1] 'Informacion envoyée (en 1453) tant par Francisco de Franco au très révérend père en Dieu Monsgr le Cardinal d'Avignon que par Jehan Blanchin et Jacques Tetaldi marchand Florentin sur la prinse de Constantinoble à laquelle le dit Jacques estoit personellement.' One version is published in *Chroniques de Charles VII roi de France, par Jean Chartier*, vol. iii., edited by Vallet de Virivalle (Paris, 1858). Another, published by Dethier with several important differences, is stated to be taken from *Thesaurus novus Anecdotorum* (Paris, 1717). Though his narrative was printed in France early in the eighteenth century, it appears to have been generally unknown and is not alluded to by Gibbon.

[2] *Ubertini Pusculi Brixiensis Constantinopoleos* : in *Analekten der mittel- und neugriechischen Literatur*, by J. A. Ellisen (Leipzig).

cipal which I have described) relating to the siege now available to the historical student which were unknown to Gibbon:

1. Zorzo (or Zorsi) Dolphin (or Zorsi Dolfin), 'Assedio e presa di Constantinopoli nell' anno 1453.' This is mainly a translation from Leonard, but the author claims to have added what he heard from other eye-witnesses of the siege. It was published by G. M. Thomas in the 'Sitzungs-berichte' of the Bavarian Academy in 1868. Another version is given by Dethier in his collection of documents relating to the siege, a collection which I refer to simply as Dethier's 'Siege.'

2. 'Rapporto del Superiore dei Franciscani presente all' assedio e alla presa di Constantinopoli.' This report was made immediately after the siege and has long been published, but apparently was not known to Gibbon. Dethier also published it in his 'Siege.'

3. 'Epistola Ang. Johannis Zacchariae,' Podestà of Pera, written within a month of the capture of the city, was first published in 1827. The version revised by Edward Hopf and Dr. Dethier is the one used by me.

4. Montaldo's 'De Constantinopolitano excidio' is reproduced in Dethier's 'Siege,' and contains useful hints by an eye-witness.

5. Christoforo Riccherio, 'La Presa de Constantinopoli,' first published in Sansovino's 'Dell' Historia Universale,' was republished with notes in Dethier's 'Siege,' and is a valuable and brightly written narrative.

6. Θρῆνος τῆς Κωνσταντινουπόλεως, was first published by Ellisen in 'Analekten,' Leipzig, 1857. If the author was in Constantinople during the siege, he has not given a single item of information which is of value to the historian. His long wail is curious and interesting, but otherwise useless.

7. The Θρῆνος of Hierax the Grand Logothetes, or 'History of the Turkish Empire,' though only written near the end of the sixteenth century, has valuable topographical hints. It was translated by H. E. Aristarchi Bey, the present Grand Logothetes, from a MS. existing in the Monastery of the Holy Sepulchre at the Phanar, and edited by Dethier.

8. 'Libro d' Andrea Cambini Florentino della Origine de' Turchi et Imperio delli Ottomanni.' I am not aware whether

this has been published at a later date than the copy in my possession, which was printed in Florence in 1529. It was then published by the son of the writer, and Book II., which treats of the siege, suggests that the author has gained his information from spectators of the siege. It contains many useful statements.

9. ' A Slavic Account of the Siege,' published by Streznevski, is judged by Monsieur Mijatovich, on account of its peculiar idioms, to have been written by a Serbian or Bulgarian. He speaks of it as the ' Slavonic Chronicle.' A translation and a slightly different version was published by Dethier as the ' Muscovite Chronicle.' Though the narrative has been largely added to by subsequent hands, there is reason to believe that it was written by an eye-witness of the siege.

10. Another Slavic version is conveniently spoken of as the ' Memoirs of the Polish Janissary.' Its author, after serving with the Turks and, according to his own statement, being present at the siege, withdrew to Poland. The original MS. was first published in 1828.

The Turkish authors available who speak of the siege are :

11. Sad-ud-din, ' The Capture of Constantinople from the Taj-ut-Tevarikh (1590),' translated into English by E. J. W. Gibb (Glasgow, 1879). This work professes to be based on the accounts of earlier Turkish historians.

12. ' Tarich Muntechebati Evli Chelibi,' a translation of which is given in the elder Mordtmann's ' Eroberung.'

13. Ahmed Muktar Pasha's ' Conquest of Constantinople and the Establishment of the Ottomans in Europe,' brought out only in 1902, on the anniversary of the present sultan's accession.

14. An Armenian ' Mélodie Élégiaque,' written by a monk named Philip, who was present at the siege. This was printed in Lebeau's ' Histoire du Bas-Empire.' Dethier published the original version in Armenian.

I gratefully acknowledge my indebtedness to Dr. Mordtmann's studies of the archæology and topography of Constantinople,[1] and to Professor A. van Millingen's ' Byzantine Constantinople,' [2] a work which is the most careful study of

[1] *Esquisse Topographique de Constantinople* (Lille, 1892).
[2] *Byzantine Constantinople : the Walls of the City and adjoining Historical Sites* (published by John Murray, 1899).

the history of those parts of the walls and other portions of the city treated of which has yet been published. I must also tender him sincere thanks for many suggestions made in the course of friendly intercourse and in the discussion of matters of mutual archæological interest, and for permission to reproduce his map of Constantinople. All future writers on the topography and archæology of Constantinople will be under obligations to Dr. Mordtmann and Professor van Millingen, who have worthily continued the work of Gyllius and Du Cange.

A few words must be added as to the title of this book. Why, it may be asked, should it be the 'Destruction of the Greek Empire'? Why not follow the example of the late Mr. Freeman, and of his distinguished successor, Professor J. B. Bury, and speak of the 'Later Roman Empire'? My plea is one of confession and avoidance.

I admit that when Charles the Great, in 800, became Roman Emperor in the West the imperial territory of which the capital was Constantinople may correctly be spoken of as the Eastern Roman Empire. But I avoid condemnation for not adopting this name and for not calling the empire Roman by pleading that I am reverting to the practice of our fathers in the West during many centuries, and by defending their practice. The Empire has sometimes been described as Byzantine and sometimes as the Lower Empire. But these names are undesirable, because the first has a vague and doubtful meaning, since no two writers who employ it use it to cover the same period; and the second has a derogatory signification which the researches of Freeman and Professor Bury, Krumbacher, Schlumberger, and other modern writers, have shown to be undeserved. The name 'Roman' has more to recommend it. The Persians and the Arabs knew the empire simply as Roman, and the overwhelming reputation of Rome led them to speak even of Alexander the Great as 'Iskender al Roumy.' The name

of Rome, or Roum, given to Roumelia, and found in other
places as far east as Erzeroum, had been applied when the
Latin element dominated the empire.   The tradition of
Rome passed on to the Turks, and the inhabitants of the
empire were and are to them I-roum or Romans.   The
Byzantine writers usually called themselves Romans.   But
the term Roman can hardly be applied to the empire
without distinguishing it as Eastern, and while it is true
that down to 1453 the empire was Roman in name, there
is some danger in employing the term of forgetting how far
the New Rome and its territory had become Hellenised,
and that a large portion of the population preferred the
name Greek.   There had been a long struggle within the
empire itself between those who wished to adopt the latter
designation and those who desired to call it Roman.   The
inhabitants of Greece were indeed for centuries preceding
and during the Crusades disloyal subjects of Constantinople.
Even during the reign of Heraclius (610 to 641), they
insisted upon being called Hellenes rather than Romans.
From that time onwards a contest was continued as to
whether the name of Greek or Roman should be applied to
the population.   The influence of the Greeks henceforth was
constantly working to Hellenise the empire.   In the reign
of Irene, at the time when the Western Roman Empire
commenced to have a separate existence, Greek influence
was especially strong.   Lascaris, four centuries later, when
he made his stand at Nicaea after the Latin conquest,
spoke of the empire as that of Hellas.   On the recovery
of the city under Michael, the Church generally employed
the term Roman, but declared that Greek and Roman might
be employed indifferently.   Various writers speak of the
Latins as Romans and of the Byzantines as Hellenes.[1]
Manuel Bryennius represents the preacher in St. Sophia as
calling upon his hearers to remember their Greek ancestors

[1] See authorities quoted in Sathas. *Documents Inédits*, i. p. xii.

and to defend their country as they had done.   At times the
people were appealed to as the descendants alike of Greeks
and Romans.

As being a continuation of the Roman Empire whose
capital was New Rome, the empire is correctly called
Roman, and the name has the advantage of always keeping
in view the continuity of Roman history.   It was the
Eastern Roman Empire which declined and fell in 1453.
But if we admit that the empire continued to be Roman
till 1453, it must be remembered, not only that its characteristics had considerably changed, but that to the men of
the West it had come to be known as the Greek Empire.
Latin had been as completely forgotten as Norman French
was by English nobles in the time of Edward III.   Greek
had become the official language, as did English in our own
country.   The inscriptions on the coins since the time of
Heraclius are in Greek.   The Orthodox Church, which aided
as much as even law in binding the inhabitants of the
country together, employed Greek, and Greek almost exclusively, as its language, and, although the great defenders of
the term Roman as applied to the population are found
among its dignitaries, the Church was essentially Greek
as opposed to Roman, both in the character of its thought
and teaching and in the language it employed.   Hence it
is not surprising that to the West during all the middle
ages, the Empire was the Greek Empire, just as the
Orthodox Church was the Greek Church.[1]   The Empire and
the Church were each alike called Greek to distinguish them
from the Empire and Church of the West.   It is in this
general use of the word Greek that I find my justification
for speaking of the capture of Constantinople, and the

---

[1] For example, Sir John Maundeville speaks of ' Constantinople, where the
Emperor of Greece usually dwells,' *Early Travels in Palestine*, p. 130 (Bohn's
edition).

events connected with it, as the Destruction of the Greek Empire.[1]

I have only in conclusion to call the attention of the reader to one or two matters connected with the authorities which I quote. I must plead that my residence in Constantinople has not allowed me to refer to the uniform series of Byzantine authors available in the great public libraries of Western Europe. My edition of Phrantzes is that published in the Bonn series ; Pachymer, Cantacuzenus, Chalcondylas, Ducas, and their contemporaries, are quoted from the Venetian edition of the Byzantine writers edited by Du Cange. My references to Archbishop Leonard are almost always to the version in the collection of Lonicerus. Dr Dethier, however, published a contemporary Italian version which has certain important variations, and to this I have occasionally referred. The editors of other authorities are mentioned in the notes to the text.

I have sometimes abstained from discussing the trustworthiness of my authorities, but have said once for all that their statements, especially in regard to the numbers they represent as engaged in battle, of victims slaughtered or captured, and the like, can rarely be regarded as satisfactory. The means of controlling them seldom exist. Even in the case of Sir John Maundeville, I have quoted him without hinting that a doubt of his very existence has been uttered. Whether he lived and was or was not a traveller, or whether his book was, as has been suggested, a kind of mediæval Murray's Guide, does not in the least affect the statements which I have reproduced from it. The work of sifting the evidence, new and old, to ascertain its value has been long and tedious, and I must leave to other students of the same period to say whether I have succeeded in selecting what is of use and

[1] See valuable remarks on the name of the empire in the Preface to Professor Bury's *Later Roman Empire*, and in the Introduction to *Documents Inédits relatifs à l'Histoire de la Grèce*, by Sathas.

in rejecting only what is valueless. To have attempted a critical examination of every important statement which I quote would have extended my book to an inordinate length, and in regard to most of them the reader will not find much difficulty in arriving at his own conclusions as to their trustworthiness.

EDWIN PEARS.

CONSTANTINOPLE, *February* 1903.

CONTENTS

ILLUSTRATIONS

DESTRUCTION

OF

THE GREEK EMPIRE

CHAPTER I

THE LATIN EMPIRE (1204–1261) AND ITS STRUGGLES WITH
AND FINAL OVERTHROW BY THE GREEKS OF NICAEA

THE later Roman Empire and its capital Constantinople
never recovered from the blow inflicted by the Fourth Crusade in 1204. A huge filibustering expedition had been
gathered together at Venice under pretext of making an
attack upon the Saracens in Egypt. Under the leadership
of Boniface, Marquis of Montferrat, and Dandolo, the famous
doge of Venice, the expedition had been diverted from its
purpose, and, in spite of the strongest possible protests by
Innocent the Third, had attacked Constantinople. The
strength of the empire had been weakened by a hundred
and fifty years' resistance to the hordes of Asia, during
which it had served as the bulwark of Europe. Its reputation had been lessened by thirty years of dynastic wars,
during which the government had allowed its fleet to decay
so that it was unable to resist the Venetians and Crusaders.
The result was that, for the first time in its long history, the
city was captured. There then followed the plunder and
division of its enormous wealth—a large part of which found
its way to the West, while perhaps a still larger portion

was destroyed—the appointment of a Latin emperor in Constantinople, and the partition of such portions of the empire as could be occupied among the conquerors.

Baldwin, 1204–1205. Baldwin, a Belgian, was elected emperor. An arrangement for the division of the spoil had been made by the leaders before the attack on the city, and this seems to have been fairly carried out. To Baldwin were assigned the two imperial palaces in Constantinople and one fourth of all that should be captured within the city and throughout the empire. The remaining three fourths were to be divided equally between the Crusaders and the Venetians. The difficulties of the conquerors began with this further division of the spoil. The task of parcelling out the empire was

Difficulties regarding division of empire. almost hopeless. It was next to impossible to accomplish such a partition, even on paper, because of the ignorance of the Western conquerors of the empire they had destroyed. Its extent was so great, the difficulty of communication so extreme, and ignorance of geography so profound, that the conquerors did not know what there was to divide. They sent into the provinces to obtain information as to the revenues and general condition of the country so that the partition might be fairly made; but, without waiting for the information, they proceeded to divide up the countries and provinces which they imagined to be within the empire. In their happy ignorance they drew lots for Alexandria and for the various countries along the north shore of the Mediterranean as well as for Georgia, Persia, and Assyria. They competed for the possession of Konia itself, the capital of the Seljukian Turks.

It was still more difficult to make a partition which should represent territory which could come at once into the occupation of the Crusaders. The one system of land tenure with which they were acquainted was the feudal. The lands of the empire must therefore be divided into fiefs and the barons and persons of higher and of lower degree must have grants according to their rank. But though Constantinople was in the possession of the men of the West, they held no more of the remainder of the empire than was within the actual sight of the barons and the comparatively small bodies of retainers who were under them. The Greeks—or, as the subjects of the later empire still generally called themselves, the Romans—had no intention of recognising either the lordship of the barons who had become their feudal superiors or the overlordship of Baldwin. They knew nothing of a feudal system, and recognised the representatives of the late empire as having a first claim to their service. They were ready to follow almost any leader against men whom they knew only as invaders, belonging to a different race, speaking a different language, and professing a form of Christianity which was hateful to them because the conquerors tried to impose it upon them.

The difficulties of the Latin empire were both internal and external.

The men from the West soon found that they were too few to hold the country. Some of the Crusaders had insisted upon leaving the city in order to proceed to the Holy Land in fulfilment of their vows and to avoid the censure of Innocent. Others were anxious to return home with their share of the spoils. 'Never since the world was created,' says Villehardouin the historian, who took an active part in the capture of the city, 'was there so much booty gained in one city. Each man took the house which pleased him, and there were enough for all. Those who were poor found themselves suddenly rich.' If they remained they had hardships to face which as the possessors of newly obtained wealth they would rather avoid. As soon as new dangers appeared the numbers of those who wished to get away increased. During the very first year of Baldwin's reign, his army on its retreat from an expedition against the Bulgarians found at Rodosto seven thousand men at arms who had quitted the capital and were leaving the country. It was in vain that a cardinal and the leaders sent by the army, among whom was Villehardouin himself, implored them even with tears to remain, for 'Never,' said these leaders, 'would they be able to succour a country in so

Dissensions among leaders.

great a need.'[1]   The most favourable answer that they could obtain was that a reply would be given on the morrow. The deserters set sail in the night without even giving the promised response to the prayer made to them.

The internal difficulties were increased by the jealousy which existed between the leaders of the Latins themselves. All through the journey to Constantinople before the capture of the city, the Crusaders and Venetians had mistrusted each other. Boniface, the leader of the Crusade, considered himself ill treated because he had not been named emperor. Though defeated, he had a large number of adherents. To him had been assigned territory in Asia Minor. He applied to exchange it for the kingdom of Salonica, alleging that as he had married the widow of the Emperor Isaac, who was the sister of the King of Hungary, he would be at Salonica in a better position to aid the emperor. His request was granted. Baldwin, however, did not trust him, and, apparently under the impression that it was the intention of Boniface to establish an independent sovereignty, insisted on accompanying him to his newly acquired capital. To this course Boniface objected so strongly that when the emperor started for Salonica, Boniface not only refused to accompany him but went off towards Adrianople, captured Didymotica, and laid siege to the former city. The Greeks flocked to his standard, possibly being induced to do so by the belief that as he had married the widow of Isaac he was entitled to their allegiance.

As soon as Dandolo, Count Louis, and the other nobles who had remained in Constantinople heard what Marquis Boniface was doing, they at once took counsel in 'parlement' as to the measures to be adopted : 'for,' says Villehardouin, they thought that they would lose all the conquests they had made.' They decided to send a knight to Boniface without delay, and the historian was himself chosen for the mission. He went at once to Adrianople and succeeded in persuading the marquis to submit the questions between him and the emperor to the arbitration of Dandolo and Count

[1] Villehardouin, ch. lxxxvi.

Louis, and for the present to cease hostilities.   Meantime the emperor had occupied Salonica.   As soon as he heard of the siege of Adrianople he at once hastened to its relief and ' pour faire tout le mal qu'il pourrait au marquis.'   On the way he met the messengers from the city, who besought him to submit his case, as Boniface had consented to do, to arbitration, at the same time plainly telling him that Dandolo, Count Louis of Blois, and the other barons would not tolerate war between him and Boniface.   The emperor hesitated and consulted his council.   Some of the members urged that the message was an outrage and advised resistance.   Violent language (' grosses paroles ') was used, but the emperor, who was unwilling to risk the hostility of so strong a combination as Dandolo and Louis, gave way to the extent of stating that he would undertake not to attack Boniface until he went to Constantinople, although he would not pledge himself to refer the questions between them to arbitration.   Shortly after, when a peace was patched up between them, it was under conditions which show that neither party trusted the other.   Villehardouin undertook to hold Didymotica until he knew by a trusted messenger that Salonica had been handed over to Boniface.

Nor were the external differences which at once presented themselves less serious.   The history of Constantinople and the Latin empire during the period between 1204 and 1260 is indeed that of a series of struggles between Baldwin and his successors on the imperial throne, on the one side, and the leaders of the Greek race who had refused to recognise the authority of the invaders, on the other.

The Western barons seemed to have thought that with the conquest of the capital the whole empire would fall to their lot.   They were soon undeceived.   In Macedonia and in Epirus Greek leaders appeared, who rallied to them all who were indisposed to accept new rulers.   At Trebizond on the Black Sea, and at Nicaea, the once famous city of the Creed, the Greeks flocked from the capital and its neighbourhood, and soon there were rulers of these cities who assumed the title of emperor.

Opposition of Greek population.

The most important of those who refused to accept the
Latin rule was Theodore Lascaris. He had been the last of
the Greek nobles to leave the city when the invaders
captured it. He made his way to Nicaea, and was followed
by many Greeks. Able, courageous, and patriotic, he was
soon recognised by the notables as the fittest man to have
rule among them, and, though without hereditary claim to the
imperial throne, he aspired to be emperor and was accepted
as best suited to receive that dignity. Two years after the
capture of Constantinople, a new patriarch was elected, who
consented to live at Nicaea and who amid as much ceremony as if the coronation had taken place in St. Sophia
placed the crown on the head of Theodore in the church o
the same name at Nicaea. The prudence and judgment of
the new emperor did much to rally the best of his countrymen around him, and justified the choice made in electing
him to the imperial throne. The Greek priests flocked to
the city from all parts of Western Asia Minor as well as
from Thrace.

Nevertheless, his task was beset with difficulties. He
had enemies on all sides, pretenders of his own race, the
Latin emperor and the sultan of the Seljukian Turks.
The latter, whose capital was at Konia, had no idea of
allowing any neighbour to become formidable. A Greek
pretender held the country to the west of Nicaea. The
Latin emperor and barons chose to regard Theodore as a
rebel because he would not make submission. After unsuccessful attempts against him by Baldwin and his successor,
Theodore was allowed in 1207 to remain in possession of
Ismidt (the ancient Nicomedia) and Cyzicus for a period of
two years. He employed the period in strengthening and
extending his empire. At the end of it, Henry the brother
of Baldwin, whom he succeeded as emperor, made an alliance
with the sultan of the Seljukian Turks : that is to say, the
Crusaders who had justified themselves to Innocent the
Third for attacking a Christian city on the ground that the
Greek emperors had allowed the Moslems to have a mosque

within the city, now found themselves under the necessity of joining forces with the infidel to attack a Christian prince.

Upon the declaration of war by the sultan, Theodore pushed forward into the valley of the Meander, and a battle was fought which, if the Byzantine authorities are to be trusted, was decided in single combat between the two sovereigns. The sultan was killed, and the empire of Nicaea was saved. The Emperor Henry, however, when he heard of the extent of the loss in Theodore's army exclaimed, ' The Greek is not conqueror : he is ruined.'

So far from being ruined, his success caused many Greeks to flock into his empire from Constantinople. When, in 1214, the Emperor Henry again declared war, Theodore was ready for him ; and as the Greeks in Epirus had commenced a vigorous attack on the crusading barons in Macedonia, Henry was glad to make a peace which left Theodore undisputed master of a territory bounded on the west by a line from Heraclea on the Black Sea to Ismidt, thence to Cyzicus and to the coast just north of Pergamos. The fruitful valleys of the Meander, the Cayster, and the Hermus marked his boundaries on the south-west.

Theodore died in 1222. The first duty of the Greeks when driven out of Constantinople was to make themselves secure against the conquerors and to prevent the progress of the crusading armies into Asia Minor. This duty had been effectually done by Theodore. During the eighteen years of his reign he had made his capital and its beautiful neighbourhood the rallying-place of what was best in the Greek-speaking populations of Asia Minor and of Thrace. He had checked the progress of the crusaders into Asia Minor and had left to his successors the task of working for the recovery of Constantinople.

Meantime, the history of the Latin conquerors of Constantinople had been one of almost continuous disaster. The first Emperor Baldwin had been lost in an encounter with the Bulgarians near Adrianople in April 1205, and was probably killed. As his fate remained doubtful, his

Henry succeeds Baldwin, 1205–1216.

brother Henry acted as regent for a year and was then crowned emperor. Shortly after the commencement of his reign in 1207, Boniface, Marquis of Montferrat and King of Salonica, was killed in a skirmish. Henry seems to have realised that in a policy of conciliation towards the Greeks lay the only hope of the continuance of his empire. He made peace with the Bulgarians and concluded an arrangement with both the emperor of Nicaea and the Greek prince who had made himself recognised as despot in Epirus. He employed Greeks in the public service. He refused to take part in the persecution of the Greeks who would not obey the decrees of the pope's legate. He allowed them to employ the Greek language in their services, and restrained the pretensions of the Roman priests. Unfortunately for the Latin empire, the reign of the chivalrous Henry lasted only ten years.

Peter succeeds, 1217–1219.

He was succeeded by Peter of Courtenay, who was invited by the barons to occupy the throne in the absence of male heirs of Baldwin and his brother Henry. Peter left France with 140 knights and 5,500 men at arms, whom he had obtained with the aid of his royal kinsman, Philip Augustus. The reports of the rich plunder which had been obtained in the capture of the city had already induced many French knights to leave their native lands to take service in the empire, but the detachment with which Peter crossed the Alps was the largest which had left the West for such purpose.

The Venetians bargained to transport them across the Adriatic on condition that they would assist in recovering Durazzo from Theodore, the Greek despot of Epirus. After a useless assault on that city, Peter started with his followers on a journey across the peninsula to Salonica. He and his host were soon lost amid the mountains of Epirus. Their provisions were exhausted. They found the passes fortified, and their only chance of life was to surrender to Theodore, who had held the country in defiance of the regent who was governing in the name of the son of Boniface. Peter was detained in captivity, and his death is as mysterious as that of the first Latin emperor. He probably perished in prison in 1218.

Peter's successor, Robert of Courtenay, succeeded in finding his way to Constantinople, though not across Macedonia, accompanied by a number of troops furnished at the request of Pope Honorius the Third. His reign was a series of disasters. He made a treaty of peace with Theodore of Nicaea in order that he might devote all his attention to the defeat of the other Theodore, the despot of Epirus. The latter had been denounced by the pope for his detention of Peter and of the legate who accompanied him. Honorius indeed had invited the princes of the West to undertake a crusade for their deliverance. When, however, the legate was released, Peter seems to have been forgotten. The despot Theodore made a well-concerted attack upon Salonica, captured it, and was proclaimed emperor in 1222. Robert led all his forces against this new claimant for the imperial title and was badly beaten. Theodore pushed on to Adrianople and hoisted his standard on the walls of that city almost without opposition.

Robert, 1219–1228.

There were thus in 1222 four persons claiming to be emperors, and occupying separate portions of what had been twenty years earlier the Roman Empire in the East. These were Robert at Constantinople, Theodore at Nicaea, another Theodore at Salonica, and Alexis at Trebizond.

The history of the next forty years (1222–1261) is that of the strengthening of the Greek empire at Nicaea and the decadence and downfall of the other so-called empires, and especially of that of the Latin Crusaders in Constantinople. The successor of Theodore Lascaris was John Ducas Vataces, who during a reign of thirty-three years fortified his position at Nicaea and increased the prosperity of his empire. He restricted the boundaries of the Latin territory in Asia Minor to the peninsula formed by a line parallel to the Bosporus from Ismidt to the Black Sea. He rendered property and life safe, and in consequence the Greek population continued to flock into his territory. Even French soldiers in considerable numbers quietly slipped away from

Nicaea, success of John Ducas Vataces, 1222–1254.

Constantinople to take service with Vataces. At the commencement of his reign he was attacked by the newly appointed emperor, Robert of Courtenay, and in the combat which ensued not only was Vataces successful, but the last of the knights who had taken part in the capture of the city were left dead on the field. ᵡ Until Robert's death in 1228, Nicaea had few troubles with the Latin empire.

Latin empire.
John of Brienne, 1228–1237.
Baldwin II., 1237–1261.

Robert's successor was a boy of eleven, who continued nominally emperor under the title of Baldwin the Second for upwards of thirty years, but the Latin knights wisely placed power in the hands of John de Brienne. Indeed, the crusading leaders seem throughout the whole Latin occupation to have assumed a large measure of the imperial authority. The period is contemporary with that of the barons who resisted King John in England, and who continued to assert their independence under the reign of Henry the Third. The French barons in Constantinople had much of the same spirit, with the additional incentive to independence that, as the emperors were of recent creation, the glamour which had already gathered about the kingly office in England and France was absent. The emperor was indeed nothing more than *primus inter pares*, and his own designs were often set aside for those of his associates. No one can doubt that they acted wisely in appointing John de Brienne, but even he, with all his experience and caution, failed as his predecessor had done when he attacked Nicaea.

The courage and ability of the old Crusader, who was already eighty years of age, hardly retarded the decay of the Latin empire. Its needs were great, and accordingly Baldwin the Second was sent on a visit to the pope and to the Western courts to obtain further supplies of men and money. Indeed, the greater part of his reign was Baldwin visits France, occupied by three of such journeys. His first visit to France was in 1237. Hardly had he arrived in Paris when he learned the death of John de Brienne. The messenger who brought the tidings told a terrible story of the distress in the imperial city. The barons and soldiers [1] dared not venture outside the walls. The supply of food had run so short that many of the gentlemen of France who were charged with its defence disguised themselves and escaped by sea or, notwithstanding that the country was full of dangers, endeavoured to make their way by land to their own country. The peril was so great that Baldwin was assured that if aid were not sent the city could not resist an attack. Upon these tidings Baldwin did his utmost to obtain aid. He was received with honour wherever he went, but he received little else. In 1238, he paid a visit to England. On his landing at Dover he was asked how he presumed to enter the country without the permission of its independent sovereign, Henry the Third. Henry had had enough trouble with Crusaders. John de Brienne, who had been in England, had obtained aid from the king and had been honourably received. On his return to France he had joined with Philip Augustus against England. Henry, however, sent word to Baldwin that as he had arrived without troops he might come on to London. After receiving this permission he paid a visit to the king and finally left England with the miserable sum of seven hundred marks.

and England.

The pope had taken Baldwin's cause greatly to heart. He enjoined all Christian princes to give him aid. He ordered the leading archbishops of the West to publish a new Crusade against the Greek schismatics. He directed part of the Peter's pence to be given for the furtherance of the Crusade and ordered that the money which St. Louis with pious zeal had extorted from the Jews as obtained by usury should be employed for the same purpose. He begged the king to direct that one third of the revenues of the churches should be thus employed, and he wrote to the king of England with a similar request. In 1238 John de Bethune started from France with men and money. The expedition, however, came to grief. Its leader died at

Pope supports Latin empire.

---

[1] The soldiers are those who received the *soldi* or pay, as distinguished from the Crusaders, who were supposed to fight only for the cause of the Cross.

Venice and the army melted away, very few ever arriving at the Bosporus.

Decay of
Latin
empire.

The character of the news from Constantinople continued constantly to be more and more distressing. The revenue was yearly decreasing. The money obtained in Europe was already spent, and the knights were driven to desperate expedients to obtain more. Copper was torn from the domes of the churches and other public buildings to be converted into coin. Empty houses were pulled down to supply fuel. The sacred relics, which in the eyes of the Crusaders constituted not only the most valuable treasures of the city but the talisman of its safety, were sold to meet

Sale of
relics.

pressing needs. The Sacred Crown of Thorns had been pledged for a sum of about seven thousand pounds, and when the time came for redeeming it, the Latins were not able to find the money. A Venetian endeavoured to obtain it in order to add to the prosperity of the Bride of the Seas, but Baldwin, possibly out of gratitude to Saint Louis of France, and with the object of obtaining a larger sum, preferred that it should be sent to France. After considerable difficulty and many negotiations, the sacred relic was redeemed and taken with solemn procession from Venice to Paris, where the king himself, clothed in penitential garments and barefoot, went out to meet it and to accompany it to its temporary resting-place. This was in 1239. Baldwin received from Louis, in recompense of his labour to obtain so valuable a prize, the sum of ten thousand marks.

Nor was this the only relic which the crusading empire was obliged to convert into money. A large portion of the true cross, the lance, the sponge, and other objects, the parting with which must have cost Baldwin and his barons many a regret, were also sent to France in order to raise money.[1]

By July 1239 Baldwin had collected in the West all the money and forces available and started for Constantinople. The number of his army was greatly exaggerated by the rumours which preceded it and greatly alarmed the Greeks at Nicaea. He arrived at Constantinople at the end of

---

[1] La Sainte Chapelle in Paris was built to receive these treasures.

December. John Vataces, in consequence of these rumours and as a precaution, allied himself with the Bulgarians. The armies of the two states attacked Constantinople. The Venetians saved the city by arriving in time to make it necessary to raise the siege. Then the Bulgarians made friends with the Latins and allowed a band of Comans (or Tur-comans) who had been driven over the Danube by the Mongols to pass through Bulgaria and take service with the Latins. The emperor of Nicaea could, however, play a similar game, and he induced a band of the same race, who formed excellent light cavalry, to settle on the banks of the Meander and in Phrygia.

John Vataces succeeded, partly by force, partly by persuasion, in inducing the despot of Salonica to abandon the title of emperor and to recognise Nicaea as the true representative of the former empire of Constantine. Vataces thereupon became acknowledged ruler of the kingdom of Salonica from the Aegean to the Adriatic.

Meantime the wealth and population of Constantinople were diminishing every day. Its commerce had almost gone. What was left was in the hands of the Venetians. No taxes could be levied on the poverty-stricken population. The Greeks of the country around Constantinople, who had been the food-producers and the source of revenue to the merchants of the capital, fled from the constant harass of war and invasions, now by Latins, now by Bulgarians, and now by Greeks, into Asia Minor, where they could labour in the fields or trade in peace and quietness.

The population in other parts of the country were in like straits. The continual money difficulties among the Latin knights and the Crusaders generally caused a widespread spirit of lawlessness. Necessity compelled them to live on the country they were passing through, and wherever they were under the command of a weak ruler, pillage was common and almost unchecked. Before men thus lawless, poor peasants fled in alarm across the Marmora to be not only among their own people but where life and property were secure.

As illustrating the lawlessness among the Latin nobles, a story told of the Emperor Robert himself is significant. He was engaged to marry the daughter of Vataces, a marriage which promised obvious advantages to the Latin empire. He preferred, however, a lady who was affianced to a knight of Burgundy. Her mother had acquiesced in her throwing over her *fiancé* in favour of the young emperor. The Burgundian and his friends forced their way into the palace, threw the mother into the sea, and brutally disfigured the face of the girl. The barons approved of the deed, and the king went whining to the pope to condemn the wrong-doers, since he himself was powerless to avenge the insult offered to him.

Under such conditions of lawlessness, capital fled the country. The Latin government had once more to resort to every possible device for raising money, and the ornaments of the churches and other public buildings were sent to the melting-pot or to auction.

While disaster and decay marked the condition of things in Constantinople, Nicaea continued to increase in prosperity. The city itself, in a healthy situation on the beautiful lake of Ascanius, had under the rule of John Vataces already become wealthy. Taxes were light because the revenue was not squandered, and the emperor had carried into the public expenditure the same habits of carefulness which he displayed in the management of his own private estates. It is recorded of him, as an illustration of his thrift, that on presenting the empress with a coronet decked with jewels he explained to her that it had been bought with money exclusively obtained from the sale of eggs produced on his own estates. He paid especial attention to agriculture, and, though distinguished as a warrior, set the example of attending personally to his farm, his flocks and herds, the cultivation of his fields, and the welfare of his labourers. We may excuse his sumptuary laws for the reason that the object was to check the luxury of the nobles and to encourage home manufactures. When he died, in 1254, after a reign of thirty-three years, Nicaea had deservedly obtained the reputation of being the chief city of all Greek-speaking people, whether in Europe or in Asia, the city to which the people lifted up their eyes in confidence of a speedy return to the queen city on the shores of the Bosporus.

The reign of Theodore Lascaris the Second, son of John Vataces, lasted only four years, and though he lacked the ability of his father, and was a sufferer from epilepsy, the empire of Nicaea continued to prosper. His military administration was able and successful. He continued the policy of Vataces in endeavouring to induce or to compel all the Greeks in the Balkan peninsula to come under his rule. It may be fairly said of him that on his death, in 1258, the position of Nicaea was stronger than on his accession. *Theodore II. of Nicaea, 1254–1258*

During these two prosperous reigns in the Greek empire that of the Crusaders had continued to go from bad to worse. In spite of the anathemas of the popes against those who should attack Constantinople, the Bulgarians and the Greeks made war upon it whenever they thought the opportunity favourable. In spite of the exhortation of the popes to Western Europe to furnish men and money, and of the fact that both were furnished, the empire grew weaker in men and its financial situation became worse.

We have seen that Baldwin returned to Constantinople with an army which is said to have numbered 30,000 men, and which in any case was sufficiently large to alarm the Nicene emperor. But these reinforcements seem to have been a burden rather than an advantage, and the chief of the crusading empire had to shock Christian Europe by consenting to give his niece in marriage to the sultan of Konia in order to secure an alliance with him against the Greek emperor. Baldwin's necessities again compelled him to visit France. He was once more received with honour, and at the Council of Lyons, in 1245, he was given the position of supreme honour, and was placed on the right hand of the pope. All, indeed, that the sovereign pontiff could accomplish in favour of his guest in this Council was done. An alliance which the Emperor Frederick had made with John Vataces was denounced, and the head of the *Second visit of Baldwin to West.*

Holy Roman Empire was solemnly excommunicated. While
nothing was said about the alliance with the Seljukian
Turk, Frederick was condemned for allowing his daughter to
be married to a schismatic Greek. Large sums were ordered
to be contributed by the dignitaries of the Church and by
the religious orders for the succour of the empire. St.
Louis again gave Baldwin a welcome, and entertained him
at his court during nearly two years while aid was being
collected. The pope gave power to absolve from sins those
who should join the Crusade or contribute to the support of
the empire. But, as Matthew Paris says, his empire
nevertheless daily decayed. It was not till 1248 that Baldwin
returned to his impoverished capital. Perhaps the lowest
depth of degradation was attained by him when in 1259 his
necessity was so great that he was obliged to put his only
son in pledge to certain Venetian nobles as security for the
payment of what he had borrowed. The unfortunate lad
was taken to Venice, and his father was unable to redeem
him until after the recapture of Constantinople.

Before the death, in 1258, of Theodore Lascaris the
Second, the ruler of Nicaea was acknowledged emperor, not
merely throughout the northern part of Asia Minor, but in the
kingdom of Macedonia, and even in a considerable portion
of Thrace. His successor, John, was a boy. John's guardian
was Michael Palaeologus, who was proclaimed emperor in
January 1259-60. Seeing that there was some disorder in
Nicaea, occasioned by the disputes between those in favour
of the boy, who, in the ordinary course of succession, would
have been emperor, and those who had recognised that the
times were too critical to allow him to reign, and had
consequently followed Michael, the Latin emperor, Baldwin,
judged the moment opportune to stipulate for concessions.
Accordingly he sent a mission to Nicaea to learn what
Michael would give in order to avoid war. The historian
Acropolitas, who was at Nicaea at the time, records what
passed. The emperor mocked the ambassadors. They
asked that he should surrender Salonica. The reply was
that that city was the emperor's birthplace; how could he

John Ducas
Emperor
of Nicaea,
1258–1260.

Michael
Palaeolo-
gus.

part with it? They suggested Seres. The emperor responded that what they were asking was neither just nor decent, since he had received it from his father. 'Give us, then, Bolero.' But that was the emperor's hunting-ground, and could not be spared. 'What, then, will you give us?' 'Nothing whatever,' replied the emperor. 'But if you want peace with me, it is well, because you know me, and that I can fight. Pay me part of the tribute collected at Constantinople, and we shall be at peace.' No better terms were to be had, and the ambassadors left.

Michael probably understood that his refusal would be followed by war. He therefore visited the fortifications already gained in Thrace by the Greeks, strengthened them, and within a few months the Latin empire was reduced to the occupation of Constantinople and a small strip around it. In the following year, 1260, Michael's general, Stratego-pulus, was entrusted with the command in Thrace. He stormed Selymbria (the modern Silivria), and tried but failed to capture Galata, which was already in the occupation of the Genoese. Thereupon a truce was made for one year.

Seeing that the Venetians, whose great power in the Levant dates from the fall of Constantinople in 1204, in which they had played so important a part, still maintained their connection with the empire on the Bosporus and, indeed, continued to be the principal source of such strength as it possessed, Michael, to the great indignation of the pope and the West, made an alliance with their rivals, the Genoese, an alliance which was the foundation of their supremacy in trade in the Black Sea.

It is not impossible that Strategopulus had been sent into Thrace in 1260 rather to form a judgment of the chances of capturing the city than of making war. It is quite possible, as suggested even by Pachymer, that the attempt on Galata was a mere feint in order that he might get into communication with friends in the capital. In consenting to give a year's truce, however, Michael seems to have been sincere. Accordingly, when, in 1261, he again sent

Capture of Constanti-nople by the Greeks.

Strategopulus into Thrace it was with instructions that he was not to attack the city. He had with him only 800 men, but as he passed through the country behind Constantinople the Greek settlers (Volunteers, as they are called, Θελημᾶτάριοι), who had friends in the city, flocked to him, and urged that he would never have a better chance of capturing it than at that time. The last detachment of troops which had come from France had left the city, with the Venetian fleet, upon an expedition into the Black Sea to capture Daphnusia. Constantinople might be surprised in their absence. In spite of the imperial orders, the chance was too good to be missed. He brought his men to the neighbourhood of the capital, and hid them near the Holy Well of Baloukli, situated at about half a mile from the Gate of the Fountain,[1] one of the important entrances into the city through the landward walls. His volunteers had not deceived him when they stated that they had friends in the city. Probably every Greek was a secret sympathiser.

George Acropolitas, who died in 1282, and whose account, therefore, must have been written while the events were fresh in his memory, gives the most trustworthy version of what happened. He says: 'But as Strategopulus had some men near him who had come from the city and were well acquainted with all that had passed there, from whom he learned that there was a hole in the walls of the city through which an armed man could easily pass, he lost no time and set to work. A man passed through this hole; another followed, then others, until fifteen, and perhaps more, had got into the city. But, as they found a man on the walls on guard, some of them mounted the wall and, taking him by the feet, threw him over. Others having axes in their hands broke the locks and bolts of the gates, and thus rendered the entry easy for the army. This is how the Cæsar Strategopulus, and all the men he had with him, Romans and Scythians (for his army was composed of these

---

[1] Πύλη τῆς πηγῆς, so called because it led to the Holy Well, is better known as the Silivria Gate. See Professor Van Millingen's *Byzantine Constantinople*, p. 75.

two peoples), made their entry into the city.'[1] Probably there were few inhabitants in that quarter, and the advance to the principal part of the city might be made in the dark. At dawn the invaders pushed on boldly, met with a brave resistance from a few—a resistance which they soon over-came—and the rest of the French[2] defenders were seized with panic and fled. While the city was thus passing once more into the hands of the Greeks, the French and Venetian ships were coming straggling down the Bosporus, on their return from Daphnusia, which they had failed to capture. Accordingly, the army of Strategopulus and his volunteers set fire to the dwellings in the French and Venetian quarters in the city and to their villas on the European shore of the Bosporus near Galata. While the foreigners were occupied in saving their own property and their women and children from the fire, Strategopulus strengthened his position in the city.

The weak and incapable Baldwin was at the palace of Blachern when the Greeks entered the city. Afraid to pass through the streets where the fighting was going on, he entered a boat, made his way down the Golden Horn, and took refuge among other fugitives with the Venetian fleet.

Flight of Baldwin II.

His flight was on July 25, 1261, and with it ends the history of the Latin empire in Constantinople. It had been established by perjured Crusaders and filibustering Venetians who were justly anathematised by Innocent the

End of Latin empire.

---

[1] P. 191. Pachymer, writing fifty years afterwards, adds that they placed ladders against the walls; and Nicephorus Gregoras, writing a century after-wards, speaks of a secret entry by an old subterranean passage for water, through which fifty men passed. Gibbon makes the mistake of saying that the entry was at the Golden Gate. Strategopulus had the Gate of the Fountain—that is, the Silivria Gate—opened for his troops. The Emperor Michael subse-quently entered by the Golden Gate; possibly, as Dethier suggests (iii. 605), by the ancient gate of that name in the Constantine Walls, which was still used for ceremonial purposes.

[2] It is unlikely that at this time there were any foreigners among the fighting men other than Frenchmen. The pope's demands for the defence of the empire do not appear to have been responded to outside France.

Third. It had always been a sickly plant in a foreign and uncongenial soil, and, though popes and kings had made quite remarkable exertions to make it grow, it never even gave a sign of taking root. The empire had succeeded, as Innocent predicted that it would, in making the Greeks loathe the members of the Latin Church like dogs, and in rendering the union of the two Churches impossible. The Crusaders, as Innocent had likewise foretold, had seized an empire which they could not defend.[1] Their expedition had broken up the great machine of Roman government which had been working steadily and, in the main, well for nearly a thousand years. It had done irreparable mischief unaccompanied by any compensatory good. In the course of two generations, the barons who had taken part in the capture had died, and though among those who, at the bidding of successive popes and of St. Louis, replaced them there must have been many actuated by worthy motives, none among them have left any evidence whatever of statesmanship or of those qualities which have enabled nations to conciliate or to assimilate the people whom they have conquered. In sixty years the peasants might have become content to acknowledge a change of rulers had they been allowed to till their fields in peace : the traders might have forgotten the hostility of their fathers if they had been permitted to exercise their industry in security; but the continued and ever increasing exactions of their masters forbade them to forget that they were under alien rulers. All that were worthy in the city had sought refuge elsewhere : the priests, the students with their priceless manuscripts, and the traders had escaped to Nicaea or to Trebizond. The oppressors had seen themselves deserted and the limits of the empire restricted almost to the boundaries of the city. The Latin empire, which had never been formidable, had become an object of contempt. When, however, its last emperor slunk away as a fugitive from his imperial city, he was hardly more contemptible than when

[1] *Epist. Inn.* viii. 133.

he was present as a mendicant at the court of St. Louis or of Henry the Third. His empire deserves only to be remembered as a gigantic failure, a check to the progress of European civilisation, a mischievous episode, an abortion among states, born in sin, shapen in iniquity, and dying amid ignominy.

CHAPTER II

CONDITION OF AND DIFFICULTIES IN RECONSTRUCTING
THE EMPIRE : DIFFICULTIES ARISING (A) FROM ATTEMPTS
BY LATINS TO RECOVER THE EMPIRE, (B) FROM CATALAN
GRAND COMPANY.

Condition
of capital
on Bald-
win's flight.

WHEN Constantinople was captured by the Crusaders and
Venetians it was adorned with the accumulated wealth of
centuries and decorated with art treasures for which not
only Greece but the whole Roman Empire had been ransacked. When the city was recaptured by the Greeks it
was a desolation. Houses, churches, and monasteries were
in ruins; whole quarters were deserted. Heaps of rubbish
marked where extensive fires had consumed houses which
no one cared to rebuild. The imperial palace itself was in
so disorderly and filthy a condition that it was some time
before it could be occupied. In place of a large population
of the most educated and highly civilised people in Europe,
was a miserably small number of Greeks who had been
reduced to poverty with a number of foreign and principally
French colonists. While the foreign captors had plundered
the city and carried off the bronze horses of Lysippus and
innumerable other objects of art and value to Western
Europe, they and their successors during the fifty-eight
years of occupation had, in their contemptuous ignorance of
the art of a conquered people, destroyed probably more than
had been taken away as plunder.

The Queen City, which during many centuries had
preserved her inviolability and had largely for that reason
become the treasure-house of the empire and even of a
large part of the Western world, had lost her reputation as

a place of safety. Amid the devastation in Egypt, in Syria, and in Asia Minor, marked and mainly caused by the advances of the Saracens and Seljukian Turks, by the struggles of the Crusaders, and the destruction of the ancient civilisations of Eastern Asia Minor occasioned by the westward movements of Asiatic hordes, the merchant had known only of one city where his merchandise was safe and where he could trade in security.

The stream of commerce between the East and the West which had flowed through the Bosporus had been diverted into other channels, and the great *emboloi* and warehouses were lying empty or in ruins. Tana or the Azof, which had been the starting-point of a great caravan route through Bokhara, Samarcand, and Balkh, now no longer contributed largely to the commerce of Constantinople. Such of its trade as was not sent overland to Western Europe was held by the Venetians, and at a somewhat later period by the Genoese or other Italians, and scarcely contributed at all to the wealth of the capital. The Danube became during the thirteenth century the highway between the Black and the North Seas. The city which had been the great centre for the collection and distribution of the furs, the hides, the caviare and dried fish, the honey, wax, and other produce which the Russian merchants collected and stored for the use of the West, was now studiously avoided. The Western traders who had met those from Novgorod, Tchernigov, and Kief at Constantinople now found their way to the mouth of the Dnieper and arranged for the transit of their goods so as to avoid the pirates whom the Latin rulers of Constantinople were unable to suppress, or the exactions levied upon their merchandise if they came within the power of the ancient capital. Trade which had come to Constantinople along the ancient roads through Asia Minor had either ceased to exist or had been diverted into other channels. The confidence arising from a sense of security which through a long series of years had attracted commerce could not be restored and in fact was never regained. The loss of her trade took from Constantinople the only external source of

Loss of its commerce.

revenue. The restored empire had thus to depend almost exclusively upon the contributions which it could levy upon the long harassed and impoverished peoples who recognised its rule.

The recapture of the capital, though an epoch-marking event, was only one step towards the restoration of the empire. It never really was restored. It never recovered the commanding position which it had occupied during even the worst periods of its history since Constantine. Its existence from 1261 to its capture by the Turks in 1453 is one long struggle.

Difficulties of restored empire.

The capital had been a centre which had kept well in touch with even the remote corners of the empire. In it had been the seat of government, the highest law courts presided over by the ablest jurists, the continuators of the work of Justinian, whose labour had formulated the law of all continental Europe. There also was the centre of the theological and religious life of the empire and the seat of the administration. Unhappily, during the sixty years of Latin rule the whole framework of this administration had been broken up. A new plan of government had to be devised. The new officials of the emperors were called upon to govern without rules, without experience, and without traditions. The forms of provincial and municipal government were hardly remembered, and there were no men trained in affairs to breathe life into them.

The influences at work in the capital had bound the empire together, but they had been exercised through local administrations. The result now was that the government became centralised : that is, that matters which previously would have been dealt with in the provinces by men with local knowledge had to be dealt with in the capital by men who were necessarily under many disadvantages. The effort of its rulers after the city was recaptured was not merely to restore to it the territory which had acknowledged its sway, but to administer good government directly from its capital.

Unfortunately, the desolation wrought in Constantinople was reproduced throughout every portion of what had been the empire before the Latin conquest. The country had been everywhere impoverished and the population diminished by successive raids of Crusaders or pretenders.

Nor were the external difficulties of the restored empire less alarming. When Michael the Eighth entered the recaptured city he found anarchy throughout his European territory and neighbouring states eager to enlarge their boundaries at his expense. The Bulgarians were a formidable power, whose dominions were not divided from his own by any natural boundary. The Serbians had utilised the period of the Latin occupation to gather strength and were rising once again to importance. The crusading families who had obtained fiefs in Greece and the southern portion of Macedonia still retained their independence. Genoese and Venetians, while struggling against each other for the favour of the emperor, were each on the alert to obtain territory as well as trading privileges at his expense. *From foreign states.*

One of the most serious evils inflicted on the empire by the Latin occupation was the fierce antagonism it had created in the Orthodox Church towards that of the elder Rome. We have seen that Innocent had foreseen this result, but even he, great statesman though he was, could hardly have anticipated that the hatred aroused would be of so long a duration. When the city had been captured a Latin patriarch had been appointed, the union of the Churches had been forced upon clergy and people, and the Church, which had always considered itself the equal if not the superior of Rome, was relegated to a position of inferiority. All attempts at re-union were henceforward regarded not merely from the point of view of religion, but from that of patriotism. Union was part of the heritage of bondage. Union meant voluntary submission to the foreign Church which had been able to impose its rule during two generations. Union, therefore, in the minds of a majority of both clergy and laity had to be resisted as a badge of slavery. *From hostility towards Roman Church.*

Though the Latin empire had perished, there still remained a Latin emperor or pretender, and he and his descendants, with the support of successive popes and aided by adventurers from France, Italy, and Spain, made many and constant attempts to regain the position which had been lost. For upwards of a century after the city's recapture there was a general scramble by the European neighbours of the empire and Western powers for adjacent territory. The dominions of the emperor were large and sparsely populated, and offered an irresistible temptation to neighbouring states. More formidable, however, than all other enemies were the Turks. Though they had been attacked in the rear and were for a while rent by internal dissensions, they were steadily increasing: adding constantly by conquests to the territory over which their emirs ruled, and increasing in numbers by the never-failing stream of immigrants and born warriors coming into Asia Minor from Central Asia.

From
Michael's
usurpa-
tion.
Among the first difficulties encountered in the reconstruction of the empire must be noted that arising from the irregularity of Michael's own position. It is worthy of note, not merely as a difficulty, but as showing the independent spirit of the Orthodox Church. The reader will have ample evidence of the inflexibility of its resistance on questions of dogma, but the very commencement of the reign of Michael illustrates how it was prepared to make a vigorous stand even against the deliverer of the empire on the simple ground of righteousness. We have seen that Michael had no legal claim to the throne. The *de jure* heir was John, a child of eight years when his father, Theodore Lascaris, died. His guardians were Michael, who had been made Grand Duke, and Arsenius the Patriarch. When a year afterwards, in 1261, the city was recaptured, it was expected by some persons of influence that Michael would either simply act as regent or associate John with him as co-emperor as soon as he became of age. Michael, however, in the same year, blinded the boy, so as to render him incapable of ascending the throne.[1] Arsenius the Patriarch, as soon as the cruel deed became known, called a meeting of the bishops and boldly pronounced against the

[1] Pachymer, iii. 10.   Greg. iv. 4.

emperor a formal sentence of excommunication. None of the bishops opposed. They did not attempt to depose him. One can only conjecture why they hesitated. Possibly it was because they considered it expedient that he should remain on the throne, or it may be that they regarded such a step as beyond their jurisdiction. The emperor was alarmed, feared the consequences of excommunication among the troops, but feared probably still more the spiritual penalties which would follow the sentence. He preferred, says Pachymer,[1] to die rather than to live burdened with the anathemas of the Church. He sought out friends of the patriarch and begged them to use all their influence to have the penalties removed. He urged that penance should be imposed, and professed himself ready to undergo any which might be deemed necessary to atone for his fault. The patriarch replied that, even if he were threatened with death, he would never remove the excommunication. The emperor went himself to visit Arsenius, and in the conversation asked whether it was his wish that he should abdicate, unbuckling his sword as he did so. When, however, the patriarch stretched out his hand to receive it, the emperor put it back. The patriarch remained firm. The emperor complained bitterly to his friends of the conduct of Arsenius, and threatened that, as his own Church would not grant him absolution, he would have recourse to the pope, who would be more conciliatory. Years passed and Arsenius constantly refused to give way. Every means thought of by the emperor of conciliating him had failed, and he at length determined to have him deposed. But threats and promises were equally unavailable. He had called together the bishops on several occasions and complained that it was impossible for him to govern the country unless he was relieved of so heavy a burden.[2] On the last of these occasions he claimed that by the law of the Church every Christian had a right to absolution on doing penance, and he asked whether such laws were to be construed less favourably for princes than for other sinners. He submitted that the patriarch had treated him not only

---

[1] Pach. iii. 16.   [2] Ibid. iv. 1.

unjustly but illegally, and concluded by inviting the bishops
to depose Arsenius.

Once more he sent to ask the patriarch whether or not
he would grant absolution, and once more Arsenius refused.
Upon this, as the bishops would not consent to declare that
he was not justified in maintaining the anathema, the
emperor had Articles of Accusation drawn against him.
The charges were not altogether of a trivial character. He
accused him of having shortened the prayer for the emperor
in matins ; of having ordered the omission of the Trisagion ;
of having conversed in a friendly manner with the sultan of
the Seljukian Turks ; of having allowed him and other
Mahometan companions to bathe in a bath belonging to
the Church, where there were crosses ; of having ordered a
monk to administer the Sacrament to the sultan's children
although he was not certain that they had been baptised.

An assembly of bishops was convoked to examine the
charges. The patriarch replied by objecting to the meeting
of the court in the palace, refused to appear, and promised
to send his answer to the charges in writing. Pachymer
recounts in some detail how the emperor endeavoured to
obtain absolution by a trick, and how Arsenius on discovering
it asked him if he thought he could deceive God. The
emperor in reply insisted that some of the charges should
be pressed on to hearing and obtained a majority of vote
condemning the patriarch.[1]

The patriarch was thereupon exiled.

His successor, Germanus, removed the anathema, but
doubts arose in the emperor's mind whether the removal
was valid. After a few months Germanus was persuaded
by the emperor to retire, and in his place the nominee of
Michael, a certain Joseph, was named. The new patriarch
was a courtier, and probably knew that the principal reason
for his election was that absolution might be effectively and
publicly given. The emperor allowed Joseph a month
within which to consider the best means of granting him

---

[1] Pach. iv. 6. Pachymer took part in these proceedings, and was in fact
one of the clerks of the court.

absolution, and then all was arranged. On the great feast of Candlemas, February 2, 1267, there was a notable function in Hagia Sophia for the removal of the anathema. The ceremony was a long and solemn one, the patriarch and the bishops, and probably the emperor and his suite, having had to pass the whole night in the church. The great church was crowded with worshippers or spectators. When the liturgy was completed the emperor, who had thus far remained standing surrounded by his guards and senators, drew near the Holy Gates [1] behind which stood the bishops. Then, uncovered, he prostrated himself to the ground at the feet of the patriarch, publicly confessed his sin, and humbly demanded pardon. While he was thus prostrate, the patriarch, and after him each of the bishops, read the formula by which he was absolved from the crime committed against the young emperor. When all had thus given absolution, the emperor rose, was admitted to Holy Communion, and, says Pachymer, henceforward treated John with every kindness. The point, however, to be noted is that even the emperor, strong-willed usurper as he was, was not merely afraid of the terrors of the Church, but found it extremely difficult to bend it to his will so as to obtain the removal of its sentence for an unjust act, although there were many obvious advantages to the state in complying with the emperor's wish.

From the first year of his accession Michael the Eighth set himself the task of diverting from the empire the attacks of Western states. It was not to be expected that Baldwin and the statesmen of the West would settle down resignedly to the loss of a Latin empire. During many years their attempts to regain the city constituted the most pressing danger to the empire and contributed more than any other cause during Michael's reign to render it unable to hold its own against the encroachments of the Turks. To Michael, as to all other statesmen in Europe, the representative of the

Difficulties arising from attempts by Latins to recover the Empire.

---

[1] The Holy Gates are in the middle of the Iconostasis or screen which separates the bema or chancel from the nave.

West was the pope. To satisfy the pope was to appease Western Europe, to divert attacks from the empire, and to cause aid to be sent against the Moslems. But the pope, on the accession of Michael, was doubly offended : first, because the Latin empire had been overthrown, and second, because the prospect of union between the two Churches was put back. Several years had to pass and many struggles had to be borne before the pontiffs reconciled themselves to the final disappearance of that Latin empire the foundation of which the great statesman Pope Innocent the Third had dreaded.

Attempts at reconciliation with Roman Church.
Michael, while resisting all attacks made or favoured by the pope, saw the desirability of being reconciled with him so as, if possible, to induce him not to lend his support to the efforts of Baldwin to recover the city. With this object he never lost an opportunity, even at the cost of alienating the sympathies of his own people and being denounced by his own ecclesiastics, of endeavouring to gain the pontifical favour by attempting to bring about the Union of the Churches.

It is remarkable that from his accession until the end of his reign these attempts fill a part of all contemporary histories quite disproportionate to what at first sight appears their importance. It is even more remarkable that during the whole period between the capture of the city by Michael and the Moslem siege in 1453 the dominant question of interest was that of the Union of the Churches. The fact that the representative of Western Europe was the sovereign pontiff accounts to a great extent, though not altogether, for the prominent part played by the religious question in nearly all the negotiations between the later emperors and the West. Not even the constant and almost unceasing struggle with the Turks occupies so much attention as do the negotiations with Rome, the embassies, the Councils, and the ever-varying tentatives to bring the two Churches into reconciliation. No true conception of the life of the empire can be formed unless it is realised how completely its citizens were occupied with these semi-religious, semi-political questions. On one side the popes were almost constant in their attempts, now to compel the Eastern Church to come in, now to persuade it; on the other, the emperors, while fully cognisant of the importance of diverting Western attacks and, at a later period, of receiving aid against the common enemy of Christendom, had constantly to meet with the dogged and unceasing opposition and bitter hostility of the great mass of their subjects to purchasing help at the price of union with the Latin Church.

A struggle began immediately on the accession of Michael and soon became a curiously complicated strife. The pope in 1262 proclaimed a Crusade against him and against the Genoese, who still remained -allied with him. The pontiff characterised Michael as a usurper and a schismatic, and granted the same indulgences to those who took up arms or contributed to the expenses of the expedition against him as to those who fought for the deliverance of the Holy Land. He urged St. Louis to collect tithes for the same purpose.[1] Michael, on the other hand, while preparing to resist invasion and strengthening the city walls, increasing his fleet, and raising new levies, yet sought to satisfy the pope by offering to do his utmost to bring about the Union of the Churches. Possibly owing to the emperor's representations, Urban the Fourth countermanded the proposed expedition, diverting it against the Tartars who were then invading Palestine. He sent friars to Constantinople to exhort the emperor to carry out his proposal for reunion. His successor, Clement, was, however, a man of a different spirit and replied to the promises of Michael that they were only fair words intended to prevent him from aiding the dethroned Baldwin. While Michael had undoubtedly this object in view, he seems to have been sincere in his desire for Union. One of his objections to the patriarch Arsenius was that he would have nothing to do with the Latins. The Greek priests clamoured to such an extent against the patriarch who succeeded Arsenius, because he was believed to be willing to follow the emperor's example in working for Union, that he was compelled to resign.

---

[1] Raynoldus and Vadingus.

As time went on, the Venetians, whose influence in the city had fallen with the Latin empire, began to lose hope of seeing Baldwin re-established on the throne, and in 1267 sent to make peace with Michael. Gregory the Tenth threatened the doge with anathema if he even made a truce with him. The emperor endeavoured, though in vain, to appease the wrath of the pope by obtaining the intervention of Louis of France. Gregory, whom Michael had congratulated on his accession upon the death of Clement, was more conciliatory. He sent legates to the capital to treat once more on Union. Pachymer gives a vivid account of the negotiations which followed, an account from which it is difficult to doubt the sincerity of the emperor's wish for reconciliation or the persistence of the opposition which he had to encounter. He states [1] that the emperor followed the example of John Ducas of Nicaea, that he sent many embassies to Rome, and that his real object was to obtain from the popes protection for the Greeks. Gregory assured him that no time was so favourable as the present for putting an end to the Greek schism. The emperor on his side did his utmost to persuade the patriarch and the bishops to aid him. The Latin delegates themselves were men of piety who showed every possible respect for the Greek rite. They were invited to discuss the differences between the dogmas of the two Churches. In their interviews with the bishops they claimed that the *Filioque* clause which constituted the great point of discussion was a divine mystery which was impenetrable, that while the difference between the Latin formula which declared that the Holy Ghost proceeds from the Father and the Son was not really at variance with the Greek that He proceeded from the Father by the Son, they ought to be content with the reasons which the Latins adduced for inserting it in the Creed. The bishops met these observations with a rugged *non possumus*. Their Creed was what had been consecrated by the usage of centuries. It was dangerous for any one Church to add to the

---

[1] Ch. v. 9. It should be remembered that Pachymer had himself joined the Latin Church.

Symbols even words which were not contrary to the Catholic faith. The bishops openly declared that, whatever the threats of the emperor might be, they would hold to the ancient formula.

News of an expedition to restore the Latin empire came pouring in, and the emperor determined to have his own way and to conciliate the pope. In an assembly in which the patriarch, bishops, and other ecclesiastics took part he spoke at great length in favour of reconciliation. The patriarch appointed Veccus, a man famous for his eloquence and learning, to reply to him. His reply is summed up by Pachymer : ' There are heretics who are so called. There are some who are not heretics and are not so called. There are some who are called but are not heretics, and lastly there are others who are not called but are heretics, and it is in this latter class that the Latins must be placed.'

The emperor dismissed the assembly and was violently angry against Veccus, whom he accused of having acted with bad faith. Having failed in substantiating a formal charge, he arbitrarily sent him prisoner to the Tower of Anemas. While in prison, however, Michael furnished him with books which favoured the Latin case, and, says Pachymer, as he was a man of singular simplicity and of sincere love for the truth he became disposed towards reconciliation. He was released. The emperor pressed the patriarch and he bishops to find a *modus vivendi* with the Latins, and was now aided by Veccus, who had discovered that the sole ault of the Western Church was that it had solely upon ts own authority added the obnoxious clause to the Creed. The patriarch and the bishops, however, were obdurate. By dint of persecution, by requiring them to pay arrears of rent for their monasteries and houses, he sought to force them o come to an arrangement. He called another assembly and finally succeeded in obtaining a declaration from them with which for the time he was forced to be content. In his very assembly, however, one of the aged bishops besought him not to press the Union, assuring him that

even if the dignitaries signed no one else would accept it.
The Arsenites and the Josephites, as the followers of the
two ex-patriarchs who would not comply with the emperor's
wish were called, had with them the great mass of the citizens, and the aged dignitary was probably right when he
stated [1] that if the emperor persisted, civil war would be
the consequence.

Meantime the emperor, who could not or would not
understand this bitter opposition to his desires, was aware
that negotiations were going on between Charles of Anjou,
king of Sicily (whose daughter had married the son and
heir of Baldwin, the ex-emperor), and the Venetians for an
attack upon his territories and the restoration of the Latin
empire. Michael sent costly presents to the pope, and
once more declared his determination to bring about Union,
and asked his indulgence. Once more he sent delegates to
the pope, who in return ordered Charles to facilitate their
passage through his dominions and to postpone hostilities.
The emperor insisted on Union, and in the following year,
1274, he and some of the bishops sent other delegates to
Lyons to complete a formal reconciliation. On their arrival
in that city they pronounced during the celebration of Mass
the obnoxious clause. Gregory the Tenth declared that
they had come voluntarily to submit themselves, to make
the Roman confession of faith, and to recognise his supremacy. After George Acropolitas had read the emperor's
profession, and the envoy of the bishops theirs, a *Te Deum*
was sung and the Union proclaimed. But whatever the
pope or the emperor might wish or even do, the Eastern
Church was not prepared to ratify a reconciliation. The
patriarch still refused to yield. He had gone as far as he
intended to go and declared that he would abdicate if the
Union were accomplished. Thereupon he was deposed by
the synod. Immediately afterwards the pope's name was
introduced into the public prayers, but with the result that
the breach between those in favour of Union and those
opposed to it became wider. The emperor pertinaciously

[1] Pach. v. 18.

persevered, and with his consent Veccus, who had now gone over to the emperor's side, was named patriarch.

On the return of the delegates from Lyons, preaching friars were sent to Constantinople by Innocent the Fifth. On his death, in 1276, his successor, John the Twenty-fifth, sent nuncios, who were received with great honour, and Michael, in return, together with the patriarch sent delegates to confirm the Union. They arrived, however, in Rome after the death of John. In 1277 Michael and his son Andronicus, the heir to the throne, who was now of full age, formally confirmed the Union of the Churches. Thereupon there began a struggle with those who opposed it. The patriarch Veccus excommunicated its adversaries, mentioning the leaders by name. John the Bastard, the despot of Epirus, who was the foremost, at once called a Council and submitted the question to its decision. This Council anathematised alike the emperor, the pope, and the patriarch. Some of the nobles and officers sent against John openly declared for him as the defender of the ancient faith.

The new pope was convinced that the emperor was doing his utmost to bring about Union, and in consequence refused permission to Charles of Anjou to send an expedition against him. When his nuncios arrived, in 1279, in the capital, they learned that, in spite of the emperor and the patriarch, the clergy and people would not accept Union. The nuncios were taken to the prisons and saw nobles, even of the emperor's own family, as well as many others, loaded with chains on account of their opposition on this question to the imperial wish. They were convinced of the emperor's good faith, but no definite statement could be obtained from the bishops. *Non possumus* remained the expression of their attitude.

When, however, Martin the Fourth learned from the nuncios what was the position in Constantinople, he seems either to have lost all hope of bringing about Union by persuasion, or possibly to have thought that his predecessor had been deceived by Michael; for in 1281 he excommunicated the emperor and all the Greeks as schismatics. By so doing he became free to assist in organising the long-threatened expedition for the restoration of the Latin empire. Michael in reply simply contented himself with the omission of the pope's name from the prayers.

Martin followed up his excommunication by joining in a league with Charles of Anjou and the Venetians in order to replace Michael by Philip, the son of Baldwin the Latin emperor. In the following year the pope in renewing his excommunication gave the emperor until May 1, 1282, within which to submit himself under pain of being deposed. Michael's position was desperate. He had alienated his own subjects ; he had risked his throne, imprisoned his nearest relations, had tried bribes, intrigues, flattery, and force. Worse than all, he had been forced to allow the various hordes of Moslems in Asia Minor—Turks, Kurds, and Tartars—to encroach on the territory of the empire at a time when, if he had had a free hand, a serious check might have been put to their progress. All was in vain. His failure with the popes was now as complete as with his own people. The threat of an expedition under Charles of Anjou was so serious that he sent thirty thousand ounces of gold to Peter of Aragon to assist him in defeating Charles and diverting his expedition from the Bosporus. He became irritable and melancholy at the obstinacy of his subjects and punished them with unreasonable severity and great cruelty.[1]

The pope's expedition was, however, put an end to by the Sicilian Vespers in March 1282. The forces of Charles of Anjou found other employment than an expedition to Constantinople. In December of the same year Michael died.[2]

Death of
Michael
VIII.

[1] Pach. vi. 24 and 25.

[2] I have relied mostly for this account of the attempt at Union on Pachymer (I agree with Krumbacher's high estimate of the value of this author's history) :

'Pachymeres ragt durch seine Bildung und litterarische Thätigkeit über seine Zeitgenossen empor und kann als der grösste byzantinische Polyhistor des 13. Jahrhunderts bezeichnet werden. In ihm erblickt man deutlich die Licht- und Schattenseiten des Zeitalters der Paläologen. Es fehlt dem Pachymeres nicht an Gelehrsamkeit, Originalität und Witz.' *Geschichte der Byzantinischen ~ ˙ᵗᵗˢᵐᵃᵗᵘᵣ.* p. 289˙ Pachymer was himself a Greek, born in Nicaea but a

During the long reign of Andronicus the Second (1282 to 1328), the son and successor of Michael, the party which the latter had headed in favour of Union with Rome fell to pieces. The older emperor's disappointment probably hastened his death. Veccus the patriarch within a few months was forced to withdraw to a monastery. His writings in favour of Union were burned. He was put upon his trial before a synod and saved himself by signing a declaration against further attempts at reconciliation with the Latin Church. The ex-patriarch Joseph was brought back in triumph, and a persecution at once commenced of those who had favoured the emperor's plans.

This hostility to the Unionist party was contemporaneous with a short period during which the fear of an attack to re-establish a Latin empire had lessened. The attention of the pontiff was directed towards sending aid to the king of Armenia, who had been for years making a brave defence against his Moslem assailants. But the attempt at Union and the re-establishment of a Latin empire was not forgotten. In 1287 Nicholas the Fourth endeavoured to accomplish these objects while allowing the Greek emperor to remain on the throne. He favoured, and perhaps suggested, a marriage between Michael, the eldest son of Andronicus, and Catherine of Courtenay, the granddaughter of Baldwin. Her other grandfather, Charles of Anjou, king of Sicily, claimed the imperial throne on her behalf.[1] The proposal of marriage had much to recommend it to the emperor, because it appeared to be a means of putting an end to the attempts to regain the imperial throne by the deposed family. The arrangements were broken off because Andronicus would not agree to recognise the pope's supremacy, without which the pontiff refused his consent. Considering the attitude of the Greek ecclesiastics, there can be little doubt that if the emperor had agreed to the pope's

member of the Latin Church. He deals with the doings of the emperor and the Greek ecclesiastics in a fair spirit. His History is essentially that of his own times and covers the period from 1261 to 1308.

[1] Pach. part 2, ii. 18.

demand the already strained relations between the Orthodox and the Roman parties would have become dangerous to the state, would have probably brought about civil war, and might have cost Andronicus his throne. The question after long negotiations was settled in 1295 by the marriage of Michael with the sister of the king of Armenia.

Popes favour project for re-establishing Latin empire.

The popes thereupon took a bolder course. They had seen the futility of the efforts to obtain Union by negotiation with the emperor, and now supported a series of attempts to recapture Constantinople and to place upon the throne a descendant of the last Latin emperor, Baldwin the Second. If the recapture could be accomplished, the Union so dear to Rome could be brought about by force.

In 1301 Catherine of Courtenay married Charles of Valois, brother of the king of France.[1] The marriage was a political one, its object being to give the hand of Catherine to a Western prince of sufficient standing to arouse an enthusiasm in all the West in favour of the restoration of the Latin empire. Charles at once entered into a treaty with the Venetians for the conquest of Constantinople, and arranged to recognise the assignment of certain portions of the empire which had already been made to other descendants of Baldwin. A Venetian was designated by the pope as Latin patriarch of Constantinople. Eighteen Venetian ships went to the capital, and were sufficiently powerful to force the emperor to grant trading concessions. Charles of Anjou and Frederic of Aragon bound themselves to aid in the attempts to recapture Constantinople.

It was in presence of this threatened attack, which

---

[1] The following table of descent will illustrate the text :

Baldwin II., emperor of Constantinople, fled the city 1261, died 1272.

Philip, married Beatrice, daughter of Charles of Anjou, king of Sicily, died 1288.

Catherine, married in 1301 Charles of Valois, son of Philip III. of France ; Charles died 1308.

| John, died without issue. | Catherine married Philip of Tarentum, son of Charles of Sicily. Philip died 1322 : Catherine in 1346. | Joanna | Elizabeth |

appeared to be far the most serious which had been contemplated since the city's recapture, that the emperor invited a certain Roger de Flor and his band of Spanish mercenaries, who came to be known as the Catalan Grand Company, to come to his aid.

Within the city itself great efforts were made, in presence of the common danger, to unite the theological factions. The patriarch, who had pronounced an anathema against the emperor, consented to withdraw it. The truce, however, between the ecclesiastics was unfortunately of short duration. As time passed, and the much-vaunted expedition did not present itself, the old rancours again showed themselves.

Indeed, the expedition to place Charles of Valois on the imperial throne made slow progress. In 1305 his brother, the king of France, gave it his support. Once more the pontiff invited the Venetians to follow the example of Dandolo and aid in the conquest of the city. It was not, however, till the end of 1306 that a treaty of alliance was made between them and Charles. The result which might have been anticipated followed when the news was received in the capital. The Latin monks, who up to this time had been tolerated within the city, were expelled, and the party in favour of Union almost entirely disappeared. Meantime the preparations for the expedition continued.

In 1308 its titular head, Charles of Valois, allied himself with the Servians. Charles himself was ready, but apparently not eager, for the enterprise. The Venetians desired speedy action; but the Western nobles only feebly responded to the pope's demand, although it was supported by the king of France. Charles of Anjou was not ready. In the course of the next year Catherine of Courtenay died, and partly on account of her death, and probably also because he despaired of leading a successful enterprise, Charles of Valois abandoned the design of capturing Constantinople. He, however, transferred what he considered his rights to the throne to his son-in-law, Philip of Tarentum.

The Venetians resigned themselves to a position which

would allow them once more to trade with the empire, and in 1310 concluded a truce with its ruler for ten years.

Philip now prepared to organise an attempt against Constantinople, and once more the pope, in 1313, weakened the position of the Latin party in Constantinople by calling upon Frederic, king of Sicily, to aid the new pretender. The king of France undertook to furnish five hundred men-at-arms, and money to pay them for a year, and called upon Louis of Burgundy to furnish another hundred. The undertaking, however, languished, and when Philip of France died, in 1314, no one, except Philip of Tarentum, seemed to have any further interest in it. He leagued himself with the king of Hungary in 1318, and two years later purchased certain rights in the principality of Achaia and what was still spoken of in the West as the kingdom of Thessalonica. But no favourable opportunity came to him, and in 1324 the doge of Venice notified the emperor that the princes of the West had no intention of attacking the imperial city. The notification turned out correct, for, until his dethronement, in 1328, Andronicus was no longer troubled with tidings of expeditions against Constantinople from Western Europe.

The Catalan Grand Company. Expedition against Constantinople.

Meantime it is necessary to return to the invitation which Andronicus had given to Robert de Flor to come to his aid. This aid was intended nominally against the Turks, but really against the expedition which Charles of Valois was preparing, with the sanction of the pope and the help of the Venetians and of all men who would respond to the pope's exhortation, to assist in restoring a Latin emperor to Constantinople. The invitation brought into the empire a band of auxiliaries from the West which, in its weakened condition, was almost as mischievous and ruinous to the empire as any expedition openly directed against its existence could have been. The evil inflicted upon the empire by the band of mercenaries invited for its defence was indeed so manifold that the story deserves telling with considerable detail.

As already stated, Philip, the son of Baldwin, the last

Latin emperor, had married the daughter of Charles of Anjou, king of Sicily. Charles promised, in 1278, to send an expedition to Constantinople, but the pope, seeing the efforts which Michael continued to make for Union, refused his sanction. Two years later, however, a new pope entered into a treaty with Venice and Naples to attack the empire, and Charles undertook to send eight hundred cavaliers to claim what he considered the rights of his grand-daughter. A body of troops was sent across the Adriatic to assist the Albanians, who were fighting against the emperor. The invaders were utterly defeated, and the empire was saved from the attack of Charles by the disorganisation produced by the Sicilian Vespers in 1283, a massacre in which 8,000 Frenchmen perished.

In the twenty years that followed, a body of Spanish mercenaries played a prominent part in the Sicilian troubles. Spain had been engaged for three hundred years in a long and almost continuous struggle against the Moors. Fathers had dedicated their sons in successive generations to the defence of Christianity and their country, and the result was already to have formed a nation of brave and disciplined soldiers, such as Western Europe had not seen since the best days of the Roman empire. Peter of Aragon had supplied a band of such soldiers to fight against France in Sicily and Calabria.

In 1301 the marriage of Catherine of Courtenay, daughter of Philip, and granddaughter of Baldwin the Second, with Charles of Valois, son of Philip the Second of France, and brother of the king, put an end to the troubles in Sicily with the French.

Now that, in 1302, peace was concluded in Sicily, their employers were anxious to be rid of the now useless merce- naries ; for, though their courage, their recklessness of danger, and their prowess were indisputable, their lawlessness, their cruelty to the inhabitants of the country where they were encamped, and their insubordination, even to their own officers, were no less remarkable. Moreover, Frederic of Sicily was unable to pay them, and they had already commenced to pay themselves by general plunder. Unaccustomed to work, and used only to a life of rapine, they were ready to take service under any leader who appeared able to offer them good chances of pillage; but woe to the country to which they were sent, and to the cause which they promised to serve !

Among their leaders was a German named Robert Blum, whose name became changed or translated to Roger de Flor. He was a typical instance of the worst kind of soldier of fortune of the middle ages. He entered the order of the Templars, but was degraded because he betrayed the Christians in return for bribes from the Moslems. Then he turned pirate, and sought foreign service. The French refused to have anything to do with him. He had therefore gone over to the enemy, and the king of Sicily made him vice-admiral. He robbed for his master wherever he could find anything to steal. If he met an enemy, he took all he could carry away, without acknowledgment; if a friend, he took what he wanted, and gave acknowledgments of a very doubtful value, which were to be paid by the king of Sicily at the end of the war.

When the Sicilian war was over, the Grand Master of the Temple urged the pope to insist that Roger de Flor should be surrendered for punishment. Roger learned that such a demand was about to be made [1] and anticipated extradition by taking service with the Greek emperor, nominally to fight against the Turks, promising to bring with him a body of Spanish troops. The alarm of Andronicus at the report of the expedition of Charles of Valois against him was great. It looked as if all Western princes were about to enter upon a new crusade for the recapture of Constantinople. Hence he was prepared to welcome aid from any source.

In 1303 Roger de Flor arrived at Constantinople with a fleet of seven ships and eight thousand men, who are described by Pachymer as Catalans and Amogavares, the latter being adventurers from other parts of Spain than

[1] Pachymer indeed states that the Pope ordered Roger to be given up.

Catalonia. This band was soon spoken of as the Catalan Grand Company.

Roger was accompanied by Fernand Ximenes, who was also at the head of a large body of retainers who were desirous of taking service under the emperor. The reputation which Roger de Flor bore as the most daring of soldiers caused him to be eagerly welcomed by the emperor, who conferred upon him the title of Grand Duke and hoped much from his services. His reckless followers knew only one virtue—that of courage. Their first adventure showed, however, the spirit of lawlessness which existed in his army. The emperor had borrowed a large sum of money from the Genoese which Roger alleged that he had employed in raising new troops. When the Genoese applied to Roger for payment it was refused. The emperor sent a high official to arrange the difficulty, and the Catalans cut him in pieces. The Grand Company were at this time encamped outside the city walls in the neighbourhood of the present Eyoub. They seized the monastery of St. Cosmas and held it as a fortress. The Genoese erected barricades on the shore of the Golden Horn, and a struggle took place between the two in which many were killed on both sides.

Shortly afterwards the Spaniards were induced to cross the Marmora to Cyzicus, and a quarrel ensued between them and the Alans, one of the first of many Asiatic tribes who had pushed their way into the valley of the Danube, and a band of whom had been taken into the imperial service. The son of the leader of the Alans was killed, and his soldiers vowed vengeance. Roger de Flor then pushed on to attack the Turks. He was seen at his best when he met the enemy. He raised the siege of Philadelphia and defeated the various armies sent against him, killing, it is said, thirty thousand Turks and driving the rest of them out of Lydia and Caria. But he was almost as terrible to the Christians whom he had been sent to protect as he was to the Moslems. His progress through Asia Minor was marked by constant plunder. Pachymer says that those subjects of the emperor who fell into his hands after they had escaped from the enemy had thrown themselves out of the smoke into the fire. Those who gave up their property had difficulty in saving their lives. The remark is made on the occasion of Roger's visit to Philadelphia, which he pillaged as if it had been an enemy's city. He treated Pergamos and Ephesus in the same way. His ships plundered the islands of Chios, Lemnos, and Mytilene. The inhabitants of Magnesia resisted his exactions, and he therefore laid siege to the city and did his utmost to capture it. It was in vain that the emperor sent orders to raise the siege and to attack Turks and not Christians. The Alans who were with him urged obedience and withdrew when Roger refused. It was only after a long siege that he recognised that he was unable to capture the city and abandoned the attempt. In retreating he plundered the Greeks as remorselessly as he did the Turks against whom he had been sent. 'Notwithstanding,' says Pachymer, 'that the emperor had prepared all that was needed for the support of Roger and his army, the peasants were robbed of everything they possessed and were left without either seed-corn or oxen for ploughing. At the news of his coming many abandoned their farms and took refuge in the islands. He appropriated to his own use the tithes and other taxes which should have gone to the emperor.' Indeed there appears no reason to doubt the assertion that this adventurer had now formed the intention of carving out a kingdom for himself. It is possible indeed, and is in conformity with his conduct, that from the first he had entertained such an intention. From this time until his death he became the enemy of the emperor whom he had come to aid.

When the Greek troops heard of the outrages on their countrymen they asked the emperor to be led against the Catalans instead of against the Turks. But the emperor himself was unwilling to break with Roger and his army, or even that they should be distant from the city so long as he expected the arrival of the great expedition intended for its capture. He still also cherished the hope that the services of the Grand Company might be employed against the Turks in case the expedition from the West did not arrive. While he was hesitating, Berenger of Catalonia arrived with new reinforcements in nine large vessels, and soon he and Roger presented themselves at the imperial court. Roger urged the emperor to subsidise Berenger, and in reply to the question why the latter had come answered, because he had heard of the liberality of the emperor's payments. In a formal assembly he reproached Roger with the lawlessness of his troops, with the injury he had done to the Greeks, and especially with the burden of expenses he had cast upon the empire. Finally, however, he consented to receive Berenger and to assign to him a portion of the tithes for the maintenance of the Catalan armies.

When, shortly after, a deputation of Catalans was sent to the emperor demanding further pay, he replied by emptying in their presence sacks full of letters complaining of exactions by the Spaniards. In spite of these complaints and of the exactions and lawlessness of the Grand Company, he appears to have been unwilling to lose their services. He recounted the money payments he had made, but promised to give them more than they had asked if only they would at once return to attack the enemy in Asia. The deputation knew the emperor's anxiety and desire to keep his own troops for the defence of the city against the expedition of Charles, and therefore refused to return without further payment. All argument was useless. Berenger was dissatisfied with the offers made to him personally and sailed away from the Golden Horn during the night for Gallipoli, which city was held by his countrymen. Roger pleaded in vain for more money to be paid at once. It was not there to be given. The tension between the Spaniards and the emperor became so great that the latter sent orders to his son Michael, encamped near Apros, to be ready against an attack by the Catalans.

Some months later, in 1307, Roger went to Adrianople under pretence that he wished to pay his respects to Michael at Apros and to take leave of him, as he declared he was about to quit the country. Pachymer, probably reflecting the popular belief, states that his real object was to learn the number of men in the Greek army and what were his chances in an attack upon it. Michael received him in a friendly manner, but the Alans in his service had not forgotten the vengeance they had vowed against him for having at Cyzicus killed the son of George their leader, and as Roger was entering the audience chamber he was stabbed by George himself. Upon news of the assassination, the Catalans fled to Gallipoli, putting men, women, and children to the sword during their flight. Michael followed them and laid siege to the city, but Berenger persuaded the Emperor Andronicus to grant the besieged time and so arranged matters that the Spaniards were able to take ship and escape. They made their way once more across the Marmora to Cyzicus, but the inhabitants stoutly resisted, and the besiegers left for Perinthos, where they killed every man they could lay hands on. When the news reached the capital the inhabitants demanded vengeance on those of the Catalans who had remained there and, taking the law into their own hands, burned their houses. The patriarch, who had in vain attempted to check their fury, with difficulty saved his own life.

Assassina-
tion of
Roger de
Flor.

Outrages
by the
Grand
Company.

The Spaniards were now at open war with the Greeks, and even Andronicus would have been glad to get rid of them. They attacked the seafaring population at Rhegium, now called Buyuk Chekmeji, burnt several men, impaled their children, and massacred those whom they had employed to carry off their booty. Their progress was checked for a while by the arrival of sixteen Genoese ships. As the Genoese had had trouble with the emperor, the Spaniards were in hopes of their aid, but the former sent secretly into the city from their fleet to learn the truth about the situation, heard the Greek version of the differences, and then declared for the emperor. The Genoese and imperial fleets attacked the Spaniards, who were led by Berenger defeated them, captured their leader, and subsequently sent him prisoner to Italy.

Gallipoli was, however, still in the hands of the Catalans

and an attempt to buy the aid of the Genoese to relieve it failed. Michael endeavoured to capture it. Both armies had secured Turkish allies. A decisive battle was fought near Apros, in which the Spaniards were successful. They followed up their victory by ravaging the neighbouring country, and in this they were joined by a band of Turks who had been invited to join them and by Alans who had quitted the imperial service.

The country between Constantinople and Adrianople was laid waste, all the inhabitants abandoning their houses to save their lives. The garrison of Catalans in Gallipoli in like manner ravaged the western part of Thrace ; men were killed, women and children, flocks and herds were carried off. The women and children were taken to be sold to, or to be held as slaves by, the Turks.

The emperor, unable either to employ or to defeat the Spaniards and being hard pressed by the Turks in Asia Minor, endeavoured now to buy them off. An embassy was sent to them, but the conditions demanded were impossible, and thereupon the scenes of violence were renewed. Bands of Spaniards and their Turkish allies made incursions in the country behind Constantinople as far as Chorlou, laid siege to Rodosto, and killed all whom they found outside the walls. Those who could escape took refuge in Constantinople. Pachymer states that the Spaniards claimed to have killed five thousand of these peasants. Adrianople was besieged and, though it was not captured, the army of the Alans, who had once more joined the Greeks, was defeated, the vineyards around the city were rooted up and the fertile country converted for the time into a desert. When the emperor again made an effort to buy the Spaniards off he found their terms higher than ever, on account of their success. They not only demanded heavy payments for services never performed, but that the Emperor should pay ransom for the towns, the fortresses and prisoners captured by them.

The two divisions of Spaniards, one under Rocafert, who had been appointed to succeed Roger, and the other under

Fernand Ximenes, were now acting separately, and while the negotiations were going on the former set out for Constantinople. They were, however, resisted by the imperial troops and compelled to retire. They continued under Rocafert to devastate Thrace. As they themselves received no food from abroad nor tilled the ground in Thrace and had already devastated the country, they were at length forced to retreat from want of provisions to Gallipoli.

Dissension in the Grand Company. Happily, serious divisions arose between the Spaniards themselves. A large number of them refused to recognise Rocafert who had been named leader with the consent of Ximenes. On the other hand, Rocafert declared that as he had conquered the country he had no intention of abandoning the leadership. The influence of Guy, the nephew of the king of Sicily, who had brought with him another detachment of foreign freebooters in seven large ships and who counted upon utilising the Grand Company for the re-establishment of the Latin empire in his own family, was unable to settle the differences between the two parties, and they were soon at open war with each other. On one side was Rocafert, on the other were Guy, Ximenes, and Berenger, who had been released by the Genoese.

In view of an attack by the imperial troops and of the necessity of finding provisions, a peace was patched up between the two Spanish factions, and they started in a body to attack Salonica and plunder Macedonia. The six thousand Spaniards were accompanied by three thousand Turks. Rocafert's division led. The van of the second division reached the camping ground of the first before it had been completely evacuated, and the two armies at once began fighting each other. Berenger hastened to put an end to the quarrel and was killed by Rocafert's brother. Ximenes was captured. Rocafert was now the sole leader. He attempted to capture Salonica but failed. He then retreated in order to return to Thrace : but his position was growing weak. He appealed to a French admiral, who had arrived in the northern Aegean as the precursor of the expected great expedition from the West, for his intervention with the Spaniards who distrusted him, but the admiral seized and carried him off to the king of Naples, where he was thrown into prison and starved to death.

When the partisans of Rocafert in the Grand Company learned of what they regarded as the treachery of the French admiral, they murdered their officers under the belief that they were parties to the capture. They elected new leaders, marched into Thessaly, and took service with the descendants of the crusading barons who had carved out territories for themselves in that province and in Greece. It is unnecessary to follow them there. It is sufficient to say that the Greek army had dogged their movements, had fought well, had defeated them in many engagements, and that what may be regarded as the last struggle with the Grand Company took place in 1315.

Its end, 1315.

The devastation caused by the attempts from the West to re-establish the Latin empire culminating in the disorders caused by the Grand Company was such that the empire's chances of recovering its strength were enormously diminished. The fall of the city in 1204 had been followed by the destruction of the organisation in Asia Minor for resisting the progress of Asiatic hordes towards Europe. One may conjecture that the great statesman Innocent the Third, who had foreseen some of the evil effects which would inevitably follow from the success of Dandolo and Montferrat, would have realised the necessity of aiding Constantinople in making such resistance. Unfortunately, Innocent's successors were less statesmanlike. Instead of seeking to strengthen the Greeks in Constantinople by condemning the wild lawlessness of the Spaniards, their dominating idea was to restore the Latin empire, so as to force the members of the Orthodox Church to enter into Union. The results of all their attempts were altogether disastrous. The empire was weakened on every side. Its component parts had always been loosely bound together. Long distances in ages of badly constructed roads had prevented the development of loyalty as a bond of union. The traditional attachment to the autocrat at Constantinople had been shaken by the

Disastrous results from attempts to restore empire.

change of dynasties. Peasants living far away from the capital, who had no other desire than to till their lands in peace, were ready to accept the rule of a Serbian or a Bulgarian, of a powerful rebel against the empire or even of the Turks themselves, provided they were undisturbed. Those who were in the neighbourhood of the capital were in worse plight. The development of trade and commerce had been hindered. Thrace had become a desolation. During five years the Spaniards had lived on the country and only deserted it when there remained nothing further to plunder. The thriving communities extending along all the northern shores of the Marmora from the city to Gallipoli were impoverished or destroyed. Flourishing vineyards and olive-yards were abandoned. The fishing and shipping communities ceased to find occupation. Great numbers of the inhabitants were exterminated.

The richest city in Europe had become poverty-stricken. The coinage, which for centuries had served as the standard for the whole Western world, had been debased in order to find money to pay foreign mercenaries. Worse than all, while the empire had been employed in resisting these invaders from the West, the Bulgarians, Serbians, and, far more important than either, the Turks had gained strength and had enormously enlarged their territories.

To the Catalan Grand Company must be attributed the introduction of the first body of Turks into Europe. It might have been expected that the traditions of Spaniards would have influenced them sufficiently to have refused Moslem aid, that Western Europe would have raised the cry of treason to Christendom when it learned that bands of Turks had been engaged to fight against a Christian though a schismatic emperor ; but the filibusters who had been invited into the empire for the defence of Christendom thought only of plunder, and Western Europe was either indifferent or thought there was little to choose between schismatics and Moslems.

The attempts to restore the Latin empire had failed, but the emperor and his people were in presence of a much more formidable enemy than the West had furnished. The Asiatic hordes whom the city had successfuly resisted for a century and a half before its capture were now constantly encroaching on imperial territory. As these hordes were destined to be the destroyers of the Empire, I propose next briefly to notice their origin and history.

CHAPTER III

THE TURKS: THEIR ENTRY INTO ASIA MINOR: NOT AT
FIRST EXCLUSIVELY MAHOMETAN: THEIR CHARACTER-
ISTICS: OTHMAN FOUNDS A DYNASTY: PROGRESS OF
MOSLEMS IN EUROPE AND ASIA MINOR: CAPTURE OF
BROUSA IN 1326.

THE great central plains of Asia, stretching almost without
an interruption from the Caspian Sea to China, have during
all historical time produced hardy races of nomad warriors.
On the three occasions in their history when they have
found skilful leaders, their progress as conquerors has been
epoch-marking. Twice their progress has been westward.
Mounted warriors and hordes of foot soldiers made their
way towards the Euxine, some going to the north and
others to the south of that sea. The first of these waves of
population thus moving westward was that led by Genghis
Khan, a Mongol belonging to the smallest of the four great
divisions of the Tartar[1] race. His followers were, however,
mainly Turks, the most widely spread of these divisions.
He had established his rule before 1227, the year in which
he died, from the Sea of Japan to the Dnieper. He and his
immediate successors ravaged a greater extent of territory
than any other conqueror. Like Alexander the Great, he and
they advanced with regularly organised armies, with apparently no other object than conquest and plunder. Their

Genghis Khan moves westward

---

[1] Dr. Koëlle has in my opinion satisfactorily demonstrated that 'Tatar' is a
incorrect spelling, due mainly to the fact that this form of the word comes t
us from the Chinese, who cannot pronounce the letter *r*.

[2] *The Mahommedans*, by J. D. Rees, C.I.E., 1894.

victories facilitated the migration of his own subjects into the newly conquered territories and hastened the departure of large bodies of men, who fled before the terrible massacres which marked the progress of their ever victorious armies.

A branch of the same great horde, under the leadership of Subutai, destroyed Moscow and Kiev in a campaign conducted with striking ability and ending in 1239, and settled in Russia. Poland, aided by French Knights Templars and the Grand Master of the Teutonic order, had put forward all her strength to resist the same division of the all-devouring army, while another wing attacked the Hungarians with half a million of men.

Their entry into Europe was in such numbers and the excesses of cruelty committed by them were so alarming that their advance everywhere created terror. The Tartars —coming from Tartarus, as some of the Crusaders believed— were so little known, says Pachymer, that many declared they had the heads of dogs and fed upon human flesh.[1] Seen nearer, they were less formidable as individuals, though infernal, terrible, and invincible as an army.

In 1258, the year before the recapture of Constantinople and the destruction of the Latin empire by the Greeks, Houlagou, the grandson of Genghis Khan, captured Bagdad, and deposed the last of the Bagdad caliphs. He extended his conquests over Mesopotamia and Syria to the Mediterranean. Damascus and Aleppo were sacked. Houlagou sought to ally himself with the Crusaders in order to overthrow the Saracens and the sultan of Egypt.

When Houlagou turned his attention to Asia Minor, he found among the Christian populations a division of the Turkish race known as Seljuks, whose sultan resided at Konia, and called himself sultan of Roum.[2] He attacked and inflicted injuries upon them from which they never recovered. It is difficult to state precisely what were the boundaries of the Seljuks and of other Moslem or partly

The Seljukian Turks.

---

[1] Pach. ii. 25.

[2] 'Roum' is still the Turkish form of 'Rome,' and exists in the names Erzeroum, Roumelia, &c.

Moslem peoples in Asia Minor and Syria, during the thirteenth century, and this difficulty arises from the fact that their boundaries were continually changing. The Saracens held certain places in Syria, but there was a Christian prince in Antioch; there were cities occupied by the western Knights Templars, a Christian prince in Caramania and a king of Lesser Armenia. There were Turcomans at Marash and in the hill country behind Trebizond, and Kurds invaded Cilicia in 1278. A large tract of country around Konia was ruled over by the Seljuks. No natural boundary marked the extent of territory occupied by any of these peoples or in Asia Minor by the Roman emperor.

It is certain, however, that the entry of the armies of the followers of Genghis Khan, continually renewed by the arrival of new hordes from Central Asia, changed the distribution of the peoples and spread terror everywhere at their approach. Even at Nicaea, within sixty miles of Constantinople, the rumour in 1267 of the arrival of a Tartar army caused a terrible panic.[1] Two years later the Tartars attacked the Saracens in Syria, whither they had been invited for such purpose by the Christians, defeated them, and carried off a rich booty. For a while they were a terror alike to Moslems and Christians. As from the followers of Genghis Khan there ultimately came the race of Ottoman Turks who conquered New Rome and its empire, it is desirable to consider them somewhat carefully.

Character-
istics of
Asiatic
invaders.

It is important to note that the first hordes who came in with the great conqueror and those who followed for at least a century were not Mahometan fanatics. Some of their leading generals were indeed Christians. Genghis himself had married a Christian wife. Mango Khan (1251–1259), one of his successors, is described by Maundeville, who visited Palestine in 1322, as ' a good Christian man, who was baptized and gave letters of perpetual peace to all Christian men,' and sent to win the Holy Land to put it into the hands of the Christians and destroy the law of Mahomet.[2]

---

[1] Pach. iv. 27.
[2] *Early Travels in Palestine*, Bohn's edition, p. 241.

His great successor, Houlagou, was the husband of the granddaughter of the famous Prester (or Presbyter) John, the king of a Christian state in Central Asia, visited by Marco Polo.[1] The army led by Houlagou contained Mahometans, but it contained also Christians, Buddhists, and professors of other creeds. Central Asiatics had up to the time which concerns us not developed any violent religious animosity. Christians, Moslems, and Buddhists dwelt together in harmony.

It is probably correct to say that the races of the great plains of Asia have never been religiously disposed. Mr. Schuyler, who was a keen observer, remarked, less than a generation ago, that the people which had been recently conquered by Russia in Central Asia were classified as to their religion with extreme difficulty. A few declared themselves Christians. The remainder were indiscriminately inscribed as Moslems, but very few among them really knew anything about the religion of Islam and did not even consider themselves as Moslems.[2] The fierce fanaticism which the early followers of Mahomet displayed and which led them within a century after his death to make the most wonderful and enduring series of conquests which have ever been accomplished by a people whose sole bond of union was religion was not shown by the followers of Genghis. They preferred to fight the Saracens and to aid the Christians rather than to do the reverse. We shall see that when, a century and a half later, another great invasion from Central Asia took place, its leader Timour the Lame's greatest activity was directed against the Mahometans, and that he

Not fanatical.

[1] Maundeville in Syria met Christians from Prester John's country, p. 189. See Col. Yule's *Marco Polo*, i. 275, a book which is a model of good editing.

[2] When, therefore, Mr. Billinski speaks of the Turks of to-day having 'millions of confederates in the heart of Russia' ready to obey the commands of the Mussulman pontiff, he is, I believe, entirely mistaken. The Mahometans under Russian rule are a comparatively insignificant part of her population, and there is no reason to believe that any but a very small portion of them would think it a religious duty to fight against the Czar at the bidding of the Sultan. It should also not be forgotten that the majority of them are Shiahs, who have never shown any disposition to aid the Sunnis, who acknowledge the caliphate of Constantinople. *Nineteenth Century*, Nov. 1891, p. 731.

demanded from them the restoration to the Christian
emperor of the cities which they had captured.

It is true that in the interval between the two invasions
under Genghis Khan and Timour, the Turkish invaders, who
had remained in Asia Minor, caught much of the fanatical
spirit. But there are many indications which show that this
spirit was of slow growth.[1] As their struggles with neighbouring and Christian peoples compacted them into a warlike nation, they all came to accept the religion of Mahomet,
and as they became better acquainted with the tenets of the
most war-inspiring religion in the world, they held to them
tenaciously, and developed the hostility towards Christians
which the spiritual pride of believers who consider themselves the elect of heaven, and their religion outside the
range of discussion, always engenders. But during the
development of their power in Asia Minor, many years
passed before they isolated themselves, and were isolated
from the Christians, on account of their religion. Their
princes sought marriage with the princesses of the imperial
and other noble Christian families. We obtain light only
incidentally upon the relations between the professors of the
two creeds at the period shortly after the recapture of
Constantinople by the Greeks. But such as we do obtain
confirms the statement that the Asiatic settlers took their
religion very easily. In 1267 certain charges were brought,
as we have seen,[2] by the Emperor Michael against the
patriarch, which give us a glimpse of interest. The relation
is made by Pachymer, who was himself one of the clerks of
the court. The patriarch was accused, not only of having
conversed familiarly with a Turkish sultan, of having
allowed him and his companions to use the bath attached
to the church, around which were the Christian symbols,
but of having ordered a monk to administer the Sacrament
to the children of the sultan without having been assured

[1] Maundeville in 1322, or a year or two later, discussed Mahometanism
with many of its professors, and goes so far as to say, ' Because they go so
nigh our faith, they are easily converted to Christian law.' *Early Travels in
Palestine*, p. 196.
[2] See *ante*, p. 28.

that they were baptized. He was charged, further, with having said the Litanies with the sultan and his followers. The patriarch replied to the two first with contempt; if the Turks had used the church bath, no harm had been done. As to giving Communion, he declared that he had been duly certified that the children had been baptized.[1] Witnesses asserted that it was true that the accused had said the Litanies with the sultan, and that he had allowed him to sit by his side during celebration, but added that they did not know whether the sultan was a Christian or not! Other persons were found who declared that he was not a Christian. The sultan, hearing of the proceedings, sent to ask, either in jest or seriously, that the emperor would give him the sacred relics which he wore round his neck, and offered to eat ham as a proof that he was not a Moslem. Pachymer adds that in thus professing his readiness to worship the relics and to eat the forbidden flesh, the sultan caused the proceedings against the patriarch to fail. As it appeared that there were eminent ecclesiastics in the court who really believed that the sultan of the Turks was a Christian, those who desired the condemnation of the patriarch tried to turn the question by suggesting that, whether he was Christian or not, it was certain that members of his suite, who had been present when Communion was administered, were unbelievers.[2] That the sultan should have been present at a Christian service at all, that his children should have been allowed by him or his Moslem followers to communicate, and that his children were baptized, or believed to be baptized, show that, whether they were Christians or not, the fanatical spirit which animated the Moslems of an earlier period, or the Turks a century later, was not present among these representatives of the Asiatics who had entered the country as followers of Genghis or his immediate successors.

The characteristics of the Turk have remained singularly like those possessed by his ancestors. The Turkish soldiers who had come in with Genghis, and the hordes of those

Permanent characteristics of Turkish race.

---

[1] Pach. iv. 3. [2] *Ibid.* iv. 6.

who followed during a century, had been for the most part
wandering shepherds, and the nomadic instinct still continued, and still continues, in the race, notwithstanding that
there has been a considerable admixture of other races.
The tent of their leader was larger than that of his followers,
and its entrance came, in the course of time, to be known as
The Lofty Gate, or The Sublime Porte. The shepherd
warriors, who were destined to destroy the empire of the
New Rome, had few of the desires, habits, or aspirations of
civilisation. Commerce, except in its simplest form of
barter, was and has always been almost unknown to them.
Among the Turks of a later period the disinclination to
change the traditional habits of the race is to some extent
due to the indifference or contempt felt for trading communities by a race of conquerors; though, perhaps, incapacity to hold their own as traders against the peoples they
subdued has had a larger share in producing their aversion
to commerce. The furniture of their huts is even yet only
such as would have been found in their felt tents. They
have no desire to possess the ordinary utensils which
Europeans of every race consider either as the necessaries of
life or as adding largely to its comfort. They have never
taken kindly to agriculture. Surrounded by fertile land, the
Turk will till only enough to supply him with the barest
necessaries of life, and the traveller in the interior of Asia
Minor is to-day, as he has been for centuries, astonished to
see that Turkish peasants who, as the owners of large tracts
of fertile land, capable of producing almost any fruits or
vegetables, and of supporting even a large number of cattle,
may be accounted wealthy, are yet content to live upon fare
and amid surroundings at which the ordinary European
peasant, and even the Turks' own neighbours of different
races, would express their dissatisfaction.[1]

---

[1] That this aversion to agriculture, and contentment amid poverty, of the
Turkish peasant are not merely the result of Mahometanism, is evidenced by the
fact that the Pomaks—that is, the Bulgarians who have accepted Islam—and
the Mahometans of Bosnia and Herzegovina, who have emigrated into Asia
Minor since the Russo-Turkish War of 1878, are noticed everywhere to be

We get few glimpses of the domestic life and manners of the Turks during the first two centuries of their emigration into Asia Minor. But such as we gain show them, in peace and war, to possess the same characteristics as distinguish their descendants at the present day. When not under the influence of their religion they are peaceful, kindly disposed, and truthful. In the hospitality of the tent or hut they are irreproachable. They possess little, but that little is at the disposal of the traveller. Judged by Western ideas, they are lazy, and lacking in intelligence. In the ordinary business of life they are singularly destitute of energy. They have learned, like their fathers, to be content with the poverty amid which they were born. They have not sufficient capacity to desire knowledge nor aspiration to make them discontented. If, as I believe the evidence to indicate, the ancestors of the present Moslems in Asia Minor were during the thirteenth and half of the fourteenth century but little under the influence of religious fanaticism, their easy-going, *dolce far niente* character may well be taken as sufficient explanation of the passing over into Turkish territories of many Christians who desired to escape from the heavy taxation under the rule of the Christian emperors.

In describing the movement of the Asiatic races into Asia Minor and Europe, but especially of the advance of the Turkish hordes who came after the death of Genghis, two facts ought never to be lost sight of. The first and most important is that from a period even preceding the recapture of the city in 1259 down to one within the memory of living men there was a constant stream of immigrants from Central Asia westward. The numbers of the immigrant settlers were thus steadily being increased. Probably at no time has the Turkish race been as prolific as the Christian races of Asia Minor, and the latter would long ago have outnumbered the conquering race had the stream of immigration been dammed. The second fact to be noted is that a constant settlement of the conquered lands was being

distinguished by their comparative energy and by the success they are achieving in various forms of agricultural pursuits.

made, a settlement which, although possibly as nomadic and
uncertain as that of the Kurds and Yuruks of to-day, was
yet a real occupation of the country at the expense of
Christian populations, who were either massacred or dispersed. It is in the nomadic character of the newcomers, in
the wasteful character of their occupation of the country, in
the substitution of sheep and cattle industry for agriculture,
in their want of intelligence, and in their expulsion and
persecution of the Christian population, that the explanation
is to be found of the destruction and, in some cases, complete
abandonment of cities still populous and flourishing when
they were captured : cities like Ephesus, Nicaea, and a
hundred others, whose ruins meet the traveller everywhere
throughout Asia Minor. The Turk has at all times been a
nomad and a destroyer. He has never been a capable
trader or even agriculturist.

When the armies led by Genghis Khan and his successors
retired, armies which were well disciplined and well led,
many of his soldiers or their followers remained and took
service with the Seljukian Turks. Others formed separate
communities. One of the chiefs who thus settled in Asia
Minor was Ertogrul or Orthogrul, the father of Osman or
Othman, the founder of the Ottoman dynasty.

During Ertogrul's life, the Seljuks had been greatly
harassed by the newer invaders. Pachymer states that
on the arrival of the Tartars the sultan of Konia (the
ancient Iconium) was surrounded by enemies, and that he
had sought the protection of the emperor. He had invited
also the aid of the sultan of Egypt, known to the Crusaders
as the sultan of Babylon, against the Tartars, by whom he
was hard pressed. Three or four years after this sultan's
death in 1277, Ertogrul died. His son Osman or Othman
by his courage and ability gave his followers the leading
place among the Turks in Asia Minor and firmly established
the dynasty named after him. He began his career by
coming to an agreement with some of the other Moslem
chiefs to divide the territory occupied by the Seljuks and
themselves in Asia Minor into eight portions. Thereupon

the combined forces of the old and new Turks commenced
a series of attacks upon neighbouring territory. During the
next twenty years, their success was almost unchecked.
In 1282, they laid siege to Tralles (the present Aidin), and,
though opposed by the son of Michael the Eighth, were
able to capture and destroy the city.[1] A short time afterwards they obtained a fleet and took into their service a large
number of sailors who had been discharged by the emperor
from motives of economy. Twelve years later, Othman and
Ali, chief of another Turkish band, pushed their raids northward and even crossed the river Sangarius and spread desolation throughout the Asiatic provinces of the Empire,
before they could be driven back. Two years later, they
laid waste the country between the Black Sea and Rhodes.

In 1299, Othman took the title of Sultan. In 1302, he
and other Turkish leaders inflicted a serious defeat upon
the imperial troops and a band of Alans on the river
Sangarius near Sabanja. The defeat was shortly afterwards
turned into a rout and the subjects of the empire with the
Alans were driven to seek shelter in Ismidt, the ancient
Nicomedia. The confines of the empire were narrowed,
and Othman established himself near Brousa and the neighbouring city of Nicaea, and came to an arrangement for
division of the newly acquired territory with the other
Turkish chiefs.

Othman,
first Otto-
man
Sultan,
1299–1327.

Alarmed for a while at the news that the emperor was
to receive help from the West, the Turks soon renewed
their attacks upon imperial territory, and the Greek population almost everywhere fled before them. They attacked
the wealthy cities on the Aegean coast of Asia Minor
and occupied several of the islands of the Archipelago.
Pachymer states [2] that they had inundated the country north
of Pergamus so completely that no Roman dared entertain
the hope of keeping his property, and all fled before the
flood of invaders : some to the city of Pergamus, others to
Adramyttium or Lampsacus, while others again crossed the
Dardanelles into Europe.

[1] Pach. vi. 21.   [2] iv. 21.

The reign of Othman is contemporaneous with one of the great periods of immigration from Central Asia. The numbers of the Turks were yearly augmented by such hordes that the Greek writers continually use metaphors derived from the torrent, from floods and inundations, to describe their overwhelming force.

Entry of Turks into Europe, 1306-7.

It was partly in order to resist this flood of invasion that the Catalan Grand Company had been invited to aid the emperor, but after having won several victories over the Turks, the lawlessness of the Spaniards forced the emperor to recognise that his Western auxiliaries were of no value for checking the progress of the enemy. The Christians of Asia Minor flocked to the capital to avoid the Company almost as much as to escape from the soldiers of Othman. Worse than all, to these Christians of Spain must be ascribed the introduction of the Turks into Europe. At the invitation of the Company, a band of them, as we have seen, crossed the Dardanelles to aid in attacking the empire which Roger and his Catalans had come to defend. About the same time, another band of Turks landed in Greece for the purpose of pillage. These invasions are epoch-marking, since from this time (1306-7), Europe was never entirely free from the presence of Turks.

Their progress in Asia Minor.

Their great progress was, however, more marked in Asia Minor. In 1308, one of the divisions of Turks not under Othman captured Ephesus, which surrendered to avoid massacre. The city still retained something of its ancient glory. Its famous church of St. John, from the ruins of which the traveller may still gain an idea of its former magnificence, was plundered, and its immense wealth in precious vessels and deposits became the prey of the victors. Many of the inhabitants were cruelly massacred, notwithstanding their submission, and the remainder were driven away as fugitives to find the means of living where they could or to starve. Other places under the rule of Constantinople were attacked, and though many victories were gained—for the imperial troops fought well—the Turks were constantly gaining cities and territory from the Christians.

It was in vain that the emperor entered into league with bands of Tartars or with other Turks to attack the armies of Othman, for the forces of this skilful leader were too numerous to be subdued. Brousa had to purchase peace from him. Othman failed, however, to capture Rhodes, which was bravely defended by the military knights from the West, and a monk named Hilarion at the head of the imperial troops gained some successes. The imperial troops succeeded also in 1310 in defeating a certain Mahomet whose dominions were in Caramania. But even with the aid of a band of Tartars who had allied themselves with the emperor, who was in command of twenty thousand of the imperial troops, little could be done to check Othman's steady progress.

Meantime in Europe, on the north shore of the Marmora, the band of Turks who had been associated with the Grand Company, but who did not acknowledge the rule of Othman, besieged Ganos and laid waste the surrounding country. The troubles which arose a few years later between the Emperor Andronicus the Second and young Andronicus, enabled the Turks steadily to encroach on the empire in Asia Minor, and their introduction as partisans in the civil war which went on in 1322 familiarised them and probably Othman himself with inroads into the country between Constantinople and Gallipoli.[1]

So far we have been concerned almost exclusively with those portions of the Asiatic army and the hordes which followed it which came westward to the south of the Black Sea. But it must be noted that the body of invaders of the same race who had come westward to the north of that sea, and who had attacked Russia, Poland, and Hungary, had constantly received additions to their numbers. This northern division was possibly more numerous than the Turks in Asia Minor. As early as 1265, a certain Timour,

[1] Gregoras states that the Turkish ships employed by Andronicus plundered all the coasts and the islands (viii. 10). Chalcondylas claims that Othman with eight thousand Turks who occupied the Thracian Chersonesus was entirely defeated.

the ruler of Tartars who were in occupation of territory on the Volga, had sent twenty thousand men to aid the Bulgarians against the Empire. Bulgarians and Tartars together had occupied all the passes into Thrace, and the emperor had saved himself with difficulty. In 1284, ten thousand Tartars came southward into Thrace from the great host which were in Hungary. In 1300, the Turks who had entered the Crimea were driven out by another horde of Tartars who had occupied South Russia. The number and strength of these invaders continued constantly to increase. Their power indeed remained firmly established in South Russia until long after the conquest of Constantinople. They had no special sympathy with the Ottoman Turks, and were ready, as were the Alans, to fight either for the emperor or against him. Cantacuzenus mentions that in 1324 one hundred and twenty thousand of them entered Thrace and were beaten in detail by his friend the young Andronicus.

Capture of Brousa, 1326.

Weakened by having to meet this huge northern army, for huge it must have been, although the number of the invaders is probably exaggerated,[1] the young emperor was forbidden or was unable to go to the relief of Brousa when, two years afterwards, Othman laid siege to that city. Its surrender in 1326 is a convenient mark of the progress made by the Ottoman Turks.

Their great leader, Othman, died in the following year.

[1] It is usually impossible to arrive at the correct estimate of the numbers of the invaders, but it may be said once for all that, while they were undoubtedly very large, the figures given by the Greek authors are seldom trustworthy.

CHAPTER IV

DYNASTIC STRUGGLES IN EMPIRE : APPEALS TO POPE FOR
AID ; REIGNS OF ANDRONICUS THE SECOND, JOHN CAN-
TACUZENUS AND JOHN ; REPEATED FAILURE OF EFFORTS
BY POPES TO INDUCE WESTERN POWERS TO ASSIST IN
CHECKING MOSLEM ADVANCE.

WHEN, in 1320, the Emperor Michael the Ninth died, the
empire was already threatened by large and ever-increasing
armies of Asiatics, both on the north and on the south. Those
on the south were steadily being incorporated into the group
ruled over by Othman.

The sixty years which had passed since the expulsion of
the Latins had nevertheless done something, though not
much, towards restoring the empire. Territory had been
recovered. The walls of the capital had been repaired. The
population had begun once again to look to the emperor at
Constantinople as their natural ruler.[1]

On the other hand the ravages of war had been terrible. Distressed
The population of those portions of the Balkan peninsula condition
which were under the rule of the empire had greatly empire.
diminished. Thousands had been murdered by the Catalan
Grand Company and their allies during their successive
devastations of the country. Land had gone out of cultivation. In Asia Minor many of the Christian inhabitants had
voluntarily submitted to the Turks to save their lives or to
obtain protection. The demand for soldiers to serve the

[1] Sir John Maundeville, who visited Constantinople in 1322, remarks on the
diminution of the empire : 'For he was emperor of Romania and of Greece, of
all Asia the Less, and of the land of Syria, of the land of Persia and Arabia,
but he hath lost all but Greece ' (*Early Travels in Palestine*, p. 130).

national cause against the many enemies who attacked the
empire, and the demands for money which was needed for
the conduct of the defence, induced the peasants both in
Europe and Asia to escape into neighbouring territories
where such demands were less rigorous. The wealth of the
empire had largely diminished. The great need of the country
was peace. Peace and security for life and property were
absolutely essential if the empire were to be restored to prosperity. The people were wearied of strife, and there are
indications which point to a general indifference as to what
became of the empire as a state. The peasant wanted to
till his land and reap his harvest in peace, the nobles to
gather their revenues in peace. The means of communication between the provinces and the capital were too few to
enable the mass of the people to take an interest in what
was passing in the capital. They had come to regard it not
so much as their protector but as the place from whence
emanated new exactions, new demands for military service,
and general harassment.

Unfortunately, the dynastic struggles which were destined
to come strengthened this desire for peace, increased the
indifference as to who was their emperor, and still further
weakened the empire.

The greatest misfortune which the struggle with the
Spaniards had brought about was the introduction of the
Turk into Europe. We have seen that each side, Orthodox
emperors and Catholic invaders, had allied themselves with
bands of Turks and other barbarians, who had overrun
Thrace and Macedonia. The destruction of the population,
the raiding of their cattle, and the laying waste of fertile
lands offered at once a facility and an incentive to the
Moslem invaders to remain in Europe. Indeed, from the
first entry of the Turks bands of nomads of that race began
to occupy portions of the desolated country.

For the next hundred and thirty years—that is, until the
Moslem conquest—the history of the empire is, so far as its
rulers are concerned, largely one of confused struggle during
which no man of conspicuous ability came to the front. To

account for this confusion it should be noted that there was
no rule of succession to the throne which was regarded as
inviolable, and that, even among the nobles and in the
Church, public opinion had little force except upon religious
questions. A few men in the city took an interest in political
questions ; the great mass of the peasants took none.
Representative institutions did not exist. The reigning
emperor, though in theory absolute, was largely controlled
by irresponsible and unorganised nobles. When a majority
of them agreed to support a rival candidate they were
sufficiently powerful to have their own way. The result was
that dynastic struggles where each rival for the throne was
supported by a party of patricians were frequent, and these
struggles contributed very largely to weaken the empire.

On the death of the co-Emperor Michael the Ninth, Quarrels
his father, Andronicus the Second, still occupied the imperial between Androni-
throne. Being now well advanced in years, he desired, on cus the
the death of his son, to break through the engagement by which Second and his grand-
Andronicus, his grandson, the son of Michael, should become son.
with him joint occupant of the throne. The relations
between the two men were far from friendly. While insisting that his grandson should present himself at the court,
the old emperor refused for four months to speak to him.
The grandson, usually known as Young Andronicus, was
supported by a powerful party and had no intention of
abandoning what he considered to be his rights. In order
to get rid of him, the emperor formally brought a charge
of treason and sought to put him upon his trial, but
Cantacuzenus, the most distinguished noble, and his other
friends rallied to the palace in such force that the elder
Andronicus was alarmed. In presence of the patriarch and
the nobles on whom he could rely, the emperor accused his
grandson of continual disobedience, and proceeded as if to
pass sentence. ' This is why,' he began—but here Young
Andronicus stopped him, asking to be allowed to defend
himself. The scene as described by his great friend and
most powerful supporter, Cantacuzenus, is a striking one.
The young man is seated on the chair and in the place

assigned to accused persons. He admits amid the silence
of the court that he has disobeyed his grandfather in such
trivial matters as going out hunting, attending races, and the
like, but claimed that he had done nothing against the
emperor's interest, and asked to be sent before independent
judges. The old man tried to shout him down, and roared
out that he believed he was not even a Christian. Young
Andronicus replied with spirit and claimed that he should
be tried. ' If you have made up your mind to condemn me
without hearing, do with me what you like and at once. If
not, judge me according to law.' That was a reply which
still appealed to all men in the city of Justinian.

When the emperor had shouted at his grandson, the
friends of Young Andronicus, who had been near but in
hiding, believing he was condemned, came forward for his
defence. A courtier warned the emperor of their presence,
telling him, says Cantacuzenus, that they were ready to do
all that was necessary for his grandson's safety. Thereupon
the emperor retired and sent word that he would pardon
him. A reconciliation was patched up, but it was only
temporary. After the lapse of a few weeks grandfather and
grandson were again openly hostile to each other. The
young man was forbidden to enter the capital, where he had
many supporters, and the two emperors remained enemies
for years. In 1326 two officers in command of the towers
above the Romanus Gate enabled him to effect a surprise.
The gates were opened and the elder Andronicus became
virtually a prisoner until his death. The contest between
them had lasted upwards of six years.

In 1328 the elder emperor abdicated and entered a
monastery, and two years afterwards the burial of a monk
named Anthony marked the end of the life of Andronicus the
Second. Andronicus the Third was now the sole occupant
of the throne, which he held until his death in 1341.

Reign of
Androni-
cus the
Third,
1328-1341.

During these thirteen years (1328-1341) war was constantly being waged against the Turks. The emperor
himself was always in delicate health, and died at the age
of forty-five. He continued his great friendship until his

death with Cantacuzenus, and invited him, even as early as 1329, to occupy the throne as co-emperor, and the offer was renewed.[1] Cantacuzenus, notwithstanding that he was pressed to accept by the only noble near him in rank, Apocaukus, who afterwards became his great enemy, refused. The emperor, however, continued to treat him as a friend, and was constantly accompanied by him on his various expeditions.

Like every emperor from the recapture of Constantinople down to 1453, Andronicus turned his attention to the West and sought to obtain aid against the Turks, even at the price of coercing his people into a Union with Rome. The Turks had invaded Macedonia and attacked Euboea and Athens. As the southern portion of the Balkan peninsula was still ruled in part by the descendants of the crusading barons and by the remnant of the Catalans, there was reason to believe that the pope would be ready to arouse the West against the common enemy of Christendom. Accordingly the emperor took advantage of the passage of Dominican missionaries through Constantinople from Tartary to convey to Pope John the Twenty-second his desire for Union and his request for aid. The pope replied by sending preachers and by urging the emperor to do all he could to accomplish his part. His successor in 1335 grew alarmed at the attacks made by the Turks by sea on various places in the Mediterranean, and finding that the Catalans had seized Athens from Gautier de Brienne, who held it as his duchy, he excommunicated them. He invited Andronicus to join the king of France and Naples in a Crusade against the Turks which the Venetians and the Genoese had promised also to aid. The emperor gladly gave his consent and sent a number of ships, but the needs of Cyprus, which was being attacked by the Saracens, were decided to be more pressing than those of the empire, and the Crusade was not proceeded with. Andronicus in 1339 sent Barlaam, the author of many controversial works, to the pope, at that time in Avignon. On his arrival he pointed out that the Turks had seized the seats

Appeals for aid to the pope.

----

[1] Cant. ii. 9, 14, 15 ; Greg. ix. 10, xiii. 3 ; Ducas, vi.

of four metropolitan sees, and he suggested that as a condition of the Union of the Churches the Turks should be expelled from Asia Minor. The pope recognised the desirability of such an attempt as keenly as many of his successors, but saw that the condition was impossible.

Death of Andronicus the Third. Reign of John (1341 to 1391), Cantacuzenus (1342 to 1355.)

Andronicus on his death, in 1341, left a son, John Palaeologus, who was then nine years old. His mother, Anne of Savoy, was a woman of ability and energy. Cantacuzenus was associated with her as regent. He held the dignity of Grand Domestic, and in the later years of his life wrote a clear and able statement of the history of his own times. He had been, as we have seen, the intimate friend of Andronicus and his great supporter when the grandfather of the same name endeavoured to exclude him from the throne. He had been named by his friend and patron as the guardian of John, but the widow of the emperor was from the first jealous of her co-guardian and never worked sympathetically with him. He tells us that from the death of Andronicus he was constantly urged to occupy the imperial throne and that he as constantly refused. He undoubtedly possessed the confidence of a large majority of the nobles. There was a general recognition that, in the existing state of the empire, it was unwise to leave the government in the hands of a boy and of a foreign princess. Ducas expressly states that Cantacuzenus ultimately allowed himself to be proclaimed emperor because his friends urged him to take the reins of government from the hands of a woman and a child and because the empress and the senate were unjust and unfair to him.[1] In 1342 he was proclaimed joint emperor under the style of John Cantacuzenus.

During the thirteen years of his reign, which lasted till 1355, the history of the empire is in the main one of civil war and consequent decadence. Distrusted by Anne, the mother of the boy emperor, his difficulties were increased by the turbulent character of his ward, whom his mother could not, or would not, restrain from wilfulness which led him even in early youth into debauchery. The result was that

[1] Ducas, i. 6.

during the whole of Cantacuzenus's reign there was a constant strain between the elder emperor, on the one side, and the empress and her son on the other. Cantacuzenus states that Apocaukus, the noble next to himself in rank, had suggested to him that he should assume imperial authority and that he had rejected the suggestion as treason to the empress and her sons and to the memory of the emperor. But Apocaukus, with the support of the patriarch, soon formed a party, nominally for the empress and her son, really against Cantacuzenus. The patriarch himself claimed to be the guardian of the infant John, excommunicated those who abandoned him, and even Cantacuzenus himself.[1] The account given by the emperor of his reluctance to accept the crown might be regarded with distrust if Nicephorus Gregoras, who after he had become a bitter enemy wrote his history of the events of the reign, were not on this point in substantial accord with Cantacuzenus. Even before his accession the troops, according to Gregoras, declared that they would recognise no other regent than the Grand Domestic, and proposed to make the oath of fidelity to the young emperor and his mother conditional upon the recognition of Cantacuzenus as tutor of John and regent of the empire.

In presence of the opposition of Anne, Cantacuzenus offered to resign, but the empress desired that he should remain, probably fearing revolt in case his resolution was carried into effect. Among much which is doubtful, it is clear that he had the confidence of the army and that the empress had not.

Civil war soon broke out between the new emperor and the partisans of John and his mother. Apocaukus was named governor of Constantinople by Anne and excited the population against Cantacuzenus apparently with the intention of having himself elected emperor by a popular vote.

Meantime the rivalries of these two nobles allowed foreign enemies to make progress. Two divisions of Turks were ravaging the empire in one direction, while a band of

[1] Cant. iv. 3

Tartars who had crossed the Danube had advanced as far as Didymotica. Stephen of Serbia had already marched southwards and was rapidly consolidating the strength of his country. In 1344 the discontent at the civil war had become so great that the nobles insisted that the empress Anne and Apocaukus should send an embassy to Cantacuzenus to make peace. When this attempt failed, Apocaukus, according to Cantacuzenus, endeavoured on two occasions to have him assassinated. Driven thus to extremities, the emperor promised his daughter Theodora in marriage to the Turk Orchan, the son and successor of Othman, who thereupon sent an army of five thousand men to assist in the struggle against the partisans of John.

Apocaukus had thrown into the prisons of Constantinople the partisans of his rival and had ordered them to be treated with unusual barbarity. He was then incautious enough to venture into prison among them. They fell upon him, slew him, stuck his head upon a spike, and showed it to the citizens. Next day, however, at the instigation of his widow, the prisoners were all killed.

Marriage of Sultan Orchan and the daughter of the emperor.

In 1346 Orchan was married to Theodora, the daughter of Cantacuzenus. Her father had stipulated that she should be allowed to remain a Christian, and the agreement was not violated. She was delivered at Selymbria to the escort of Turkish cavalry which had been commissioned to accompany her. Amid much pomp and ceremony, with music, torches and display of various kinds, the first imperial princess of the Orthodox Church was handed over to the eunuchs of her barbarous lord. We may pass over the father's excuses for consenting to this marriage, which doubtless appeared to many of his subjects a gross act of wickedness. All that they amount to is that he believed the necessities of state required him to obtain the aid of Orchan and that it could not be obtained in any other way.

Marriage of the emperor John to another daughter of Cantacuzenus.

The next year, a much more promising marriage took place, namely that of his daughter Helen with the young emperor John Palaeologus. It had been brought about in the following manner. Cantacuzenus had approached the capital, and though the empress had been warned that he was in the neighbourhood, she had taken no precaution to prevent his being admitted, believing, indeed, that the story of his being near was an invention to gain time so as to prevent the condemnation of a new patriarch who was known to be a partisan of Cantacuzenus and was then on his trial before a Council of the Church. The friends of Cantacuzenus were in possession of the Golden Gate and opened it to him and his band of a thousand trusted followers. He marched in triumph to the Palace of Porphyrogenitus. The empress, as soon as she heard of the entry, shut herself up in the Palace at Blachern and called to her aid the Genoese of Galata. When the latter saw that the population were on the side of her rival, they refused to aid her. John advised his mother to treat, and after considerable hesitation she consented and articles of peace were agreed to. An amnesty was to be granted by both sides, and John was during ten years to permit Cantacuzenus to be the dominant ruler. Thereupon the latter proposed that his daughter Helen should become engaged to John, and, though the young man was unwilling, his mother accepted the arrangement. Helen was thirteen years old and her proposed husband fifteen.

Peace and prosperity appear to have been anticipated from the cessation of civil war which it was hoped this marriage would produce. Europe, if not, as Gibbon asserts, 'completely evacuated by the Moslems of Asia,' [1] was yet at peace with the empire. Within its borders all parties were supposed to be reconciled, and at the church of Blachern (the *bema* of Hagia Sophia having been destroyed by an earthquake) a remarkable coronation service was held in May 1347. Two emperors, namely the young John Palaeologus and John Cantacuzenus, and three empresses— Helen, wife of the Palaeologus, Irene, wife of Cantacuzenus, and Anne of Savoy, the dowager—were crowned with

[1] Vol. vii. p. 30, edition of Dr. J. B. Bury. The Tartars were still in the Balkan peninsula, and Orchan in 1347, probably just after the marriage of John, sent six thousand Turks to aid Matthew, son of Cantacuzenus, in fighting against the kral of Serbia.

unusually elaborate ceremonial. The bystanders, however, noted that the jewels were many of them false and the trappings of far less value than had previously been displayed on similar occasions.

Ducas notes that the young emperor, who had been forced to marry the daughter of Cantacuzenus, instead of taking part in the manly exercises of arms which were still practised by the youth of the empire, plunged into debauchery and soon disgusted his adherents by his drunkenness and by the depravity of his private life. The narrative of Gregoras declares that John complained bitterly of having been insulted by his father-in-law, and the statement is probably true that, seeing his debauchery, Cantacuzenus urged him to lead a better life and devote himself to duty.[1]

Pressed as he was for money in every direction, Cantacuzenus endeavoured to obtain it by a popular vote. The notice of the incident is almost unique in the later history of the empire and on that account merits attention. Cantacuzenus himself tells its history. Finding that the state had been greatly weakened by civil war, that the treasury was empty, the cities reduced to poverty by domestic divisions or by the invasions of the various foreign enemies who had ravaged the country, and his own private fortune expended, he determined to summon a meeting in Constantinople of the wealthy classes in order that they should contribute to the public necessities. He expressly states that he had no intention of making a levy by force. In the meeting thus called together there were representatives of all ranks—soldiers, shopkeepers, artisans, heads of monasteries, and priests. Cantacuzenus in addressing it declared that he had no desire to act against the Palaeologi but recognised that the civil war had exhausted the treasury, and promised that the money collected would be employed and his effort directed against the attacks of Serbians, Bulgarians, and Turks. He added that it was not he who had sought the alliance of the Turks, though he had given his daughter in marriage to Orchan, but that the aid of these barbarians had

[1] Greg. xxvii. 49.

been forced upon him by his enemies within the empire. The partisans of John had been the first to ask the Turks for assistance. They had delivered cities to the Turks, had paid them, and had made it necessary that he, in his own defence, should ask for their alliance. He concluded by urging the great assembly to consider in what manner means might be found of preserving the empire.[1]

The nobles returned answer that they recognised the necessity of contributing for the safety of the state, and advised that every person should give what was in his power. The emperor, believing that he had accomplished his purpose, then dismissed the assembly.

Very little result appears to have been produced. Nor does the voluntary taxation appear to have yielded any considerable sum. In the meeting itself there were many who were opposed to Cantacuzenus personally, and within a short period the animosity between the partisans of the two emperors became as rancorous as ever. Among the most violent of his own partisans was his son Matthew, who, under the belief that Anne, the empress-dowager, was conspiring against his father, boldly took possession of several cities.

Wearied out by constant struggle, Cantacuzenus states that he wished to abdicate and retire to a monastery, and that his wife approved of his design. His writings show that he felt great interest in the discussion of theological questions. The part which he himself took in several religious controversies, the anxiety that he underwent to have the excommunication against him annulled, first by the Patriarch John and afterwards, 'for greater safety,' by John's successor,[2] Isidore, his negotiations with the pope for Union, and many other circumstances, show that the withdrawal to a monastery was a not unnatural development of his life.

While he was making preparations to carry his design into execution, news came of the progress of Stephen of Serbia, which forced him to postpone it. Salonica, 'one of

---

[1] Cant. iv. 5 and 6.   [2] ἕνεκα ἀσφαλείας πράττειν, iv. 3.

the eyes of the empire,' was in danger of surrendering to
Stephen. The partisans of the Palaeologi among the
population of that city were numerous. The neighbouring
country was, however, under the power of the great Serbian,
and unless Stephen were checked without delay the city
would be given over to him. The old emperor sent word
to his followers to remain steadfast, promising that he would
come to their relief. In order to do so, he took a step which
is sometimes incorrectly treated as the first important introduction of the Turks into Europe.[1] He induced his son-in-
law, Orchan, to send a body of twenty thousand cavalry, under
his son Suliman, across the Dardanelles to march against
Stephen. The emperor left the capital as soon as he had
heard that the Turks had crossed the straits to co-operate
with them, and took his co-emperor John, who was obnoxious
to the Turks, with him. For some reason which is not clear,
the Othman or Ottoman Turks withdrew after they had
crossed the Maritza, but the two emperors with another body
of Turks went to Salonica and put an end to any design to
surrender it. This was in 1349.

The history of the empire during the next six years is
a medley of incidents, due to the hostility between the two
emperors. John refused to address his elder colleague as
emperor, and even proposed to join Stephen of Serbia,
whose power in the Balkan peninsula was now greater
than that of any other ruler. The Bulgarian king, appealed
to by Cantacuzenus to enter into alliance against Stephen,
refused his co-operation, and shortly after joined the Venetians to attack the empire.

Genoese
and
Venetians.

Cantacuzenus asked for the aid of the Genoese, who
joined him in order to resist the Venetians. The rivalry
during this reign between the two republics of Venice and
Genoa was great. Each was at the height of its power, and

[1] Even Gibbon (vii. 30) says, ' It was in the last quarrel with his pupil
that Cantacuzenus inflicted the deep and deadly wound which could never be
healed by his successors and which is poorly expiated by his theological dia-
logue against the prophet Mahomet.' But the Moslems, both from the north
and south, had been fighting in Europe fifty years earlier, sometimes on the
side of the Greeks, oftener, as with the Catalans, against them.

the commerce and dominions of the empire were the principal objects of their rivalry. A hundred and fifty years earlier there had been colonies of Amalfians, Pisans, Anconans, Ragusans, and even Germans, within the walls of the city. All these had disappeared,[1] and Genoa the Superb and Venice, Queen of the Seas, were the sole Italian competitors for domination in or a share of the empire. At the period with which we are concerned they were about equally matched in strength, and the two brave republics were constantly fighting the battles of their great duel in the waters of the Greek empire. Within a few months the Genoese were alternately the allies and the enemies of Cantacuzenus. In 1350 a fleet of fourteen Venetian galleys, and another of Catalans, prevented the Genoese from entering the Bosporus. Two years later another formidable fleet of Venetian galleys joined one of twenty-six Spaniards in order to attack the Genoese. After Pisani, the Venetian admiral, had rested his men for two days on the island of Prinkipo, he joined the imperial ships at Heptaskalion, and with a fleet of sixty-eight vessels attacked the Genoese. The fleet of the latter, numbering seventy ships, was at Chalcedon, and tried to intercept the enemy when they endeavoured to make their way to the Golden Horn. In a battle which was fought at the mouth of the Bosporus while a strong south wind was blowing with a heavy sea—a battle which continued all night—both sides lost heavily. Eighteen Genoese ships were sunk. Pisani withdrew to Therapia, with a loss of sixteen ships. Galata, held by the Genoese, was not attacked, on account of the prevalence of Black Death,[2] or possibly because he heard that seventy or eighty other galleys were on their way to aid the Genoese.

---

[1] Heyd's *History of Commerce in the Levant.*

[2] The Black Death (πανούκλα) was the terrible disease which spread throughout Europe and depopulated most of its large cities between 1346 and 1370. Cantacuzenus, whose son Andronicus fell a victim, gives a vivid and terrible picture of its symptoms, and of its effect upon the population (iv. 8). Dr. Mordtmann, who is not merely distinguished as an archæologist well acquainted with the Byzantine writers, but as a physician of great experience, believes it to have been a black form of smallpox, and not what is usually known as plague, and a well-known specialist in plague, to whose attention 1

Immediately afterwards the Genoese joined with the Turks, and transported across the Bosporus a body of them to attack Constantinople. Cantacuzenus, in consequence, was obliged to make peace with his rivals in Galata by allowing them to include a large portion of additional territory within new walls,[1] as well as to take possession of Selymbria and Heraclia in Thrace. The Genoese thereupon once more became his allies. Orchan was ready to assist him, and again promised to send twenty thousand Turks to resist the party of John.

Once more Cantacuzenus endeavoured to come to terms with his colleague. The latter had also endeavoured to gain the aid of Orchan, but failed. John's reply to the overture of his father-in-law was again to refuse to recognise that he had any right to the title of emperor. The followers of the rival emperors, Cantacuzeni and Palaeologi, were more bitter in their opposition than the leaders themselves, and the former in 1353 proclaimed Matthew, the son of Cantacuzenus, co-emperor with his father.

It is clear from the statement of Cantacuzenus himself that, as John grew older, his own party became weaker. The hopes of the people and of the nobles for a peaceful reign had been disappointed. Instead of having peace, the country had been disturbed by civil war. Serbia and Bulgaria had both recovered strength. The Turks had encroached on the imperial territories.

The emperor's greatest offence was rightly considered to have been the employment of Turkish auxiliaries, and the permission granted to the captors to sell the captured Christians as slaves, or the inability to prevent them from doing so.[2] The patriarch Philotheus remonstrated with him on this account, and Cantacuzenus declares that he

---

have submitted the account of Cantacuzenus, is disposed to accept the same view.

[1] The walls of Galata, both before and after this enlargement, which doubled the area of the city, may still be traced.

[2] The demand for slaves, and especially for girls for the harems, was always great. Slaves, indeed, usually formed the most valuable part of the booty in a raiding expedition.

received the admonition as the voice of God, and promised to conform to it.[1] Probably because he recognised that his own popularity was waning, he had allowed his eldest son, Matthew, to be associated with him in the government, but though the son displayed great activity, and gathered round him a strong party, both he and his father were condemned by the popular judgment.

The account given by Cantacuzenus is that he was asked by the nobles to nominate his successor, that he deferred giving his answer, but went to consult the patriarch, who retired to a monastery and after a week sent word that he would not return to the court nor to his church unless the emperor would swear never to proclaim his son Matthew. Thereupon Cantacuzenus called together the senate, who declared for Matthew. Cantacuzenus protests that in the struggle going on between John, his son-in-law, and Matthew he was always neutral, but that as the nobles wanted the latter he consented to name him as his colleague and successor. Thereupon Matthew was allowed to wear the purple buskin and the other imperial insignia. His name, as well as that of his father and Anne, the mother of John, was mentioned in the public prayers, while that of John was omitted.[2] The patriarch, however, remained obdurate. Matthew had not yet been consecrated. An assembly of bishops declared that, notwithstanding the patriarch's opposition, he ought to be asked to perform the ceremony. The answer of Philotheus was to decree excommunication against any one who should attempt to lay upon him such a duty. The patriarch was threatened with dismissal. He replied that he would be glad of it, and was dismissed accordingly.[3]

The great anxiety of Cantacuzenus until, and even after, his abdication was to see his son recognised as emperor. Matthew, however, fell into the hands of John, who generously offered him his liberty on condition that he would renounce all claim to the throne. Cantacuzenus states that he counselled his son to accept this offer. After

---

[1] Cant. iv. 39.   [2] Ibid. iv. 37.   [3] Ibid. iv. 37.

some hesitation he took his father's advice. Articles of peace were accepted, and among the stipulations it was provided that Matthew might wear any buskin he liked except in purple. It was a relief to both parties when John saved himself from the reproaches of his father-in-law by leaving for Italy and Germany. His party appears to have increased in strength during his absence.[1]

He remained abroad for two years. On his return he encountered at Tenedos a Genoese adventurer, with a considerable number of followers, who was on the look-out for an island which he might seize as the Venetians had seized Chios. John proposed to employ the adventurer to aid him in becoming sole emperor. They came together to Constantinople, where the citizens had already risen in revolt against Cantacuzenus, who had in consequence to shut himself up in the Blachern Palace with a foreign guard. During the night John's friends asked to be admitted at the postern of Hodegetria, pretending that they were merchants with a cargo of olive oil, and that the sea was rising and dangerous. They promised the guardians that if they were admitted half the cargo should be paid for the favour. They rushed the postern as soon as it was open, and two thousand men entered the city, took possession of the walls, and made a demonstration in favour of John. When morning broke, the Hippodrome was crowded with citizens, and the city in a tumult. Cantacuzenus apparently lost his head, entered the monastery of Peribleptis, and assumed the habit of a monk. He at once made submission to his young rival, asked and, after some weeks, received permission to retire to Mount Athos, and there passed nearly twenty-five years in the composition of his voluminous History. He died in 1380.

Cantacuzenus, like his predecessors, looked to the West and especially to the pope to aid him in checking the progress of the Turks. Throughout the whole of his reign

Cantacuzenus submits and retires to Mount Athos, 1355.

---

[1] The statement that he visited Italy and Germany is made by Ducas (i. 11), but it is remarkable that Cantacuzenus makes no mention of it. Muralt (p. 640) suggests that he left Tenedos in the spring of 1352. But Cantacuzenus, writing of the events of 1254, represents John as having passed a whole year in Tenedos. Possibly this would be a year terminating in January 1355.

the attempts to obtain aid from the West and to bring about the Union of the Churches, two objects which had become inseparable, are constant. The zeal with which successive popes sought to obtain the Union found a ready response in Cantacuzenus.

News travelled slowly from the Levant to Italy, but such as reached the West made it known, not merely that Moslems were encroaching on Christian territory; that the victories obtained in the great crusades had largely become fruitless; that almost every inch of territory which had been won in Syria at the sacrifice of so many lives and so much treasure had been captured by the infidels, but that the Christian populations had been everywhere treated with the barbarity that has always followed Moslem conquest. The history indeed of Egypt, Syria, and Asia Minor had been a long series of massacres, culminating perhaps in that of Egypt where in 1354, when the Christians were ordered to abjure their faith and to accept Mahometanism and refused, a hundred thousand were put to death.[1]

Under such circumstances, Clement the Sixth was not less anxious than his predecessors had been to check Moslem progress. Encompassed as he was with a host of difficulties, and insecure even in his own position, he constantly kept before him the desirability of attaining the two results which for nearly three centuries were prominent objects of papal policy: resistance to the Mahometans and the Union of the two great Christian Churches. In 1343, the year after his appointment to the pontifical throne, he persuaded the queens of Sicily and Naples to send a fleet with one fitted out by himself against the Turks. Two years later he urged all Christians to aid in the defence of Caifa and, in return for their services in defending that city, permitted the Genoese to trade with the infidels at Bagdad. When he learned that the Christian expedition which he had authorised was massacred by the Turks near Smyrna, he proclaimed a crusade and appealed to Edward the Third of England not to prevent Philip of France from taking

Attempts by pontiff (a) to resist Moslems, (b) to effect union.

[1] Gregoras, xxix. 25.

part in it by making war against him, an appeal which was unsuccessful and which was followed six months later by the victory of Crécy. In the same year Clement sent two nuncios into Armenia to persuade the members of the ancient Church of that people to enter into union with Rome. In 1347 he wrote to congratulate Stephen of Serbia on his having expressed the desire to enter the Roman Communion.

During the early years of the reigns of John and Cantacuzenus, Clement does not appear to have had direct communication with Constantinople. He had apparently a dislike to or prejudice against the elder emperor, for in 1345 he wrote to the dauphin of France not to treat with Cantacuzenus but only with the Dowager Empress Anne.[1] He had seen with indignation the employment of Turks by Cantacuzenus against his enemies and considered him a usurper of the throne which ought to be occupied only by John, the son of a mother whose predilections in favour of Union were well known. His information, according to the emperor's narrative, was derived from an Italian lady who had lived with the Empress Anne and whose sympathy would naturally be with the cause of her mistress.

Cantacuzenus determined to explain to the pontiff his own position, to justify his conduct and at the same time to offer his aid in any expedition that might be formed for attacking the Mahometans and to express his desire to accomplish the Union of the Churches.[2]

Accordingly he sent a deputation to Clement consisting of the protovestarius and an Italian in his service who was known to the pope. On their arrival they had long interviews with Clement and were astonished at his detailed knowledge of the condition of the empire. According to Cantacuzenus, the pope expressed great satisfaction at the clemency shown by him to his enemies and especially at the marriage between his daughter and John, in which he saw the prospect of a united empire and one which would be able to aid in resisting the Moslems. Clement sent the

[1] Rayn. iv. lxiii.   [2] iv. 9.

deputation back to Constantinople accompanied by two bishops as nuncios distinguished alike by their piety and learning. They arrived in the capital in 1347. After expressing the satisfaction of the pope for the emperor's moderation towards his enemies and his kindness towards Anne, the nuncios declared that the pontiff was even more zealous than any of his predecessors for an attack upon the Turks and that he had already endeavoured to induce the Italian princes to join in an expedition by promising them aid in men and money, but that his zeal was still further increased by the offer of the emperor to aid in such undertaking. If in addition to this he could procure the reconciliation of the Churches, he would gain the approval not only of the pope but of God and His angels.

Cantacuzenus in his reply expressed his thanks to the pontiff for his promised aid against the infidels and in reference to the Union of the Churches declared that he would willingly die if by his death he could secure the object for which both ardently longed. He pointed out, however, that the differences between the Churches related to doctrine, and that Catholic teaching recognised that these could only be settled by a Council of the whole Church. He himself could accept no new dogmas nor force others to accept them before they had been definitely accepted by a Council. He therefore suggested that one should be called, being confident that its deliberations and its decisions would receive divine guidance. As the pope could not come to Constantinople and Cantacuzenus could not go to Rome, the emperor proposed that the Council should be summoned to meet in some maritime city, midway between the two capitals.

The nuncios found, or professed to find, the proposal of the emperor reasonable, and returned to Rome. The pope expressed his satisfaction, but declared that he could not suggest a place of meeting till he had communicated with the princes of the West. After some time he sent word that though he regarded the Union of the Churches as the most important question with which Christendom had to deal, he was obliged to defer fixing the time and the place for the Council until he had secured peace among the Italian princes. The death of Clement, in 1352, delayed the execution of this project.

Character of Cantacuzenus.

It is difficult to form an impartial judgment of the characters of Cantacuzenus and John, whose reigns cover the period during which, if it had been possible, the empire might have recovered its strength. The history of the reign written by the former, as well as the narrative of Ducas, places the conduct of the elder emperor in a favourable light. The charge most commonly brought against him, of having introduced the Turks into Europe, can only be accepted with considerable reserve. As we have already seen, he was not the first to introduce them. The Spaniards must bear the responsibility of this charge. Once it became necessary to fight, whether against Serbians, Bulgarians, or internal enemies, an emperor can hardly be blamed for obtaining auxiliaries. The mercenaries most easily obtainable were the Turks. All contending parties in the Balkan peninsula were ready to accept their aid. The excuses of Cantacuzenus are evidence which proves that he realised the danger of their obtaining a permanent foothold in Europe. A more valid justification is furnished by the fact that, with the object of preventing them crossing into Thrace without his permission, he endeavoured to close the two passages which they had been accustomed before his time to employ—namely, from Lampsacus and between Sestos and Abydos.

When his own conduct during the time of their joint emperorship is compared with that of John it is seen that in love of country, in devotion to its interests, as well as in sagacity, he is greatly his superior. The difficulties that arose between them were in fact largely due to the jealousy weakness, debauchery, and incompetence of John. When youth he was simply a drunken reprobate. That a young emperor, who believed that he had been supplanted by another in his right to the sole occupancy of the throne should resent references to his profligacy and his irregular life was natural enough, but Cantacuzenus cannot justly be blamed because he refused to surrender the government into his hands.

Our estimate of the character of Cantacuzenus has to be based mainly on his own writings. But through them we know the man better perhaps than any other emperor. When dealing with events illustrating his own motives and conduct, he is an unconscious hypocrite. He gives us his version of all the principal events of his reign. His despatches and his speeches are reported at weary length, but they usually leave the impression of having been revised and modified by the light of his subsequent experience. His own narrative is confirmed to a considerable extent by that of Ducas, who, however, is open to suspicion as a partisan. His grandfather had belonged to the party of Cantacuzenus and had escaped into Asia Minor to avoid the vengeance of Apocaukus. Ducas describes Cantacuzenus as distinguished by the soundness of his judgment and by his great courage.[1]

Cantacuzenus is great in accounting for his failures. Judged by his own narrative, which may be described as an *apologia pro vita sua*, he appears a respectable ecclesiastically minded man of mediocre talent, seriously desirous of the good of the people whom he governed, but anxious, above all, not only to become emperor but to found an imperial family.

The vanity of Cantacuzenus leads him seldom to lose an

---

[1] The History of Nicephorus Gregoras, as written by an enemy, is a useful corrective. Krumbacher in his account of Byzantine literature speaks of Gregoras as ' die Hauptperson des 14. Jahrhunderts ' (p. 19). His narrative is described by Cantacuzenus as stamped with ignorance, partiality, and falsehood. Its chief accusation against him is not merely false but improbable (iv. 24). In his own History Cantacuzenus declares that he has never departed from the truth either on account of hatred or the desire to say pleasant things (iv. concluding chapter). What he finds most fault with in Gregoras is the statement that, even during the lifetime of Andronicus, Cantacuzenus had become possessed of a burning desire to become emperor, and that he had consulted certain monks at Mount Athos who were supposed to have the power of divination, in order to learn whether he would accomplish his desire. The story, he declares, is absolutely false. It is brought up because he as emperor protected Palamas in his religious controversies where Gregoras took the opposite side.

occasion of reporting what friends or enemies say in his favour. When he sent the embassy to Pope Clement the Sixth to explain why he had employed Turks and to propose to render aid to the sovereigns of the West in the expedition which Clement contemplated, he remarks that the pontiff spoke in the highest terms of his moderation and kindness in not having treated his ungrateful enemies with more severity.[1] In his many negotiations with Rome he never fails to report expressions complimentary to his own sagacity, character, and conduct. In like manner he records the flattering expressions used regarding him by the Ottoman sultan, expressions which then, as now, are nearly destitute of all meaning, as if they were a serious representation of the sentiments of the writer. He cannot resist pointing out that Nicephorus Gregoras, whose History he declares to be false and malicious, had at one time awarded him unbounded praise.[2]

When the chief of the Genoese forces which had captured Heraclia and were flushed with victory proposed to attack the capital, Cantacuzenus makes him abandon his design because he knew that it was defended by the emperor, who was the equal in wisdom and experience of any commander of the age.[3] It is in the same spirit of self-laudation that he declares that in the struggle with the Serbians before Salonica he had exterminated some by the simple terror of his name and others by his army.[4]

Reign of John after retirement of Cantacuzenus (1355 to 1391).

John occupied the throne after the retirement of Cantacuzenus for upwards of thirty-five years. A youth largely spent in selfish pleasures gave little promise that the young man of twenty-three would be able to cope with the difficulties by which the empire was beset. With the aid of his mother, Anne of Savoy, and of partisans whose only hope was in the patronage of the new ruler, he had succeeded in ridding himself of his elderly, respectable, and patriotic colleague. He had now to face the difficulties with which the empire was beset. Of these the dynastic struggle which

[1] iv. 9.   [2] iv. 24.   [3] iv. 28.   [4] iv. 17.

still continued with Matthew, the son of Cantacuzenus, was soon disposed of. An agreement had been arrived at before the withdrawal of his father by which Matthew should retain the title of emperor and remain in possession of certain districts of the Rhodope mountains, and of the island of Lemnos. A few months later the island was exchanged for a lordship in the Morea. Shortly afterwards Matthew was made prisoner by the Serbians, delivered to John, and, after he had been kept for a while prisoner in Tenedos, abdicated and retired in 1358 to the Morea.

John had no liking for religious controversies within his own Church, and although Cantacuzenus in his retirement wished that the most important of them should be continued John forbade it. There was a curious theological controversy, related by the writers of the time, which is of value as showing that in the midst of the most grave political difficulties the Byzantine people had not yet lost their interest in religious questions. Barlaam, a Calabrian abbot of the Greek Church—who, as we have seen, had been sent to Rome to negotiate for Union and aid because, among other reasons, he was well acquainted with Latin, ' better indeed than with Greek '[1]—charged certain monks at Mount Athos and their followers, known as Bogomils, with heresy, called them Omphalopsychae, Messalians, men who believed that by looking long at their navel they could see God with mortal eyes,[2] or at least with the uncreated light of Mount Tabor. Barlaam's great opponent was Palamas, archbishop of Salonica. The party headed by Palamas was favoured by Cantacuzenus, whose mother, indeed, was a Bogomil. The controversy waxed fierce and bitter, but Barlaam was unable to obtain the condemnation he desired. It raged for fifteen years until forcibly put an end to by John on the withdrawal of his colleague.[3]

[1] Greg. xi. 10.   [2] *Ibid.*
[3] The Bogomils still exist in Eastern Rumelia. One may be sceptical as to the doctrines in which, according to their enemies, they believed. Apparently they were quietists, searchers after the Inner Light, who would have nothing to do with the worship of Eikons, were possibly Unitarians, and had a tendency in many directions towards what may be called reformation principles. Their

By far the most important difficulty which John had to face was the constantly increasing encroachments by the Turks. Their influence at the beginning of his sole occupancy of the throne is shown by the consent he was forced to give to the engagement of his infant daughter to the son of Orchan, the great Turkish leader and successor of Othman. Their influence at a later period, in 1374, is shown by his having been forced into an alliance with Murad and, towards the end of his reign, by his having to destroy a part of the walls of the capital at Murad's bidding.

At no period of his life did the emperor show that he possessed ability above the average. Neither he nor any of his ministers rose above mediocrity. He nevertheless recognised the danger to his empire from the advance of the Mahometans, the powerlessness of his own unaided subjects to resist that advance, and the expediency of obtaining help from the West. In dealing with some of the questions which disturbed his subjects he possessed a certain aloofness

teaching was imbued with the Slavic mysticism which is characteristic to-day of Russian literature.

The Bogomils became first noticeable in Bulgaria in the days of King Peter (927–968). Even a few years earlier they are alluded to as certain ' Pagan Slavs and Manichaeans.' Later on the Bogomils are spoken of as Paulicians. In Bosnia they became so powerful that the whole country was described as Bogomil. The pope in 1407 promised help to Sigismund against the ' Manichaeans and Arians ' in Bosnia, and they were beaten and the kingdom dismembered in 1410–11. The Council of Bâle received a deputation from the Bogomils in 1435 and dealt at the same time with them and with the Hussites. In 1443 they lent valuable aid to Hunyadi against the Turks. Persecuted by both the Catholic and Orthodox Churches, many of the magnates who had been forced to become Catholics in order to retain their lands turned Mahometans, and their example was largely followed by the smaller landholders. Among the Mahometans of Bosnia there still exist many customs of Christian origin. Mr. Evans, in *Through Bosnia and Herzegovina*, states that there are still many thousands of Bogomils in these countries. Herr Asboth, who has been over the country, declares the statement to be too general, and says that he was never able to find any, although he admits that they recently existed. Subject in Bulgaria to persecution from the Orthodox Church, many of them sought escape about a century ago by joining the Church of Rome. Bogomilism spread from Bosnia into Europe, where it gave rise to the Cathari or Albigenses, who acknowledged the Church of Dragovitza in Macedonia as their mother Church. The best account I know of the Bogomils in Bosnia is in J. de Asboth's *Official Tour through Bosnia and Herzegovina*, London, 1900.

which made him examine them as a statesman. It is probably true, as Gibbon suggests,[1] that in his appeals to Rome he was greatly influenced by his mother, Anne of Savoy. She had been brought up as a member of the Latin Church and, though compelled on her marriage to change her name and her religion, she yet remained attached to the Church and country of her childhood. Her struggles during the minority of her son had not tended to make her look with favour on the Orthodox, and her influence upon her son's mind was probably sufficient to make him regard with as much favour the Church to which his mother had belonged as that of which he was now the temporal head. He had come to regard the differences between the two Churches as matters rather for ecclesiastics than for statesmen. He personally was ready to accept the Union of the Churches and even papal supremacy in religious matters, provided that in return he could obtain aid from the West against the enemies of the empire. But, whatever were his own sentiments towards the Church of Rome, his conduct during the long period of thirty-five years showed that he felt the need of external aid if the empire were to be saved. His reign is one long series of efforts to obtain it. He was ready to humiliate himself, to use all his powers of persuasion for Union, provided that the pontiffs would induce Western rulers to fight the Turks.

Hope was probably stimulated in the empire by the fact that the pope and the West generally seemed at last to recognise that, in their own interest, measures should be taken to defend the empire. Moreover, the danger was now so pressing, not only to the Greeks but to Europe, that it appeared possible to obtain aid without submitting to the humiliating conditions hitherto imposed. While John knew that to persuade the Orthodox Church to acknowledge any of its doctrines as heretical, and especially to induce the ecclesiastics to accept the supremacy of the pope, was almost impossible, he professed himself ready to make his own submission. The Union of the Churches could be

Renewed efforts by popes against Moslems.

accomplished at a later day. There appeared reason to hope that the pope regarded the danger from the Moslems mainly from the statesman's point of view and desired mutual action. John was so far justified in this hope that it may be confidently asserted that had the counsels of more than one of the popes during his reign been followed there would have been a concerted action against the common enemy sufficient to have delayed the Turkish progress, and possibly to have altogether arrested it. We shall see, however, that, although all the states of Western Europe still acknowledged the supremacy of the pope, their interests and jealousies were as diverse as they have been in modern times, and that the pontiff was able neither to induce nor to compel the nations acknowledging his supremacy to act in concert.

Knowing from his own visit to Italy and from the negotiations carried on by Cantacuzenus that Rome was predisposed to aid, John, immediately he became sole ruler, sent an embassy to the pope. His delegates were authorised to make the emperor's submission to the papal authority in exchange for the undertaking by the pope to furnish galleys against the Turks.

In the following year, 1356, John sent a golden bull to the pope at Avignon containing the terms of his submission.[1] The pope thereupon expressed his satisfaction by a reply to the emperor, and while communicating the good news to the knights of Rhodes, the king of Cyprus, and the doge of Venice, invited them to make preparations to aid the Christian cause. So far, however, as the empire was concerned, the series of efforts made at the pope's instigation were without any satisfactory result. Ill planned, inadequately supported, unenergetically pursued, they were all almost useless. Six years afterwards—namely, in 1362—John was invited to join the kings of France and Denmark and Guy de Lusignan of Cyprus in a Crusade against the Saracens, an expedition

---

[1] Raynaldus, N. xxxii., professes to give the text of his submission. I his text is genuine it shows that John was under the same delusion as Michael had been : namely, that he could force the Orthodox Church to accept what he wanted.

of quite secondary importance to the empire. To the men
of the West, Turks and Saracens were all the same. The
Greeks knew better. Two years passed and a new pope, Urban
the Fifth, was still organising a plan against the Saracens.
In reply to the pontiff's invitation John promised all the aid
possible to the new Crusade, though pointing out that the
benefit to the empire would be slight. But the sovereigns
of the West had had enough of Crusades and would not
respond to the call from Avignon. The companies of military monks who were in France equally refused to take part
in the proposed undertaking, and the efforts of the pope only
succeeded in inducing a few English adventurers to join with
Peter of Lusignan in a fruitless attack upon Egypt.

At length, in 1366, a more hopeful Crusade, or at least
one more likely to result in advantage to the empire, was
proclaimed. At the bidding of the pope, Louis, king of
Hungary, and Amadeo of Savoy proposed to attack the
Turks and to aid the emperor. Once more the condition
was attached that John should complete the Union of the
Churches. But, once again, the crusading army was
weakened by the division of forces judged necessary for an
attempt at the same time upon the Saracens. Nor would
other states join. In vain the pope threatened the Genoese,
Venetians, and Spaniards with all the terrors of an interdict
if they gave aid to the enemy. They continued to trade
with the Saracens as before. In vain he exhorted the
sovereigns of Western Europe to go to the aid of Cyprus
and Rhodes, and promised them indulgences if they would
take part in this war of the Cross. They turned deaf ears
to his summons.

In 1367 Urban had entered Rome, and one of his first
acts on taking possession of the chair of St. Peter was to
exhort the Genoese and Venetians to facilitate the voyage of
John to the imperial city. The emperor was willing enough
to go to Rome, provided that there was a reasonable chance
of obtaining substantial aid. He had made submission once
and was ready to do all that he could to complete the Union
the pope so greatly desired, but he knew much better than

the pope how difficult it would be to induce his people to accomplish the proposed task. His needs, however, were great, and the summons of the pope was urgent. Accordingly, in 1369, he ventured on the dangerous step of leaving Constantinople. He was received with every honour in the elder Rome, and made a profession of faith which satisfied the four cardinals who had been deputed to receive it. An encyclical notified the great news to all Christian princes. The pope allowed John to negotiate with English mercenaries then in Italy for service, granted him religious privileges, loaded him with presents, and requested the rulers of the states through which he had to pass on his homeward journey to receive him with the respect due to his rank. Urban at the same time addressed a letter to the Greek clergy urging them to accept the Union.

John, however, found little or no material help. He left Rome in debt, and on his return to Venice, where, on his Romeward journey, he had been received in great state and promised four galleys, he was detained until he paid his debts. The emperor urged his son Andronicus, who had been appointed regent during the absence of his father, to find the means of releasing him. The son declared that as the treasury was empty and the clergy would not help, he was unable to obtain ransom. His younger son, Manuel, contrived however, to find in Salonica sufficient money for his father's release.

Both Urban and his successor, Gregory the Eleventh displayed a great desire to aid the empire to stem the tide of Moslem progress. Gregory in 1371 urged the kings of France and England to join with the Genoese to save the remnant of Christians in the Holy Land from the Saracens All their efforts were fruitless.

The Turkish invasion had meantime become more serious than the Saracenic conquests, as the invaders had now penetrated by land and sea respectively as far as Albania and Dalmatia. The pope once more urged Louis of Hungary, the successors of the crusading nobles who still held territory in Greece and along a portion of the coast of the Adriatic, the knights of Rhodes, and the king of Sicily to combine in a great movement with John against the common enemy. Once more he caused a new Crusade to be preached and promised indulgences to those who took up the Cross. He begged the Emperor Charles to make peace with Bavaria so that the empire in the West might join the Crusade. On all sides, however, there was a reluctance to enter upon it. In spite of the pope's influence and promise to arm twelve galleys for despatch against the Turks, John's ambassador returned from the West having completely failed in obtaining aid.

Gregory the Eleventh was equally persevering in his efforts to bring about the Union of the Churches. Franciscan and Dominican missionaries were sent into the East to expose the wickedness of the schism caused or persisted in by the Orthodox Church. Nuncios were despatched to complete the reconciliation. The emperor was reproached, quite unjustly, because he was unable to persuade or compel his subjects to accept Union and to become reconciled with the Latin priests.

The pontiff, however, did not lose sight of his political object. Louis of Hungary fell under his condemnation because he had neglected to engage in the Crusade. But Louis had seen the great defeat of Bulgaria and Southern Serbia on the Maritza in 1371 and was not prepared to make war hastily against so formidable a foe as the Turk had then shown himself to be.

In 1374 the pope returned to the charge and urged the king of Hungary to be on watch against the incursions of the Turks into the empire until the fleet prepared at the pontiff's expense should arrive in the Marmora. At the same time he invited John once more to visit Rome in order to discuss measures for the accomplishment of Union.

In 1375 he again urged Louis of Hungary to do his duty as chief of the Crusade. He sent five hundred knights of Rhodes and an equal number of squires to defend the Greeks. He authorised the bishops in Western lands to apply large sums from the Church revenues for the purpose

of resisting the enemy of Christendom. His influence fell
far short of his desire. The Hungarian king was reported
to have misappropriated the money he had been allowed to
acquire from the Church, and the great fleet which the
Genoese had collected for the purpose of attacking the
Turks endeavoured to depose John in favour of his son
Andronicus.

Difficulties
with
Sultan
Murad. John himself was in serious difficulties with the Ottoman
sultan,. Murad. These two sovereigns were now, indeed,
the two great actors on the stage during several years, but
the character of Murad dominated over that of the commonplace John. To avoid possible treachery, the Christian
emperor, who was not trusted by Murad, was in 1374
compelled with his son Manuel to follow the sultan in a
campaign. During his absence he entrusted the government to Andronicus, his eldest son. Thereupon an accident
occurred which seems greatly to have impressed contemporaries. Andronicus entered into an arrangement with
the son of Murad by which the two swore to be friends and
to act together, when one should become emperor and the
other sultan. A definite arrangement may well be doubted
and possibly all that passed was due to the impulsiveness of
boyish friendship without any likelihood of practical result.
Murad, however, when he heard of the agreement, blinded his
son, insisted that John should treat Andronicus in the same
manner, and threatened war if he did not comply. According
to Ducas, John blinded not only Andronicus, but also his infant
son.[1] Probably the sight of one eye only was destroyed.
Andronicus was imprisoned in the Tower of Anemas with his
wife and son, and John's younger son, Manuel, was crowned as
co-emperor. Two years afterwards Andronicus escaped to the
Genoese in Galata. With their aid he succeeded in entering
Constantinople, proclaimed himself emperor, and shut up
his father in the same prison in which he had himself been
confined. Two years afterwards the prisoner escaped to
Scutari, and Andronicus had the sense to avoid civil war by

[1] Ducas, xii. Chalcondylas makes a similar statement (i. 45) ; Canale says
that a Genoese doctor restored sight to Andronicus.

coming to an arrangement with his father by which John was once more placed on the throne with his son Manuel. Andronicus in compensation received certain of the towns on the north side of the shore of the Marmora.

When Andronicus had succeeded in obtaining possession of the city with the aid of the Genoese, almost his first act was to arrest all the Venetians, with whom the Genoese were again at war. With their aid, John endeavoured to take Tenedos from his enemies, but failed. In the following year (1379) the Genoese united themselves with Louis of Hungary and defeated the Venetians at sea. They were still sufficiently influential in 1382 to compel the emperor to make peace with Andronicus.[1] Constantly strengthening themselves, they entered into a treaty in 1387 with the Bulgarian prince of the Dobrutcha.

During this time the Turks were making steady and almost unchecked progress in Greece, on the eastern shore of the Aegean, and in Bulgaria and Macedonia. The inhabitants were becoming weary of the constant struggle and it is significant that in 1385 the patriarch Nilos wrote to pope Urban the Sixth that the Turks left complete liberty to the Church. Even Rome appears to have been in despair. Urban the Sixth like his predecessors had so completely made his action against the Turks conditional upon the renunciation by the Greeks of their heresies and upon Union with Rome that all hope of aid from him or from Western Europe had for a time died out.[2]

The last years of the reign of John Palaeologus were once more disturbed by domestic troubles. His eldest son, Andronicus, had died in 1385, but his grandson, John, had many friends and was supported by the Genoese. His party was sufficiently powerful to gain an entry into the city by the Chariseus or Adrianople Gate and to compel the old Emperor John to associate his grandson of the same name as emperor with Manuel, his younger son, and himself. After a few months, however, Manuel, who had never

---

[1] Sauli, *Colonia dei Genovesi in Galata*, ii. 260.
[2] Urban the Sixth died in 1389.

Death of
John.

accepted the arrangement, entered by the Golden Gate and his nephew fled. In 1391, the elder Emperor John died after a reign of fifty-one years.

During his long occupancy of the throne the power of the Turks had enormously increased and the empire had almost become a vassal of Murad. In the last year of his reign there occurred an incident, already alluded to, which illustrates at once the weakness of John and his practical vassalage to the Turks. Wishing to strengthen the landward walls and especially at and near the Golden Gate, where the defences had fallen into decay, he gave out that he was about to clear the city of its accumulated rubbish and to ornament that gate. Bajazed, who was now the Ottoman sultan and successor of his father, Murad, when he learned what had been done, insisted that the new defensive works should be destroyed, threatening that if his wishes were not complied with he would put out the eyes of John's son Manuel, who had gone by the Sultan's orders to accompany the Turkish army on a campaign in Pamphylia. John obeyed the orders he had received.[1]

[1] Ducas, xiii.

CHAPTER V

REIGN OF ORCHAN : STRUGGLES WITH EMPIRE ; ITS SUC-
CESSES AND REVERSES ; INVASIONS OF TARTARS. REIGN
OF MURAD : DEFEAT OF SERBIANS AND BULGARIANS BY
TURKS ; BATTLE OF COSSOVO-POL AND ASSASSINATION
OF MURAD.

THE death of John, in 1391, is a convenient period to resume
the narrative of the progress of the Turks.

Othman had died the year after the capture of Brousa,
in 1326. He had succeeded in making his division of the
Turks the most formidable in Asia Minor, in conquering or
absorbing the Seljukian Turks, in destroying many flourishing cities and strongholds on the Black Sea, in entirely
preventing the reorganisation of the power of the empire in
the north-west portion of Asia Minor, and, above all, in
organising a fighting race into a formidable army.

His successor was his son Orchan. Nicaea is only
distant four or five hours from Brousa, and had hitherto
been able to resist all attacks by the Turks. Its population
was fairly secure within its extensive and strong walls ; the
beautiful lake of Ascanius adjoins one side of it, and furnished a constant supply of water and of fish. Once, indeed,
an emperor had sent up a fleet to assist a great army of
Western Crusaders, and to receive from their hands the city
which they were about to capture from the Seljuks.[1] Orchan
laid siege to it, and its citizens defended themselves with

Reign of Sultan Orchan, 1326–1357.

---

[1] This was in 1097, when, on the invitation of Godfrey de Bouillon, Alexis
had reached the city on its water side by taking his boats, in part at least,
overland from the Gulf of Moudania to the lake. The object of Godfrey was
to prevent the Crusaders being exposed to the demoralisation of plundering a
hostile city.

courage until relief came. Cantacuzenus and his sovereign hastily gathered together an army, and acting upon the advice of the imperial Grand Huntsman Godfrey, the bearer of the illustrious name which had won its first renown in the Crusade before this very place, successfully drove back the Turks. Unfortunately, on the evening of the same day, a panic seized the imperial troops, and the enemy, taking advantage of it, struck hard, captured the baggage, changed the panic into a rout, and captured the great and important city in the very hour of its triumph.

Master of the two cities, Brousa, a natural stronghold which had been strengthened by successive emperors, and Nicaea, whose ancient reputation and importance as the City of the Creed had been increased by its having served during two generations as the rallying place of the exiles from Constantinople during the Latin occupation, Orchan now assumed the title of sultan, made Brousa his capital, and struck the first Ottoman coins to replace those of the Seljukian sultans.

During his reign of thirty-two years he enlarged the territory occupied by the Ottomans, and greatly improved their national organisation. While constantly engaged in war, and though not less bent on conquest than his father, he neglected no opportunity of inducing the Christian subjects of the empire to come under his rule. He took care that the taxes levied were less than those paid in the empire. Although by this time Turkish armies were probably almost exclusively Moslem, Orchan formed one of his best regiments out of Christians who had voluntarily entered his service.

Orchan was far from obtaining uniform successes against the empire. He was often and bravely opposed by the imperial troops. In 1329, a large army, which had been transported into Thrace in a fleet of seventy ships, was destroyed near Trajanopolis, and most of the Turks were either killed or reduced to slavery. In 1330, a new invasion into Thrace of Turkish cavalry was defeated, and fifteen thousand Turks were slain. Orchan's attempt in the following year to capture Ismidt failed, and he was obliged to sue for peace. In spite of these disasters, he was always able within a few months to assemble new armies, and to renew the struggle. Already he had succeeded in exacting tribute from nearly the whole of Bithynia. His troops, within two years, invaded Macedonia, Euboea, and Athens, and while Cantacuzenus was with difficulty holding his own against them, another army met Andronicus the Third in Thrace, and took possession of Rodosto—an army, however, which the emperor shortly afterwards destroyed.

New recruits were continually making their way across the Dardanelles or the Marmora into Thrace, until, in 1336, the Turkish army in that province met with disaster in an unexpected manner. A band of Tartars from the north made a descent upon them when they heard that they had been successful in a raid upon the Christian population and were carrying off an enormous mass of booty.[1] Three months after the departure of the Tartars a new descent into Thrace was attempted by the Turks. Once again the Greeks were successful, and, in the same year, an army which ravaged the environs of Constantinople was destroyed and the Turkish fleet which brought them captured.

The efforts of Orchan were more successful in Asia Minor. A division of his army had laid siege again to Ismidt, and the inhabitants, in order to avoid imminent starvation, surrendered. The acquisition, in 1337, of this city, the most important seaport on the Asiatic side of the Marmora, and the head, then as now, of all the roads leading from the capital to every part of Asia Minor, Persia, and Syria, was of the utmost importance.

Nicomedia taken (1337).

During the stormy joint reigns of John and Cantacuzenus (1342 to 1355), the empire was attacked both by Tartars on the north, and by the Turks in Asia Minor. The Bulgarian and Serbian kingdoms had both gained strength during the Latin occupation at the expense of the empire, and were ready to avail themselves of the aid alike of Turks and Tartars in

[1] Greg. ix. 2 says the Turks had carried off three hundred thousand Christian captives. The Turks fought well, but were exterminated.

their endeavours to capture territory from the empire. When, in 1342, Cantacuzenus was attacked by the Bulgarians, a division of the Turks, whose emir had taken the title of sultan of Lydia, was induced to come to his aid. Twenty-nine thousand arrived at the mouth of the Maritza, the ancient Hebrus, and with their aid a temporary relief was afforded; but for some reason, possibly a severe winter, they withdrew to Asia Minor. The Bulgarians on this occasion were not aided by the Tartars, probably because the latter were occupied in the Crimea, and throughout what is now southern Russia, in fighting the Genoese, who had blockaded the northern coast of the Black Sea. Apocaukus, the rival of Cantacuzenus, succeeded in the following year in hiring a Turkish fleet and army. Both sides, indeed, in the civil war then going on, as well as the Bulgarians and Serbians, never hesitated to increase their armies by employing Turks or Tartars as auxiliaries.

When, in 1344, Cantacuzenus promised his daughter Theodora in marriage to Orchan, he received at once the aid of a body of five thousand Ottoman Turks, and this number was increased when the marriage took place, two years later. But the young emperor John met him with another body of Turkish auxiliaries. Orchan would have made short work of John; for in an interview which took place with much ceremony and cordiality at Scutari to congratulate his father-in-law on his second coronation, he appears to have decided upon following the Turkish method of getting rid of a rival to the throne of his father-in-law. Cantacuzenus, however, would not sanction assassination. Orchan apparently could not understand any such scruples, and shortly afterwards sent a number of Turks to the capital on a pretended political mission, but really with the object of aiding Cantacuzenus by murdering John. The elder emperor, as soon as he learned the design, at once put his foot down, and declared that he would not permit John to go outside the palace except accompanied by him.[1]

In the attacks by Stephen, the kral of Serbia, who had

---

[1] Cant. iv. 16.

taken the title of emperor of the Serbians and the Greeks, or emperor of Serbia and Romania—for both forms are used—Orchan once more sent troops to aid his father-in-law. In the struggles which took place at this time between the Genoese and the Venetians, Orchan aided the first. When the emperor wished to employ both, he was obliged to concede to the Turks a stronghold on the Thracian Chersonese. They, however, always proved to be dangerous allies, and the inhabitants of the whole northern coast of the Marmora were so harassed by them that great numbers deserted their farms and fled to the capital or elsewhere.

It was in 1355 that Cantacuzenus left the government in the hands of John. His policy and his influence had been directed towards coming to an agreement with the leading group of Turks—that, namely, ruled over by his son-in-law. Almost the last act before his withdrawal was to persuade Orchan and his son, Suliman, to give up the cities in Thrace which the Turks had occupied, on his behalf, during the struggle with John.[1] Orchan, on his part, was to all appearances disposed, on the retirement of Cantacuzenus, to be on friendly terms with John, and, in consequence, each party assumed the attitude of an ally. It may be suggested that if a policy of friendliness had been continued, the Turks might have been content with their territory in Asia Minor. But such a solution was not possible. The Turkish nomad warriors, to whom the cultivation of the soil was distasteful, required new lands to roam over, and wanted new territories to plunder. The arable lands, which had supported large populations, were too small for nomad shepherds, and the latter were always being pressed forward to the north and west by a constant stream of immigrants behind them. Indeed, in the year when Cantacuzenus abdicated, Suliman, the son of Orchan, had to lead his armies and defend his territories against a newly arrived horde of Tartars in the north-east of Asia Minor. His successful defence was, at the same time, one more blow against the empire, for in this campaign he succeeded in

Cant. iv. 39.

Angora
taken
1354).
capturing the important stronghold of Angora, which commanded the great highroad to Persia.

But Orchan and John, though nominally on friendly
terms, distrusted each other, and indeed Orchan's character
and conduct compare favourably with John's. When
Halil, the son of Orchan and of John's sister-in-law
Theodora, was captured by pirates from Phocaea, at the
head of the Gulf of Smyrna, and then in the occupation of
the Genoese, it was with difficulty that John could be
induced to join in the siege of that city in order to release
his nephew. He endeavoured to make a bargain with
Orchan before he consented to co-operate. Finally Halil
was ransomed, Orchan and John each paying half of the
amount. On his release the two rulers met, and at Chalcedon, the present Kadikeuy, John promised his infant
daughter to Halil, and the two rulers swore to establish a
perpetual peace.

In 1359 Orchan died. During the thirty-two years of
his reign, he had planted the Ottoman state firmly in Asia
Minor. The landmarks of its progress were the important
cities of Nicaea, Ismidt, and Angora, each of which dominated a large tract of country. He had compacted the Turks
together, had attracted to his rule many of those who had
previously acknowledged other emirs, and every year of his
reign had seen the number of Ottoman Turks increasing by
defections from his rivals and by immigrants from the eastward. He was an able commander and an exceptionally
good administrator. While Othman is the founder of the
Turkish dynasty, Orchan is the sovereign who caused his
people to be recognised as forming a separate nationality,
and was thus the maker of the Turkish nation.

Sultan
Murad the
First,
1359-1389.
Orchan was succeeded by his son Amurath or, adopting
the modern orthography, Murad. He was the younger
brother of Suliman, who died two months before his father.
The new sultan was not influenced by any tie of relationship
with the imperial family. Moreover, the influence of Islam
was now becoming much more serious than it had hitherto
been. Mahometanism had become the religion of most of

the Turks, and Murad, stimulated by a certain mufti, soon learned to become a fanatical persecutor of even his own Christian subjects. He increased the amount of taxes which they had to pay, and generally made their burdens heavy. But by far the heaviest of those burdens was caused by the organisation of the body of 'New Troops' established by Orchan and known as Janissaries. He decreed a law, said to be founded upon the sacred text of the Koran, that the Christians should be required to give to himself absolutely one in five of their children. From the boys thus obtained, he established the famous corps whose deeds were to make them for ever famous.[1]

At the commencement of his reign, Murad turned to conquest. The work of Orchan had been to establish and compact Ottoman rule in Asia Minor. That of his successor was mainly to carry out a similar policy in Europe. After capturing Heraclia on the Black Sea, he crossed over into Thrace and occupied Adrianople, seized Didymotica and Chorlou, overran the whole country between Constantinople and Bulgaria, and sent his ships to plunder the Greek islands. In return for the fanaticism with which they had inspired him, he promised that one fifth of the spoil captured by land and sea should be given to the mollahs. When the sale of Christian captives took place, he took care, says Ducas,[2] that the young, the well set-up, and the strong men should be bought at a low price to be added to the Janissaries.

The few remaining Turkish emirs in Asia Minor whose territories had not been gained by the Ottomans joined forces to resist the new sultan. At the same time the Serbians, Bulgarians, and Hungarians, all of whom had become alarmed at Murad's progress, declared war upon him. Compelled in 1363 to defend himself against the emirs to the east and south of his territories in Asia Minor, he was sufficiently strong to force the emperor to bind himself not merely to give aid to him in Asia but not

---

[1] I reserve my description of the Janissaries for a later chapter.
[2] Ch. xxiii.

to attempt to recover any of the cities or territories which
he had conquered in Europe. When he had broken the
strength of the rebel emirs he crossed rapidly back into
Thrace and near Adrianople defeated a combined army of
Hungarians, Serbians, and Bulgarians. Two years afterwards, in 1366, an army of fifty thousand Serbians
endeavoured in vain to drive Murad out of Adrianople. The
lowest degradation which the empire had yet reached was
when the miserable John consented to become the tributary of
Murad in order that he might enjoy his remaining possessions in Europe. In 1373 he formally recognised the sultan
as his suzerain, bound himself to render him military service
and to give his son Manuel as a hostage.[1]

The only palliative which can be offered for John's conduct is that he felt resistance to be useless. The empire
wanted peace. The cities and towns had been devastated,
not merely by successive wars, civil and foreign, but by the
terrible Black Death, a plague which since 1346 had
demanded everywhere its large quota of victims. He had
seen Turkish armies defeated, but everywhere and always
reappearing in greater numbers than ever. Asiatics were in
overwhelming numbers on every side. The Egyptian
Moslems had captured Sis, the capital of the Lesser Armenia,
in 1369. Not only was every district in Asia Minor overrun with Turks, but they had penetrated Europe at many
points. Bands of them had been left in the country when
the armies, invited into Macedonia or Thrace or crossing
over for plunder, had withdrawn. 'For my part, I believe,'
says Ducas, 'that there is a greater multitude of them
between the Dardanelles and the Danube than in Asia
Minor,' and although Ducas wrote three quarters of a century
later, his remarks are applicable to the reign of John. He
describes how Turks from Cappadocia, Lycia, Cilicia, and
Caria had sailed into Europe to pillage and to ruin the land
of the Christians. A hundred thousand had laid waste the
country as far west as Dalmatia. The Albanians from
being a large nation had become a small one. The Wallachs

[1] Chalc. i. 51, and Phrantzes, i. 11.

the Serbians, and his own people, the Romans, had been completely ruined. Amid his lamentations over the evils inflicted by the invaders, his saddest thought and gravest source of complaint is that the victories gained by the Turks had been won by men who were the offspring of Christian parents, by Janissaries who were of Roman, Bulgarian, Serbian, Wallachian, or Hungarian origin. It is in the hopelessness of further resistance to such overwhelming forces that the only explanation of John's acceptance of the position of a tributary prince is to be found.

The ruin of the South Serbians and Eastern Bulgarians of which Ducas speaks had really taken place. They had each ventured to declare themselves empires. With the indifference which characterises the Greek writers in regard to the conduct of other nations, they allude to rather than mention how that ruin had been brought about. In 1371, a great battle took place on the plains of the river Maritza which sealed the fate of the Eastern Bulgarians and of the Serbians who were in Macedonia. The three sons of the kral took advantage of the absence of Murad in Asia and, having collected an army of sixty thousand men, marched almost as far as Adrianople without opposition. While they were feasting in front of a bridge over the Maritza near Harmanli, fully assured of their safety by reason of their superiority in numbers, suddenly a night attack was made upon them by a small division of the Turkish army. It was soon joined by the entire army of seventy thousand Turks. Wild confusion was followed by a terrible slaughter. One of the three sons of the kral was killed and the other two were drowned in the Maritza. Hundreds of soldiers perished in attempting to cross it. The army was simply annihilated.[1]

To assist him in his conquest of Hungary, Serbia,

Battle of Harmanli, 1371.

---

[1] Du Cange, *Familiae Dalmaticae*, 230, Venetian edition. The story of this battle is fully described in *Die Serben und Türken im XIV. und XV. Jahrhundert* S. Novakovich (Semlin, 1897) and also in Ireček's *History of the Bulgarians* (. 430). Ireček states that as late as the seventeenth century the stone monument of the despot Uglisha's tomb still existed. Uglisha was one of the three brothers.

Bulgaria, and Moldavia, Murad allied himself, in 1373, with the Tartars north of the Danube, and both prepared to attack these states.

Meanwhile in the troubles which arose in 1374 between John and his son Manuel on the one side and Andronicus the grandson of John by his eldest son of the same name, Murad exercised his right as suzerain. Shortly after Manuel was associated with his father, the two were ordered to accompany their lord on an expedition. It was during their absence that the eldest sons of the emperor and sultan, as already mentioned, either swore friendship and common action, when each succeeded to his father's throne, or were considered by their fathers to have done so. It may have been believed that they had entered into a conspiracy to hasten such succession. Countouz, the obnoxious son of Murad, raised a rebellion against his father when he heard of his cruel resolve, but his troops passed over to the side of their sultan. He fled to Didymotica and joined Andronicus, who was also a fugitive from his father. Murad followed his son, and laid siege to that city. The inhabitants, pressed by famine, opened the gates to him. Countouz was blinded by his father, but Andronicus escaped ; all the garrison was drowned and a large number of the inhabitants had their throats cut, Murad adding to his barbarity by compelling the fathers to be the executioners of their sons.[1]

In 1379, as already mentioned, John and his son Manuel, who had been captured and imprisoned by his grandson Andronicus, escaped to Scutari and took refuge with Bajazed, the son of Murad. The sultan, after assuring himself that the inhabitants of Constantinople preferred Manuel to Andronicus, made a bargain with John and his son by which, in return for aid in restoring them, the empire should pay a large annual tribute, furnish a contingent of twelve thousand soldiers, and surrender to him Philadelphia, the last remaining city in Asia Minor which still acknowledged the rule of Constantinople. John and Manuel entered Constantinople by the

---

[1] Chalc. i. 44 says that the sultan immediately beheaded his son ; Ducas that Countouz was blinded (xii.).

Adrianople Gate, and Andronicus escaped across the Golden Horn to the Genoese in Galata. Much as the two emperors may have regretted their bargain, Murad held them to it, and they, Christian emperors, marched to Philadelphia, in order to compel their own subjects to open its gates to the Turks.

Philadel-
phia sur-
rendered,
1379.

Everywhere the Moslem flood was becoming irresistible. The sultan of Bagdad, in 1376, invaded Armenia and took prisoners both its king and queen; at the other extreme of the empire the Turks were in Epirus and were holding their own in many parts of Morea. The Knights-Hospitallers surrendered Patras to them in order to purchase the release of their Grand Master. One of the few strongholds in Thrace which Murad had not hitherto obtained was Apollonia, the present Sissipoli, which, partly built on an island in the Black Sea and in an otherwise strong position, had so far avoided capture. It was taken, however, by Murad in 1383, and, as usual, its garrison was cruelly massacred. In 1385, Murad captured Sofia, and then sent two armies, one to take possession of Cavalla and other places on the north shore of the Aegean, and the other to capture Monastir and various towns in Macedonia. In the same year a Turkish army took Belgrade and pushed on to Scutari in Albania, taking possession of it and of other strongholds. In 1387, after a siege lasting four years, Salonica was captured.

The Serbians, by their defeat at Belgrade and elsewhere, were compelled to become the vassals of Murad, and, following his usual custom, the sultan compelled their kral in 381 to send two thousand men to aid him in subduing a revolt of his brother-in-law, the emir, in Caramania, the ancient Cilicia. Many subjects of the empire had to render like military service.

On the return of the Serbians, their discontent was so great that the kral Lazarus, son of the famous Stephen, collected a large army and made an effort for freedom. But, though his armies succeeded in killing twenty thousand of the enemy, Ali Pasha compelled them again to submit to the Turkish yoke. The brave Serbians soon, however, recovered,

First battle
of Cossovo-
pol, 1389.
and Lazarus succeeded in making alliances with his Christian neighbours which promised success. In 1389, with a large army of his own subjects, of Hungarians, Wallachs, Dalmatians, and Albanians, he once more endeavoured to crush the common enemy. A decisive battle was fought on the Plain of Black Birds or Cossovo-pol, in what is now called Old Serbia.[1] Murad and his son Bajazed were in command. The Christians broke the right wing of the Turks, but the issue of the battle was turned by the daring of Bajazed. Lazarus and his suite were taken prisoners, and the triumph of the enemy was complete. The latest historian of Serbia observes that as the battle on the Maritza in 1371 sealed the fate of the Eastern Bulgarians and of the Serbians in Macedonia, so did this battle of Cossovo-pol in 1389 determine that of the Northern Serbians and the Western Bulgarians.[2]

Assassina-
tion of
Murad.
During or immediately after the battle, there followed a dramatic incident. A young Serb ran towards the Turkish army, and when they would have stopped him declared that he wanted to see their sultan in order that he might show him how he could profit by the fight. Murad signed to him to come near, and the young fellow did so, drew a dagger which he had hidden, and plunged it into the heart of the sultan. He was at once cut down by the guards.[3] The Serbians, according to Ducas, did not know of the sultan's death for a considerable time, and did not defend themselves with their usual courage. Lazarus was captured, and was hewn in pieces.

[1] Cossovo-pol, the Plain of Blackbirds, is between Pristina and Prisrend, to the north-east of Uskub. The town of Cossovo is due south of Prisrend, and about thirty miles distant.

[2] Novacovich, p. 335. 'Gleichwie durch den Krieg an der Maritza das Schicksal Ost-Bulgariens und der serbischen Staaten in Macedonien, ebenso ist durch die Schlacht aus Kossovopolje, den 15. Juni 1389, das Schicksal der nördlichen serbischen Länder und des westlichen Bulgarien entschieden worden, namentlich der Länder des Fürsten Lazar und Buk Brancovic's.'

[3] Sad-ud-din. See also Halil Ganem's Les Sultans Ottomans, Paris, 1901 Upon the assassination of Murad the custom grew up, which continued till about 1820, of not allowing any Christian belonging to a foreign state to enter the presence of the sultan except with Janissaries holding each arm.

CHAPTER VI

REIGN OF MANUEL: ENCROACHMENTS OF TURKS; MANUEL
  VISITS WEST, SULTAN BAJAZED SUMMONED BY TIMOUR;
  FRIENDLY RELATIONS BETWEEN MANUEL AND MAHOMET
  THE FIRST; JOHN ASSOCIATED WITH MANUEL. SIEGE
  OF CONSTANTINOPLE BY MURAD; ITS FAILURE. EFFORTS
  AT UNION; MISCONCEPTIONS IN WEST REGARDING
  GREEK CHURCH CONSTANCY OF ATTEMPTS AT UNION;
  NEGOTIATIONS FOR MEETING OF COUNCIL OF CHURCH.
  INTERNAL STRUGGLES IN LATIN CHURCH. EMPEROR
  INVITED BY BOTH PARTIES; ACCEPTS POPE'S INVITATION;
  MEETING OF COUNCIL AT FERRARA AND FLORENCE;
  UNION ACCOMPLISHED; JOHN RETURNS TO CAPITAL;
  DIVISIONS IN GREEK CHURCH.

MANUEL was with the Turkish army at Brousa when he
learned the death of his father in 1391. He escaped secretly,
hastened to Constantinople, and succeeded in being proclaimed as the sole occupant of the imperial throne.
Bajazed, who had become sultan on the assassination of his
father, Murad, in 1389, taken by surprise at the escape of his
hostage, at once presented alarming demands. He asked
that the Turks should have a resident cadi within Constantinople itself and that Manuel should declare himself to be
the sultan's vassal and pay tribute. After a year of fruitless
negotiations, which Manuel had protracted in order that he
might send to the West to implore aid, Bajazed attacked the
empire on every side. Within a few months Turks were
pillaging the Adriatic coast, were exterminating or carrying
off prisoners from Thrace, and were laying siege to the
capital. Their leader before the city urged the citizens to

declare for Manuel's nephew, John, the son of Andronicus, who had, indeed, been compelled by Bajazed to come forward as a pretender. In 1395 John joined the Turks in attacking the capital, but was defeated. The Turkish leader returned across the Bosporus, strengthened his position on the Gulf of Ismidt, by building a castle or fortress, probably the one now seen at Guebseh, and another on the Bosporus known as Guzel-hissar,[1] and then once more summoned Manuel to surrender the city. Thereupon the emperor took a step which, if the version of Ducas is correct, justifies his historian for attributing it to wisdom and patriotism. He arranged to share the empire with John, to leave the city himself, and to allow him to enter on condition that he would not hand it over to the Turks. John, however, on his side had agreed with Bajazed that Selymbria and the other places on the north shore of the Marmora which he had held since the death of his father should be delivered to the Turks, and, this arrangement being concluded, the city was saved from attack.[2]

Meantime the spread of the Turks over new territories once more alarmed the West, and in 1394 Boniface preached a Crusade and urged in what is now Austria and the states of Venice that immediate action should be taken against them. The danger was pressing and the pope's call to battle was this time responded to. Sigismund, the Hungarian king informed the emperor that he had fifty-two thousand armed men, and invited his co-operation.

Battle of
Nicopolis,
1396.

But the men of the West had not yet learned how formidable the Turks could be. In 1396 at Nicopolis on the Danube the united Christian army was met by Bajazed who inflicted upon it a crushing defeat. How that defeat was accomplished will be told when giving the story of Bajazed's life. Bajazed recaptured all the places in

---

[1] Now called Anatolia-hissar. The word *hissar* means castle.

[2] The version of Ducas differs from those of Chalcondylas and Phrantzes the first of whom knows nothing of the arrangement suggested, but states that Manuel left the city for Italy, while Phrantzes declares that John, having lost the favour of Bajazed, fled to his uncle, who entrusted the city to him during his absence (Phr. pp. 61–3.)

Hungary which he had previously lost, threatened to besiege Buda, boasted that he would annex Germany and Italy and feed his horse with oats on the altar of St. Peter at Rome. So serious was the disaster of Nicopolis and the impression it produced that at length the Venetian senate recognised the necessity of joining their traditional enemies the Genoese in order to send a powerful fleet against the common enemy. Boucicaut, a skilful sailor who was named admiral, took command. He arrived at Gallipoli with a fleet containing fourteen hundred knights. They met near the Dardanelles seventeen well-armed Turkish galleys and defeated them. Shortly afterwards Boucicaut was proclaimed by Venetians and Genoese admiral-in-chief. He pushed on to the Bosporus and arrived just in time to relieve Galata, which was being besieged by the Turks. Manuel named him Grand Constable. Boucicaut next endeavoured to recapture Ismidt but without success. Elsewhere, however, he succeeded in inflicting several losses on the Turks and especially harassed their settlements on the eastern shore of the Bosporus. Finding he was powerless without further aid to inflict serious damage upon them, he urged Manuel to acknowledge the king of France as his suzerain, in order that he might receive aid. His project met with the approval of the Venetians, the Genoese, and of Manuel himself. Boucicaut returned to France to obtain assistance and to employ his own influence in favour of the project, but Charles the Sixth, being unable or unwilling to protect his proposed vassal, refused to receive his submission.

Manuel, at the end of 1399, decided to follow the example of his predecessor and to see whether his own efforts would not be more successful in obtaining aid from the West. He was received, as they had been, with imperial honours in Venice and elsewhere, but neither from that city nor from Florence, Ferrara, Genoa, or Milan did he secure any assistance. His public entry into Paris was with a display that was intended more to please the Parisians than to be of use to him, and he soon learnt that there was as little to be hoped from France as from Italy. Nor was he more successful on his visit to Henry the Fourth in England. After an absence of two and a half years, Manuel returned to his capital. He found that the Turks had employed the time with energy and had made great progress in their raids on the empire. His own people were almost in despair. The Turks were once more besieging the capital and were securely established on the opposite shore of the Bosporus. The population of Constantinople had decreased. Many of its buildings had fallen out of repair, and its territory in Thrace was almost limited by the walls of the city.

On the other hand, he arrived at a moment when if Christendom had been united a great and possibly a fatal blow might have been struck against the common enemy. The lieutenant of Boucicaut was defending Constantinople against the third attempt by Bajazed to capture the city, when the tidings from the great Timour or Tamarlane gave the besieger pause. Bajazed withdrew. Timour, indeed, had summoned the sultan to give up to the Greeks all territory that he had taken from them and had asked the Genoese to co-operate and obtain the co-operation of other Western powers against the Turks. Bajazed not only refused to obey the summons but went forward to attack Timour and, as we shall see when dealing with the life of Bajazed, was in the great battle of Angora, on July 25, 1402, defeated and made prisoner. He died in the following year. The defeat of the sultan gave a new lease of life to the city, but no aid came from the Christians of the West. The Venetians and Genoese were again at war with each other and Western Europe was as divided and as powerless for concerted action against the Turks as it has so often been since.

The Turks in less than a generation after the withdrawal of Timour recovered all their influence and territory. Manuel was compelled even as early as 1403 to recognise Bajazed's successor, Suliman (to whom, indeed, he gave his granddaughter in marriage), as lord of a large portion of Thrace. Suliman, however, proved himself a weak and worthless leader of the Turks, and in 1409 the Janissaries preferring his brother Mousa, arrested and killed him. He was succeeded by Mahomet, the first of that name in the Ottoman dynasty, who had been aided by Manuel and who in return gave back to the emperor the fortified places on the Marmora and Black Sea which had been in the occupation of the Turks : an almost solitary instance of this kind of generosity on the part of the Turks, who hold as a religious principle that they must only surrender territory to force. Mahomet had, however, given his promise to Manuel and, says Ducas, he faithfully kept it.[1]

During the next few years and until the death of the sultan, Manuel's relations with him were friendly. In 1415 the two sovereigns had an interview at Gallipoli. Although the Turks were pursuing their encroachments in Hungary and Dalmatia, Mahomet abstained from attacking the empire. When they carried off nearly two thousand captives into slavery from Euboea, its Venetian rulers were compelled to seek the mediation of Manuel in order to obtain peace. Five years afterwards, Mahomet in passing to his dominions in Asia Minor went by way of the capital, and Phrantzes testifies that, in spite of suggestions to seize him, Manuel refused to violate the right of hospitality. So great was the sultan's trust in the emperor that Mahomet named Manuel as the guardian of his two younger sons.

Murad, the eldest son and successor of Mahomet, who became sultan in 1420, proposed a renewal of the alliance with Manuel. The. latter would probably have consented. He was overruled, however, by the senate, which was in favour of a policy of war and decided that John should be associated with his father. A demand was made to Murad to send his two younger brothers to Constantinople, and the grand vizier returned the answer which might have been expected, that the education of two Mussulmans could not be entrusted to the enemies of their faith—believers to be educated by infidels.[2]   War followed, and the Greeks

---

[1] Ducas, xx.; Chalc. iv. p. 183. Phrantzes, p. 89, praises Mahomet very highly.
[2] Ducas, xxiii.

supported a pretender to the Turkish throne, who was soon defeated and hanged by Murad.

Siege of
Constanti-
nople by
Murad,
1422.

Thereupon, in 1422, siege was laid to Constantinople. The walls had largely 'fallen out of repair and the three thousand men who were sent as a first detachment sat down before it in hope of an easy capture. A few days later Murad himself appeared, bringing with him in chains the Greek ambassadors who had been sent to treat of peace. A large army of two hundred thousand men, together with a great crowd of bashi-bazouks, encamped before the landward walls and built an earthwork for their protection from the Golden Gate to the Xyloporta at the end of the walls on the Golden Horn. Among them, or arriving shortly afterwards, was a certain Mersaite, a Madhi, a half-mad fanatic at the head of five hundred dervishes. He claimed to be of the blood of Mahomet and to possess prophetic powers. He foretold that the capture of the city would happen when he gave the signal, for which all were to be ready. The sultan had sat down before the walls in the middle of June, but his primitive bombs, his wooden towers, and his attempts to undermine the walls were of no avail. Mersaite prophesied a capture on August 24. On that day the defenders of the foss were rained upon with showers of arrows and a general assault was made, but the two Theodosian walls, which were defended by crowds of citizens, were far too strong to be captured by the simple fanatical onslaught of dervishes. The Greeks fought valiantly, the young Emperor John being at their head and on horseback, in the peribolos outside the Romanus Military Gate, formerly known as the Pempton. Upon the failure of the attack by the dervishes, Murad suddenly raised the siege and the Greeks pursued the retreating army and captured some of their rude guns.[1] The immediate cause of the raising of the siege of Constantinople is variously stated. Manuel had sent aid to the adherents of Mustafa, the younger brother of Murad, aged only six years, and had thus strengthened the revolt which had been raised

---

[1] Mersaite declared he failed because of the presence of a noble lady evidently the Holy Virgin, walking upon and guarding the walls.

in his favour in Asia Minor. It was of more importance to
Murad to put an end to this Turkish rising than to persist
in his attempt to capture the city.[1]

In 1425 Manuel, whom Ducas describes not incorrectly
as a wise and moderate prince, died, after a reign of thirty-
four years.

Death of Manuel, 1425.

John, sometimes called the Fifth and sometimes the
Seventh of that name, now became sole emperor, and
reigned from 1425 to 1448. The two features of his reign

John, 1425–1448.

which make all incidents in it that are not connected with
them of comparative insignificance, are, first, the steady
almost unchecked progress of the Turks in south-eastern
Europe and in Asia Minor : the encroachment of an overwhelming flood, now apparently receding in one direction,
but again sweeping over every obstacle in another, and in
reality always steadily advancing and submerging all the
Christian populations in the Balkan peninsula : and, second,
the efforts of the emperor and those about him to save the
remnant of the empire by obtaining the help of Europe.

John's reign was spent in one continous effort to obtain
assistance from the West to save the city and to check
the progress of the Turks. Like his predecessors, he
addressed himself to successive popes. Perhaps nothing
brings more vividly before the reader of European history
the power of the occupants of the pontifical chair than the
fact that it was taken for granted that from the pope, and
the pope alone, that Western aid could be obtained. We
have seen that former emperors had looked to the kings of
France and England and to other princes, but their aid was
sought only on the advice and with the support of Rome.
In justice also it must be admitted that no princes recognised
so completely as did a long series of popes the expediency and
duty of defending Constantinople as the first outwork of the

---

[1] According to another version he withdrew on account of the famine and
plague which prevailed in his army. It is, however, certain that the Turkish
revolt in favour of Mustafa took place, and in the following year, 1423, Murad
captured the leader, Elias Pasha, and bowstrung both him and the young
Mustafa at Nicaea. Before the end of the year he returned to Thrace and took
possession of Adrianople.

defences of Europe against the forces of Asia, and of aiding its emperors in their efforts to check the Turkish invasion. They were the prime ministers of Western Europe and almost the only persons who regarded the Eastern question as statesmen.

Unfortunately, while the popes saw the necessity of preventing the progress of the barbarians, they attached conditions to their offers of help which made them unacceptable and which indeed were impossible : namely, that the Greeks should accept the Union of the Churches, with which Union was associated the supremacy of the pope.

A succession of pontiffs during the two hundred years preceding the Moslem conquest of the city worked for Union with marvellous persistency. The same passionate desire for reunion is not less manifest now in the occupant of the chair of St. Peter ; but modern efforts are made with this essential difference, that while in the period which concerns us it was believed that reunion could be imposed, every one now recognises that if it is to be brought about, it must be by voluntary and full consent.

Errors in West regarding Orthodox Church.

In the fourteenth century it never seems to have occurred either to popes or emperors that people cannot be compelled to change their religious opinions. The idea was that the great mass of people were ready to accept any opinion sanctioned by the ordinary civil authorities. The early negotiations leave the impression that the Churchmen of the West thought that the emperor and the patriarch could bring about a Union by their simple decree, could change the profession of belief and obtain the admission of papal supremacy without the voluntary consent of even the Greek ecclesiastics. It never appears to have dawned upon Roman Churchmen that the members of the Orthodox Church might refuse to accept Union and a change in belief when these had been accepted by the civil and religious chiefs. Such a view showed ignorance at once of the character, always intensely conservative, and of the history of the Orthodox Church. Without entering into a discussion how far the population of the capital and the empire was

Greek by race, it is sufficient to recall that Greek was the language of the people, that all that they knew of history and philosophy, all their methods of thought, their theology and literature, had come to them in Greek forms. They thought and spoke as Greeks. Most of them gloried in being Greek. In matters of philosophic and religious speculation the Greek mind was more acute, and more subtle, than the Western mind. In theological questions, probably all classes were more interested than the corresponding classes in the West. If in the course of centuries the common people had ceased to take that keen interest in matters of theological speculation which caused the artisan or tradesman to neglect his immediate occupation in order to ask his customer's opinion on the merits of the latest heresy, it was largely because the great formulas of Christian belief had, as it was believed, received their final adjustment. If any questions were unsolved—as, for example, that of the Inner Light—the population was always ready to take an interest in them; but it deeply resented any attempt to dogmatise without full discussion. It especially resented the determination of such questions by a foreign authority. The Greek Churchmen considered themselves, and probably rightly, as better versed in theology than those of Rome. They had the tradition of being admittedly superior in learning to their brethren in the West, and, though ready at all times to discuss, would not consent to be dictated to by the bishop of Rome.

The Catholic Church not only made the mistake of disregarding the traditional susceptibilities of the Eastern people, who invariably, after 1204, associated the rule of Rome with the abominations of the Latin occupation; of disregarding also the universal interest felt in the Orthodox Church on theological questions, but it greatly underrated the authority and influence of the Orthodox clergy when such authority and influence were in conflict with the emperor or even with the emperor and patriarch combined. Much has been written of what is called Caesaropapism : that is, of the combination of the secular and ecclesiastical powers which were supposed to be vested in the emperors. At various times the autocrat undoubtedly assumed much of the power which in the Holy Roman Empire in the West was left to the popes. At other times, however, and in some matters at all times, the patriarch of Constantinople exercised a jurisdiction independent of the emperor. The religious sanctions possessed by the Church were not to be set aside even by or for him. We have seen, for example, that when the Emperor Michael the Eighth had usurped the crown and blinded the infant John so as to prevent him coming to the throne, though the ecclesiastics seemed to have considered it expedient that he should retain the office he had usurped, the patriarch Arsenius and the prelates associated with him could not be either coaxed or frightened into granting him absolution, and that it was not until Arsenius and his successor, Germanus, had ceased to occupy the patriarchal throne that the emperor could succeed in having the anathema removed.[1]

Many other examples could be given which show that it is an error to suppose that the patriarchs were merely or even usually the creatures of the emperors. When questions of dogma arose the head of the Orthodox Church supported by his clergy was jealous of the secular power. The history of Constantinople during the time between the Latin and the Moslem conquests of the city abounds in illustrations showing that the Church would not consent to dictation from the emperors, and that the clergy would not blindly follow the patriarch. But, when dictation was supposed to come from Rome, the great mass of clergy and people were, as they had been from the time of Photius, on the side of their Church and, if need be, against the emperor.

It must be remembered also that the Eastern Church had steadily refused to admit the supremacy of the Western. It had never regarded the phrase 'under one fold and one shepherd' as indicating that the whole Church of Christ should be under the government of one bishop. It had never admitted that the 'One Shepherd' should be other than Christ, and had therefore constantly denied the

[1] See *ante*; and also Pachymer, iii. 10 to iv. 25.

supremacy of the pope. One Empire, one Church, one
Head of the Church was a Western theory which had never
made much way in the later Roman empire. The movements in the West which placed the imperial power in
commission, giving to the emperor the supreme secular, and
to the bishop of Rome the supreme ecclesiastical, authority
had no corresponding movement in the East. The emperors
were only heads of the Church in the same sense as the king
of England is in all matters ecclesiastical supreme. The
emperors and ecclesiastics were usually agreed in not allowing the supremacy of the bishop of the elder Rome.

To the popes, however, the Union of the Churches was
indissolubly associated with the admission of papal supremacy. It would be going too far to say that they desired
Union exclusively to obtain recognition of such supremacy,
but it may safely be said that they never lost sight in all
their negotiations for Union of the necessity of obtaining its
recognition, and that, in the opinion of many ecclesiastics
both Western and Eastern, such supremacy was the most
important object aimed at.

Murad's unsuccessful attempt, in 1422, to capture Constantinople made it evident to the emperor that aid from
Western nations was absolutely necessary if the empire or
even the city was to be saved. The pope also recognised
both the importance of saving the empire and its extreme
danger, and held out hopes of aid if Union were accepted.
The imminence of the danger was patent to all. When
John became sole occupant of the throne, in 1425, the
empire was surrounded by Turkish armies. Nearly the
whole of Asia Minor was in their hands. Large armies had
invaded Hungary; Bulgaria had ceased to exist; Serbia
was a vassal of the sultan. In Macedonia and even in
Thrace the Turks had made a desolation and held many
cities. If the city of Paris were worth a Mass, the
empire was worth a tenfold acknowledgment of the pope's
supremacy.

The emperor, the nobles, and a considerable part of the
clergy came to believe that they must purchase aid on any

conditions or see the city captured. Questions of dogma, the addition of the *Filioque* clause, the use of unleavened bread, the condition of souls in purgatory, were to them matters of secondary importance when the very existence of their country was at stake. Even papal supremacy appeared to John and many laymen worth accepting in return for the despatch of soldiers who would resist the Turkish invasion.

We have seen that many attempts at Union had been made by all the emperors since the recapture of the city, but that they had all failed, that the traditional conservatism of the Orthodox Church, its stubborn resistance to the slightest change of dogma or ritual, all intensified by the traditions of the Latin occupation, had been more powerful than the energy and influence of popes and emperors combined.[1]

The great attempt at Reunion.

The last and greatest attempt to bring about a Union was now about to be made, and deserves fuller notice than has been given to any which preceded it.

In 1429, in the fourth year of his reign, John sent to request the pope to despatch a messenger to Constantinople to treat of Union. Eugenius gladly complied and sent a friar to arrange conditions with the emperor and patriarch. It was agreed that the canonical method of arriving at a binding conclusion on matters of dogma should be adopted. The matters in dispute were to be submitted to a Council of the Church at which John and the patriarch were to be present.

Meantime Eugenius employed his influence during the next three or four years to induce the Venetians and Genoese to unite against the common enemy, to give aid to the knights in their defence of Rhodes, and to prevent any

---

[1] 'The Greek Church has had a fossilised aversion to change ; boasting that it follows the doctrines and practices of the Apostolic Church, it believes that it has no need of reform.' *Eighteen Centuries of the Orthodox Greek Church,* by Rev. A. H. Hore, p. 553 (Jas. Parker & Co. : London, 1899).

The expression ' fossilised aversion ' is perhaps too strong, though I should be prepared to admit that the Eastern *non possumus* was at least as obstinate as the Western. The Orthodox Church in countries where it is free, as in Greece and Russia, shows signs of growth, and therefore hardly deserves the adjective ' fossilised.' Since 1453 in Turkey it has been comatose.

attacks upon une empire from the West. So far all looked promising. Unfortunately, however, at this time the Latin Church itself was divided. Rival popes, one in Italy, the other at Avignon, had denounced each other as pretenders. A Council of the Church opened at Bâle in March 1431 was by a papal Bull ordered to be transferred to Bologna after the expiry of eight months. The principal reason assigned for the transfer was the greater convenience of John and the imperial party. Eugenius had taken this step without consultation with the cardinals, and the change of place was at once strenuously opposed. A majority of the Council refused to obey and replied that as the Bohemians, the followers of John Huss, had been formally cited to appear at Bâle, the place of meeting could not be changed. As to the convenience of the representatives of the Greek Church, 'the peace of Germany is not to be sacrificed for the old song which has rung in the ears of Europe for three centuries and ended in nothing, the reconciliation of the Greek and Latin Churches.' [1]

The Council was supported in its opposition to Eugenius by the Emperor Sigismund, by the duke of Milan, and by many kings, princes, bishops, universities, and cities. Only four cardinals remained on his side. Nevertheless he fearlessly denounced the Council as a Synagogue of Satan. For a while the more he threatened the more the dignitaries of the Church flocked to Bâle. Eugenius in vain endeavoured to extort from the Emperor Sigismund the dissolution of the Council as the price of his consent to place the imperial crown on his head. Sigismund would not yield, and Eugenius had to crown him. With the exception of Venice and Florence, all Western Europe was against Eugenius. An insurrection in Rome forced him to leave the city, and he escaped in a mean disguise. He was driven for a while to withdraw his denunciations and to admit the legality of the Council and of its acts.

A temporary reconciliation was of short duration. The claims of the rival parties were incapable of reconciliation.

[1] Milman, *History of Latin Christianity*, 3rd edition, vol. viii. p. 348.

The Council was determined to limit the power of the pope ; the pope would endure no limitation.

Two years were lost in useless negotiations. John strongly urged that the Council should consider the question of Union without delay, and sent a representative to Bâle in October 1433. When the members refused by a two-thirds vote to remove to Italy the emperor's representative suggested that the meeting-place should be Constantinople. The Council in 1434 declared against this proposal, but offered to pay the expenses of the Greeks if they would come to Bâle. The latter, possibly from their ignorance of the geographical situation of the city, refused to go thither. Other places were suggested and the pope again gave his approbation for Bologna or some other place in Italy.

Representatives arrived in Constantinople from both the Synod at Bâle and the pope, who were again in opposition to each other. To such an extent had these hostilities grown that the Council declared Eugenius guilty of perjury and schism and incapable of holding any ecclesiastical office. Eugenius retorted by calling them an assembly of devils.

The deputies from Bâle brought with them to Constantinople a comminatory decree of the Council against the pope. The emperor and patriarch had therefore to choose between the Council and Eugenius. Each had invited them, had offered to bear the expenses and menaced them in case of refusal. The deputies from Bâle were heard at a public session of the Synod and threatened that if the Council were not recognised, the nations of the West would make war upon the empire, and this notwithstanding the aid of the pope, whose decrees they insisted were null and void. The ambassadors from Eugenius, who had arrived with a band of three thousand crossbowmen, offered terms as to transport and convoy similar to those which the messengers from Bâle had proposed, and suggested that the proclamation calling the meeting of the Council might be issued in the emperor's name. They were also heard in a public sitting of the Synod in September 1437, a few days after the audience of the deputies from Bâle. John and the patriarch decided to accept the proposal of Eugenius.[1]

When the news reached the pope he at once issued a Bull fixing Ferrara as the meeting-place of the Council. In November 1437, the emperor, with a large suite, embarked. The imperial party arrived at Venice in the following February. The Venetians had been excommunicated by the Council of Bâle as adherents of Eugenius, who was their fellow-citizen, and, probably with a desire to induce the Greeks to throw in their lot entirely on the side of the pope, received John and the patriarch with unwonted honour. The doge and the senate in the ' Bucentaur,' with the galleys belonging to the republic and a crowd of gondolas, went out to receive them. Lodging was found for their followers on the Lido. Syropulus, who attended the patriarch and whose history from the Greek point of view is the most trustworthy narrative of these proceedings, was amazed at the display on the reception in Venice. ' You could as easily number the leaves on the trees or the sands of the sea as the gondolas and galleys of the Venetians.' Phrantzes is not less enthusiastic. He speaks of ' Venice the marvellous, the most marvellous : Venice the wise, the most wise ; the city predicted in the psalm, " God has founded her upon the waters." ' [2]

The Greeks were shown the treasures of St. Mark, but Syropulus remarks that as they gazed upon them arose the thought, ' These were once our own. They are the plunder of Hagia Sophia and our holy monasteries.'

Their departure for Ferrara was with a like magnificence. Twelve noble galleys and an innumerable number of gondolas, whose occupants and sailors were bright with silks of various colours, attended them. The imperial eagles were mingled with the gonfalons of St. Mark, and the city which more than any other lends itself to display has seldom presented a more brilliant spectacle.

[1] While the rival representatives were in Constantinople Murad suggested to John that his friendship under the circumstances would be of greater value than that of the pope. Chalc., Syropulus, and Phrantzes.

[2] Phrantzes, pp. 181-6.

Meantime the pope had threatened excommunication against the fathers of the Church who should continue to sit at Bâle, and had given them four months within which to present themselves at Ferrara. Their reply was a formal deposition of Eugenius.

First meeting of Council.

Upon the arrival of the imperial party at Ferrara and after long negotiations regarding questions of precedence, it was decided that the first meeting of the Council should be held on March 9, 1438, and it was so held, the business being merely formal. Four cardinals, twenty-five bishops, and other nobles had previously received the patriarch and conducted him to the pope, who rose from his throne, embraced him, and led him to a seat near him similar to those occupied by the cardinals. No decision could be taken during the four months' delay. As the recalcitrants did not come in at the appointed time, a further postponement of two months was granted, probably for the reason that the pope knew that the princes of the West were still disposed rather to sympathise with the Council than with him. All this delay was in the highest degree irksome to the Greeks. Many of them had left their homes without much hope of arriving at a reconciliation, but when on reaching Ferrara they realised the discord which existed in the Roman Church itself not a few concluded that before anything could be done to complete the Union a reconciliation must take place among the Catholic factions themselves. During their long wait the restrictions imposed upon their movements aroused their suspicions. They complained that they were treated as prisoners. They could not leave the city without a permit. Three of the leading men who escaped to Venice were ignominiously brought back. They again escaped and this time found their way back to Constantinople. Nor was the treatment of the ecclesiastics such as might have been expected from hosts to guests. The bishop of Ferrara refused to allow the Greeks to celebrate in one of his great churches, declaring that he would not permit it to be polluted. The emperor and patriarch, for political reasons among others, were impatient to return, and did their utmost to urge on the work for which they had left their homes.

In October the second meeting of the Council was held. By this time a considerable number of the fathers of the Church had made submission to Eugenius and had arrived in Ferrara. Gibbon's remark that 'the violence of the fathers of Basil rather promoted than injured the cause of Eugenius'[1] is just. The delay had undoubtedly strengthened the papal authority. Hence at the second meeting of the Council its business began at once to progress. Six Latin and six Greek theologians were selected to formulate the questions in difference. These related to the Procession of the Holy Ghost ; the nature of the penalties of purgatory ; the condition of souls before the last judgment ; the use of unleavened bread in communion, and lastly, the supremacy of the pope.

Business of Council commences.

Meantime plague had broken out in Ferrara. Five only out of the eleven cardinals remained, and all that had been done was to formulate the points of difference. For some reason which is not quite clear, the Council was transferred to Florence. The unhealthiness of the city was alleged, but Syropulus says that the plague had ended. The Greeks were extremely reluctant to go to so remote a place as Florence, but they finally consented, in the hope of speedily concluding their mission.

At Florence the Council got fairly to work. Cardinal Julian Cesarini, who had been president of the Council at Bâle, and John, the head of the Dominicans in Italy, were the champions on the Latin, and Isidore of Russia, Bessarion, and Mark, bishop of Ephesus, on the Greek side. Long, weary, and profitless discussions took place on the subject of the Double Procession. Two questions were involved : first, was the doctrine itself orthodox—that is, did the Holy Ghost proceed from the Father alone or from the Father and the Son ; second, assuming the Double Procession to be orthodox, by what authority had the Latin Church, claiming to speak as the Universal Church, presumed

[1] Vol. vii. p. 108.

to add to the Nicene Creed the words *Filioque*, which proclaimed the disputed dogma, before the decision of a General Council had been pronounced. After many meetings among the Greeks alone, it was decided that as the Latin Church held that the Procession was not from two ' principles ' but from one, and this by one operation, its teaching was in accord with that of the Orthodox Church, which acknowledged that the Procession is from the Father but through the Son. The scholars who brought about this agreement were Bessarion and George Scholarius, the latter of whom was destined afterwards to play an important part during the siege of Constantinople. The declaration of the Greeks was approved at a meeting of the Council.

Greater difficulty arose on the second point, of the conduct of the Latin Church in adding the clause to the Creed. The emperor was at length convinced, or professed to be, that the clause had formerly existed in the Creed at the time of the Seventh Council,[1] but it required all his influence to persuade some of the Greek ecclesiastics who were not convinced of this fact to avoid an open rupture. The debates were obstinate and angry. But emperor and pope were determined on Union, and each used all his influence and authority to convince or compel the more refractory to obedience. Finally, it was decided that the words *Filioque* had been lawfully and with good reason inserted in the Creed.

The question of purgatory and the condition of souls in the intermediate state occasioned little or no difficulty. On the use of unleavened bread, however, the controversy became so violent that on five different occasions the Greek bishops were with difficulty prevented from leaving the Council. It was at length decided that each Church might maintain its usage in regard thereto.

The most dangerous question, after that of the Double Procession, regarded the pope's supremacy, and was apparently not made the subject of a public discussion.

In July 1439, after twenty-six sittings of the Council, the

---

[1] Second Council of Nicaea, in 787.

Union was signed and all was ready for its formal proclama- tion. Earth and heaven were called upon to rejoice that the dividing wall between the Churches of the West and East had been broken down. In August, the Act of Union was published with imposing solemnity in the cathedral and a *Te Deum* was sung in Greek.

The embassy from Constantinople had been greatly impressed by the dissensions among the Latins. No French or German bishops had taken part in the meetings at Ferrara or Florence. Fifty out of the sixty-two bishops who were present were Italians, the remainder Spaniards or Burgundians. When the latter were admitted to the Council they saluted only the pope, doing this with the manifest intention of slighting the emperor. The adherents of Bâle were, indeed, openly hostile, and as they were known to have great influence among the princes of the West, the Greeks lost the illusion that if they came to an agreement with the pope, aid would gladly be sent from the great Catholic states.

It had been with difficulty that the emperor and the court party in Constantinople had persuaded the Churchmen to go to the West. While the former were willing to make many sacrifices, even perhaps to accept the pope's supremacy, in the hope of obtaining aid against the Turks, when they recognised that the influence of Eugenius was not what they had believed it to be, they were less urgent, and certainly less able, to coerce the distinguished ecclesiastics who had been persuaded to accompany them. All were, indeed, miserably disappointed and disillusionised. Though the emperor never wavered in his determination to come to an agreement which would aid in the preservation of his empire, his own brother, Demetrius, refused to sign the Act of Union. Mark of Ephesus would not attend at the solemn proclamation, nor were George Scholarius or Gemistes or any of the bishops from Georgia present. The bishop of Heraclia, on his return to Venice, was required to recite the Creed in St. Mark's, but he did so with the omission of the *Filioque* clause. The same bishop declared on his return to Constanti-

nople, that he would rather his right hand had been cut off
than that it should have subscribed the Union. In order to
avoid the scandal of an open rupture, the four copies of the
decree did not mention the supremacy of the pope. Other
copies signed only by the Latin bishops were not recognised
as authentic by the Greeks.[1]

The patriarch, a man of eighty, died just before the
decree of the Union was signed, and was buried in the Bap-
tistery of Florence. Religious animosity dogmatised over his
grave about his opinions. Some of the Greeks subsequently
pretended that his death was one of the several causes which
rendered the Council illegal. Some of the Latins maintained
that he had left a declaration of his acceptance of the Roman
doctrine, and even of the supremacy of the pope.

John re-
turns to
Constanti-
nople,
August
1439.

The two persons who had shown themselves sincerely
desirous of accomplishing a Union were the pope and the
emperor. The former, who had paid the expenses of the
Greek mission, now urged foreign states to prepare and send
forth armies in aid of the Greeks. On the departure of John,
in August 1439, for his capital, the pontiff not merely promised
all the aid he could furnish, but undertook to maintain, at his
own expense as long as he lived, three hundred men in the
imperial service. He at once sent two well-armed galleys,
and declared that he would furnish twenty ships of war
during a period of six months. Eugenius and John had
loyally stood by each other, and so far as depended upon
them the Union had been accomplished.

With the object of giving effect to the decisions arrived
at, the pope retained Bessarion and Isidore, both of whom
he made cardinals. The latter, we shall see, was present at
Constantinople during the final siege. He was metropolitan
of Russia, and on his return to Moscow proclaimed the

---

[1] The copies sent to London and Karlsruhe, as well as the diptych of Rome
(the official record) consulted by Niches, signed by the emperor of Constantinople
and by thirty-six Latin prelates, contain on this point only the following : ἔτι
ὁρίζομεν τὴν ἁγίαν ἀποστολικὴν καθέδραν καὶ τὸν ῥομαϊκὸν διάδοχον εἶναι τοῦ μακαρίου
Πέτρου. The pope and forty-two Latin prelates, on the other hand, signed the following : Item definimus S. Ap. sedem et romanum pontificem in universum orbem
tenere primatum et ipsum pontificem romanum successorem esse S. Petri.

Union. He gave dire offence by naming the emperor before the grand duke, and the pope before the patriarch.

In 1442, the pope once again summoned certain princes, and especially Ladislaus, king of Poland and Hungary, to aid Constantinople, Cyprus, and Rhodes against the Turks. He, however, was at war in Italy, and consequently unable to furnish the aid which he had promised. Ladislaus was permitted to retain the Peter's pence on condition that he would employ it in raising troops against the infidels. The pope persuaded Alphonse of Aragon to furnish armed galleys, and granted indulgences to all who sided in the struggle against unbelievers. But all attempts to arouse a general crusading spirit failed. With a few exceptions, those who went to fight the battles of Christendom against Murad belonged to nations whose vital interests were at stake. Many causes contributed to this result, and among them the awakening to new life in Italy. The Renaissance which was now in progress substituted the classic spirit for the Hebraic. Paganism itself, among scholars and statesmen, was in competition with Christianity, and the great movement which was destined to give birth to modern Europe and which was greatly assisted, as we shall see, by the Greek scholars from Constantinople, was antagonistic to the crusading spirit. A common Christianity was no longer a bond of union to those who were dreaming of a classic revival and of a return to pagan ideals. Except to men who were outside the influence of the new movement, the pope and churchmen appealed in vain.

News of the accomplishment of the Union was received in Constantinople with mingled feelings. Hopes had been damped. The advantages to be gained by sacrificing their Orthodox Faith were found to be doubtful. The conservative party, led by Mark of Ephesus, gained greatly in strength. Finding that the emperor had consented to the appointment of a new patriarch who accepted the Union, Mark resumed his denunciations both of it and of the Latin Church. The patriarchs of Syria and Egypt refused to recognise the decisions of Florence and threatened with excommunication the priests ordained by the patriarch of Constantinople.

Death of
John,
October
1448.
John lived nearly eight years after his return to Constantinople from Florence and died in October 1448. The events which happened during this interval relate principally to the marvellous success of the Turks over the armies of Central Europe, and will be better told in the story of their progress. It is sufficient to say that these disasters hastened his death.

During his reign the condition of the empire had undergone little change. Though when first associated with his father he had headed the war party, he recognised after the siege of the city in 1422 that his father's dying counsel to keep on friendly terms with the Turks was wise. This policy, as we have seen, did not prevent him from doing all he could to obtain aid from the Western powers. He had paid the price which Rome exacted and never lost hope that such aid would come. At the same time he was ready to join with the Hungarians and other Christian nations, even at considerable risk of precipitating an attack upon the city. His power, however, was too small to make any co-operation outside the capital and the Straits of much value. He did what he could. He repaired and strengthened the city walls.[1] He kept the fleet in at least as good a condition as he had found it. He was probably justified in believing that his wisest course was to obtain all the aid possible from the West, to be ready to co-operate, and in the meantime to keep quiet. His pliant policy delayed the siege of the city and thus for a while averted the final calamity.

[1] Many of the towers near the Golden Gate bear inscriptions showing that they were repaired during John's reign. For the inscriptions see Paspates' Βυζαντιναὶ Μελέται.

CHAPTER VII

PROGRESS OF TURKS BETWEEN 1391 AND 1425 : SULTAN
BAJAZED'S REIGN : CONQUESTS IN EUROPE : BULGARIAN
KINGDOM ENDED : WESTERN ARMIES DEFEATED AT NICO-
POLIS : ANATOLIA-HISSAR BUILT : CAPITAL THREATENED :
SUMMONS BY TIMOUR TO BAJAZED : TIMOUR'S PROGRESS :
REPLY OF BAJAZED : BATTLE OF ANGORA AND CRUSHING
DEFEAT OF TURKS : FURTHER PROGRESS OF TIMOUR :
DEATH OF BAJAZED, 1403 : ALARM IN WESTERN EUROPE :
DEPARTURE OF TIMOUR : STRUGGLE BETWEEN THE SONS
OF BAJAZED : ULTIMATE SUCCESS OF MAHOMET : HIS
GOOD UNDERSTANDING WITH MANUEL : DEATH OF
MAHOMET, 1420 : ACCESSION OF MURAD : WAR WITH
EMPIRE : SIEGE OF CONSTANTINOPLE, 1422 : DEATH OF
MANUEL, 1425 : TRIUMPHAL PROGRESS OF MURAD : HE
BESIEGES AND TAKES SALONICA : BESIEGES BELGRADE
BUT FAILS : COMBINED MOVEMENT UNDER HUNYADI
AGAINST MURAD : BATTLE OF SLIVNITZA, 1443, AND
DEFEAT OF TURKS : MURAD SUES FOR PEACE : TREATY
MADE WITH LADISLAUS : VIOLATED BY CHRISTIANS :
BATTLE OF VARNA, 1444 : MURAD RAVAGES MOREA :
ISKENDER BEY, HIS ORIGIN : CAPTURES CROIA : HUNYADI
AGAIN ATTACKS MURAD : DEFEATED AT COSSOVO-POL,
1448 : REASONS FOR FAILURE OF CHRISTIAN ATTEMPTS :
JOHN HAS TO FOREGO JOINING WESTERN COMBINATION
AGAINST TURKS : DEATH OF MURAD, 1451 : MAHOMET
THE SECOND BECOMES SULTAN.

T is convenient to halt here and to retrace the steps of the
Ottoman conquerors from the accession of Manuel, in 1391,
with more care than was necessary in describing their direct

attacks upon the empire. The number of Turks in Asia Minor and in Europe had now so much increased that their leaders began to dream, perhaps were already planning, the conquest of as wide a territory as had fallen before the immediate successors of the prophet. They had already almost succeeded in completing a ring of conquered states round Constantinople itself. The defeat of the Bulgarians and South Serbians on the Maritza, the great victory over the Serbians at Cossovo-pol, in 1389, enabled them to join forces with the Turks in the Morea and at isolated places on the eastern shore of the Adriatic. Nearly all Asia Minor acknowledged the rule of the Ottomans, and it was to the European portion of the empire that the attention of the Turk would now be turned.[1]

An observer looking back upon all that was going on in Eastern Europe during the first half of the fifteenth century can now see that all the great events were part of a gigantic struggle against the hordes of Asia, represented by the Turks on the south of the Danube and in Asia Minor and the races whom it is convenient to call Tartars to the north of that river. The humiliation of the emperors to obtain aid from the West, the proceedings at Florence, the repeated calls upon Hungary and other Christian nations, were all incidents of that struggle. The statesmen of the West were gradually learning that the Ottomans had developed into a nation of fighters, and that it was not merely the remnant of the Greek empire which was threatened, but Christendom itself.

Reign of
Sultan
Bajazed,
1389–1403.

Upon the assassination of Murad at Cossovo-pol, his son Bajazed became sultan. He had already acquired, or acquired shortly after his accession, the nickname of *Ilderim* or the Thunderbolt.

He commenced his reign by strangling his elder brother, Jacoub. Ducas declares that he was an irreconcilable enemy

---

[1] Caramania was the Turkish state which remained longest outside Ottoman dominion. At one period it extended from the river Sangarius to Adana. Ordinarily its boundaries did not extend further north than Konia. See Stanley Lane-Poole's *Mohammedan Dynasties*, p. 134.

of the Christian name and a passionate follower of Mahomet. During the reign of his predecessor, the struggle between the empire and the Turks had taken a theological character, and it is beyond reasonable doubt that religious animosity of a kind which had not shown itself among the first armies of the Turks had now diffused its baneful influence among the Ottoman armies. Under Bajazed, this fanaticism was intensified to such an extent that it led to cruelties of which it may be said that it is hardly possible to believe that even Mongol barbarity was ever greater than that exercised by the followers of the successor of Murad against Christians.

The commencement of his reign was marked by a series of rapid movements which were crowned with success. He stands out in Turkish history as the maker of swift marches and as the striker of sudden and effective blows. It was on this account that he received the name of ' Ilderim.' He forced Stephen of Serbia, the son of Lazarus (whom he had caused to be hewn in pieces upon the assassination of Murad), to become his vassal and to give him his sister in marriage. Bulgaria, Wallachia, Albania, and Macedonia with Salonica as its capital acknowledged his rule. His fleet plundered the islands of the Archipelago and burnt the town of Chios.[1]

The last message the emperor John had received before his death, in 1391, from Murad was that unless he destroyed the work he had executed in repairing the towers of the Golden Gate, he would put out the eyes of his son Manuel, who was then at Brousa. Happily, his threat came to naught. On learning of the death of his father, Manuel, as we have seen, escaped to the capital. Thereupon Bajazed, upon the rejection of his impossible demands, commenced a series of attacks upon the empire.

Bajazed carried war into every part of the Balkan peninsula. Durazzo was threatened by a Turkish army, and the Venetian senate was compelled to send aid to the relief of its signor. His armies employed themselves in

Reign of Manuel.

---

[1] The island of Chios had for several years been held by a Commercial Company, mostly if not exclusively of Genoese, each of whose members was, apparently, known by the name of Justiniani.

Thrace in raiding cattle and in capturing the Christian inhabitants, thousands of whom were either killed or sold into slavery. Tirnovo was taken, and Shishman, the king of Bulgaria, made prisoner in 1393. With his death, in the same year, the kingdom of Bulgaria came to an end. Ali Pasha, the grand vizier of Bajazed, blockaded Manuel in Constantinople, and urged the citizens to dethrone him and declare for John, the son of Andronicus, the elder son of the late emperor John. But after the Turks had continued near the capital for upwards of a year, Manuel attacked and defeated both them and his nephew John.

End of Bulgarian kingdom.

The greater part of the Morea was still under the rule of the empire. Bajazed organised a great expedition of fifty thousand men for its conquest. He captured Argos, plundered the country nearly as far as Coronea and Methone, in the Morea, and exterminated or brought away thirty thousand captives.

In consequence of the success of these various expeditions, the pope and the other princes of the West became thoroughly alive to the necessity of putting forward all their strength to check the Thunderbolt's progress. Their hopes centred in the leadership of Sigismund, king of Hungary and brother of the emperor in the West. The Venetian senate decided to treat with him for an alliance. The pope and the chief of the Holy Roman Empire did their best to engage the Christian powers to place themselves under his leadership. In 1393, Sigismund had beaten the Turks at Little Nicopolis, and hope rose high of greater successes. In the spring of 1396, the duke of Burgundy, at the head of a thousand knights and nine thousand soldiers—French, English, and Italians—arrived in Hungary and joined his forces. German knights also came in considerable numbers. The Christian armies defeated the Turks in Hungary, and gained victory in several engagements. The emperor Manuel was secretly preparing to join them. Then the allies prepared to strike a decisive blow. They gathered on the banks of the Danube an army of at least fifty-two

housand—and possibly a hundred thousand—men, and encamped at Nicopolis. The *élite* of several nations were
present, but those of the highest rank were the French
knights. When they heard of the approach of the enemy,
they refused to listen to the prudent counsels of the Hungarians and, with the contempt which so often characterised
the Western knights for the Turkish foe, they joined battle
confident of success.

Battle of
Nicopo
1396.

Bajazed, as soon as he had learned the presence of the
combined Christian armies, marched through Philippopolis,
crossed the Balkans, made for the Danube, and then waited
for attack. In the battle which ensued (1396), Europe
received its first lesson on the prowess of the Turks, and
especially of the Janissaries. The Christian army, with
rash daring, broke through the line of its enemies, cut down
all who resisted them, and rushed on irresistible to the very
rearguard of the Turks, many of whom either retreated or
sought refuge in flight. When the French knights saw
that the Turks ran, they followed, and filled the battlefield
with dead and dying. But they made the old military
blunder, and it led to the same old result. The archers,
who always constituted the most effective Turkish arm,
employed the stratagem of running away in order to throw
their pursuers into disorder. Then they turned and made a
stand. As they did so, the Janissaries, 'Christians of origin,
from many Christian nations,' as Ducas bewails, came out
of the place where they had been concealed, surprised and
cut to pieces Frenchmen, Italians, and Hungarians. The
pursuers were soon the pursued. The Turks chased them
to the Danube, into which many of the fugitives threw
themselves. The defeat was complete. Sigismund saved
himself in a small boat, with which he crossed the river,
and found his way, after long wandering, to Constantinople.
The duke of Burgundy and twenty-four noblemen who
were captured were sent to Brousa to be held for ransom.
The remaining Burgundians, to the number of three
hundred, who escaped massacre, and refused to save

their lives by abjuring Christianity, had their throats cut by order of the sultan.[1]

The battle at Nicopolis gave back to Bajazed almost at once all that the allies had been able to take from him. The defeat of Sigismund, with his band of French, German, and Italian knights, sent dismay to their countrymen and the princes of the West.

In the same year, Bajazed gained successes over the Moslem prince of Caramania and a Turkish pretender at Sinope, rebels who had been induced to rise in the hope that they might take advantage of the attack of Sigismund and his allies.

The sultan's great object, however, was to complete his triumphs by the capture of Constantinople. His grand vizier had, in 1396, while blockading the city, urged the inhabitants to declare for the young Prince John, who was the Turkish *protégé*. On refusal, Bajazed sat down to besiege the city, and only abandoned the idea of an assault when it was pointed out that to do so would make enemies of all the Christian powers.

In 1396, apparently immediately after the battle of Nicopolis, and as an essential step towards the capture of the city, he built on the Bosporus the castle still remaining at Anatolia-Hissar, about six miles from the city. It served at once, and continued to serve until 1453, as a useful base of operations. After having completed it, says Chalcondylas, he went to besiege Byzance, and summoned Manuel to surrender the city.[2] The emperor, who had just welcomed six hundred French knights, sent by Charles the Sixth of France, did not deign to reply. Two years later, in 1398, in order to avoid an attack by the Turks, who were drawing near the capital with an army numbering ten thousand, nominally to support John, Manuel consented, as we have seen, to share the throne with his nephew, an

---

[1] Gibbon suggests, on the authority of the *Hist. Anonyme de St-Deny,* that the French had murdered their Turkish prisoners on the eve of the engagement, and that the sultan was merely retaliating (Gibbon, vii. 37).

[2] Chalc. ii. 807.

thereupon went to Western Europe to endeavour to secure help.

The aid sent to Sigismund from the West and that now sent to the Bosporus under Boucicaut show that many statesmen had awakened to the need of checking Turkish progress. The empire was able for a while to hold its own against the attacks made by the sultan.

Bajazed, whose life was alternately one of great activity in warfare and of indescribable debauchery in the intervals between his campaigns, had kept the capital under terror of sieges during six weary years. In 1402, he summoned John to surrender the city, and swore by God and the Prophet that if he refused he would not leave in it a soul alive. John gave a refusal. Chateaumorand, the lieutenant of Boucicaut, who, as we have seen, had gone west to endeavour to obtain aid, took charge of the defence, and waited for an attack.

At this time, remarks Ducas, the empire was circumscribed by the walls of Constantinople, for even Silivria was in the hands of the Turks.[1] Bajazed had gained a firm hold of Gallipoli and thus commanded the Dardanelles. The long tradition of the Roman empire in the East, save for the capture of the city itself, seemed on the eve of coming to an end. No soldier of conspicuous ability had been produced by the empire for upwards of half a century: one who was capable of inflicting a sufficient defeat, or series of defeats, on the Turks to break or seriously check their power. The empire had fought on for three generations against an ever increasing number of Turks, but without confidence and almost without hope. It was now lacking in sufficiency of men and money. The often promised aid from the West had so far proved of little avail. The armies defeated by the empire, either alone or aided by Italians, were renewed by the constant stream of emigrants from Asia. The power of Serbia had been almost destroyed. Bulgaria had perished. The two states had been alternately at the mercy of hordes of infidels from

[1] Chap. xv.

the north or those under the Turkish sultan. From
Dalmatia to the Morea the enemy was triumphant. The
men of Macedonia had everywhere fallen before Bajazed's
armies. Constantinople was between the hammer and
anvil : Asia Minor, on the one side, was nearly all under
Turkish rule; the European part of the empire, on the
other, contained as many Turks as there were in Asia
Minor itself. The insolent tyrant passed in safety between
his two capitals—one at Brousa, the other at Adrianople—
and repeated his proud boasts of what he would do beyond
the limits of the empire. It seemed as if, with his overwhelming force, he had only to succeed once more in a task
which, in comparison with what he and his predecessors had
done, was easy, and his success would be complete. He
would occupy the throne of Constantine, would achieve that
which had been the desire of the Arab followers of Mahomet,
and for which they had sacrificed hundreds of thousands of
lives, and would win for himself and his followers the
reward of heaven promised to those who should take part
in the capture of New Rome. The road to the Elder Rome
would be open, and he would yet feed his horse on the altar
of St. Peter.

We have seen what was the insolent message he sent
in his arrogance, in 1402, to John. The answer given
would have completed a dramatic story if it had seemed well
to the gods. ' Tell your master we are weak, but that in our
weakness we trust in God, who can give us strength and can
put down the mightiest from their seats. Let your master
do what he likes.' Thereupon Bajazed had laid siege to
Constantinople.

Suddenly, in the blackness of darkness with which the
fortunes of the city were surrounded, there came a ray of
light. Had there been an interpreter there as of old time,
Bajazed might have learned the significance of the hand-
writing on the wall. All thought of the siege was abandoned for the time, and Constantinople breathed again
freely.

What had happened was that Timour the Lame had

challenged, or rather ordered, Bajazed to return to the Greeks
all the cities and territories he had captured. The order
was categorical and, given to a ferocious barbarian like
Bajazed, drove him to fury. The man who gave it was,
however, accustomed to be obeyed.

Timour [1] or Tamarlane was a Mahometan and a Turk,
though he claimed to be of the same race as Genghis, who
was a Mongol. Under him the warrior shepherds of the
south plains of Asia came westward in even greater numbers
than they had done under his famous predecessor. They
advanced in well-organised armies, under generals who seem
to have had intelligence everywhere of the enemy's country
and great military skill. After having annexed Kharizon
and Persia to Transoxiana and reduced Turkestan to
obedience, Timour turned westward. In 1386, he appeared
at Tiflis, which he subsequently captured at the head of an
enormous host estimated at eight hundred thousand men.
At Erzingan he put all the Turks sent there by the sultan
to the sword.

Bajazed seems from the first to have been alarmed and
went himself to Erzingan in 1394, but returned to Europe
without making any attempt to resist the invader, probably
believing that Timour had no intention of coming further
west.[2] He soon learned his mistake. Timour was not
merely as great and cruel a barbarian but as ambitious as
Bajazed himself. In 1395, while the emperor was in the
Balkan peninsula, Timour summoned the large and populous city of Sivas to surrender. The inhabitants twice
refused. Meantime, he had undermined the wall. On their
second refusal, his host stormed and captured the city. A
hundred and twenty thousand captives were massacred.
Bajazed's son was made prisoner and put to death. A large
number of the prisoners were buried alive, being covered
over in a pit with planks instead of earth so as to pro-
ng their torture. Bajazed was relieved when he learned
that from Sivas, which had been the strongest place

[1] The word *timour* is the same as the ordinary Turkish word for iron, *demir*.
[2] Leunclavius, 250.

in his empire, the ever victorious army had gone towards Syria.

Timour directed his huge host towards the frontier city of the sultan of Egypt—namely, Aleppo—his object being to punish the sultan for his breach of faith in imprisoning his ambassador and loading him with irons. On his march to that city, he spread desolation everywhere, capturing or receiving the submission of Malatia, Aintab, and other important towns. At Aleppo, the army of the Egyptian sultan resisted. A terrible battle followed, but the Egyptians were beaten, and every man, woman, and child in the city was murdered.

After the capture of Aleppo, Hama and Baalbek were occupied. The latter, which, like so many other once famous cities, has become under Turkish rule a desolation with only a few miserable huts amid its superb ruins, was still a populous city, and contained large stores of provisions. Thence he went to Damascus and in January 1401 defeated the remainder of the Egyptian army in a battle which was hardly less bloody than that before Aleppo. The garrison, composed mostly of Circassian mamelukes and negroes, capitulated, but the chief was put to death for having been so slow in surrendering. Possibly by accident, the whole city was burned.

Timour was stopped from advancing to Jerusalem by a plague of locusts, which ate up every green thing. The same cause rendered it impossible to attack Egypt, whose sultan had refused to surrender Syria.[1]

From Damascus, Timour went to Bagdad, which was held by contemporaries to be impregnable. Amid the heat of a July day, when the defenders had everywhere sought shade, Timour ordered a general assault, and in a few minutes the standard of one of his sheiks, with its horsetai and its golden crescent, was raised upon the walls.[2] Ther

---

[1] Leunclavius, pp. 250-1, Ven. edition, makes the conquest of Damascus in 1399 ; Chalcondylas and others, in 1402 ; the Turkish authors quoted by Von Hammer, in 1401. The statement of the hindrance due to locusts I take from Muralt, 772, who quotes as his authority 'Bizar,' a name unknown to me.

[2] The Crescent, which Gibbon and other writers assert to have only bee

followed the usual carnage attending Timour's captures.
The mosques, schools, and convents with their occupiers were
spared : so also were the *imaums* and the professors. All
the remainder of the population between the ages of eight
and eighty were slaughtered. Every soldier of Timour, of
whom there were ninety thousand, as the price of his own
safety, had to produce a head. The bloody trophies were, as
was customary in Timour's army, piled up in pyramids
before the gates of the city.

It was on his return northwards from Damascus that, in
1402, Timour sent the message to Bajazed which at once
forced him to raise the siege of Constantinople. Contemporaneously with this message, Timour requested the
Genoese in Galata and at Genoa to obtain aid from the West
and to co-operate with him to crush the Turkish sultan.

Timour organised or sent a large army on the Don and
around the Sea of Azof on the Cimmerian Bosporus,
connecting that sea with the Euxine, in order that, in case of
need, it might act with his huge host now advancing
towards the Black Sea from the south. His main body
passed across the plain of Erzingan, and at Sivas Timour
received the answer of Bajazed. The response was as
insulting as a Turkish barbarian could make it. Bajazed
summoned Timour to appear before him and declared that
if he did not obey, the women of his harem should be
divorced from him, putting his threat in what to a Mahometan was a specially indecent manner. All the usual
civilities in written communications between sovereigns
were omitted, though the Asiatic conqueror himself had
carefully observed them. Timour's remark when he saw

Bajazed's
reply to
Timour's
summons.

employed by the Turks after the capture of Constantinople, had probably been
used by them for many centuries previously. It is true that it had been made
use of in Constantinople at an early period, and figures on several coins of
Constantine, but I doubt whether it was used as the symbol of Constantinople
in the later centuries of its history. The Crusades are not incorrectly described
s wars between the Cross and the Crescent. The symbol is an ancient one
and figures with the star on several coins belonging to about 200 B.C. The
Abassid dynasty so used it. Professor Hilprecht considers it a remnant of
moon-worship and connects it with the subsequent cult of Ashtaroth, Astarte,
or Aphrodite.

the sultan's letter contained the name of Timour in black writing under that of Bajazed which was in gold, was ' The son of Murad is mad ! ' When he read the insulting threat as to his harem, Timour kept himself well in hand, but, turning to the ambassador who had brought the letter, told him that he would have cut off his head and those of the members of his suite if it were not the rule among sovereigns to respect the lives of ambassadors. The representative of Bajazed was, however, compelled to be present at a review of the whole of his troops and was requested to return to his master and relate what he had seen.

Meantime, Bajazed had determined to strike quickly and heavily against Timour and by the rapidity of his movements justified the name of Ilderim. His opponent's forces, however, were hardly less mobile. Timour's huge army marched in twelve days from Sivas to Angora. The officer in command of that city refused to surrender. Timour made his arrangements for the siege in such a manner as to compel or induce Bajazed to occupy a position where he would have to fight at a disadvantage. He undermined the walls and diverted the small stream which supplied it with water. Hardly had these works been commenced before h learned that Ilderim was within nine miles of the city Timour raised the siege and transferred his camp to th opposite side of the stream, which thus protected one side o his army while a ditch and a strong palisade guarded th other. Then in an exceptionally strong position he waite to be attacked.

Disaffection existed in Bajazed's army, occasioned by h parsimony, and possibly nursed by emissaries from Timou Bajazed's own licentiousness had been copied by h followers, and discipline among his troops was noted as f less strict than among those of his predecessor. In leadir them on what all understood to be the most serious ente prise which he had undertaken, his generals advised him spend his reserves of money freely so as to satisfy followers ; but the capricious and self-willed Ilderim refuse They counselled him, in presence of an army many tim more numerous than his own, to act on the defensive and to avoid a general attack. But Bajazed, blinded by his long series of successes, would listen to no advice and would take no precautions. In order to show his contempt for his enemy, he ostentatiously took up a position to the north of Timour and organised a hunting party on the highlands in the neighbourhood, as if time to him were of no consequence. Many men of his army died from thirst under the burning sun of the waterless plains, and when, after three days' hunting, Bajazed returned to his camping ground, he found that Timour had taken possession of it. The enemy had almost altogether cut off his supply of drinking water and had fouled what still remained.

Under these circumstances, Bajazed had no choice but to force on a fight without further delay. The ensuing battle was between two great Turkish leaders filled with the arrogance of barbaric conquerors, each of whom had been almost uniformly successful. Nor were pomp and circumstance wanting to impress the soldiers of each side with the importance of the issue. Each of the two leaders was accompanied by his sons. Four sons and five grandsons commanded the nine divisions of Timour's host. In front of its leader floated the standard of the Red Horse-tail surmounted by the Golden Crescent. On the other side, Bajazed took up his position in the centre of his army with his sons Isa, Mousa, and Mustafa, while his eldest son Suliman was in command of the Asiatic troops who formed the right wing. Lazarus of Serbia was in command of his own subjects, who had been forced to accompany Bajazed and formed the left wing of the army. The Serbians gazed in wonder and alarm upon a number of elephants opposite to them, which Timour had brought from India.

At six o'clock in the morning of July 28, 1402, the two armies joined battle. The left wing of Bajazed's host was the first to be attacked, but the Serbians held their ground and even drove back the Tartars. The right wing fought with less vigour, and when the troops from Aidin saw their former prince among the enemy, they deserted Bajazed and

went over to him. Their example was speedily followed by
many others, and especially by the Tartars in the Ottoman
army, who are asserted by the Turkish writers to have been
tampered with by agents of Timour.[1]

Defeat of
Bajazed. The Serbians were soon detached from the centre of the
army, but Lazarus, their leader, at the head of his cavalry,
cut his way through the enemy, though at great loss, winning
the approval of Timour himself, who exclaimed, ' These
poor fellows are beaten, though they are fighting like lions.'
Lazarus had advised Bajazed to endeavour, like himself, to
break through, and awaited him for some time. But the
sultan expressed his scorn at the advice. Surrounded by
his ten thousand trustworthy Janissaries, separated from
the Serbians, abandoned by a large part of his Anatolian
troops and many of his leading generals, he fought on obsti-
nately during the whole of the day. But the pitiless heat
of a July sun exhausted the strength of his soldiers, and no
water was to be had. His Janissaries fell in great numbers
around him, some overcome by the heat and fighting, others
struck down by the ever pressing crowd of the enemy. It
was not till night came on that Bajazed consented to withdraw. He attempted flight, but was pursued. His horse
fell, and he was made prisoner, together with his son Mousa
and several of the chiefs of his household and of the Janissaries. His other three sons managed to escape. The
Serbians covered the retreat of the eldest, Suliman, whom
the grand vizier and the Aga of the Janissaries had dragged
out of the fight.

The Persian, Turkish, and most of the Greek historians
say that Timour received his great captive with every mark
of respect, assured him that his life would be spared, and
assigned to him and his suite three splendid tents. When
however, he was found attempting to escape, he was more
rigorously guarded and every night put in chains and con

---

[1] Though the Turks were a branch of the Tartar race, the Greek author
by this time had acquired the habit of calling the nation which Othman had
formed Turks, and all others from Central Asia Tartars, and it is convenient
to follow this nomenclature.

fined in a room with grilled windows. When he was conveyed from one place to another, he travelled much as Indian ladies now do, in a palanquin with curtained windows. Out of a misinterpretation of the Turkish word which designated at once a cage and a grilled room, grew the error into which Gibbon and historians of less repute have fallen that the great Ilderim was carried about in an iron cage.[1] Until his death, in 1403, he was an unwilling follower of his captor.

After the battle of Angora, Suliman (the eldest son of Bajazed), who had fled towards Brousa, was pursued by a detachment of Timour's army. He managed to cross into Europe and thus escaped. But Brousa, the Turkish capital, fell before Timour's attack, and its inhabitants suffered the same brutal horrors as almost invariably marked either Tartar or Turkish captures. The city, after a carefully organised pillage, was burned. The wives and the daughters of Bajazed and his treasure became the property of Timour. Nicaea and Ghemlik were also sacked and their inhabitants taken as slaves. From the Marmora to Caramania, many towns which had been captured by the Turks were taken from them. Asia Minor was in confusion. Bajazed's empire appeared to be dropping away in every part east of the Aegean. Suliman, however, established himself on the Bosporus at Anatolia-Hissar, and about the same time both he and the emperor at Constantinople received a summons

---

[1] Von Hammer has shown conclusively that the story of an iron cage is a mistake. It arises from the misinterpretation of the Turkish word Kafés, which has the two significations given above. Two contemporary authors made the blunder, Phrantzes and Arab Schah. A Bavarian, who was made prisoner at the battle of Nicopolis, named Schildberger, and who was present at the battle of Angora, has given a detailed account of the massacre of the Christians, but he does not mention the cage. (His travels between 1394 and 1427 have been translated and published by the Hakluyt Society, 1879.) Neither do Ducas, Chalcondylas, or Boucicaut, though they state that Bajazed died in irons, which he had to wear every night after his attempt at escape. Six Persian authors who wrote the history of Timour are silent about the cage. The oldest Turkish historian recounts, upon the evidence of an eye-witness, that Bajazed was carried about in a palanquin ' like a Kafés,' or in the usual kind of grilled palanquin in which ladies of the harem travelled. Sad-ud-din, one of the most exact of Turkish historians, states that the story of the iron cage given by many Turkish writers is a pure invention.

from Timour to pay tribute. The emperor had already
sent messengers to anticipate such a demand. Timour
learned with satisfaction that the sons of Bajazed were dis-
puting with each other as to the possession of such parts of
their father's empire as still remained uncaptured by him.

Timour
captures
Smyrna.
In 1402, the conqueror left Kutahia for Smyrna, which
was held, as it had been for upwards of half a century, by the
Knights of Rhodes. In accordance with the stipulation of
Moslem sacred law, he summoned them either to pay
tribute or become Mahometans, threatening them at the
same time that if they refused to accept one or other of these
conditions all should be killed. No sooner were the proposals rejected than Timour gave the order to attack the
city. With his enormous army, he was able to surround
Smyrna on three sides, and to block the entrance to it from
the sea. The ships belonging to the knights were at
the time absent. All kinds of machines then known for
attack upon walled towns were constructed with almost
incredible speed and placed in position. The houses within
the city were burned by means of arrows carrying flaming
materials steeped in naphtha or possibly petroleum, though,
of course, not known under its modern name.

After fourteen days' vigorous siege, a general assault was
ordered, and the city was taken. The knights fought
like heroes, but were driven back into the citadel. Seeing
that they could no longer hold out, and their ships having
returned, the grand master placed himself at their head, and
he and his knights cut their way shoulder to shoulder
through the crowd of their enemies to the sea, where they
were received into their own ships. The inhabitants who
could not escape were taken before Timour and, without
distinction of age or sex, were butchered.

The Western settlers hastened to come to terms with
Timour, who, like his great predecessor, was not opposed to
any Christians on account of their religion. The Genoese
in Phocaea, in the islands of Mitylene and Scios, sent to
make submission, and became tributaries of the conqueror.

Smyrna was the last of Timour's conquests in western

Asia Minor. He went to Ephesus, and during the thirty
days he passed in that city his army ravaged the whole of
the fertile country in its neighbourhood and in the valley of
the Cayster. The cruelties committed by his horde would
be incredible if they were not continually repeated during
the course of Tartar and Turkish history. In fairness, it
must also be said that the Ottoman Turks, although their
history has been a long series of massacres, have rarely been
guilty of the wantonness of cruelty which Greek and Turkish
authors agree in attributing to the Tartar army. One
example must suffice. The children of a town on which
Timour was marching were sent out by their parents reciting
verses from the Koran to ask for the generosity of their conqueror but co-religionist. On asking what the children were
whining for, and being told that they were begging him to
spare the town, he ordered his cavalry to ride through them
and trample them out : an order that was forthwith obeyed.

Timour, wearied with victories in the west, now determined to leave Asia Minor and return to Samarcand. This
resolution he carried out. He contemplated the invasion of
China, but in the midst of his preparations died, in 1405,   Death of
after a reign of thirty-six years.   Timour.

Bajazed the Thunderbolt died at Aksheir two years
earlier, and his son Mousa was permitted to transport his
body to Brousa.[1]

The battle of Angora gave the greatest check to the
Ottoman power which it had yet received. Considering the
number of men engaged and the complete victory obtained
by Timour, one might have expected it to have been fruitful
in more enduring consequences than it produced. But its
immediate results, though not far-reaching, were important.
The fourteen years' victorious career of the Thunderbolt was
brought suddenly to an end. The empire of the Ottoman

[1] I have relied for the account of the battle of Angora and the subsequent
progress of Timour, mainly upon Von Hammer (vol. ii.), who is at his best in
describing this period of Turkish history. The authorities are carefully given
by him. Zinkeisen, in his *History of the Turks*, calls attention to the deterioration of the Ottoman armies during the reign of Bajazed, and attributes it to the
profligacy of the sultan.

Turks which he had largely increased, and especially by the
addition to it of the north-west portion of Asia Minor, was
for a time shattered to pieces. The sons of the vanquished
sultan, after the departure of Timour and his host, were
quarrelling over the possession of what remained. Three of
them gained territories in Asia Minor, while the eldest,
Suliman, retook possession of the lands held by his father
in Europe. Most of the leaders of the Ottoman host, the
viziers, governors, and scheiks, had been either captured or
slain, and in consequence the sons of Bajazed fighting in
Asia Minor found themselves destitute of efficient servants
for the organisation of government in the territories which
they seized on the departure of Timour.

The progress of the great Asiatic horde created a profound impression in Western Europe. The eagerness of
the Genoese to acknowledge the suzerainty of Timour gives
an indication of their sense of the danger of resistance. The
stories of the terrible cruelties of the Tartars lost nothing in
their telling. When the news reached the neighbouring
nations of Hungary and Serbia and the republics of Italy
of the defeat of Bajazed, the capture of Brousa, of Smyrna,
of every other town before which the Asiatic army had sat
down, and of the powerlessness of the military knights, it
appeared as if the West were about to be submerged by a new
flood from Asia. No terror so great had threatened Europe
since the time when Charles Martel defeated the Moslem
hordes on the plains around Tours, or since the even more
threatening attack upon Christendom when the main body
of the Arab armies sat down for successive years before
Constantinople and were signally defeated by the obstinacy
of its defenders.

Then, when news came of the sudden departure of the
Asiatics and of the breaking up of the Ottoman power, hope
once more revived, and it appeared possible to the pope and
Christian peoples to complete the work which Timour had
begun by now offering a united opposition to the restoration
of an Ottoman empire. Constantinople itself when Bajazed
passed it on his way to Angora was almost the last

remnant of the ancient empire, and seemed as if it required
only one more attempt, and that not needing that the sultan
should put forth all his strength, to secure its capture.   The
battle of Angora saved it and gave it half a century more of
life.

A struggle which lasted for six years began between the
sons of Bajazed.   Suliman, in 1405, sought to ally himself
with the emperor, and his proposals show how low the
battle of Angora had brought the Turkish pretensions.   He
offered to cede Salonica and all country in the Balkan
peninsula to the south-west of that city as well as the towns
on the Marmora to Manuel and his son John, now associated
as emperor, and to send his brother and sister as hostages
to Constantinople.   The arrangement was accepted.

Suliman, having thus made himself secure, attacked his
brother Isa in 1405, defeated and killed him.[1]   Another
brother, Mousa, in the following year, attacked the combined
troops of Suliman and Manuel in Thrace, but the Serbians
and Bulgarians deserted the younger brother, and thereupon
Suliman occupied Adrianople.   Manuel consented to give
his granddaughter in marriage to Suliman, who in return
gave up not merely Salonica but many seaports in Asia
Minor : a gift which was rather in the nature of a promise
than a delivery, since they were not in his possession.
Unhappily, Suliman, like many of his race, had alternate
fits of great energy and great lethargy, and was given over
to drunkenness and to debauchery.   This caused disaffection
among the Turks ; and Mousa, taking advantage of it, led
an army in 1409, composed of Turks and Wallachs, against
him.   The Janissaries, who were dissatisfied with the lack
of energy displayed by their sultan, deserted and went over
to the side of Mousa.   Suliman fled with the intention of
escaping to Constantinople, but was captured while sleeping
off a drinking bout and killed.

[1] Chalc. iv. p. 170. Ducas says he disappeared in Caramania ; Phr. p. 86,
that he was bowstrung.   There was, according to Chalcondylas, another son
of Bajazed, the youngest, also named Isa, who was baptised and died in Constantinople in 1417.   This was probably the son given over as hostage to
Manuel.

Then Mousa determined to attack Manuel, who had been faithful to his alliance with Suliman. He denounced him as the cause of the fall of Bajazed and set himself to arouse all the religious fanaticism possible against the Christian population under the emperor's rule. According to Ducas, Mousa put forward the statements that it was the emperor who had invited Timour and his hordes, that his own brother Suliman had been punished by Allah because he had become a giaour, and that he, Mousa, had been entrusted with the sword of Mahomet in order to overthrow the infidel. He therefore called upon the faithful to go with him to recapture Salonica and the other Greek cities which had belonged to his father, and to change their churches into mosques for the worship of God and Mahomet.[1]

In 1412, he devastated Serbia for having supported his brother, and this in as brutal a manner as Timour had devastated the cities and countries in Asia Minor. Then he attacked Salonica. Orchan, the son of Suliman, aided the Christians in the defence of the city, which, however, was forced to surrender, and Orchan was blinded by his uncle.

While successful on land Mousa was defeated at sea, and the inhabitants of the capital, in 1411, saw the destruction of his fleet off the island of Plataea in the Marmora. In revenge for this defeat he laid siege to the city. Manuel and his subjects stoutly defended its landward walls, and before Mousa could capture it news came of the revolt of his younger brother, Mahomet, who appeared as the avenger of Suliman. The siege of Constantinople had to be raised. Mahomet had taken the lordship of the Turks in Caramania shortly after the defeat of his father at Angora, and had been unattacked by Timour. The emperor proposed an alliance with him, which was gladly accepted and the conditions agreed to were honourably kept by both parties. Mahomet came to Scutari where he had an interview with the emperor. An army formed of Turks and Greeks was led by Mahomet to attack his brother. But Mousa defeated him in two engagements. Then Manuel, after a short time,

[1] Ducas, xix.

having been joined by a Serbian army, attempted battle against him, and with success. The Janissaries deserted Mousa and went over to Mahomet and Manuel, and his army was defeated. He was himself captured and by order of Mahomet was bowstrung.[1]

Mahomet was now the only survivor of the six sons of Bajazed, with the exception of Isa, the youngest, who was still living with Manuel as a hostage. Three of his brothers had been the victims of fratricide. In 1413, Mahomet proclaimed himself Grand Sultan of the Ottomans.

Sultan Mahomet the First, 1413-1420.

He had been loyally aided by Manuel and the Serbians, and in return loyally respected the agreements he had made with both. He gave up, as we have seen, Salonica and the fortified towns on the Euxine, the Marmora and in Thessaly which had been taken from the Greeks.

In 1415, the Turks, who had remained nearly undisturbed on the western side of the Balkans, entered Bosnia. The inhabitants were mostly Bogomils, who had been constantly persecuted by their Catholic neighbours in order to force them to Union with the Church of Rome, were menaced, on account of their refusal, by the king of Hungary, and in reply threatened that they would coalesce with the Turks. Upon such an intimation, the Turks entered the country.[2]

The two rulers, Manuel and Mahomet, continued on friendly terms. It was probably due to the emperor's influence that the sultan consented, in 1415, to allow the Knights of Rhodes to build a strong fortification on the boundaries of Caria and Lycia as a place of refuge for Christians who should escape from the hands of the Moslems. Ducas gives an account of the interview which took place between the grand master and Manuel and adds that the emperor went so far towards conciliating the Christians that he contented the rulers of Chios, Mitylene, and Phocaea. In returning from the Morea in 1416, Manuel met Mahomet at Gallipoli, the sultan going on board Manuel's galley and eating with him.

[1] Chalc. iv.; Phr. i. 29; Ducas, 19.
[2] *Official Tour in Bosnia and Herzegovina*, by J. de Asboth.

Two years later, the good understanding between Mahomet and the emperor was interrupted by an incident which is creditable to Manuel. A Turkish pretender who claimed to be Mustafa, the elder brother of the sultan, who is supposed to have been killed at Angora, aided by a ɔdy of Wallachs, attempted to dethrone Mahomet. They were attacked and beaten back and then took refuge in Salonica. Manuel declined to give them up, but promised that he would prevent the pretender and the leader of the Wallachs from making further attacks upon Mahomet. To accomplish this, he sent the pretender Mustafa to the island of Lemnos and imprisoned the chief of the Wallachs in the monastery of Pammacaristos in Constantinople. But Mahomet would not be satisfied with any punishment less than the death of the pretender, and from this time ceased to trust Manuel. Nevertheless, when, in 1420, the sultan was in passage through Constantinople towards his Asiatic possessions, Manuel behaved loyally. All the members of his council, says Phrantzes,[1] advised the emperor to seize him. Manuel refused and declared that, though the sultan might violate his oath of friendship, he would rather trust to God and respect his own. On Mahomet's return to Europe through Gallipoli, the council again urged the emperor to capture him. Again, however, he refused, and sent a trusty general to escort him from the Dardanelles to Adrianople.

Death of Mahomet.

A short time after his arrival, in 1420, Mahomet died. His death was kept secret for forty days, in order to give time for the arrival of his son, Murad, who was then at

Reign of Murad, 1420-1451

Amasia. Murad was proclaimed at Brousa and began his reign by proposing to Manuel the renewal of the alliance which had existed with his father. We have already seen that this proposal was rejected, and that, after fruitless negotiations for the surrender of two of Murad's sons, war was declared. The emperor thereupon sent to Mustafa the pretender, who still remained prisoner at Lemnos, and, giving him assistance, recognised or appointed him governor of Thrace and of all the places in that province held by the Turks

[1] i. 37.

which he could occupy. In return, Mustafa swore to deliver Gallipoli, which had been taken by the Turks in the reign of Bajazed, to the emperor as soon as he had captured it, as well as certain towns on the Black Sea. Mustafa succeeded for a while and with the aid of the imperial troops captured Gallipoli (1420). A number of its Turkish garrison joined his army. Manuel's general now claimed the fulfilment of his promise to deliver this important town, but Mustafa stated what has often been advanced in our own time as a generally recognised rule in Islam, that a true believer could not surrender to unbelievers territory held by Moslems except by force, that his religion bound him to build a city on the ruins of the Christian city, and that he would rather break his oath than violate the duty imposed by his religion. It was in vain that the emperor's representative reminded him of his past history: how he had sought refuge at Salonica, how the emperor had risked the anger of Mahomet by insisting upon his refusal to give him up; how at Lemnos he had still been protected. The pretender was obdurate.[1]

When Manuel heard of the bad faith of Mustafa, he endeavoured to re-establish the same friendly relation with Murad which had existed with his father. He offered to assist the sultan to recover all that his father possessed, provided he would send his sons to Constantinople. According to Phrantzes (who from this time takes an active part in many of the incidents he relates), the sultan was equally ready to be friendly, provided that no further aid should be given to Mustafa,[2] but no understanding could be arrived at.

The perjured Mustafa was probably a very poor creature. He soon lost the confidence of his followers, and shut himself in Gallipoli, giving himself up to pleasures and paying little attention to the measures which Murad was taking against him. The latter passed over into Asia, made arrangements with the Genoese at Phocaea to send him a fleet and a number of Italian and French soldiers, and,

[1] Ducas, xxiv.   [2] Phr. i. 38

when they arrived, crossed the Dardanelles from Lampsacus to Gallipoli.[1]

The troops who remained faithful to the pretender attempted to prevent the landing of Murad and his native and foreign troops, but failed. Thereupon Mustafa fled. Murad took possession of Gallipoli and then followed the pretender to Adrianople with all possible speed. Mustafa hastened towards Wallachia on the approach of the sultan. A band of young soldiers followed and captured him. He was brought before the sultan, condemned, and hanged like an ordinary malefactor.

Then the sultan thought himself strong enough to take up the task which Bajazed had undertaken when summoned by Timour. He decided at once to attempt the capture of Constantinople. He laid siege to it in the second week of June 1422 and ended in failure, as we have already seen, at the end of August in the same year.

One at least of the reasons why the siege in 1422 had been abandoned was a rising against Murad on behalf of his younger brother named Mustafa. One of his two brothers, had been strangled by his orders, but Mustafa was saved by Elias Pasha. Murad had ordered Elias to bring the boy to Brousa. Elias, however, succeeded in having him recognised in that city and at Nicaea as sultan. The rebellion, therefore, had assumed alarming proportions. Murad with a trusty band of followers went to Nicaea, gained access to the city, and the boy Mustafa, who was only six years old, was bowstrung, possibly without the consent of his brother. Then Murad in great haste crossed again to Europe,[2] occupied Adrianople, and made it his European capital.

[1] In reference to this passage across the Dardanelles, Ducas (ch. xxvii. gives an interesting piece of information as to the size of the Genoese vessels There were seven large ships. Murad was in the largest, which containe 1,300 Turkish and Frank soldiers. These ships 'covered the sea like floatin cities or islands.'

[2] Ducas mentions expressly that in the same year three Mustafas died first, the pretender, who claimed to be the son of Bajazed; second, his brother and, third, the grandson of Atin (ch. xxviii.).

We have now arrived at the period when many of those who were destined to be great actors in the tragedy of the Moslem conquest of Constantinople appear on the scene. The young emperor John, who had become co-emperor with his father in 1420 and who now alone possessed power, owing to the debility of his father, went, in 1423, to Hungary to seek help against the common enemy. He left his brother Constantine, who was destined to be the last Christian emperor of the city, in charge of the capital with the title of Despot. A few months later, Phrantzes, the historian of the conquest, and Lucas Notaras, afterwards made Grand Duke, who also took a prominent part in the events of 1453, were sent by Constantine to Murad and arranged terms of peace, subject to ratification by John, when he returned from Hungary. The associated emperor came back by sea to his capital in October and terms of peace were ratified by which the empire had to pay a heavy tribute and to surrender many towns on the Black Sea.

In July 1425, Manuel died. He was seventy-seven years old and had reigned thirty-four years—or, counting the eighteen years when he was co-emperor with his father, fifty-two years. In his old age, he had become hopeless of saving the empire, or even the capital. He counselled John to make the best of the situation, to try to live on good terms with the sultan, and to be content to remain the vassal of Murad.

The Turks had now largely recovered from the disorganisation produced by the invasion of Timour. Everywhere they were regaining territory, and their internal divisions were disappearing. Those occupying the south and south-west of Asia Minor were the first to recover from the blow of the Tartars. As early as 1415, Manuel had to resist them in the Morea. They had defeated the Venetians, had plundered Euboea and carried off thousands of Christian captives. Others had invaded Dalmatia and the Adriatic coast. Their numbers in Hungary and south Russia had been enormously increased by the conquests of Timour, the Turks of south Russia fleeing before his host. In 1419, the

Hungarians had defeated an army of three hundred thousand who entered the great plain north of the Danube. Most of the Turks in Asia Minor, if not all willing subjects of Murad, still rendered him at the time of the death of Manuel, in 1425, a nominal submission. The prince of Caramania was, however, always a troublesome feudatory.

Murad's reputation may be judged by the fact that in the year in which Manuel died he made a triumphal progress. Having traversed Thrace, he went to Brousa, to Pergamos, Magnesia, Smyrna, and Ephesus. While at the last-mentioned city, homage was done to him by the ambassadors of the emperor John, of Lazarus, king of Serbia, Dan, prince of the Wallachs, and the signors of Mitylene, Chios, and Rhodes. He was, in fact, the almost undisputed lord of Asia Minor and of all places in the Balkan peninsula, with the exception of a few fiefs in Greece, and of Constantinople, with a small territory behind it. With the exception of the Venetians and the Hungarians, he was at peace with all the world. But the Venetians were still holding their own. They had supported the insurrection in Caramania. Their fleet had been sent to prevent Murad from crossing into Asia, and they were masters of Salonica. But even in that city Murad had still a triumph to achieve. Pressed by famine when the inhabitants were besieged by the Turks, shortly before Murad's siege of the capital, the population had offered the city to the Venetians, who gladly accepted it and sent a fleet to its relief. But the Turks had constantly claimed that they had been improperly deprived of their intended prey, and the answer given by Murad to proposals of peace made by the republic were: Surrender Salonica first. In 1428, Murad determined to fight for it. While he went south-west into Macedonia, the whole population, including the southern Serbs and southern Bulgarians, submitting to his rule, one of his leading generals laid siege to Salonica. Ducas says that the besiegers were a hundred to one, and there can be no doubt that there was a fatal discrepancy in numbers. On the arrival of Murad, the Janissaries were promised permission to pillage the city. In a general assault, they captured it without much difficulty, and the brutalities, the atrocities, the wanton and useless cruelties inflicted upon the population made a profound impression upon Western Christians. Probably they learned more of the nature of these cruelties, owing to the presence of Italians and the comparative proximity of Salonica to Western Europe, than ever before. But though women were violated, houses pillaged, churches profaned, and seven thousand of the captives sold into slavery, Europe did not yet understand that these were the ordinary incidents of Turkish conquest. Upon the capture of the city, in 1430, Murad and the Venetians made peace.[1]

Great efforts, however, were yet to be made to check the progress of Murad, and if in the course of his triumphal progress to Ephesus he was under the illusion that the European nations were content to allow Moslem invasion to remain unchecked, he was soon undeceived. Hungary, Serbia, and Poland now formed the great line of defence against a Turkish advance, and when, in 1428, the first two states were invaded by the Turks, it became evident to the West that Catholic as well as Orthodox nations would have to resist the progress of Turkish arms. Before the nations attacked were ready, Murad struck swiftly and heavily, and Sigismund, king of Hungary, not having received the aid he expected from Ladislaus, king of Poland, suffered a serious disaster on the Danube.

On receiving news of the Turkish advance, the pope once more preached a new Crusade and called upon all Christians to go to the aid of the Poles and Hungarians. But messengers travelled slowly, and preparations were long. Four years afterwards, in 1433, Murad again invaded Hungary, but was stoutly resisted by Elizabeth, mother of the infant Ladislaus,

Preparations to resist Murad.

---

[1] De la Brocquière, whose narrative was finished in 1438, states that, when in Galata, the ambassador of the duke of Milan, the protector of the Genoese, told him that 'to do mischief to the Venetians he had contributed to make them lose Salonica taken from them by the Turks;' and he adds, 'Certainly in this he acted so much the worse, for I have seen the inhabitants of that town deny Jesus Christ and embrace the Mahometan religion.' *Early Travels*, pp. 335-6.

and had to retire. In withdrawing he attempted to annex
Serbia, on the pretext that Bajazed having married the
sister of Stephen, the former sovereign, the crown belonged
to him as the heir of Ilderim. In 1435, he laid siege to
Belgrade, and put out the eyes of two sons of the kral,
under the pretext that they had attempted to escape to their
father. The siege lasted six months, but the attempt failed.
The Serbians defended the city bravely. The Turkish army
suffered from malarial fever, and a relieving army under a
Polish general compelled them to raise the siege.

It is worthy of note that during the absence of the
emperor at Ferrara and Florence in order to treat of the
Union of the Churches—an absence from his capital of two
years and two months (November 1437 to February 1440)—
Murad proposed to attack the city and was advised to do so
by all his council with the exception of Halil pasha,[1] who
pointed out that as John had gone to confer with the representatives of the Christian powers on questions of religion, at
the request of the pope, they would feel bound to come to
his aid, if advantage were taken of his absence to attack
the capital. Halil's advice was taken.[2]

Immediately on John's return, he and other European
Christian rulers began to make more or less combined
movements against Murad. The influence of the pope was
energetically used to make an alliance successful. The
question was no longer one merely of defending a schismatic
though Christian emperor, but of preserving the existence of
great Catholic states. Nor were the means for offering
a strong resistance to Turkish advance wanting. The
crown of Hungary was worn by Ladislaus, the young king
of Poland, who was crowned in 1440. Almost immediately
after his accession, his army succeeded in defeating a
Turkish detachment in Hungary. In the same year Scanderbeg—that is, Alexander Bey—at the head of a large body of
Albanians, declared war on Murad. Though John on his

---

[1] Halil was the one Turkish leader in 1453 friendly to the Greeks. Even
at this early date he showed a similar spirit. Chalc. 136, Venetian edition.

[2] Phr. ii. 13, p. 180.

return from Florence sent an embassy to the sultan to protest that he was a loyal vassal, he was only waiting for the ships and aid promised by the pope and by Western princes in order to join in a combined attack. Although the ships promised were long in arriving, the West was known to be full of anxiety, and preparations were being hurried forward. On New Year's Day 1442, the pope again preached a Crusade and called on all Christian princes, and especially on Ladislaus, king of Poland and Hungary, to help in the defence of the three bulwarks of Christendom—Constantinople, Cyprus, and Rhodes.[1] Cardinal Julian was commissioned to advise Ladislaus, and the king was ordered to render every aid possible to him as the legate of Eugenius. George Brancovich of Serbia bound himself to aid the Hungarian king and for this purpose to send twenty-five thousand men and large sums of money, the produce of the Serbian mines. The combined army of Hungarians and Serbs, with the co-operation also of Scanderbeg, was placed in June under the command of John Corvinus Hunyadi, the waywode of Transylvania. Hunyadi had already distinguished himself as a brave and skilful leader against the Turks. In a short campaign of less than half a year, he had captured five strongholds north of the Danube, won as many battles, and had returned laden with booty and trophies of victory. In 1442, at the head of twelve thousand chosen cavalry, he chased the Turks out of Serbia and defeated in succession several armies. Christians from France, Italy, and Germany hastened to enrol themselves under his leadership. Not even before the terrible disaster at Nicopolis in 1396 had so powerful an army been gathered together to attack the common enemy as was now collected under Hunyadi. It represented all the force that the pope and Western Europe could muster, and the presence of Cardinal Julian gave it the sanction of an international army representing Christendom. Seldom have soldiers had more confidence in their leader, and apparently that confidence was well bestowed.

Hunyadi leader of Christian armies.

---

[1] Possibly Hungary was not mentioned, with the object of leading the Turks to believe that the place of attack would not be nearer than Constantinople.

His
victories.

Near Nisch the army of twelve thousand chosen cavalry under Hunyadi was joined by that of Ladislaus, consisting of twenty thousand men, with whom were the king and the cardinal. The first and most important battle of the campaign with the united army was fought between Sofia and Nisch, probably near Slivnitza on November 3, 1443. The Turks were completely defeated, and thirty thousand of them are said to have been left on the field. Four thousand were made prisoners and nine standards captured. Thereupon the Christian army advanced to Sofia, which it captured, and then pushed on towards Philippopolis. At Isladi near Ikhtiman, the beginning of the pass about midway between Sofia and Philippopolis, Hunyadi found that Murad had arranged for making a stand. The natural strength of the pass, the principal entrance to which is the Gate of Trajan, and the measures taken on the high tableland at the head of this pass to make the frozen ground impassable to cavalry, made Hunyadi hesitate. A second pass appeared more practicable. On Christmas Eve, the Christian army forced a passage, triumphing over the Turks and over the equally serious obstacles of rocks and ice. Murad's strong entrenchments were carried by brilliant and persistent attacks, the Christians having to make their way through snowdrifts, while the enemy rolled rocks and masses of ice from the heights. The Turks were driven from their stronghold and the Christian army followed them down the slopes of the Balkans into the plain. Once more the Turks stood, and again they were beaten.[1] Upon this, the triumphant Christian army halted and waited for reinforcements before further advance.

It was probably immediately after this campaign, or possibly during the halt in Roumelia, that Murad hastened into Asia, where the prince of Caramania had engaged in a conspiracy with others of the emirs of Anatolia to rise against the sultan and to attack his territory simultaneously with the attacks made by Christians in Europe. Konia and many other cities had been sacked and desolation carried

[1] Callimachus, who describes the battle, took part and was wounded in it.

far and wide even among the Turks wherever they had stood for Murad.[1] The sultan suppressed the rising with his usual cruelty, treating the Turks as he had done the Christians.

The successes of Hunyadi compelled Murad, and this for several reasons, to sue for peace. He sent an embassy to the Hungarian, but as the latter was awaiting new troops to pursue his campaign, he at first declined to treat, and sent Murad's delegates to Szegedin, then occupied by the king and the cardinal. Finding, however, that his reinforcements did not arrive, Hunyadi consented to retire and take part in the negotiations. The Turks on their side agreed to terms. Murad was to give up to George Brankovitch all the places in Serbia which he had captured, to allow Wallachia to be added to Hungary, to leave Scanderbeg in possession of Albania and Macedonia, and to give up the two lads whom he had blinded and the other hostages. Ladislaus and Hunyadi on the return of the latter to Hungary made a triumphal entry into Buda. Thirteen pashas, nine Turkish standards, and four thousand prisoners bore testimony to the success of the campaign. The mission from Murad had gone forward into Hungarian territory to complete the formalities of peace which had been agreed to at Szegedin. A formal truce for ten years was concluded in June 1444 between Murad and the king of Poland and Hungary and his allies. The treaty was not, however, signed by Hunyadi, who declared that he was only a subject. Each party swore that the army of his nation would not cross the Danube to attack the other. Ladislaus took the oath to this effect solemnly on the Gospels and Murad on the Koran.[2]

Peace solemnl accepte

The treaty of June 1444 thus solemnly ratified was almost immediately broken.[3] To the eternal disgrace of

---

[1] I have followed here the version of Ducas (xxxii.). It is doubtful, however, whether this expedition into Caramania ought not to be placed a year earlier. See the authorities quoted by Muralt, p. 856.

[2] Chal. vi.; Ducas, xxxii. The latter states that Hunyadi refused either to sign or to swear.

[3] The treaty was made in June. According to Muralt, it was broken in the same month. If so, the account of Ducas is incorrect. Murad was informed

M

Treaty
violated by
Christians.
Ladislaus and of the cardinal legate, Julian Cesarini, who had accompanied Hunyadi on the campaign just described, and who figures as the evil genius of Ladislaus until his death, it was broken by the Christians. History furnishes few examples of equally bad faith.

All the evidence goes to prove that the Turks intended to respect the treaty. The sultan, indeed, had taken the opportunity of abdicating and of formally handing over the government to his son, Mahomet, a boy fourteen years old, and had already retired to Brousa with the intention of going on to Magnesia, to live in peace and quietness. Murad wanted rest. Even when he was seen by La Brocquière, probably in 1436, he was 'already very fat.' A short, thick-set man with a broad brown face, high cheek-bones, a large and hooked nose, he looked, says the same writer, like a Tartar—that is, like a Mongol. Voluptuous in the worst Turkish sense of the word, he also loved wine and banished a believer who dared to reprove him for drinking it. 'He is thought,' adds La Brocquière, 'not to love war, and this opinion seems to me well founded.' [1] Just about this time also he lost his eldest son, Aladdin, to whom he was much attached, and was overcome with grief. Hence his determination to get rid of the cares of government.

The opportunity to the Christians seemed tempting. News had arrived that a powerful fleet of seventy ships had appeared in the Bosporus, ten triremes having been sent by the pope and ten others at his request by Latin princes. The duke of Burgundy and a French cardinal had arrived at Constantinople to urge John to join in a Christian league. The cities of Thrace were undefended by the Turks, and the fleets, it was believed, could prevent Murad with his army from crossing into Europe. The only obstacle to vigorous and successful action was the newly signed treaty.

Pretexts were found that Ladislaus had had no right to

by George of Serbia of the renewal of war and again took the government into his own hands 'at the beginning of summer, when the dog-days were commencing.' Ducas, xxxii.

[1] *Early Travels*, pp. 346–347.

agree to a truce without the consent of the pope, and that Murad had not executed his part of the treaty. Ladislaus hesitated to break his oath, but Cardinal Julian urged that his league with the Christian princes of the West was better worth respecting than his oath to the miscreant. According to more than one author, he maintained the proposition that no faith need be kept with infidels.[1] Finally, the cardinal called down upon his own head all punishment due to the sin, if sin there were, in violating the oath. But in the name of the pope, the vicar of God on earth, he formally released the king from the obligations to which he had sworn.[2]

The action of Ladislaus was in reality not merely wicked and immoral, but ill-advised and hasty. Even in the short interval between the conclusion of peace and the declaration of war, the French, Italian, and German volunteers had gone home. John was not ready to aid him. Phrantzes had been sent to Ladislaus, to the cardinal, and even to the sultan, to temporise and to prevent an outbreak of war before a coalition could be formed. Hunyadi very reluctantly gave his consent to the violation of the truce, and then only on condition that the declaration of war should be postponed until September 1. George of Serbia not only refused to violate the engagement into which he had solemnly entered with Murad but refused to permit Scanderbeg to join Ladislaus. The whole business was ill-considered and ill-managed, and the fault lies mainly with the cardinal.

[1] Lonicerus, p. 18, speaking of the cardinal, does not go so far. He says, ' qui Pontifici licere juramenta praesertim hostibus Christiani nominis praestata rescindere contendebat.' Thurocz (quoted by Von Hammer, p. 307, vol. ii.) and Cambini, p. 13, make similar statements.

[2] *Liber Jurium*, xxii. 57, xxvi. 24, 26 Chalc. vi. Aeneas Silvius states that Eugenius, when he was informed of the treaty, wrote to Cardinal Julian that it was null as having been signed without the papal sanction; that he ordered Ladislaus to disregard it, and that he gave him absolution for so doing. At the same time, he directed the cardinal to do his best to renew the war, in order that the great preparations he had taken in hand might not be fruitless. The statement may be true, but it is difficult to believe that the report of the signature could have reached Rome and that his answer could have arrived to the cardinal before war was declared.

When Murad's dream of quiet days at Brousa was disturbed by the news that the treaty solemnly accepted a few weeks earlier had been violated by the faithless Christians, who in this case are justly characterised by the Turks as infidels, he at once resumed the duties of a ruler and prepared to go to the aid of his son, young Mahomet. With the aid of the Genoese he crossed the Bosporus, probably at the extreme north end below the Giant's Mountain, where the entrance into the Black Sea was, and long continued to be, known, from the number of temples which had existed there from pre-Christian times, as the Sacred Mouth. The Italian and Greek fleets near the capital were unable successfully to resist the passage, the ascent of the Bosporus being almost impossible for sailing vessels during the continuance of the prevailing north winds. From thence Murad hastened to meet the army of Ladislaus.[1]

Battle of
Varna,
Nov. 11,
1444

The place of rendezvous for the Christian armies was Varna. Ladislaus took the field in the autumn, with only ten thousand fighting men. He marched along the valley of the Danube, and was joinèd by Drakul, prince of Wallachia, with five thousand of his subjects. The total of the two armies probably never exceeded twenty thousand men.

The Wallachian prince advised prudence and delay. He

---

[1] The Turkish accounts agree that the crossing was at the Bosporus. Barletius, Book II. p. 38, with whom Leunclavius agrees, says : ' Si vera est fama,' merchant vessels transported the army over the Bosporus, receiving a gold coin per man. Bonfinius likewise gives this story of payment and says it was made to the Genoese. Lonicerus, p. 18, says the fleet crossed the Dardanelles. Ducas, whose account I have adopted, states that the fleet only crossed with great difficulty and against the will of the emperor. Chalcondylas makes the transit take place at Hieron, near the Dardanelles (Chalc. 135) ; one writer, at Asomaton. There is a church of the Asomatoi (the Bodiless, i.e. of Angels) at Arnaoutkeui still existing. See The Constantiade, where the Patriarch gives an account of it. Phrantzes identifies the position on the Bosporus (namely, opposite Anatolia-Hissar) by saying that it was near the narrow part of the Bosporus above the village of Asomaton or Arnaoutkeui : κατὰ τὸ στενὸν ἐγγὺς τοῦ ἀνωτέρου μέρους τῆς τῶν Ἀσωμάτων κώμης (Ph. ch. II. p. 223), which is conclusive as to the locality he wishes to indicate. Ducas also in several places gives the name of Hieron to the straits between Anatolia and Roumelia-Hissar. It is therefore clear that two places on the Bosporus were known as Hieron. The safest passage would be at the Hieron below the Giant's Mountain.

pointed out that even a hunting party of the sultan contained as many men as were now collected to oppose him. Hunyadi, however reluctant he had been to enter on the campaign, seems to have thought that, once the armies had started, their only hope of safety lay in expedition and in being able to obtain a strong position for fighting. The discussion between the two brave leaders led to a quarrel, in which Drakul drew his sword, but was immediately overpowered and compelled to purchase safety by the promise of a further reinforcement of four thousand men.[1] Drakul then retired, and his place was taken by his son. Many of the towns and villages passed through on their march were held by Turks, but the Christian armies, in most cases, easily overcame all opposition, and in their course plundered the schismatic Bulgarians and their churches as if they had been enemies.

At Varna the army proposed to rest. Further advance, if desirable, was difficult, on account of the illness of Ladislaus.[2] Hunyadi took up a strong position.

Varna is at the head of a bay. On the south side was situated, at a distance of about four miles from the town, a village named Galata. Between the two stretched a long line of marsh, which is the termination of a lagoon, bounded on the south side by a steep range of hills.[3] Between the end of the marsh and the bay the Christian army encamped with the hill on its rear. Hardly had it taken up its position when scouts brought the startling news that Murad's army was encamped at a distance of four thousand paces. The night was bright and clear, and by ascending the hill they could see the fires, and make even an estimate of the number of their enemies. Their astonishment at the rapidity with which Murad had advanced added to their alarm. They found that he was at the head of an army of at least sixty thousand men—a hundred thousand men are

[1] Callimachus.

[2] 'Morbo detentus,' Lonicerus, 18. Chalc. and others also mention his illness. He was suffering from an abscess in the thigh.

[3] On the opposite shore of the lagoon now runs the railway from Varna to Rustchuk.

said to have crossed into Europe—while their own consisted only of eighteen or twenty thousand. Guards were doubled, and a council at once held, to decide upon what was to be done. Cardinal Julian's advice was that they should entrench themselves, make a barrier around them of their carts, and await attack. Their machines, or guns, the alarming effect of which had already been seen at Belgrade, would be of value for their defence. He also urged that probably a fleet would soon come to their aid. The bishops with the army, and a few others, agreed with him.

On the other hand, Hunyadi and the leader of the Wallachs declared the proposal to be absurd. The great Hungarian urged that the enemy was only to be conquered by daring and dash. Every sign of hesitation, especially at the beginning of a campaign, was fatal. Suppose the Turks also chose to play the waiting game, were the Christians ready to stand a siege? Their only salvation lay in audacity. He characterised what was said about the coming of a fleet as ridiculous. Ships would be of no more use in their present position than cavalry at sea. Even if the sailors landed, what could they do against horsemen?

The advice of the experienced soldier carried the day. The young king, though he was suffering great bodily pain, supported Hunyadi, and declared against delay.

Hardly was the council of war over before the scout announced that the Turks had settled the question for them and were preparing to attack. Though the alarm was false, or at least premature, Hunyadi at once made all arrangements for defence, and strengthened his position. His army had its back to a hill; on one side was the marsh, and on the other he placed his baggage and other wagons so as to make a rampart. He blocked up the passes through the marsh as well as he could with carts and chariots. He placed four companies of Wallachians on the left, where the marshes afforded protection, while the Hungarians formed the right wing, of which he himself took command. This was the position of greatest danger, as being least protected. Ladislaus was placed in the safest

place in the centre, surrounded by Hungarians and Poles.
The great black standard of Hungary floated over Hunyadi,
while the flag of St. George marked the place near the king
occupied by the cardinal and the Wallachian chief. A
reserve of Wallachs was stationed to act wherever there was
necessity. Murad, however, did not begin his attack as
soon as the Christians expected. He took four days before
he completed his preparations. He came down further into
the plain, and carefully formed his plan of battle. The
invincible Janissaries occupied the centre, with the sultan
in their midst. They formed what may be called a zariba.
Around them was a ditch or trench. Behind that stood the
camels, while behind them was a breastwork formed of
shields fixed to the ground immediately in front of the
Janissaries surrounding the sultan. The Anatolian troops,
some of whom were armed with arquebuses, were on the
Sultan's left, and the European or Rumelian troops on his
right. In front of the sultan, hoisted on a long spear, was
placed the violated treaty.

The Turks sent forward six thousand of their cavalry,
who occupied the hill near the Christian army. Their
purpose was to examine the ground, and to take note of the
numbers of the enemy, and of their position. Nevertheless,
they discharged showers of arrows against the Christians,
their archers being, as usual, their best troops.[1] When
Franco, one of the standard-bearers of Ladislaus, prevented
his men from attacking them, the Turks, believing that the
Christians were overawed by their superior numbers and
dared not leave their entrenchments, came down into the
plain and began the battle. Then Franco let his troops go,
and with such effect that the Turkish cavalry were soon in
full retreat. Murad thereupon brought forward the main
body of his army, and the fight became general. Hunyadi
sustained successfully the shock of the Anatolian division,
drove it back and put it to rout. . The remainder of the
Christian army in the plain were attacked at the same time,
but the Turkish horsemen were hard pressed, and fled.

[1] *Early Travels*, 361

One of the bishops who, says Callimachus, was more skilful
in ecclesiastical than in military matters, seeing the Turks
retreating, hastened after them with a band of soldiers, and,
arriving at the densely packed host, was soon floundering in
the marsh, and he and his men were of no further use in
the fight. But the Turks were pursuing their usual method
of fighting; 'for,' remarked La Brocquière only half a dozen
years before this battle, 'it is in their flight that they are
most formidable, and it has been almost always then that
they have defeated the Christians.' [1]

Meantime, Hunyadi, who knew their tactics well, on
returning from his fight with the Asiatic division, strictly
charged the young king not to allow the troops around him
to move, to remain with them, and to wait for his return
after attacking the European division, or at least until he
knew the issue of the fight, because, if successful, he would
then have to deal with the Janissaries.[2] The Christians of
the left wing and even around the standard of Ladislaus
were hard pressed. The cardinal and Franco, with the son
of Drakul, had to fall back to the barricade of wagons. A
fierce struggle took place near and among the wagons, and
the Turks for a while gained ground. Hunyadi hastened to
the aid of the Christians, and his arrival changed for a while
the tide of battle. The Turks retreated from the wagon,
and were driven back two thousand paces. Hunyadi and
his men were fighting splendidly and manifestly succeeding
In their attack, Caradja, the leader of the European
division of the Turks, was killed.

At this moment occurred an incident which in a
probability influenced and perhaps altogether changed the
fortunes of the day. According to Chalcondylas, some who
were near the king and were jealous of the fame of Hunya
persuaded Ladislaus not to leave the glory of the day to the
Hungarian, as if he were the only leader. 'His would be
the sole renown; ours the ignominy of having remaine

---

[1] *Early Travels*, 366.
[2] Chalc. p. 138. The account by Phrantzes, p. 198, of the intervi
between Hunyadi and the king is very well given.

idle.' Influenced by these taunts, the king led his followers
into the fight while Hunyadi was attacking Murad's right,
and made direct for the sultan himself in the midst of his
entrenchments. Hunyadi, who during the day was always
at the point of greatest danger, on galloping back after the
retreat of the Turks before the troops forming the left wing,
found that the brave but too impulsive young king had left
his post. Hunyadi immediately went to his aid. He found
that Ladislaus and his followers had broken through the
entrenchments, the line of camels and the shields, and were
among the Janissaries. Struggling desperately, he had laid
low many of the enemy, but had become separated from his
own men.

His absence caused many of the Christians to believe
that he had been either captured or killed and, in consequence, many of them began to give way. The fortune of
the day was at this time doubtful. Many among the Turks
and Christians were in flight, neither party being able to
judge how the battle was going. The unconquerable
Janissaries, however, remained firm and resisted the young
king's attack vigorously. In the crisis of the battle,
according to the Turkish annals, Murad prayed, ' O Christ,
Thou art God, as Thy followers say, punish their perfidy.' [1]

Hunyadi was in despair. He saw his men deserting and
that his army had already been greatly reduced in numbers,
but he managed to reach the king. Ladislaus was still
fighting when his general drew near, but his horse fell
forward with him, in consequence of a great blow from an
axe. As the king fell, says Callimachus, he was instantly,
not merely pierced, but simply buried beneath the weapons
the Janissaries. His head was taken to Murad, who had
it at once hoisted upon a lance.[2]

The issue of the battle had been at various stages doubtful. Two divisions of the Turks had been beaten and fled,
but both had rallied and returned. At one moment the

---

[1] Bonfinius states that it was at this moment also that he unfurled the treaty
Szegedin.
[2] Leunclavius, 256.

sultan himself contemplated flight, but was stopped by a
Turk who cursed him as a coward and prevented him from
leaving the field. Hunyadi attempted to recover the king's
body, but when he saw one after another of the small
number of Wallachs who were with him struck down, he
looked to his own safety and made good his escape. The
battle was lost. He, Julian, Franco, and as many as could,
when darkness came on, retreated across the hills into the
great neighbouring forest.

The fortune of battle had so often changed that it was
not until the following day that the Turks recognised how
great was the success they had gained. The slaughter in
the small army of the Christians had been heavy. Many, too,
had perished in the marsh or had been drowned in the lagoon.
Others, among whom was Julian, were afterwards caught in
the forest. The remnant of Huns and Wallachs had the
utmost difficulty in making their way across the Danube.
On his way home, Hunyadi was taken prisoner by his old
enemy, Drakul, prince of Wallachia, but was set free when
the Hungarians threatened war, as they immediately did,
unless he was at once released.

The great effort from which the emperor and the West
had hoped so much had proved futile. The fleets had been
powerless. The struggle was over before aid was received
from the emperor or the Western princes. The remark of
a careful traveller is justified, that the bad faith of the
Christians did much to intensify among the Moslem
dislike and distrust, and led to reprisals commonly justified
by the Turkish teaching that 'no faith is to be kept with
infidels.'[1]

The part which the emperor John played, if he took any
in this campaign, is doubtful. Chalcondylas states that he
had declared war against the sultan, but he is the only
contemporary who makes this assertion. Probably he was
ready, though unable, to aid the Western ships in preventing
Murad from crossing the Bosporus.

<hr>

[1] Eton's *Travels*, p. 332.

Murad had inflicted a crushing defeat upon the Christians, was weary of fighting, and readily promised the emperor that, if he abandoned all concerted action with the Western powers, he should not be attacked. He once more abdicated the throne in favour of his son Mahomet, and withdrew to his beautiful gardens and palace at Magnesia, hoping once more for peace in retirement.[1]

The same year—always 1444—he was forced by the Janissaries, who were already beginning to claim a share in the government, and who had marked their discontent by burning a large part of Adrianople, to resume the guidance of the state.

After reducing them to complete submission, he turned his attention to Greece, which on the death of the previous emperor had been divided between three of his seven sons.

Constantine, brother of John, and afterwards the last emperor, had shown energy in the Morea. He was in possession of a large part of the Peloponnesus, and had chased the Turks out of Boeotia, Pindus, and part of Thessaly. This weakening of their hold compelled Murad to bestir himself. In November, 1446, he started for Greece at the head of an army of sixty thousand men.

[1] Gibbon adopts the statement of Chalcondylas (145) that Murad joined the dervishes after Varna, though on other matters regarding his life he relies upon Cantemir, who by implication discredits the story. Chalcondylas states that in the crisis of the battle of Varna, the sultan had vowed that if he were successful he would abdicate and join one of these religious orders. Von Hammer knows nothing of the story, and the whole course of Murad's life is against the belief that 'the lord of nations submitted to fast and pray and turn round in endless rotations with the fanatics who mistook the giddiness of the head for the illumination of the Spirit' (Gibbon, VII. p. 140). Neither Phrantzes nor Ducas mentions his having become a dervish, as they probably would have done the fact had been known to them. Indeed, the one point in favour of the story was unknown to Gibbon: namely, that some of the dervish sects are liberal or philosophical. They are all religious or pietistic, but many claim that their tenets are independent of Islam. Their explanation of the turning dancing is that they first look towards Mecca and reflect, God is there; then they make a turn and reflect, He is there also; and so in the complete circle. should be noted also that there are many dervishes who neither turn nor dance in their devotions. On the subject of the dervishes in Turkey, two useful books are *The Dervishes*, by J. P. Brown (London, 1868), and, better still, *Les Confréries Musulmanes* par le R. P. Louis Petit, supérieur des Augustins de l'Assomption à Kadikeuy (Constantinople, 1899).

Constantine sent an ambassador, the historian Chalcondylas, to propose terms, which were, however, rejected. Murad then advanced and attacked Constantine, who held a strong position behind the famous rampart of the Hexamilion, extending across the Isthmus of Corinth. Murad carried it by assault, and killed all the garrison. His principal general then ravaged the Morea, and carried off sixty thousand Christians into slavery. Patras was captured and burnt, and Constantine, who had fought well but whose army was much smaller than the Turkish, had to pay tribute and surrender all territory that he had conquered from the Turks beyond the Isthmus of Corinth. He was still, however, able to retain possession of a large part of the Morea.

Iskender Bey and the Albanians.
After the campaign in Greece, Murad marched northwards to attack the Albanians, and endeavoured to capture Kroya,[1] the capital of the country. But it was held by the Albanian leader, George Castriotes, whom we have already met under the name of Iskender (or Alexander) Bey, a man who was a military genius, and who in some respects recalls the adventures and characteristics of Garibaldi. But he was unscrupulous as well as energetic. Devoting himself like a new Hannibal to the salvation of his country, he held and continued to hold absolute, but willingly rendered, sway during twenty-five years over the Albanian mountaineers. Christian by birth, but given over with his brothers to the Turks as hostages, and forcibly converted to Mahometanism, he had become a favourite of Murad for his handsome appearance, his strength of body, and his courage. He had gained power over his countrymen in the first instance by a ruse as bold as it was relentless. Scimitar in hand, he offered as an alternative to the reis-effendi, or commander in-chief, either immediate death or the affixing of his signature and seal to a document ordering the governor of Kroy to hand over to him the fortress and the adjacent country. Having obtained the document in due form, he then killed the reis-effendi. At this time Iskender Bey was only ninetee

[1] Kroya or Croia, now called Ak-Hissar or the White Castle, is a few mil to the north of Durazzo and a short distance from the Adriatic.

years old. Gathering a small band of Albanians about him, he hastened across the peninsula and obtained possession of Kroya by a stratagem even more desperate and dangerous than that by which he had obtained the order for his appointment as Turkish governor. Leaving his followers outside the city and in hiding, he presented his credentials and obtained the keys of the fortress. During the night, he personally admitted his followers, and the Turkish garrison were murdered while they slept. Then he rapidly made his preparations for defence against the attack of Murad which he knew would follow. It is sufficient for our purpose to say that he was successful, and that at the approach of the winter of 1447–8, Murad's attempt to recapture Kroya entirely failed, and the great sultan withdrew to Adrianople.

Meantime the Christians north of the Danube were preparing to make a greater effort than ever to strike at the power of the sultan. The new pope, Nicholas the Fifth, urged the duty of aiding the Hungarians and the Poles as vigorously as his predecessor. But his appeals to other states were of little avail. Hunyadi, notwithstanding the defeat at Varna, was named lieutenant-general of the kingdom almost immediately on his return, and at once set himself to reconstruct an army. In less than four years he possessed the best-disciplined host which Hungary had yet seen. But it was far too small for the purpose on hand. Among its twenty-four thousand men were two thousand German arquebusers and eight thousand Wallachians. With this force Hunyadi crossed the Danube near Turn-severin and invaded Serbia, because its ruler, whose sister was married to the sultan, refused to break the engagement with Murad.

When the sultan, who was preparing for another attempt to defeat Iskender Bey and the Albanians, heard that George of Serbia was on the point of being attacked, he at once made all haste to go to his assistance. Hunyadi encamped near Cossovo, on the same Plain of Blackbirds where, in 1389, Murad the First had been assassinated after his victory. The Turkish army, probably numbering a hundred and fifty thousand men,[1] occupied three days in crossing the Sitnitza, a small river which runs through the plain into the Vardar. Hunyadi, for some reason which is not evident, left his entrenchment and crossed the stream, apparently with no other object than of forcing on the fight. Why he should have done so, since he was hourly expecting the arrival of a detachment of Albanians under Iskender Bey, it is impossible to understand.

The battle commenced on October 18, 1448. The Turks were drawn up in the same order as at Varna, the Janissaries in the centre surrounded by a trench, behind which were ranged the camels, and behind them again a belt of shields or bucklers fixed in the ground. To the right of the Janissaries was the European, and to the left the Asiatic, division of Murad's army. On the other side, the centre of the Christian army was occupied by the German and Bohemian arquebusers and some of the best troops of Transylvania. The right wing was formed of Hungarians with a few Sicilian auxiliaries, while the Wallachs were on the left

The first day's fight was not general. But at noon or the second, the whole lines on both sides were engaged, and continued till sunset, when, in spite of the superiority in numbers on the Turkish side, no advantage had been gained Hunyadi, indeed, believed that during the night his enemy intended to break up his camp and commence a retreat For this reason, he determined upon a night attack—one c the measures, as General Skobeleff testified after fightin in Central Asia under somewhat similar circumstances, i which the best-disciplined army almost necessarily win All the valour of the Hungarian army was powerless t break through the line of the Janissaries, and the attac consequently failed. On the morning of the third day, th fight was again renewed, and victory appeared doubtfu But the Wallachs turned traitors, and in the midst of th fight, their leader having obtained terms from Murad, pass over to the Turkish side. The army of Hunyadi was no

---

[1] Aeneas Sylvius gives the number at 200,000; Chalcondylas at 15,0 which Von Hammer reasonably suggests is an error for 150,000.

attacked in front and rear, but contrived to reach its entrenchments. Judging that its condition was hopeless, Hunyadi made his escape in the evening, leaving the Germans and Bohemians to hold the central position of his encampment. This they did with magnificent courage, but the battle was already lost. Out of the army of twenty-four thousand, seventeen thousand men, including the flower of the Hungarian nobility, are said to have been left dead on the field.[1] But the victory had been dearly bought by Murad. During the three days' fight, forty thousand Turks had fallen.[2]

The Christians had lost the battle through the rash courage and confidence of their leader. Hunyadi had refused to wait for Iskender Bey and his Albanians, had abandoned a strong position in order to attack an enemy largely superior in numbers, and his desertion of the best of his auxiliaries is inexplicable or unjustifiable. The defeat at Cossovo-pol, following that at Varna, made men forget for a time the series of brilliant victories which the great Hungarian had gained over the Turks in Transylvania and elsewhere. But in the glorious defence of Belgrade against Mahomet after the capture of Constantinople, Hunyadi recovered greater reputation than ever, and the West recognised in that city the first bulwark of Christendom, and in its defender the greatest soldier of the age.[3]

The effect in Hungary and Constantinople of these victories of Murad was appalling. The sultan and his successors for many years had nothing to fear from the enemy north of the Danube.

The great combined efforts of the West to break the Ottoman power and, incidentally, to save Constantinople had failed disastrously. Nor are the reasons for such failure difficult to understand. They are mainly two : underestimating

Reasons for failure of Western attempts against Turks.

[1] Bonfinius makes Murad state in a letter to Corinth that eight thousand Hungarians were left dead on the plain : a much more likely number.

[2] Von Hammer gives the numbers I have adopted.

[3] For the siege of Belgrade see a paper in the *English Historical Review*, 1892, by Mr. R. N. Bain.

the power of the enemy, and dividing their own forces. First and above all, neither the pope nor the statesmen of Europe had realised the enormous number of fighting men which the Turk could bring into the field. They knew that the empire of Constantinople had been dismembered by Turkish armies, but they attributed this loss to secondary causes, and do not appear to have realised that Turkish armies beaten again and again constantly reappeared. The empire's loss, in their opinion, was due to the incapacity of some of its emperors, to civil war, to the pressure of Serbia and Bulgaria, and to the judgment of Heaven upon the Greeks for having refused to come within the one Christian fold, and to acknowledge the one shepherd. The Turks were the instruments of divine justice to punish schismatics, but, having done their work against the empire, they would, now that they ventured to attack Catholic states, no longer be permitted to make further encroachments.

The failure of the men of the West was largely due to the fact that they despised the common enemy. They were under the curious delusion that the Turk was not a fighting man ; that, though he had been successful in beating Greeks, Serbs, and Bulgarians, he was no warrior, and that he had thus far succeeded because he had never encountered European soldiers. This delusion lasted for at least two centuries after the capture of the city. Almost every Western writer who visited Constantinople spoke of the defeat of the Turks as a task well within the power of a European state. That such a blunder influenced the men of the West before the capture of the city, may be illustrated by the statement of two contemporaries. In an oration by Aeneas Sylvius, who afterwards became Pope Pius the Second, delivered at Rome in 1452, before Pope Nicholas, King Ladislaus, and a number of cardinals, the orator appealed to the knowledge of his audience to recognise that the Turks were ' unwarlike, weak, effeminate, neither martial in spirit nor in counsel ; what they have taken may be recovered without difficulty.' [1]   A like testimony is given by La Brocquière

---

[1] 'Novit majestas imperatoria, Turcorum, Assyriorum, Aegyptiorum gentem : imbelles, inermes, effaeminati sunt, neque animo neque consilio martiales ;

in 1438, but with much more caution, since he had been through Asia Minor and had seen the Turks. Nevertheless, this Western traveller states that, though he would not depreciate them, he is ‘ convinced that it would be no difficult matter for troops well mounted and well led to defeat them,’ and, in regard to himself, he adds, ‘ I declare that with one half of their numbers I should never hesitate to attack them.’ [1] He fully realised, as he explains again and again, that their victories had been gained by their enormous superiority in numbers, but though he was very far from despising them as soldiers, he regards them individually as greatly inferior to the soldiers of Western states. His estimate of the inferiority of the Turk was shared by his countrymen and Western statesmen generally,[2] but they did not recognise to the same extent as he did how great and ever increasing was the host which had to be fought. Nor did they recognise, as did he, the wonderful mobility of the Turkish army. It was the same error of forgetting their mobility which brought disaster upon Hunyadi at Varna and at Cossovo-pol.

While the first mistake was in underrating the might of the enemy in regard to numbers, warlike spirit, and mobility, the Western powers blundered also in dividing their forces. The sermon before the pope already referred to, on New Year’s Day 1452, called for international concerted action to defend Constantinople, Cyprus, and Rhodes. The mistake was in trying to do too much. On many occasions, as we have seen, the forces sent against the Turk were divided, and an army which might have been sufficiently strong to strike an effective blow against one of the Turkish divisions was defeated in detail when split into two or three, to be sent against Saracens, or to the aid of the military knights, as well as against the Turks.

The one chance of safety for Constantinople now lay in

sumenda erunt spolia sine sudore et sanguine.’ Oratio Romae habita anno 1452 de passagio Cruce signatorum contra Mahometanos suscipiendo. Edita apud Reynaldum [by Dr. Dethier].

[1] La Brocquière, 366.   [2] Θρῆνος, line 720.

the inhabitants themselves, with such forces as, at the instigation of the pope, should be sent to the aid of the emperor.
But to add to the chagrin and difficulties of the aged John
at seeing the Christian armies defeated, he had once more
formally to promise the sultan that he would not assist
any of the enterprises set on foot from the West. Nor
did the influence of the disasters upon the emperor and
people of Constantinople stop here. A formidable party in
the city, headed by the bishop of Ephesus, which was opposed
to the Union, and which strongly resented the proceedings
at the Council of Florence, was greatly strengthened. Its
members pointed to the victories of Murad, and asked, with
scorn, what had been gained by the abandonment of their
faith. They knew that they had the support of Murad in
their opposition to the Unionists, and the fact that they were
not forcibly suppressed by the Court party during the reign
of John's successor can probably be best accounted for on
the ground that any strong steps taken against their members would be represented to the sultan as a violation of
the engagement to have no further intrigues with the
West.

Death of
John, Octo-
ber 1448.

The disaster of Cossovo-pol hastened the death of John,
which took place on the last day of October 1448, within a
few days after he had heard the news.[1]

Of Murad,
February
1451.

In February 1451, his great contemporary, Murad, died at
Adrianople. He had been a successful warrior, and, with the
exception of his failure to capture Belgrade, had succeeded
in most of his enterprises. Gibbon is perhaps justified in
speaking of him as a philosopher in matters of religion,
but he was relentless in imposing his creed. Cantemir, his
eulogist, relates that in Epirus he converted all the churches
into mosques, and ordered every male Epirot, under penalty
of death, to be forcibly made a Mahometan. He deserves the
praises of Turkish writers. Chalcondylas and Ducas recognise in him certain good traits of character. The first says

---

[1] According to Scholarius and Manuel the Rhetorician, John shortly before
his death declared against the Union. In such a matter, however, both these
witnesses are suspect.

that he was a just and equitable man, and Ducas gives him credit not undeserved for having scrupulously respected the treaties which he made with Mahometans or Christians.   His son Mahomet, who now becomes the second sultan of that name in the Ottoman dynasty, was at Magnesia when he heard the news of his father's death.

CHAPTER VIII

CAUSES LEADING TO DECAY OF EMPIRE : NOT DUE TO DE-
MORALISATION OF COURT ; INTERNAL AND EXTERNAL
CAUSES ; LATIN CONQUEST AND FORM OF GOVERNMENT
HAD PRODUCED INTERNAL DISSENSIONS AND CHECKED
ASSIMILATION OF HOSTILE RACES ; METHOD OF TURKISH
CONQUEST AND ITS FATAL CONSEQUENCES ; RAVAGES OF
BLACK DEATH ; POPULATION OF CAPITAL IN 1453 ; ITS
COMMERCE ; RELATIONS OF PEOPLE WITH GOVERNMENT ;
RESEMBLANCE TO RUSSIA ; DIFFICULTY OF OBTAINING
IDEA OF DOMESTIC LIFE.

As the later Roman empire is now drawing to a close, it
is worth while endeavouring to realise what were the immediate causes of its weakness, and what was its actual
condition immediately preceding the final siege.

The empire to which Constantine Dragases succeeded
on the death of his brother John was over the city and a
strip of land behind it which may be estimated roughly at about
a hundred miles in length from its walls towards the north
and west.   To this and about half of the Peloponnesus still
held by his brother had the realm of Theodosius been
reduced.

How far
was popu-
lation de-
moralised ?

It has often been stated that the fall of the Empire was
due to, or at least largely contributed to by, the demoralisation
of the Court, the nobles, and the citizens.   This view had its
origin largely, though not exclusively, in the religious
animosity of Latin Churchmen.   The Court has been
described as given over to gorgeous displays, to meaningless
ceremonies, to luxury, and to effeminacy ; the nobles as
partakers in such displays and themselves effeminate ; the

citizens as idle, delighting in spectacular shows, and asking only to be amused. I know of no evidence which supports any such conclusion and believe that, on the contrary, such evidence as exists is against it. The population of the city, nobles and people alike, were religious—given over to superstition, according to our modern view—but they were not luxurious or mere pleasure-seekers. Their superstition corresponded with that of their fellow Christians in the West. 'I believe,' says La Brocquière, who visited Constantinople in 1433, ' that God has spared the city more for the holy relics it contains than anything else.' [1] But the same writer adds the qualification that ' the Greeks have not the like devotion that we have for relics.' Nor is this religious or superstitious spirit the necessary companion of either luxury or effeminacy. The effeminacy and the luxury associated with Constantinople, in so far as they existed, belong to the period before the Latin conquest. When any displays are recorded after the recapture of the city—as, for example, at coronations—they are merely the traditional ceremonies which survived as such observances do in the coronation of our own sovereigns or at great historical courts like the Austrian and papal. The trials and sufferings, the long struggles against external and internal enemies which had gone on for nearly two centuries, had divested nobles and people alike of any love for idle ceremonies or mere diversions. The miracle plays which the people crowded to see in Hagia Sophia do not show that they had degenerated. The writer just quoted saw a representation of the three youths cast by Nebuchadnezzar into the burning fiery furnace,[2] which, while it may have served to increase the congregation's trust in God, can hardly be regarded as a frivolous amusement.

The hippodrome was no longer used by the people for the shows which had pleased their ancestors at an early period. La Brocquière, indeed, records that he saw the emperor's brother and a score of nobles amusing themselves on horseback within its walls, but they were training them-

---

[1] La Brocquière, p. 341. [2] *Ibid.* p. 340.

selves for war by practising archery, and endeavouring to make themselves masters in it.[1] He records also that he was present at a tournament which the emperor and empress witnessed. Neither in his account nor in that of any contemporary with which I am acquainted is there anything to show that the diminished population of the city were other than an industrious and sober people, to whom a question of religious dogma was of greater interest than any other, except perhaps those relating to the progress of their great enemy.

But though the demoralisation of the Court and people in the usual sense of the term ought not to be counted among the reasons for the decay of the empire, the attitude of mind in the Court, in the Church, and among the masses is indicative of decay. In any country, but especially in one under absolute monarchy, the poorer classes of the people know and care little about politics. Among them there was under the empire a general indifference as to what was likely to happen. They were heavily taxed, were called upon to send their sons to the wars, and if there were to be a change of masters, it did not much matter. Their attitude was, indeed, not unlike that which exists to-day among the poorer Turks. A change of rulers would be welcomed by many, perhaps by most, though at the last moment religious sentiment might and probably would come in to rouse opposition. Present evils are so burdensome that the hope of a change of rulers is constantly expressed.

There was also among the subjects of the empire, as among those of the sultan, an underlying sentiment that the inevitable was happening. Ἀνάγκη ἦν was the belief among the Greeks almost as firmly as the Turks of to-day hold that it is their *kismet* to be driven out of Europe.

The poorer classes may be disregarded when we are considering the public opinion of the empire. Such opinions as existed among them were a reflection of those of the nobles, and especially of the Churchmen. Both clergy and nobles were intensely conservative, and had become by habit

[1] La Brocquière, p. 339.

averse to any change. The energy had gone out of the Church. There was no fervour of belief. The missionary spirit was absolutely extinct. No instances are recorded of abandonment of self-interest for the common good. The great body of idle monks contrast unfavourably with those of the West of the same period. The patriotism of the priest Hilarion and his small following had not been imitated. A dead level of contented mediocrity characterised the clergy. An enthusiasm for Christianity, if it could not have saved the empire, might at least have prolonged its existence. But enthusiasm was dead. It would be a relief to read of wild enthusiasts leading crowds into hopelessly impracticable schemes, for such things would at least indicate life. Nothing of the kind exists. The life of the Church was suspended, and it could only arouse itself to resist change. Even in the greatest religious question of the two centuries preceding 1453, that of the Union of the Churches, the Orthodox Church had to be stimulated into action by the emperors and nobles.

The nobles themselves were, however, hardly less conservative than the Churchmen. A lack of energy, an absence of vital force, is the distinguishing characteristic of both. Until the Latin conquest, their conservatism was that of a civilised and wealthy class, who had enjoyed for centuries the advantages of peace and of security. In the two centuries after the recovery of the city the nobles had regained much of their old influence, and up to the final conquest felt, in Constantinople, much of the same security as before and the contentment of acquired or inherited wealth. Commerce had largely passed into the hands of the Genoese and Venetians, but the loss hardly affected the nobles. To all appearance they remained as contented as ever. Even in presence of the enemy which had constantly been lessening their incomes and drawing an iron circle around the empire, they appear to have been hardly conscious of the life and death character of the struggle.

So long as the emperor and nobles could employ their own peasantry or could hire auxiliaries, they had resisted the

Turks with a certain amount of success. From Dalmatia to Matapan, from Durazzo to the capital, as well as in Asia Minor, the progress of the enemy had been contested. The Greek armies were destroyed by overwhelming numbers rather than defeated by superior courage. When the capital was cut off from its supply of soldiers from the provinces, it was in grievous straits, and to this condition it had come on the accession of the last Constantine.

Priests and nobles appear to have gradually drifted into the belief that resistance was hopeless. Their acquiescence in what they believed to be the inevitable suggests the mediocrity of their leaders. Their merits and faults were alike negative. They were not given over to vice and profligacy ; they were not cruel tyrants ; they were not wanting in courage ; but they were without ability or energy, incapable of initiating or executing any successful plan of campaign against the enemy or of making arrangements for securing efficient foreign aid.

It is, of course, easy to suggest after the event that the empire might have been saved, but it is difficult to believe that among the governing class there was not a lack of vitality which contributed to its fall. Looking across the centuries, we may, perhaps, conclude that the empire followed the natural course of evolution under despotic rule : struggle for existence, success, wealth, contentment to the point of stagnation, a general slackness and loss of energy and a reluctance to struggle of any kind. But whether such conclusion be justified or not, it cannot be doubted that weariness of strife and general enervation characterised all classes of society. In remembering this, it may be said that the morale of the empire was destroyed and its population demoralised.[1]

Three causes mainly contributed to the diminution and ultimate downfall of the empire : first, the establishmen

---

[1] Perhaps it could be contended successfully that the relaxing climate of Constantinople had much to do with the enervation of its population, and that every race which has possessed the city has suffered from the same cause.

of the Latin empire, with which must be associated (*a*) the internal dissensions among the Greeks themselves, and (*b*) the increased difficulty in assimilating the races occupying the Balkan peninsula ; second, the attacks, literally from every side, by hordes of Turkish invaders, who usually, beginning by raids upon their cattle, ended by expelling or exterminating the conquered people and taking possession of their lands ; and, third, the depopulation of the Balkan peninsula and of the cities in Asia Minor held by the empire caused by Black Death or Plague.

Causes of decay of empire.

The history of the empire subsequent to the Latin occupation bears evidence of the weakness which that occupation had caused. The whole framework of government administration had been broken up. The imperial system was in ruins. The ancient forms of administrative organisation were restored, but there never existed sufficient strength in the capital to put new life into them, and the old traditional spirit of municipal life and to a certain limited extent of self-government had during two generations of hostile rule and the subsequent series of attempts at the restoration of Latin rule been forgotten. The empire was, indeed, kept together by obedience to law, but it was rather a traditional obedience than one due to a strong administration. When a man defied law it was public opinion which he had to face rather than dread of the emperor. The Latin conquest and the growth of neighbouring states consequent upon such conquest made it impossible for the emperors ever to obtain a strong and sufficient hold over the territories which they recaptured.

Latin conquest.

The divisions among the Greeks themselves, especially those regarding the occupancy of the throne, led to civil wars and gave the Turks opportunities of entering the country and occupying it. They were due in the first place to the change in the succession when Michael the Eighth seized the imperial throne, and were therefore also directly caused or contributed to by the Latin conquest. Though the rules of succession had never been so strictly observed as in the West, his usurpation weakened the office of emperor and

Internal divisions.

manifestly increased the power—not of a regularly constituted body like our House of Lords, or the American
Senate, but—of an irresponsible body of nobles. In the next
place, the dissensions may be attributed to the existing and
traditional form of government.

It is a commonplace to say that uncontrolled autocracy
is the best government if a succession of able men can be
assured. The difficulty is that, if the ordinary rules of
succession are observed, the successor of a Justinian or a
Julius Caesar may be a fool. In Constantinople effective
control over the appointment of an emperor was wanting,
The senate or council of an absolute ruler, be he called emperor
or sultan, is usually weak in proportion to the strength of
the ruler, and if, in the customary order of succession, the
heir to the throne is unsuited to the office, the ring of
creatures, by whatever name it is called, which his predecessor
has gathered round him is pretty sure to support the heir,
irrespective of his merit or ability. Others acquiesce for the
sake of peace, or are drawn to support a pretender. The
nobles usually gained strength during the reign of a weak
prince, and in the support they gave to rival claimants the
empire bled.

Democratic government in the modern sense of the term
had not yet been born. Sir Henry Maine claims that the
modern doctrines of popular government based on democracy
are essentially of late English origin. It is certain that
nothing like them had existed in the Roman empire, either
in the East or West. Any traditions of self-government
which the Greeks had retained—a form of self-government
which was never upon modern democratic lines—had been
entirely overshadowed, not merely by the autocratic govern
ment of the emperors, but by that of the Church. Th
government was that of an absolute sovereign moderated b
irresponsible nobles.

Without, however, seeking further to discover the reason
for the internal divisions and the consequent civil war
their existence and baneful effects are the most manifes

though not the most important, of the evils which weakened the Empire.

The second fact associated with the mischief caused by the Latin conquest, which contributed to the decay of the empire, is that such conquest prevented the assimilation of the various peoples occupying the Balkan peninsula. Even at the best period of the empire that population had always been strangely diversified. Albanians and Slavs had been there from very early times, side by side with Greeks and the race known as Wallachs, each of the four races having a distinct language. *Divisions of race in Balkan peninsula.*

The influence of good administration and the strong hand of the central power kept these races in order. They had the usual tendency to hostility one towards the other, but until the Latin conquest good government and the Greek language, that of the Church and administration, were always a force tending to break down the boundaries between them and to incorporate isolated sections in the Greek-speaking community. But at all times their mutual jealousies constituted, as indeed they do now, the most difficult factor in the problem of the government of the Balkan peninsula.[1]

This difficulty had been enormously increased by the Latin conquest. The populations were harassed everywhere by native rebellions and by foreign invaders : Greek pretenders to the empire who refused to recognise the crusading kings : crusading knights who settled in Greece after the expulsion of Baldwin : adventurous soldiers of fortune from Italy : freebooters from the Catalan Grand Company : Venetians and Turks : and lastly by dissensions between the emperors themselves, the most hurtful of which were between Cantacuzenus and John.

---

[1] Mr. D. G. Hogarth in *The Nearer East* (London, 1902), on pp. 280-1, speaks of the country as a ' Debateable Land distracted internally by a ceaseless war of influences, and only too anxious to lean in one part or another on external aid.' . . . 'Macedonia has been torn this way and that for half a century.' The whole chapter on ' World Relation ' is valuable and suggestive. The same diversity of interests and hostility arising from differences in race and religion is well brought out in the best recent book on *Turkey in Europe*, by Odysseus.

The various invaders found their task easier from the
hostility which existed between the various groups. Racial
animosity was fostered by inducements held out by the newcomers to one group to join them in attacking another.
These troubles destroyed the work of assimilation which
had been going on for centuries. Communities now of
Greeks, now of Slavs, were driven from the localities they had
occupied for long periods, and the constant movement left
the Balkan peninsula with its various races intermingled in
strange confusion. To adopt chemical nomenclature, hundreds
of villages were mechanically mixed with those of other
races but never chemically combined. There were Slav
villages in the neighbourhood of Athens itself, Albanians in
Macedonia: Greeks, Serbians, and Bulgarians largely replaced
the Latin race of that province, which in the times of the
Crusades was known as Wallachia Proper. Language and
race had taken the place of subjection to the empire as a
bond of union, and as the Turks gradually pressed forward
their advances into the interior, literally from every side, they
found the conquest of these isolated and generally hostil
communities greatly facilitated by the disunion existing
among them.

Throughout Macedonia, Thessaly, Epirus, and Greece th
boundaries were changed oftener even than allegiance, an
though the Greek element predominated in the south an
along the coast as far as Salonica and around the coasts c
the Aegean and the Marmora, other communities were inter
spersed among them in great numbers.

The subjugation of the Macedonian Serbs and the Sout
Bulgarians can be roughly stated as having been accomplishe
at the battle on the Maritza. The defeat of the Serbian
and Bulgarians was a harder task. But Serbia and Bulgar
were the two portions of the Balkan peninsula where th
people were almost all of the same race and could organi
themselves for defence. No such organisation was possib
south of their territory.

System of
Turkish.
conquests.   The second cause which had contributed to the dimin
tion of the empire and of its population was the system

Turkish conquests. Large numbers of the Christian population were killed ; larger numbers were driven away to wander houseless and homeless and either to die of starvation or find their way into the towns.

Conquest of a territory or capture of a city, forcible expulsion of the inhabitants or massacre of most of them and occupation of the captured places followed each other with wearisome regularity. The military occupation was that of nomads who replaced agriculturists. Everywhere the cattle of the Christians were raided. Arable lands became the wasteful sheep-walks of nomad Turks.[1]

Lastly, the depopulation caused by the terrible diseases which visited Europe in the century preceding the Moslem conquest aided greatly in destroying the empire. The prevalence of Black Death or Plague killed in the Balkan peninsula and especially in the towns hundreds of thousands and possibly millions of the population. In 1347 this scourge, probably the most deadly form of epidemic that has ever afflicted humanity, made its appearance in Eastern Europe. The cities of the empire contained large populations crowded together, and their normal population was increased by many fugitives. These crowded cities, with their defective sanitary arrangements and poverty-stricken inhabitants, offered a favourable soil for a rich harvest of death. The disease had followed the coasts from the Black Sea, where, says Cantacuzenus, it had carried off nearly all the inhabitants. At Constantinople it raged during two years, one of its first victims being the eldest son of Cantacuzenus himself.[2] Rich as well as poor succumbed to it. What proportion of the inhabitants of the city died it is impossible to say, but, judging by what is known of its effect elsewhere, we should probably not be wrong in suggesting that half the people perished. But its ravages were not conned to the towns, and from one end of the Balkan peninsula

Marginal note: Black Death.

[1] The Turkish system of occupying conquered territories by military colonies and driving away the original inhabitants excited great opposition among the Serbians and led, says Von Ranke, to the struggle which ended in 1389 on the plains of Cossovo. (*History of Serbia*, Bohn's edition, p. 16.)

[2] Cantacuzenus, iv. 8.

to the other it swept the country in repeated visitations and probably carried off nearly the same proportion of inhabitants.[1] Cantacuzenus, in a vivid description of the disease, adds that the saddest feature about it was the feeling of hopelessness and despair which it left behind.

The first visitation of the disease continued during two years in the capital. In 1348 it spread throughout the empire. We have seen that in 1352 the victorious Venetian and Spanish fleets dared not venture to attack Galata for fear that their crews would be attacked by the malady. It raged in Asia Minor as fiercely as in Europe. Trebizond was ruined. The Turks themselves suffered severely. Between its entrance into Europe and 1364 the Morea had three visitations, and what remained of the Greek population became panic-stricken. Further north, at Yanina its ravages were equally terrible. In 1368 so many men died that Thomas, governor of the city, forced their widows to marry Serbians whom he had induced or compelled to enter the city for that purpose. A further outbreak seven years later took place in the same city, and among its victims was Thomas's own daughter. During the same period Arta, which adjoins the ancient Cyzicus, suffered severely. It is useless for our purpose to inquire whether Black Death and Plague were identical, but one or the other continued to depopulate town and country. We have seen it at Ferrara in 1438, but in the interval since it first made its appearance it had visited the capital on seven different occasions, the latest being in 1431 when the whole country from Constantinople to Cape Matapan suffered severely.[2]

---

[1] The tradition of its destructiveness even in England, which it reached in 1348, and the panic-struck words of the Statutes which followed it, have, says J. R. Green, ' been more than justified by modern researches. Of the three or four millions who then formed the population of England more than half were swept away by its repeated visitations' (Green's *Short History of the English People*), p. 241.

[2] According to one contemporary writer, Murad had to relinquish the siege of Constantinople in 1422 on account of the appearance of plague in his army (*Historia Epirotica*). Mahomet the Second, however, according to Critobulus, attributed the necessity of raising the siege to hostility within his own family, doubtless alluding to the rising already mentioned in Asia Minor. He says, in

It may safely be assumed that the Turks, who lived in the open air, and in the country rather than in towns, suffered less than the Christians. Though they are reported to have lost severely, the process of depopulation scarcely told against them. The places of those who died were taken by the ever-crowding press of immigrants flocking westward. The successors of the Greeks who perished were not Christians but Turks. In other words, while the Christians died out of the land, there were always at hand Turkish nomads to take their place.

It is when contemplating the devastation produced by successive attacks of disease, one of which was sufficient to kill half the population of England, when remembering the weakening of the empire by the Latin occupation and the subsequent attempts to recapture the city, and when recognising that the empire was the bulwark against a great westward movement of the central Asiatic races which forced forward the Turk to find new pastures in Christian lands, that we can understand how the diminution of the Empire and of its population and its ultimate downfall came to be inevitable.

Those who have travelled most in the Balkan peninsula and in Asia Minor recognise most completely how densely populated and flourishing these countries once were, and how completely they have become a desolation. Everywhere the traveller is even now surprised at the sight of deserted and fertile plains and of ruined cities, of some of which the very names have been forgotten. From Baalbek to Nicomedia the ancient roads pass through or near places whose names recall populous and civilised towns which are but the ghastly shadows of their former prosperity. Ephesus, which when visited by Sir John Maundeville in 1322, after it had been captured by the Turks, was still ' a fair city,' is now absolutely deserted. Nicaea, the city which has given its name to the Creed of Christendom, was also at

Desolation on accession of last empire and now.

substance, 'The city was almost in the hands of my father, and he would certainly have taken it by assault, if those of his own family in whom he had confidence had not worked secretly against him.' Crit. xxv.

the time of the Turkish occupation populous and flourishing. It now contains a hundred miserable houses within its still standing walls. Hierapolis and Laodicea are heaps of uninhabited ruins. A scholarly English traveller remarks that his search has been in vain for the sites of many cities once well known, and that he met ruins of many cities which he was unable to identify.[1] The same story of depopulation and of destruction was and is told by the condition of the Balkan peninsula. The observant traveller La Brocquière, who made his journey through Asia Minor to Constantinople and thence to Budapest, noted that desolation was everywhere. In the district between the capital and Adrianople he adds that ' the country is completely ruined, has but poor villages, and, though good and well watered, is thinly peopled.' He found Chorlou ' destroyed by the Turks.' He visited Trajanopolis and describes it as once ' very large, but now nothing is seen but ruins with a few inhabitants.' He found Vyra, to whose church three hundred canons had been formerly attached, a poor place with the choir of the church only remaining and used as a Turkish mosque.[2] All contemporaries bear witness to the depopulation and ruin of the country. From pestilence and the results of the Latin conquest it might have recovered, but when to these disasters was added that of conquest by successive hordes of barbarians whose work was always destructive, its ruin was complete.

Population of Constantinople on accession of Constantine.

It is impossible to arrive at an accurate estimate of the population of the city on the accession of the last Constantine. La Brocquière, in 1433, describes Constantinople as formed of separate parts and containing open spaces of a greater extent than those built on.[3] This is one of many intimations that the population had largely decreased.[4] Some of the nobles as well as the common

---

[1] *Travels and Researches in Asia Minor,* by Sir Charles Fellows. Professor Ramsay has also the same story to tell, though his own success in identifying lost cities has been exceptionally great.

[2] La Brocquière, 340-7. [3] *Ibid.* 337.

[4] Compare this with Villehardouin's statement that in 1204 Constantinople had ten times as many people as there were in Paris.

people had left the city as soon as they saw that a siege was probable.[1] To make an estimate we must anticipate our narrative of the siege. Critobulus makes Mahomet appeal to the knowledge of his hearers in proposing to besiege the city when he states that the greater number of the inhabitants have abandoned it ; that it is now only a city in name and contains tilled lands, trees, vineyards, and enclosures as well as ruined and destroyed houses, as they have all seen for themselves. As his hearers could see as well as he whether this statement was correct, there can be little doubt of its accuracy. He further declared that there were few men in the city and that these for the most part were without arms and unused to fighting, and that he had learned from deserters that there were only two or three men to defend each tower, so that each man had to guard three or four crenellations. Tetaldi states that there were in the city from twenty-five thousand to thirty thousand men [2] and six to seven thousand combatants and not more.[3] The actual census taken at the request of the emperor and recorded by Phrantzes gives under five thousand fighting men, exclusive of foreigners. Assuming the statement of the French soldier and eye-witness Tetaldi to be substantially correct, there would apparently be something like eighteen thousand monks and old men incapable of bearing arms. The only other indications which assist in forming an estimate of the population are furnished by the number of prisoners. These are probably exaggerated. Archbishop Leonard estimates them at above sixty thousand. Critobulus gives the number of slaves of all kinds, men, women, and children, as fifty thousand citizens and five hundred soldiers, estimating that during the siege and capture four thousand were killed.[4] Probably all captives are included as having been reduced

---

[1] Phrantzes, 241.

[2] Another version says from 30,000 to 36,000 men.

[3] P. 23. The 'not more' is from the edition of Dethier, p. 896. The version published in the *Chronique de Charles VII* gives 25,000 to 30,000 armed men. Dethier's omits 'armed.'

[4] The Superior of the Franciscans says that 3,000 were killed on May 29 (Dethier's *Documents relating to the Siege*, p. 940).

to slavery. The complete desolation of the city and the strenuous efforts made by the sultan to repeople it after the capture raise a strong presumption in favour of the existence of a comparatively small population at the time of the siege. Gibbon judged that 'in her last decay Constantinople was still peopled with more than a hundred thousand inhabitants,' forming his estimate mainly upon the declaration of the archbishop as to prisoners. I am myself disposed to think that this number is rather over- than under-estimated. Taking the prisoners to be fifty thousand, and allowing for the escape of ten thousand persons and another ten thousand for old men and women who were not worth reducing to slavery, probably eighty thousand would be about right.

Within the narrow limits of what had been possible, the citizens over whom the new emperor was called to rule had done their duty to the city itself. They had kept fourteen miles of walls the most formidable in Europe in good repair and they had preserved the wonderful aqueducts, the cisterns, the great baths and churches.

Its commerce. Commerce still continued to be the principal support of the inhabitants. This was now largely shared by the Genoese in Galata and by the Venetians who occupied a quarter in Constantinople itself. The familiarity of the Italian colonists with Western lands and their superiority in shipping, in which indeed at this time they led the world, enabled them to achieve a success in what was then long-voyage travelling which was denied to the Greeks ; but the latter collected merchandise from the Black Sea ports and from the Azof which was either sold to the Frank merchants in Constantinople or transhipped on board their vessels.

Emperor and nobles. It is difficult to realise what were the relations between the government and the governed during the two centuries before the last catastrophe. The empire was the continuator of the autocratic—or rather the aristocratic—form of government which had been derived from the elder Rome. Emperor and nobles governed the country. The nobles formed the senate. Like our own Privy Council, it met rarely and had ill-defined functions, but upon occasions of emergency it had to be consulted.   Its co-operation gave to any measures edicted by the emperor an important sanction. When the decision of the senate was acquiesced in by or coincided with that of the Patriarch and his ecclesiastical council, the emperor may be said to have possessed all the approval that could be derived from public opinion.

Though the senate met rarely, its support was never altogether dispensed with.   The emperors did not claim to reign by divine right, nor was any such pretext put forward on their behalf.   The succession passed in the usual manner and the emperor reigned with almost autocratic powers so long as the nobles and the patriarch and ecclesiastics were content.   In the period with which we are concerned the nobles sometimes preferred to associate a younger man with the occupant of the throne.   Such association was usually, though not always, in accordance with the desire of the reigning emperor, and had the conspicuous advantage of allowing the elder to train his younger associate in state-craft.   In some cases, as in those of young Andronicus and of John during the reign of his father, Manuel, it was imposed upon the emperor in order to bring about a change of policy.

No form of popular representation existed.   The mass of the people had nothing to do with the laws except to obey them.   So long as their lives and their property were protected and the laws fairly administered they were content.

So far as can be judged from the silence as well as from the writings of the Byzantine writers, there was little fault to find with the administration of law.   When cases of the miscarriage of justice are mentioned they are generally brought forward to show the scandal they had produced or in some other connection which suggests that such cases were exceptional.   It was not only that the keen subtlety of a long succession of Greek-speaking lawyers had preserved the traditions of their great ancestors of the time of Justinian and had guarded law in admirable forms, but the still better traditions of an honest administration of law had continued, and this with the result—simple as it may

*Adminis-
tration of
law.*

appear to Western readers; strange as it would have sounded to a Turkish subject at any time since the capture of Constantinople—that people believed that the decisions of the law courts were fairly given.

Interest in religious questions.

The inhabitants of the capital retained until the last days of its history as a Christian city their intense interest in religious questions. It is of less importance to qualify such interest as superstitious or fanatical than to try to understand it. That theological questions possessed a dominating influence over the people of Constantinople is one of the facts of history, and represents an important element in the education of the modern Western world.

An able modern writer says with justice that ' religious sentiment was down to the fall of the empire as deep as it was powerful. It took the place of everything else.' [1] Probably the exclusion of the great bulk of the inhabitants from all participation in government and the consequent want of general interest in political questions or those regarding social legislation helped to concentrate attention upon those relating to religion. The Greek intellect—and, though there were large sections of the population which were not Greek, the Greek element as well as the Greek language gave its tone to all the rest—was essentially active and philosophical. The investigation of theological questions was not conducted lightly. The same spirit which made scholars of Constantinople espouse the study of Plato as they had done for two centuries before 1453—a study which caused Pletho, on his visit with John at the Council of Florence, to be regarded as an authority to be eagerly sought after by those awakening to the new learning in Italy—had been applied to many questions of philosophy and theology. The examination of such questions was more speculative, thorough, and scientific than in the West. [2]

[1] Bikelas, *La Grèce Byzantine et Moderne*, p. 153. His essays express this opinion in many other places.

[2] ' Les schismes sont chez eux [the Greeks] la conséquence du même esprit de tous les temps; c'est la théologie soumise au contrôle de l'intelligence pure, le dogme éprouvé par le mécanisme de leur logique brillante et rapide. Ces

While it is true that Constantinople had for centuries produced few ideas and little of original value in literature, it had rendered great service to humanity by preserving the Greek classics. Its methods of thought, its civilisation as well as its literature, were on the model of classical antiquity, but these were all modified by Christianity. Part of the mission of the empire had been to save during upwards of a thousand years, amid the irruptions of Goths, Huns and Vandals, Persians and Arabs, Slavs and Turks, the traditions and the literary works of Greece. It had done this part of its work well. Amid the obscurity of the Middle Ages in the West, Constantinople had always possessed writers who threw light on the history of the empire in the East. No European people, remarks a recent writer, possesses an historical literature as rich as do the Greeks. From Herodotus to Chalcondylas the chain is not broken.[1] The Greek historians of the period with which the present work is concerned, Pachymer, Cantacuzenus, Gregoras, Ducas, Critobulus, and Phrantzes are in literary merit far superior to the contemporary chroniclers of the West. Though their works are written in a style which aims at reproducing classical Greek and imitating classical models, they were not intended merely for Churchmen. Nor was Constantinople rich only in historians.

Though intellectual life was never wanting in the city, many of whose people possessed the quick, ingenious, and piercing intellect of the Greek race, the reader of the later historians feels that the civilisation amid which they lived was not that of modern times. It is difficult to realise what it was like. It has often been compared with that of Russia, and writers of reputation have spoken of that empire as preserving the

Civilisation not modern.

discussions théologiques, appliquées uniquement à la recherche de l'essence divine, à l'explication du fait divin, du mystère, prennent chez eux un caractère exclusivement scientifique.' Montreuil, *Histoire du droit byzantin*, i. 418.

[1] Krumbacher, *Geschichte der Byzantinischen Litteratur*, p. 219, says : ' Kein Volk, die Chinesen vielleicht ausgenommen, besitzt eine so reiche historische Litteratur wie die Griechen. In ununterbrochener Reihenfolge geht die Überlieferung von Herodot bis auf Laonikos Chalkondylas. Die Griechen und Byzantiner haben die Chronik des Ostens über zwei Jahrtausende mit gewissenhafter Treue fortgeführt.'

succession of the political and religious systems of Byzantium as well as of its mission to the non-civilised nations of Asia.[1] Allowing for the difference between the Greek and the Slav intellect, the analogy in a general sense holds fairly good, and is especially noticeable in two points, the religious spirit of both peoples and their contented exclusion from all active participation in the government.

It is, however, difficult to determine how far the conditions of existence in the first half of the fifteenth century among the citizens of the capital resembled those found in Russia. The difficulty arises, not merely from distance of time, but from the fact that in the empire manners, usages, the conception of life, and the influence of religion were neither Western nor modern. The people were governed much as Russia is governed now : but there were important differences due to race, tradition, and environment. Nevertheless, the condition of the empire reminds one of the Russia of fifty years ago. There were the same great distances between the capital and the provinces and the same difficulty of communication. News travelled slowly ; public opinion hardly existed. There were in the country a mass of ignorant peasants tilling the ground and caring little for anything else, peasants who were in a condition of serfdom, thinking of the emperor as a demi-god and rendering unquestioning obedience to his representatives ; thinking of the Church as a divine institution entrusted with miraculous powers to confer a life after death, but far too ignorant to trouble themselves about heresies or dogmas. Among these peasants probably only the priests and monks were able to read, although among a people naturally intelligent this would not necessarily imply a want of interest in what was going on around them. The analogy to Russia must not be pushed too far. Religion and language, a common form of Christianity and the traditional duty of submission to the rule of Constantinople were the bonds which held the empire together, but the Greek tendency to individualism

[1] Rambaud, *L'empire de Grèce*, p. 367. Bikelas and Finlay make the same comparison.

and the political development of the empire which destroyed the belief that allegiance was necessarily due to the ruler in the capital had been for two centuries a disintegrating element which prevented the growth of the apathy on political and social questions, and the deadly contentment which has been a characteristic of the great Slavic race.

In the cities there was intellectual life: Salonica, Nicaea, Smyrna, and other centres of population had in times past vied with the capital in general culture and still retained something of their attachment to it. To the last hour of the empire there was, as we have seen, general and absorbing interest in the question of the Union of the Churches. But interest in other questions which had once kept religious thought from stagnation had largely died out. The more pressing questions of life interested the citizens. Moreover, the people believed that all questions of Christian belief had been settled. The Creed was final and had no more need of revision than the style of the Parthenon. The practices adopted from Paganism had become so generally accepted as to pass without dispute. Iconoclasts and Paulicians can hardly be said to have left any representatives. A Pagan Christianity with a Pantheism accepting holy springs, miraculous pictures, miracle-working relics, had become the accepted form of faith, a form which we of the twentieth century find it as difficult to understand as the earlier belief which had regarded the emperor as divinity.

One of the difficulties of the student of political and social history of the thirteenth and two following centuries is that of being unable to get glimpses of personal characteristics or domestic life. The men who figure in contemporary writings are too often little better than dummies who move and turn, but do not suggest vitality. An historical novel of the period written upon the lines of Scott or Dumas, of Kingsley or Charles Reade, or better still, anything corresponding to Chaucer's 'Canterbury Tales,' would be of priceless value in giving indications not merely of what was the environment of a Constantinopolitan but of the characteristics of an individual of the period. The writers on whom we have to depend are mostly Churchmen, who describe the persons of whom they write as if they felt bound to make them correspond with one of half a dozen approved models.

The absence of better indications may be accounted for. The subjects of the empire during the century and a half preceding 1453 lived in the midst of alarms. Its boundaries had been constantly changing and continually narrowing. Disaster followed disaster; usurpations, dynastic struggles, inroads of Genoese and Venetians; struggles with them and between them; ever encroaching Turks, battles, triumphs, defeats, hopes of final success, but territory still decreasing; hope of aid from the West or from Tamerlane; illusions all: finally the last siege and extinction. The writers in the midst of such times thought they had more important matter to deal with than the depiction of scenes of domestic character or delineations of prominent persons.

CHAPTER IX

ACCESSION OF CONSTANTINE DRAGASES; PATRIARCH GRE-
GORY DEPOSED; RENEWED ATTEMPT TO OBTAIN AID
FROM THE WEST; EMPEROR MEETS WITH LITTLE
SUCCESS; ARRIVAL OF CARDINAL ISIDORE; RECONCILIA-
TION SERVICE DECEMBER 12, 1452, IN HAGIA SOPHIA;
DISSENSIONS REGARDING IT.

THE emperor John left no son, and the succession had therefore to pass to one of his three brothers, Constantine,
Demetrius, and Thomas. Constantine, the eldest, was at the
time of the emperor's death at Sparta, but Demetrius claimed
that as his elder brother was not born in the purple, while
he had inherited that honour, the crown ought to be placed
on his head. The dowager empress, the widow of Manuel,
the clergy, senate, the troops and people generally, declared
in favour of Constantine.[1]

While the matter was still under debate, Thomas, who had
learned at Gallipoli the death of his brother, arrived in the
capital and immediately supported the nomination of
Constantine. An embassy was sent to the Morea and on
January 6, 1449, placed the crown on the head of Constantine Dragases, the last Christian emperor of Constantinople.[2]

On March 12, he arrived in the capital and his brother
Thomas, who had been appointed despot, went after some

[1] Constantine is usually called the Eleventh. Gibbon, however, counts the
son of Romanus the First as Constantine the Eighth, and thus makes the last
Emperor Constantine the Twelfth. He is often spoken of as Constantine
Dragases, because his mother, Irene, belonged to a family of that name. She
was a South Serbian princess.

[2] Phrantzes, p. 205, represents Constantine as crowned. Apparently this
ceremony was not regarded as a definite coronation, and hence Ducas calls
John the last Emperor.

days to the Morea. There he was shortly afterwards joined by Demetrius who had withdrawn his opposition and accepted the situation.

The party opposed to the Union had now become sufficiently strong to call together a Synod, which met in the autumn of 1450. The three patriarchs of the East were present, and under their guidance the assembly declared the patriarch Gregory to be an enemy of the Orthodox Church and deposed him. In his stead they appointed Athanasius.

During the interval between the death of John and that of Murad, on February 3, 1451, the Christian cause looked more hopeful. Scanderbeg had maintained himself successfully in the field, Murad had been compelled a second time to raise the siege of Croya. In four separate battles the Turkish armies had been defeated. In the siege of Sventigrad they lost thirty thousand men, and, though the brave Albanian failed in capturing the city and had to raise the siege, his campaign was a triumph.

It seems to have been generally recognised that young Mahomet, the successor of Murad, had even before his accession determined to lay siege to the city. The emperor, therefore, once more renewed the efforts of his predecessors to obtain foreign aid. Once more the insuperable obstacle to the Union of the Churches, the rigid refusal of clergy and people, came to the fore. Constantine, like his predecessors, tried and failed to coerce the Church. Athanasius, the new patriarch, declared himself ready to maintain the Orthodox faith and declined to recognise the acts of the Council of Florence. When Constantine asked aid from Rome, he found that the deposed Gregory had taken refuge there, and while the patriotism of the latter led him to seek the pontiff's help against the Turks, his Catholicism compelled the pope to espouse his cause. Nicholas the Fifth summoned the emperor, as the price of his support, to replace Gregory and to take the measures necessary for formally completing the Union agreed to at Florence. Constantine was willing to do what he could, but knew the temper of his subjects. He knew himself to be distrusted by them for

what they regarded as his Romanising tendencies. When
Mahomet was at Magnesia, where the news of the death of
his father reached him, the Christians around regarded the
new emperor unfavourably on account of his predilection for
the Union, and spoke of him as a usurper. Constantine, who
was on the look out for a wife [1] and had employed Phrantzes
on various expeditions to find one, had been compelled, on
account of the opposition of his subjects to any further
relationship with the Latins, to abandon his intention of
marrying the daughter of Foscari, the doge of Venice. He
had thus given offence to a powerful state, and, though he
had offered all sorts of concessions, Venice would only promise
to send ten galleys to the help of the city.

The emperor temporised. He begged the pope to send
ships and also learned and capable ecclesiastics who could
aid him to make the Union acceptable to the clergy. In
reply Nicholas promised to send a fleet, although he was
powerless to persuade other Christian princes to follow his
example. In answer to his second request he deputed
Cardinal Isidore, Metropolitan of Russia, whom we have
seen at the Council of Florence, to be his legate.

In November 1452, a great Genoese ship with the
cardinal accompanied by Leonard, archbishop of Chios,
arrived at the city and was received by the emperor with
very honour. Isidore at once pressed for a formal recognition of Union. The emperor and some of the nobles
assented, but the majority of the priests, monks, and nuns
refused. Ducas says that no nun consented and that the
emperor only pretended to do so. It is not unlikely that he is
right. Mahomet had declared war. Preparations for the siege
of Constantinople were already being made, and not only the
emperor but many priests, deacons, and laymen of high rank
were ready to accept everything that Isidore proposed, provided only that the city could obtain additional defenders.
It was in this spirit that they consented to be present on
December 12, 1452, in the Great Church in order to celebrate

[1] Constantine's wife, Catherine Catalusio, died in 1442, after being married
but ten months.

the Union and by so doing obtain aid in their time of mortal anguish.[1] The service was destined to be memorable. The party which would not accept the Union took offence at the reconciliation service. While the emperor and a host of dignitaries were present in Hagia Sophia a crowd went to the monk Gennadius, better known as George Scholarius, and asked what they should do.

The man whom they went to consult was not a mere monk who had won the popular ear. He was a scholar with a European reputation, the most distinguished advocate in the long contest between the rival systems of Aristotle and Plato which marks the transition from mediaeval to modern thought. He was the last of the great polemical writers of the Orthodox Church whose works were studied in the West as well as in the East. His great rival in the controversy was Pletho, a celebrated Platonic scholar. Both these writers had accompanied John Palaeologus to the Councils of Ferrara and Florence.[2]

The reply of Gennadius, who was now a monk in the monastery of Pantocrator (a little over a mile distant from the Great Church), whither they had gone to consult him, was distinct enough. He handed from his cell a paper asking why they put their trust in Italians instead of in God. In losing their faith he declared that they would lose their city. In embracing the new religion they would have to submit to be slaves.

Something like a riot followed, and drunken zealots ran through the streets declaring that they would have no Union with the Azymites—that is, with those who celebrate with unleavened bread.

---

[1] Ducas, xxxv.

[2] As they were opposed in philosophy, so also were they on the great question before these Councils. Pletho insisted that the Union should be effected by the submission of the Greek Church to the Latin formula, wh... Scholarius endeavoured to frame a form of words which could be accepted both parties. Had his advice been acted upon, it is possible that he and h... companions would on their return to the capital have been able to persua... their countrymen to accept the Union in sincerity. For the life and writir... of George Scholarius, afterwards the Patriarch Gennadius, see Krumbache... *Geschichte des Byzantinischen Litteratur*, p. 119, and works there quoted.

Meantime the congregation in the Great Church, after listening to a sermon from the cardinal, formally gave their consent to the Union on condition that the decrees of Florence should be again examined and, if need be, revised. A Mass was celebrated in which Roman and Greek priests took part; the names of Nicholas the Fifth and the restored Patriarch Gregory were joined in the prayers, and both the cardinal and the patriarch shared in the celebration in token that the old schism was at an end and that the great reconciliation had been accomplished.

The reconciliation was, however, a delusion and a sham. Many who accepted it, says Ducas, gave utterance to the thought, ' Wait until we have got rid of Mahomet, and then it will be seen whether we are really united with these Azymites.' Notaras, the grand duke and subject of highest rank in the city, was reported to have declared that he would rather see he phakiola of the Turk than the veil of the Latin priest. Those who conformed did so under compulsion. They agreed with the mob in regarding the Latin priests as the representatives of a foreign tyranny. The most devout among the citizens were the most opposed to a change of belief in order to obtain a temporal advantage. Without going so far as Lamartine, who says ' L'Église avait tué la patrie,' we may safely admit that it had greatly divided the people in presence of their great enemy.

We have now arrived at a period within a few months of the final siege of the city and have to limit our attention to the struggle which is about to take place over against its walls, to the incidents of this epoch-marking event, and to the *dramatis personae* of the contest.

CHAPTER X

CHARACTER OF MAHOMET THE SECOND; RECEIVES DEPUTA-
TION FROM CITY; RETURNS TO ADRIANOPLE FROM ASIA
MINOR; HIS REFORMS; BUILDS ROUMELIA-HISSAR; RE-
JECTS OVERTURES FROM EMPEROR; CASTLE COMPLETED,
AUGUST 1452; WAR DECLARED; MAHOMET RETURNS TO
ADRIANOPLE; HE DISCLOSES HIS DESIGNS FOR SIEGE OF
CITY. CONSTANTINE'S PREPARATIONS FOR DEFENCE;
ARRIVAL OF SIX VENETIAN SHIPS; AID REQUESTED FROM
VENICE; JUSTINIANI ARRIVES, JANUARY 1453; BOOM
ACROSS HARBOUR PLACED IN POSITION. TURKISH ARMY
ESTIMATE OF; NOTICE OF JANISSARIES; MOBILITY OF
ARMY; RELIGIOUS SPIRIT OF; CASTING OF GREAT
CANNON; TURKISH FLEET ARRIVES IN BOSPORUS
DESCRIPTION OF VESSELS COMPOSING IT. MAHOMET'S
ARMY MARCHES TO CITY; OFFER OF PEACE.

Character
of
Mahomet.

As Mahomet plays the principal part in the great traged
of the Capture of Constantinople, we may turn aside from
the narrative in order to form a general estimate of th
young man, leaving until after the conquest of the city th
attempt to make a more complete sketch of his character.

As he was only twenty-one years old when he becam
sultan, the events of his subsequent life inevitably colou
any attempt to delineate him in his youth. There exis
many notices in regard to his character drawn by con
temporary writers, and though Gibbon's remark, that it
dangerous to trust either Turkish or Christian authors whe
describing Mahomet, is useful as a warning, these notice
and especially the Life of Mahomet by Critobulus [1] enab

[1] The MS. of Critobulus was found in the Seraglio Library about thirt
five years ago by Dr. Dethier. It was published by Karl Müller with excelle

us to get a fair view of the man.   He was well-formed and
handsome, about the middle height, with piercing eyes and
arched eyebrows.   His most conspicuous feature was his
long aquiline nose, which seemed to overhang his thick red
lips and made the Turks describe him in after years as
having the beak of a parrot surmounting cherries.

The dream of his boyhood was to capture Constantinople.
He would succeed where Bajazed and Murad had failed.
Ducas gives a striking picture of his sleeplessness and
anxiety while at Adrianople before the siege of the city
commenced.   His one thought was how he might obtain
his object.   He passed his days in active preparations.   He
went in disguise among his men accompanied by two
soldiers to hear what they had to say of him and of his
enterprise, and is said to have killed any man who ventured
to recognise and salute him.   He passed his nights arranging
the plan of his attack—where he should place his cannon ;
where he would endeavour to undermine the walls ; where
the attack with scaling ladders should commence.   The
anxiety he displayed when on the eve of this and many
subsequent undertakings ; his desire to learn the opinion
formed of him by his own men and by foreigners; his many
hasty acts and the many legends which grew up during his
lifetime and after his death representing him as a rash and
impulsive ruler, all indicate that he was of a highly strung
and nervous temperament.   .

There are two sides to his character, each well marked
and distinct ; the man lived a double life, whereof one aspect
would almost seem to be irreconcilable with the other.   In
one he presents himself as a student, sicklied o'er with
the pale cast of thought, doubting of everything and anxious
to learn what answers the best men of his time and of
former ages, philosophers and theologians, had to give to
the greatest problems of life.   In the other aspect he is a

notes.   Dr. Dethier also prepared an edition with notes and documents
relating to the siege, which were printed by the Academy of Buda-Pest
but never published.   Through the courtesy of the Council and of Dr.
Arminius Vámbéry I have been presented with copies.   They are especially
valuable for their topographical criticisms.

bloodthirsty tyrant, a *hunkiar* or drinker of blood ; one who recked nothing of human slaughter and who seems even to have delighted in human suffering. Yet the two lives are inseparably blended. He would turn from study to slaughter, and after slaughter and torture would show himself to be full of pity for the sufferings of his victims.

Nature had endowed him with intelligence far above the average of that possessed by men of his race He was the son of a slave, and probably of a Christian, and like so many of the sultans before his time and until the middle of the eighteenth century probably owed his intelligence to the non-Turkish blood in his veins. His early struggles while yet a lad, and the great responsibilities he had to assume in order to protect his very life, had quickened his faculties and had made him both suspicious and self-reliant. His environment, among men who were simply soldiers of the original Turkish type ; the tradition of his house and race, in accordance with which any slaughter or any cruelties might be committed ; the religion to which he belonged, which regarded all non-Mussulmans as enemies of the true faith, who were to be subdued : all tended to make him regardless of human life. But amid his cruelties his better nature and his more thoughtful side occasionally asserted itself.

In one respect his characteristics are those of his race No man can show himself more cruel and relentless in slaughter than the Turk whenever his religious sentimen comes into play. The unbeliever is an enemy of God and o Mahomet, and it is a sacred duty when he is fighting agains the Moslem to slay him. Those who are at war agains Islam must be utterly destroyed, root and branch, unles indeed they will accept the faith. Men, women, and childre must alike suffer the penalty. But when no religiou sentiment obscures the natural feelings of humanity, the same Turk is goodnatured and kindly. Probably no rac is more charitable towards its own poor or treats animal with more kindness. Mahomet the Second both in hi cruelty towards his enemies and in his spasmodic kindness was a not unfair representative of his race.

But in another respect the characteristics of Mahomet are quite un-Turk-like. His interest in questions of philosophy and theology, in science and even in art, recall the names of Western rather than of Turkish rulers. It was indeed his interest in theological questions that led to various reports that he was an atheist,[1] that he was an unbeliever in the dogmas of his own religion and that he contemplated embracing Christianity. That he felt an interest in such questions separates him at once from the mass of his race : for, probably more completely than the professors of any other religion, Moslems accept their creed without question.[2]

Phrantzes notes that when as a mere boy he had been entrusted with kingly power, some of the old viziers had warned Sultan Murad that it was not prudent to leave the government to his son.[3] Their warning was not altogether disregarded, and the viziers who gave it paid dearly for their counsels.

His father, Murad the Second, had died in February 1451 at Adrianople. When Mahomet learned the news he was in Magnesia. Calling upon all who loved him to follow, he hastened as rapidly as possible to Gallipoli. During the two days he remained there a great crowd flocked to his standard. Then he pushed on to Adrianople. On the day after his arrival he was proclaimed sultan. Halil Pasha the grand vizier and Isaac Pasha were in attendance, but as they were the advisers who prevented the young sultan from retaining supreme power, they were doubtful of their reception and kept themselves in the background.

Mahomet's accession.

---

[1] Lonicerus, p. 22.

[2] M. Léon Cahun, in his introduction to the *History of the Turks and Mongols*, says : 'L'Islamisme est une règle qu'on respecte et qu'on défend, mais qu'on ne se permettrait pas de discuter. Les Turcs ont toujours été trop inaccessibles au sentiment religieux pour jamais devenir hérétiques ; ils sont les derniers des hommes capables de comprendre *Oportet haereses esse*. Ils ne demandent pas mieux que de croire, mais ils ne tiennent pas du tout à comprendre.'

[3] Phrantzes, i. 30.

Mahomet, however, ordered Halil to take his place as grand vizier and appointed Isaac Pasha governor of Anatolia or Asia Minor.

Mahomet commenced his reign by one of those acts of cruelty which at once proclaimed the brutal and the treacherous side of his character. Being himself the son of a slave mother and having a younger brother, named Ahmed, an infant still at the breast, who was the son of Murad by his marriage with the sister of the Serbian kral, he ordered a certain Ali to drown the young Ahmed in his bath. His predecessors had killed their brothers, but the latter, as we have seen, were in open revolt. Von Hammer states that there are Turkish historians who praise Mahomet the Second for this act of cruelty, and this for the reason that it is easier to kill a babe than a boy who is grown up.[1] Fearing apparently the effect so wanton an act of cruelty would have upon his followers, Mahomet disclaimed all participation in it and put Ali to death.[2]

Mahomet is entitled to be classed among the men who at an early age showed exceptional military skill. This skill was developed during almost continual warfare to the end of his reign. His industry, his boundless desire for conquest, his careful attention to every detail that was necessary to secure success, and his confidence in his own judgment, recall the names of Alexander and Napoleon. From his first and most important enterprise against Constantinople itself down to the last expedition of his reign he was not merely the nominal but the actual commander of the Turkish troops. He would brook no interference. He allowed no council or other body of his subjects to thwart his designs. The New Troops or Janissaries, flushed with victory and already conscious of that solidarity which in later years made them the terror of sultans, exacted from him a donative on his accession, but they paid dearly for their temerity and soon learned that their new master would neither be dictated to nor divide his sovereignty.

[1] Von Hammer, note iii. p. 429.
[2] Ducas, p. 129; Chalcondylas says, ' Peremit, cum, aqua infusa, spiritum ejus interclusisset ; '   Montaldo, ' fratre obtruncato.'

For the present we must be content to note that the young sultan was a man of unusual intelligence, who as a boy had accepted responsibility with eagerness; that he still had in 1452 the alternate confidence and hesitancy of youth; that he was of great energy, of studious habits, of nervous temperament, painstaking in the formation of his designs, ready to obtain the judgment of others, but otherwise quick in arriving at a decision. His maxim in later years was that in warfare secrecy and rapidity are the main elements of success. In reply to an officer of high rank who asked why great warlike preparations were being made he answered, 'If a hair of my beard knew, I would pluck it out and burn it.'[1] His ambition was great. He proposed to attack Naples, dreamed of leading his armies to the elder Rome, and regarded his conquests as stages in a great design of conquering the world.[2] These objects were however in the future. The immediate one before him was the capture of the city, and to its accomplishment he directed all his thoughts and all his energy without wavering until he had attained it.

Within a few weeks of Mahomet's arrival in Europe from Magnesia ambassadors were sent to his court at Adrianople from Constantine and other rulers in Europe and Asia Minor who were under his suzerainty to congratulate him on his accession. As his first care was to make sure of his own position and to gain time, Mahomet received them all with apparent cordiality and promised to observe the treaties made by his father. At the request of the representatives of the emperor he not merely confirmed the existing treaties, but declared his willingness to pay an annual sum of three hundred thousand aspers chargeable upon the produce of the Strymon Valley for the maintenance of Orchan.[3]

Then he returned to Caramania, where Ibrahim Bey, who

Con-
ciliating
embassies

---

[1] Von Hammer, iii. 68. [2] Zorzo Dolfin, p. 986.

[3] Orchan was the Turkish member of the house of Othman who still remained in Constantinople and was either the son or grandson of Suliman, brother of Mahomet I.

had already shown himself ready to join Hunyadi and other enemies of the Turks, was in revolt.[1] There must be no repetition of the incident which had made Murad's attempt to capture the city a failure. No sooner had the sultan left Europe than, with an indiscretion which Ducas condemns, ambassadors from the emperor were sent to ask that the pension promised for the support of Orchan should be doubled and at the same time to demand leave, if the request were refused, that Constantine might be at liberty to set him free. The messengers insinuated that in such case Orchan would be an acceptable candidate for the Ottoman throne. The request was of course a threat, and was so treated by Halil Pasha—who had been friendly to the late emperor and who continued his friendship to Constantine—and by Mahomet himself. When Halil heard their demand he bluntly asked them if they were mad. He told them that they had a very different man to deal with from the easy-going Murad; the ink on the treaty was not yet dry, and yet they came as if they were in a position to demand better conditions than had been already granted. 'If you think,' said Halil, 'you can do anything against us, do it: proclaim Orchan prince; bring the Hungarians across the Danube and take from us, if you can, the lands we have captured; but I warn you that you will fail and that if you try you will lose everything.'[2] The account given by Ducas has every appearance of truthfulness. Halil felt that his own attempts to save the city were being thwarted by the emperor himself. He, however, promised to report to Mahomet what they had said and kept his word.

His master dealt with the ambassadors much more diplomatically. He was outside Europe, and it would be inconvenient if any attempt should be made to prevent him returning to Adrianople. Besides, he must have time to come to terms with Caramania. He therefore represented that he was quite disposed to accede to the demands submitted to him, but that, as he was going to Adrianople in a short time, it would be better that they should submit to

him there that which was judged best for the empire and
the citizens.

Thereupon the sultan with all haste made terms with
Ibrahim Bey of Caramania and returned to his European
capital. When there he at once gave orders that the
pension to Orchan should no longer be paid, and sent to
arrest all the tax-gatherers in the Strymon Valley who were
collecting the money to pay it.

Returns to Adrianople, and begins his active preparations.

He had quieted one possible ally of the empire. He
addressed himself next to another opponent who had shown
that he could be terribly formidable. He made a truce with
John Hunyadi for three years and concluded arrangements
with the rulers of other states. He strengthened his army.
He amassed stores of arms, arrows, and cannon-balls. He
superintended the thorough reform of the administration of
the revenue, and in the course of a year he accumulated a
third of the taxes which would otherwise have been
squandered.

Then he determined to carry into execution a plan
which would give him a strong base for operations against
the city he was resolved to capture. He was already master
of the Asiatic side of the Bosporus. At what is now
Anatolia-Hissar he possessed the strong fortification built
by Bajazed. It is at the place where Darius crossed
from Asia into Europe and where the Bosporus is narrowest,
being indeed only half a mile broad. Mahomet already
possessed by treaty, made with his father, the right to cross
the straits and to march through the peninsula behind
Constantinople to his capital at Adrianople. He now,
however, proposed to build another fortification at some
point on the opposite—that is the European—shore. It
would serve the double purpose of enabling him to command the straits and of giving him a base for obtaining his
supplies from Asia and for the attack by sea upon the city.
With a fleet already large at the Dardanelles and with the
command of the Bosporus, he hoped to isolate Constantinople so far as to prevent it from receiving any aid
in men or supplies of food. The command of the Bosporus

Purposes building fort on Bosporus.

would be a blow to the trade of Venice and Genoa as well as to the emperor. Ships would be prevented from trading freely with, and bringing supplies from, the Black Sea. It might have been expected that the emperor would have put forth all his strength to oppose the execution of such a design. The all-sufficient explanation is, that, even if his naval strength had been sufficient to delay the crossing of Mahomet's crowd of builders, the army was too hopelessly insignificant to hold the shore against that which could soon arrive from Adrianople on its rear.

Remon-strances against project When the emperor and citizens learned, in the spring of 1452, the preparations which were being made by the collection of building materials and the bringing together of crowds of workmen, they recognised all the importance of the project and its danger to the city. Ambassadors were sent to the sultan at Adrianople to learn whether it was possible in any way to divert Mahomet from his purpose. They urged the existence of treaties with the grandfather, the father, and even with Mahomet himself: treaties which had expressly stipulated that no fortification or other building should be erected on the European side of the Bosporus.[1] They claimed that these stipulations had hitherto been scrupulously observed, that armies had been allowed to pass, but Mahomet's predecessors had prevented any of their subjects putting up fortifications or other buildings. The messengers urged upon the sultan that to break the treaties was to commit an act of injustice to the emperor.

Mahomet's reply. In reply, the sultan, who was determined to avoid war till he was ready, declared to the messengers that he had no intention of breaking treaties: a statement which was, of course, in flagrant violation of the truth. He pointed out, however, that in the time of his father the Italians had tried to hinder the passage of his troops when it had become necessary to fight the Hungarians, and urged that it had become essential for the protection of his European possessions that he should be in a position to prevent such detention in future. He claimed that the land on which he

[1] Crit. vii.

proposed to build his fortress belonged to him, and professed
to think it strange that the emperor should wish to place
any difficulties in the way of the execution of so necessary a
project. If indeed, he significantly added, the emperor was
not peaceably disposed, that would be a different matter.[1]

When the messengers reported their interview, the
emperor's first idea was to fight, and he was only prevented
by the entreaties of the clergy and people from sending a
detachment of his troops to destroy the builders and their
work. Some indeed of the inhabitants were in favour of
such action, but the emperor[2] had to come to the miserable
conclusion that it was impossible to prevent the young
sultan from carrying out his project except by war in the
open country, and that for such war he was not prepared.

When the spring of 1452 was further advanced the
sultan himself took the lead in the execution of his project.
He assembled thirty well-armed triremes and a large number
of transports and sent them from Gallipoli to the Bosporus.
At the same time he himself marched at the head of a large
army towards its European shore.

Selects a site at Roumelia-Hissar.

On his arrival he selected, with the aid of his engineers,
the most advantageous position for his proposed fortifications.
This was found immediately opposite Anatolia Hissar.[3]

Once the plan had been decided upon, every available
man seems to have been set at work to aid in its speedy
execution. Mahomet himself superintended the construction
of the new fortification and pushed on the works with the
energy that characterised all his military undertakings.

Building begins.

At the beginning of the operations Constantine with the

[1] Crit. viii. The account given by Ducas represents the reply of the sultan
as much more brutal. He dismissed the ambassadors with the remark that he
would not have the question reopened ; he was within his rights, and if they
returned he would have them flayed alive.

[2] Phrantzes, p. 233 ; Ducas, xxxiv. ; Crit. ix.

[3] Critobulus gives the width at seven stadia. It is really half a nautical mile.
Probably it is unwise to suppose that Critobulus had any means of measuring
with any degree of accuracy, or the distance given by him would be very
valuable as indicating what contemporary writers meant by a stadium. It is
important, however, in reference to other statements of distance given by Critobulus which will be noted later.

object of saving the crops of the peasants around the city, and of appearing to be reconciled to the project which he could not prevent, sent provisions to the workmen. Mahomet in reply, and probably with the intention of forcing on war in the open, permitted his men to scour the country and gather or destroy the crops. All the neighbouring churches and houses, including the famous church of the Asomatoi at Arnoutkeui, were destroyed to furnish material.[1]

The land enclosed, says Critobulus, was rather a fortified town than a fort. The walls and towers still remain and form the most picturesque object which the traveller sees on his passage through the Bosporus. Each of two peaks is crowned with a strong tower. These are connected by a long high wall interrupted with smaller towers, and from the two largest towers similar walls at right angles to the long wall connect them with great towers on the shore at the end of another line of walls parallel to the channel. Small guns or bombards enabled the enclosure to be defended against any attack by land. On the sea shore and under the protection of the walls were stationed large cannon which threw heavy stone balls and commanded the passage.

Completed
middle of
August
1452.

The work had been commenced in March 1452. It was completed by the middle of August of the same year. The city had hoped to maintain peace and Turks had entered and left it apparently without difficulty. When the fortification was finished and Mahomet's army had robbed the peasant of their crops, this hope vanished. Constantine closed the gates, making the few Turks within its walls prisoners. They were, however, a few days afterwards sent to the sultan. Upon the closing of the gates, Mahomet formally declared

War
declared.

war and followed up his declaration by appearing with an army of fifty thousand men before the walls. But his preparations for a siege were far from ready. After remaining three days he withdrew on September 6 to Adrianople and at the same time the fleet returned to the Dardanelles.[2]

---

[1] Ducas, xxxiv.

[2] Phrantzes, 234, and Barbaro, p. 2. Barbaro was a Venetian ship's doctor who was in the city before and during the siege and who kept a diary which

Within the next few weeks the city as well as the **Capture of ships at Roumelia-Hissar.** Venetian and Genoese colonies learned how greatly the new fortification of Roumelia-Hissar had strengthened Mahomet's position. On November 10, two large Venetian galleys under the command of Morosini were fired at as they were passing and captured. A fortnight later, on November 26, another Venetian ship was fired at and also captured. Some of the crew were sawn in halves. These captures, says Barbaro, led to the beginning of the war with the Venetians. For the first time the Turks commanded the Bosporus.

Now that he had provided himself with a safe base of operations against the city and withdrawn to Adrianople, Mahomet threw off all disguise, and calling together the principal officers of the army announced to them the **Mahomet's address to the pashas.** object of his preparations, which, in accordance with his habitual practice, he had hitherto kept secret. Critobulus gives us an address which he represents Mahomet as making to his leaders. He describes the progress made by his ancestors in Asia Minor, how they had established themselves at Brousa and had taken possession of the Hellespont; had conquered part of Thrace and Macedonia, Bulgaria, Serbia, and even Selymbria, and had overcome nearly every obstacle. The great barrier to their progress was the city and the army of the Romans. Whatever the sons of Othman wanted to do was opposed at Constantinople. The citizens had fought them everywhere pertinaciously and continually. This opposition must be ended; this barrier removed. It was for his hearers, said Mahomet, to complete the work of their fathers. They had now against them a single city, one which could not resist their attacks; a city whose population was greatly reduced and whose former wealth had been diminished by Turkish sieges and by the continual incursions made by his ancestors upon its territory, a city which was now only one in name, for in reality

simply invaluable, though for the part written day by day, internal evidence shows that it was subsequently revised after the siege. It was published in 1856.

it contained cultivated lands, orchards, and vineyards. Its buildings were useless and its walls abandoned and for the greater part in ruins. Even from its weakness, however, they knew that from its favourable situation, commanding both land and sea, it had greatly hindered their progress and could still hinder it, upsetting their plans, and being always ready to attack them. Openly or secretly it had done all it could against them. It was the city which had brought about the attack by Tamerlane and the suffering which followed. It had instigated Hunyadi to cross the Danube and on every occasion had been in every possible manner their great enemy. The time had now come when in his opinion it should be captured or wiped off the face of the earth. One of two things : he would either have it within his empire, or he would lose both. With Constantinople in his possession the territories already gained could be safely held and more would be obtained ; without it, no territory that they possessed was safe.

Critobulus professes that the sultan claimed to have information that the Italians in Constantinople would not give any aid to the emperor, and were indeed his enemies and that on account of the difference of religion there was bitter strife between them and the Greeks. Mahome concluded by urging that there was great risk in delay and that the city should be attacked before any aid could be sent to its relief. He gave his vote for war, and nearly all the assembly followed his example.[1]

Mahomet now pushed on his preparations for the siege with the utmost activity. The general commanding the European troops was ordered to take a portion of them into the neighbourhood of Constantinople and clear the country This he did, and attacked in the usual Turkish fashion all the villages on the route which still remained under the ru

---

[1] The speech of Mahomet, of which I have given the substance, can course only be taken as a reproduction of what Critobulus had heard or possil of what an intelligent writer who knew the Turks well thought it probal Mahomet would say. As such it is valuable. It is of course formed Critobulus, following the example of the Greek Byzantine historians general on the model of those given by Thucydides and other classical authors.

of the emperor. Selymbria, Perinthos, and other places on the north shore of the Marmora were sacked.

The inhabitants of Constantinople seem at first to have hoped against hope, notwithstanding the construction of the fortress at Roumelia-Hissar, that the sultan would have remained content with his position on the Bosporus thus strengthened. They soon realised that an attempt was about to be made to capture the city far more serious than any that had been made within living memory. They knew their weakness and the strength of their foe. They knew that in a siege they would be under greater disadvantages than ever before ; that conquest would mean falling into the hands of implacable enemies, the slaughter of their young men, the loss of all their property, the plunder of their churches, and the enslaving of their women. The statement of Critobulus is probable enough that the inhabitants remarked to each other that in former sieges the position of the city was better, because it had command of the sea and the inhabitants had therefore only need to defend the walls on the landward side. We may dismiss, as being merely curious and characteristic of the period, the stories of supernatural events which increased the tribulation of the inhabitants, of earthquakes, and strange unearthly groanings, of lightning and shooting stars, of hurricanes, torrential rains and floods, and of other signs which indicated the wrath of God against the city. Those of the inhabitants who did not believe in omens had something more serious to think about than perspiring pictures, men and women possessed of the devil, and mad enthusiasts who prophesied misfortune to the city, and helped to depress the spirits of the fighters. Those who kept their heads, with the emperor as their leader, behaved like men and met the danger bravely. They set themselves in the first place to strengthen the defences. Their first task was to repair the walls, for which purpose tombstones and all other materials available were freely employed. Arrows and all other kinds of arms were collected.

During the whole of the winter the emperor and his

Hopes that siege could be avoided

Arrival of
Isidore
with 200
soldiers;
of
Venetian
ships;
of Cretans.

people pushed on their preparations. In November 1452, as we have seen, Cardinal Isidore had arrived with two hundred soldiers sent by the pope. Six Venetian vessels— not, indeed, intended for war but capable of being adapted to such purpose—came to the city, and their captains together with those of three large ships from Crete yielded to the request and promises of the emperor and consented to render help. The leading Venetian commander was Gabriel Trevisano, who, in reply to the imperial request, consented to give his services ' per honor de Dio et per honor de tuta la Christianitade.' [1] When the Venetian ships coming from the Black Sea were destroyed by the Turks at Hissar, the emperor and leading nobles, the cardinal and Leonard, with the 'bailey ' of the Venetian colony and its leading members, held a council to arrange conditions on which Venice should be asked to send aid. Their deliberations took place on December 13, the day after the famous service of reconciliation in Hagia Sophia, and on several following days. Trevisano and Diedo, the most important sea captains, were also present. An agreement was concluded and messengers were sent to Venice to ask that immediate aid should be sent to the city. Finally the council decided that no Venetian vessel should leave the harbour without express permission.[2]

Arrival of
Justiniani.

On January 29 the city received the most important of all its acquisitions; for on that day arrived John Justiniani. A Genoese of noble family, he was well skilled in the art of war and had gained great reputation as a soldier. On board his two vessels were four hundred cuirassiers, whom he had brought from Genoa, and others whom he had hired at Chios and Rhodes, making together with his crew in all seven hundred men.[3] A soldier of fortune, he had come on his own accord to offer his sword when he heard of the straits in which the emperor found himself, and had received a promise that in case of success he should receive the island of Lesbos. He was cordially welcomed by the emperor and nobles and was shortly afterwards, by the consent of all named commander-in-chief, with the powers of a dictator in

[1] Barb. p. 14.   [2] Barb. p. 11.   [3] Barb., and Crit. ch. xxv.

everything that regarded the war. He at once took charge of the work already begun of strengthening the defences. He distributed small guns upon the walls where they could throw their stone balls to greatest advantage. He classified the defenders and appointed to each his station.

In the last days of March Trevisano with his crew, aided also by Alexis (or Aloysius) Diedo, whose three galleys had come from Tana on the Azof, reopened a foss from the Golden Horn in front of the landward walls as far as the ground remained level, and at the same time repaired the walls in the neighbourhood.[1] A few days later the Italians were assigned to the most important positions on the landward walls. Barbaro, with the enthusiasm of a Crusader, gives a list of Venetian nobles who took part in the defences, and this ' for a perpetual memorial ' of his brave countrymen.

Justiniani appears at first to have chosen to defend the walls at Caligaria.

On April 2 the chain or boom which defended the entrance to the Golden Horn was either closed for the first time or strengthened.[2] It extended from the Tower of Eugenius near Seraglio Point to the Tower of Galata,[3] within the Galata Walls, and near the present Moumhana, and was supported on logs. Ten large ships, of which five were Genoese, three from Crete, one from Ancona, and an imperial ship, were stationed at the boom, bows towards it, and with long triremes near them for support. The guardianship of the boom was entrusted to the Genoese.[4]

Closing the harbour.

[1] La Brocquière says this foss, on his visit, was two hundred paces long.

[2] Barbaro says that the emperor employed an Italian to place the boom in position.

[3] The present Tower of Galata was called the Tower of Christ. See Paspates, *Meletai*, p. 180.

[4] Barb. p. 25. Tetaldi states that there were nine galleys and thirty other ships (p. 25). The fact that the Turks soon found that it was impossible to take possession of the chain or to drive away the defending fleet tends to show that the Greek fleet was respectable in number of ships. On the other hand, when it became of extreme importance to send ships outside the chain to aid ships from Genoa coming to the relief of the city, the fact that none were sent out is evidence to show that no ships could be spared from the defence of the chain or that no sufficient number of galleys, triremes, or other vessels inde-

By the end of March Mahomet's preparations were
nearly complete. He had already summoned all available
cavalry and infantry from Asia and the parts of Europe
under his control. As they arrived he drilled, classified, and
formed them into bodies of cuirassiers (or men with breast-
plates), slingers, archers, and lancers.

The
Turkish
army.

While it is impossible to state with anything like
certainty what was the number of fighting men whom
Mahomet was shortly to bring before the walls of the city,
the materials for forming a general computation are not
wanting. The Turkish army was composed of regulars and
irregulars. The first and most important division of
regulars were the Janissaries. After them came a great
horde of Turks from those who had occupied Asia Minor
and Europe. Every Turk was bound to serve, and a call had
been made on all. The Turkish nation was the Turkish
army. Among them were many men who represented the
class subsequently known as Derrybeys, chieftains who
held their lands from the sultan on condition of bringing a
number of retainers into the field during war. The
irregulars, or, as they may be conveniently called, the Bashi-
Bazouks, consisted partly of the poorest class of Turks, who
did not possess a horse, and partly of Christians attracted by
the hope of plunder.

Amid the estimates of the number of men in Mahomet's
army, that of Barbaro may be taken as safe and substantially
correct. He takes note of both regulars and irregulars—that
is, of all the combatants—while he disregards the camp-
followers as non-combatants. He states, when speaking of
the siege, that there were a hundred and fifty thousand men
stationed between the Golden Horn and the Marmora. As,
excluding the men on the fleet, all Mahomet's followers took
part in it, the number mentioned may be taken as Barbaro's
estimate of the whole Turkish army. Cheirullah, a
Turkish chronicler, affirms that there were not more than

pendent of wind for propulsion were at hand to take the offensive. There were
probably many smaller merchant ships and boats of which no account was
taken.

eighty thousand effective fighting men, excluding in this estimate apparently the Bashi-Bazouks.[1]

Barbaro's estimate of one hundred and fifty thousand fighting men is substantially confirmed by Tetaldi, who states that there were two hundred thousand men under Mahomet, of whom a hundred and forty thousand were effective soldiers including thirty thousand to forty thousand cavalry, the rest ' being thieves, plunderers, hawkers, and others following the siege for gain and booty.'[2] Taking the estimate of Cheirullah and Tetaldi, we may perhaps safely say that in the army of one hundred and fifty thousand men there were at least twenty thousand cavalry.

In this great army the Janissaries played the most important part and formed beyond all doubt the most efficient division. These were at least twelve thousand in number.[3] The name Janissaries signifies ' New Troops,' and was given by a famous dervish and saint, Hadji Bektash, when they were formed, in 1326, into a new infantry by Sultan Orchan. From their institution they constituted a fraternity governed in religious matters by the rules of Hadji Bektash.[4] Under the care of the first Murad, the son of Orchan, their organisation had been developed, and by the time of Mahomet the Second they had already acquired high repute for discipline and daring.

The part they played in the capture of the city and their

---

[1] The elder Mordtmann makes the suggestion that the Bashi-Bazouks are in this estimate excluded, and I agree with him. The same remark applies also to Philelphus who gives 60,000 foot and 20,000 horse. Other writers include all those who were present with Mahomet and thus make the number of the besiegers very much higher. Ducas's estimate is 250,000 ; Montaldo's, 240,000 (of whom 30,000 were cavalry, ch. xxvii.). Phrantzes states that 258,000 were present; Leonard the archbishop, with whom Critobulus and Thysellius agree, gives 300,000 men, while Chalcondylas increases this to 400,000.

[2] Tetaldi's *Informacion de la prinse de Constantinoble*, p. 21.

[3] Leonard and others say 15,000, but the smaller estimate is in accord with many Turkish statements that the number of Janissaries was, until the time of Suliman, limited to 12,000.

[4] The connection between the Dervish order of Bektashis and the Janissaries endured as long as the Janissaries themselves, and when the latter were massacred, in June 1826, with the cry of ' Hadji Bektash ' on their lips, the order of Bektashis was also suppressed. *Etat militaire Ottoman*, par Djavid Bey (Constantinople, 1881), and Walsh's *Two Years in Constantinople* (1828).

subsequent renown deserve a somewhat complete notice. The order took its origin in a long recognised Moslem rule, that when a people at war with Mahometans is summoned to make submission and refuses it may be enslaved, and that in such a case one fifth of the property captured should belong to the sultan. Christian captives fell within the limit of this rule. In practice, however, the sultans by no means considered themselves bound to restrict themselves to the prescribed one fifth. They held that as many of the children as the conqueror thought fit should be given over to him to be trained for the public, and especially for military, services. Accordingly, without regard to the fact that the parents had already surrendered one or more sons to the ruler, they were often called upon to furnish others. The demand for Christian children to be given up absolutely to the sultan was regular and methodic. No tithe or other tax required for the service of the Church was ever claimed with more regularity and insistence than this blood tax for the service of Islam. A formal examination of Christian children available for service was made every five years, when a Turkish inspector, at the head of a troop of soldiers and bearing an imperial firman of authorisation, visited the portions of the empire assigned to him. The registers of the churches were carefully examined to see how many children ought to be brought forward for inspection, and the priests, under the penalty of death, were bound to show a correct list. The boys selected were usually between the ages of ten and twelve years. Those were preferred who were distinguished either by their strength, intelligence, or beauty. In addition to these regular and legal contributions to the services of the state, it was the custom of the pashas, on returning from the provinces to bring presents of Christian children to their imperial master.

The boys thus taken away from their parents and their homes were forcibly converted to Mahometanism. From the day of their reception into Islam they were kept under strict surveillance and instructed with the object of making them useful servants of the sultan. After a while they were divided according to their aptitudes and told off for special training for different branches of civil and military service. It is with the latter that we are most concerned, though it may be mentioned that many of those who had been Christian slaves rose to the highest positions in the civil service and greatly increased the efficiency of Turkish rule. All were thoroughly drilled in the observances and taught the precepts of the Moslem religion. All were subjected to a severe discipline, were trained to practise self-denial, to endure hardships cheerfully and not to repine at scantiness of food or loss of sleep. Day and night they were under supervision. The obedience exacted from them towards their superiors was absolute, prompt, and, in appearance at least, willing. All were taught to be expert in archery, and to ride well.

After a probation lasting usually six years, those who were drafted into the military service were still subject to severe restraints. Bertrandon de la Brocquière bears witness to the excellence of their discipline, and the same testimony is borne by a series of other witnesses for two centuries later. What may be called the Articles of War to which they were subject, besides prescribing absolute obedience to every command of their chief, required abstinence from every kind of luxury and the strict performance of the many rules of devotion laid down by Hadji Bektash.[1] All men who were not within barracks at the hour fixed were detained for punishment. No Janissary was allowed, until long after the conquest, to marry.[2]

On the other hand, the same Articles contained regulations which enable us to understand how in time service among the Janissaries came even to be coveted. Though discipline was strict, punishment could only be inflicted upon a Janissary by one of his own officers. It is true that, after receiving the bastinado, the offender had to rise, bend low, and salute the officer who had superintended the punishment,

---

[1] Djevad, p. 55.

[2] Permission to marry was not granted to Janissaries till the time of Suliman, a century later.

but no disgrace was attached to this act of discipline. The boy who was admitted into the brotherhood of the Janissaries was provided for as completely as if he had become a monk. When by reason of age or wounds he became weak, he was retired from active service and received a pension of three aspers daily more than he had received when on service.

In times of warfare the sternest features of the barracks were relaxed. Camp life was the recreation, and furnished the joy and hope, of the Janissary. War was for him a delight. His regiment marched to battle with every sign of rejoicing and of military display compatible with discipline.

The effect of the long training, with its strictness on the one hand and its relaxations on the other, was to develop an *esprit de corps* among them such as has rarely existed in any other army. Everything was done that could be done to cultivate this spirit. Every means was employed to make the Janissary live his life in and look only to the interests of his regiment. He was forbidden to exercise any trade or occupation whatever, lest he should possess an interest outside his regiment. In the time of Suliman the sultan ordered the aga of a regiment of Janissaries to be beheaded because one of his men was found mending his clothes. The officer was spared at the request of his comrades, but the private soldier was dismissed from the service. The regiment was to be everything to the Janissary; the outside world nothing. No man was allowed to accumulate wealth, although his regiment could do so. Each man followed the good or ill fortune of the powerful body of which he was a member.

The result was that the regiment represented to the Janissary everything that he held dear. He became jealous of its honour, and the regiment in its turn became exclusive towards outsiders. The Janissary came before long to think of his position as privileged and to regard entrance into his corps as only to be allowed under severe restrictions. So careful indeed did he become of the rights of his regiment that before long no person born of Mahometan parents was admitted, even though his father had been one of themselves. As a consequence of this cultivation of regimental rights, the popularity of the New Troops became so great that many young Christians of adventurous spirit voluntarily sought to join their ranks.

The Janissaries developed into a species of *imperium in imperio*. Perhaps the body in Western Europe to which they may most aptly be compared is the Order of Knights Templars. Each was a partly religious, partly military Order. Each was jealous of its own privileges and constituted a fraternity largely isolated from the rest of the community. But the isolation of the Janissary was more complete than that of the Templar at any time. The Moslem had been cut off from his own family and had forgotten all the Christians he had known as a child, and his regiment had taken the place of father and mother, wife and home. His individual rights had been merged in those of his regiment. The resemblance between the Janissaries and the Templars might be noted in one other respect— namely, that their religion sat lightly upon them. Though the former were bound by the precepts of Hadji Bektash, these precepts were, from the Mahometan point of view, extremely latitudinarian.[1]

All their discipline and training tended to make them devoted to the sultan as commander-in-chief. The Janissary had nothing to gain and nothing to fear from any person except his military superiors. Each man's promotion depended on the arbitrary will of his commanding officer, or ultimately of the sovereign. Each man saw before him a career in which he could rise to the command of an army or to other high office, provided he won the approval of his sultan.

Such a military organisation had never been seen in the world's history, and furnished to the early sultans a force

[1] When, contemporaneously with the murder of the Janissaries in 1826, the Order of Bektashis was suppressed, Sultan Mahmoud assigned as a reason that jars of wine were found in the cellars of their convents stoppered with leaves of the Koran. The statement was probably false, but was intended to create the worst possible impression against the Bektashis.

which was almost irresistible. Wholly Christian and largely
European in origin, it was yet completely Mahometan in
spirit and in action. It was indeed an army which would
have satisfied Frederick the Great or any other ruler who
has desired to model a force according to preconceived ideas.
Take a number of children from the most intelligent portion
of the community ; choose them for their strength and
intelligence ; instruct them carefully in the art of fighting ;
bring them up under strict military discipline ; teach them
to forget the home of their childhood, their parents and
friends ; give them a new religion of a specially military
type ; saturate them with the knowledge that all their hope
in life depends upon their position in the regiment ; make
peace irksome and war a delight, with the hope of promotion
and relaxation from the hardships and restraints of the
barracks : the result will be a weapon in the hands of a
leader such as the world has rarely seen. Such a weapon
was the army of the Janissaries.

The success of Mahomet's predecessors in the Balkan
peninsula had been largely due to the New Troops. Though
their numbers appear to have been limited to twelve thousand, they had already proved their value. We have seen
that when John Hunyadi had put the Turks under Murad
the Second to rout, it was the Janissaries who saved the
day and turned the disaster of Varna into a great victory.
Their discipline and strength were even more triumphant
in the defeat of the great Hungarian on the plain of Cossovo
in 1448. Black John, as the Turks named him from the
colour of his banner, succeeded in putting to flight the
Anatolian and the Rumelian divisions of his enemy. But
the attack on the Janissaries failed utterly. They stood
like a wall of brass until the moment came for them to
become the attacking force, and through their efforts the
triumph of the sultan was complete.

The force which had thus shown its quality only five
years previously was by far the most important division
under Mahomet's command. The ablest, bravest, most
terrible portion of the army of the arch-enemy of Christendom

was composed exclusively from Christian families. The most formidable instrument employed by the Turks for the conquest of the Christians of South-eastern Europe and for attacking the nations of the West was formed of boys born of Christian parents, enslaved, forcibly converted to a hostile religion, who yet became devotedly attached to the slavery to which they had been condemned. It was their boast in after years that they had never fled from an enemy, and the boast was not an idle one.

The remainder of the Turkish forces which may be classed among regular troops came from all parts occupied by the Turks but mainly from Anatolia. Their organisation, discipline, and powers of endurance probably made them as formidable an army as any which a European power of the period could have put into the field.

The Bashi Bazouks constituted an undisciplined mob who were good enough to be employed where numbers and wild courage were of use in annoying or weakening the enemy. La Brocquière states that the ' innumerable host ' of these irregulars took the field with no other weapon than their curved swords or scimitars. ' Being,' says Philelphus, ' under no restraint, they proved the most cruel scourge of a Turkish invasion.'

In speaking of the Turkish host it must not be forgotten that in 1453 hardly any European power can be said to have possessed a standing army. It is with no surprise, therefore, that we note that contemporary European writers from the West speak with astonishment of the discipline which prevailed. ' Their obedience to superiors,' says La Brocquière, ' is boundless; none dare disobey even when their lives are at hazard, and it is chiefly owing to their steady submission that such great exploits have been performed and such conquests gained.' The same writer bears testimony to the great mobility of the Turkish army. ' Ten thousand Turks on the march will make less noise than a hundred men in our Christian armies. In their ordinary marches they only walk, but in forced marches they always gallop, and, as they are lightly armed, they will

thus advance further from evening to daybreak than others
in three days. It is by these forced marches that they
have succeeded in surprising and completely defeating the
Christians in their different wars.' [1]

The army which Mahomet commanded was not merely
endued with the fatalism and confidence of an ordinary
army of Islam ; it was engaged upon a work in which many
generations of Moslems had longed to take a part. The
prophet himself was represented in the Sacred Traditions
as holding converse with Allah respecting the capture of
New Rome, and was told that the Great Day of Judgment
would not come before Constantinople had been captured
by the sons of Isaac. On another occasion Mahomet
declared that 'the best prince is he who shall capture
Constantinople, and his the best army.' The inspired words
had filled his immediate followers with the determination to
capture the city. The Arabs attempted the task no less than
seven times. At the third, in 672, they were accompanied
by the aged Eyoub, who in his youth had been the standard-
bearer and favourite of the Prophet. The huge army had
sat down before the city during seven years, sowing the fields
on the neighbouring coasts and gathering in the harvest
but determined to win the reward which Mahomet had
promised to those who should capture the New Rome
Eyoub's death before its walls and the failure in these Arab
attempts of the largest and most powerful army and flee
which Islam could ever collect had not rendered the word
of the Prophet void. The sacred promise still held good
and served to stimulate every soldier to increased exertion
Seven centuries had passed since the long struggle against
the Arabs, in which the Queen City saved European civilisation, and now, once again in the fulness of time, that which
the early Moslems had desired to see was within the reach
of those who fought under a leader who bore the same

---

[1] *Early Travels in Palestine*, p. 365. La Brocquière made a careful study
of the Turkish methods of fighting and of how they might be defeated by
combination of European troops among which he would have placed from
England a thousand men at arms and ten thousand archers. As his visit was
in 1433, it is not improbable that Agincourt was in his mind.

name as the Prophet. Among those who in the army were under the influence of religious ideas or traditions the coming attempt to capture the city was looked forward to hopefully and joyfully. To the ignorant and thoughtless among his barbarous followers the promise of unlimited plunder which Mahomet the Second held out was a stronger inducement; but to the better informed and more religious, and to some extent to all, the hope of winning paradise furnished a powerful allurement to battle or at least a compensatory consolation at the prospect of death.

After this digression I return to the preparations which Mahomet was making at Adrianople for the execution of his great design, and to those which the emperor had in hand for the defence of the city.

In the first weeks of January, the fame reached Constantinople of a monster bombard or gun which was being cast in Adrianople. Ducas gives interesting information of its history and describes it as the largest possessed by the Turks.

Urban's great bombard.

In the autumn of 1452, while Mahomet was finishing the castle on the Bosporus, a Hungarian or Wallachian cannon founder named Urban, who had offered his services to the emperor and had been engaged by him, was induced by higher pay to go over to the enemy. He would have been content, says Ducas, with a quarter of the pay he received from Mahomet.[1] After learning from him what he could do, the Turks commissioned him to make as powerful a gun as he could cast. Urban declared that if the walls were as strong as those of Babylon he could destroy them. At the end of three months he had succeeded in making a cannon which remained for many years the wonder of the city and even of Europe, and marks an epoch in the

---

[1] The Turks have rarely failed in obtaining able European soldiers. Moltke was in the Turkish service. The first Napoleon narrowly escaped taking a like service. (See Von Hammer.) More recently they have had in General Von der Golz one of the ablest German soldiers.

continually increasing power of guns. The casting was
completed at Adrianople.[1]

In January it was started on its journey to the capital.
Sixty oxen were employed to drag it, while two hundred
men marched alongside the wagon on which it was placed to
keep it in position. Two hundred labourers preceded it to
level the roads and to strengthen the bridges. By the end of
March[2] it was brought within five miles of the city. But,
though the fame of this monster gun has overshadowed all
the rest, we shall see that it was only one amongst many.[3]

Turkish
fleet.

Above all, says Critobulus, Mahomet had given special
attention to his fleet, ' because he considered that for the siege
the fleet would be of more use than even his army.'[4] He
built many new triremes and repaired his old ones. A
number of long boats, some of them decked over, and swift
vessels propelled by from twenty to fifty oarsmen were also
ready. No expense had been spared. The crews of his fleet
were gathered from all the shores of Asia Minor and the
Archipelago. He selected with great care the pilots, the men
who should give the time to the oarsmen and the captains.

At the beginning of April, his fleet was ready to leave

---

[1] Dethier suggests that the casting of the largest gun was done at Rhegium
the present Chemejie, about twelve miles from Constantinople, and that th
transport spoken of by Ducas was either of smaller ones or of the bras
required for the large one (p. 991; Dethier's notes on Z. Dolfin).

[2] Phrantzes, p. 237, gives the arrival on April 2.

[3] Critobulus, xxix., gives the description of the construction of a canno
the barrel of which was forty spans or twenty-six feet eight inche
long. The bronze of which it was cast was eight inches in thickness in th
barrel. Throughout half the length its bore was of a diameter of thirty inche
Throughout the other half, which contained powder, the bore was on
one third of that width. The σπιθσμὴ or *palmus* or span was in the Midd
Ages, says Du Cange, eight inches long. Two stone balls still existing at To
Hana (that is, the Cannon Khan) are forty-six inches in diameter. These wou
answer the description of Tetaldi, that the ball reached to his waist. A gre
Turkish cannon which is now in the Artillery Museum at Woolwich weig
about nineteen tons. It was cast fifteen years after the siege of Constantino
and is an excellent specimen of the great cannon of the period (*Artillery;*
Progress and Present Stage, by Commander Lloyd and A. G. Hadcock, R.
p. 19).

[4] Crit. xxi.

Gallipoli, which had been the place of rendezvous. Baltoglu, a Bulgarian renegade, was placed in command. A flotilla of a hundred and forty sailing ships started for the Bosporus.[1] Of these, twelve were fully armed galleys, seventy or eighty were *fustae*, and twenty to twenty-five were *parandaria*. Amid shouts from one ship to another, the beating of drums, and the sound of fifes, all marking the delight of the Turks that their period of inactivity was at an end, the fleet made its way through the Marmora. The sight carried dismay to the remnant of the inhabitants of the Christian villages along the shores, for within the memory of none had such a fleet been seen. Within the city itself the news of the enormous number of vessels on their way was not less alarming.

The fleet arrived in the Bosporus on April 12 and anchored at the Double Columns or Diplokionion just below the present Palace of Dolma Bagtche.[2]

At the Double Columns the detachment of the fleet which had come from the Dardanelles was joined by other vessels which had been swept in from the Black Sea and the Marmora. Phrantzes gives the total number at four hundred and eighty.[3] Many of the vessels from the Black Sea were laden with wood or with stone balls.

The Turkish fleet under Baltoglu's command thus consisted of a number of vessels from all the shores of the Marmora, the Bosporus, and the Black Sea. Among them

[1] Barbaro.

[2] Barbaro gives the arrival on April 12. Dr. Dethier maintains that Diplokionion was at Cabatash and that subsequently to the Conquest the people and the name were transferred to Beshiktash. Barbaro says it was two Italian miles, equal to one and a third English mile, from the city, which is in accord with Dethier's view, but in presence of Bondelmonti's map, drawn in 1422 and given in Banduri, showing the Two Columns, and of other evidence, it is difficult to credit Dethier's statement.

[3] Phrantzes, p. 241; Ducas gives the total number as 300, Leonard as 250, Critobulus as 350. The independent accounts of two men who had been at sea, like the French soldier Tetaldi and the Venetian Barbaro, are not far apart. The first says there were 16 to 18 galleys, the second 12. The estimate of the long boats is 60 to 80 by Tetaldi, as against 70 to 80 by Barbaro; while the transport barges or parandaria are described by one as from 16 to 20, by the other as from 20 to 25. Chalcondylas (p. 158) states that 30 triremes and 200 smaller vessels arrived from Gallipoli. Leonard says that there were 6 triremes and 10 biremes.

were triremes, biremes, *fustae, parandaria*, and galleys. As
we shall find these terms recurring, it will be well to realise
what they signified. The trireme of the fifteenth century
was a long and fast vessel which had usually two masts,
was very low in the water and, though employing sails, was
mainly dependent for propulsion on her oars. The arrangement of oars from which she derived her name was not in
tiers one above the other and thus requiring oars of different
length. The ' banks ' or benches, unlike those in ancient
ships, were all on the same level. The oars were short and
all of the same length : but three oars projected through one
rowlock port, each oar working on a tholepin. ' One man
one oar ' was the invariable rule. Three men occupied one
bench or seat. Down the middle of the trireme ran a
central gangway called the *histodokè*, primarily intended as
a rest for the mast, but upon which the officer passed to
and fro to keep time for the oarsmen. There were thus
three upon each side of him, or six men nearly abreast
throughout the length of the trireme. The arrangement
upon a bireme was of a similar character, except that two
men instead of three occupied one bench. There was also
but one mast. The *fusta* resembled the bireme in having
two oarsmen on each bench on each side of the *histodokè*
from the stern to the one central mast, but only one on each
side from the mast forward.[1]

The *fusta* was a lighter boat than the trireme, and could

[1] The following illustration shows the arrangement of the boats.

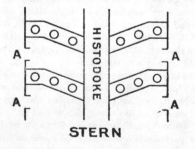

A.A.A.A. represent four rowlock ports, through each of which three oars pass, in
the case of a trireme, pulled by three men on the seat marked with circles.

thus be propelled more rapidly. The *parandaria* were heavy boats, probably not differing much from the sailing barges or *mahoons* still used in the harbour of Constantinople, the Bosporus, and Marmora. The name 'galley' was in the fifteenth century applied to war vessels propelled by a single bank. of long oars on each side. Leonard employs the term *dromon*, not, as it had been used in earlier days from about 500 A.D., as a generic term for war ships,[1] but to indicate the large *caiques*, usually of twelve oars, which could not be classed as triremes, biremes, or fustæ.

Probably the majority of the vessels in Mahomet's fleet were not larger than the ordinary bazaar caiques which ply between Constantinople and distant villages on the Bosporus or the Marmora or are employed in deep-sea fishing.[2]

Mahomet, leaving Adrianople in the early days of April with the whole of his army, overspread and ravaged the country which had not already been swept by the vanguard of his force and arrived on the 5th of that month before the city. He encamped at about a mile and a half's distance from the landward walls.

Turkish army arrives before the walls, April 5.

Apparently, before the arrival of the main body of Mahomet's army, a sortie was made by the Greeks and Italians against those who had arrived, and this was possibly led by Justiniani.[3] They met at first with success, wounded many and killed a few Turks, but when Mahomet arrived the advantage of the besiegers in numbers was so overwhelming that no further sorties were attempted. The bridges leading across the foss to the Gates were broken down ; the Gates were closed and were not again opened so long as the siege lasted.

will be noticed that the second man sits a little forward of the first, and the hird of the second.

[1] *Ancient Ships*, by Mr. Cecil Torr.

[2] I have been indebted to Yule's valuable notes on Marco Polo for his esearches on the construction of ships. Unfortunately, Mr. Cecil Torr's ionograph on *Ancient Ships* (Cambridge, 1896) does not bring their history so ate down as the fifteenth century. For the period of which it treats it is imply perfect.

[3] Crit. xxv.

The Turkish army on April 6 advanced three quarters of a mile nearer to the walls, and on the following day again approached still closer. The imperial guard extended from the height crowned by Top Capou [1] to the Adrianople Gate, and thus occupied the valley of the Lycus. This district was known as the Mesoteichion. Their camp was so near to the walls as only to be just out of range of missiles discharged by the besieged.[2]

Formal
offer of
peace.

The law of the Koran requires, or is believed to require, that before war is definitely declared there shall be a formal offer of peace, and accordingly before the siege commenced Mahomet made such a proposal. To men who knew their own weakness and the tremendous odds against them any such offer must have been tempting. He sent messengers to declare that if the city were given up to him he would consent to allow the citizens to remain ; he would not deprive them of their property, their wives or their children, but take all under his protection. As the inhabitants knew well the fate of a population when conquered by a Turkish army, they might possibly have accepted the proposal, if they had had any confidence in the oath of the proposer. The answer sent was that they would consent to other conditions, but never to the surrender of the city.[3]

Upon this refusal Mahomet at once made his dispositions for a regular siege.

[1] As may be seen from the note in the Appendix on the position of the St. Romanus Gate, I believe that when Top Capou, which beyond doubt had been known as the Gate of Saint Romanus, was closed, the Pempton was generally spoken of as the St. Romanus Gate. The Italians, who had the largest share in the defence in the Lycus valley, probably ignorant of any name for the Military Gate which led from the city into the peribolos, called it by the name of the nearest Civil Gate. Hence I propose to speak of the Pempton as the Romanus Gate and of the Civil Gate crowning the seventh hill by its present Turkish name of Top Capou—that is, Cannon Gate—a name which it probably acquired by a reversal of the process which had led the Italians to speak of the Pempton as St. Romanus.

[2] Crit. xxvi.   [3] Crit. xxvi.

CHAPTER XI

TOPOGRAPHY OF CONSTANTINOPLE; DISPOSITION OF MAHO-
MET'S FORCES AND CANNON; ESTIMATE OF FIGHTING MEN
UNDER EMPEROR; VENETIANS AND GENOESE : DISPARITY
IN NUMBERS: ARMS AND EQUIPMENT: ATTACKS ON
THERAPIA AND PRINKIPO.

IN order to understand these dispositions and the operations *Topo-graphy of Constanti-nople.* of the siege which had now begun it is necessary to take account of the topography of the city. Constantinople in modern times comprises not only Stamboul but the large and even more populous district situated on the northern shore of the Golden Horn. This district was known in mediaeval times as Pera.[1] On the slope of Pera hill towards the Horn the Genoese were in possession of a walled city called Galata. Sometimes this city is described as Galata of Pera. In modern times, however, Pera is the name of the city on the north of the Golden Horn, exclusive of Galata. In 1453 what is now known as Stamboul was the only portion of the present city to which the name Con-stantinople was applied.[2]

The city about to be besieged is situated on a peninsula at the south-west extremity of the Bosporus. It is, roughly speaking, an isosceles triangle with its base to landward. One of the sides is bounded by the Marmora and the other by the Golden Horn. It was surrounded by walls, which, with a few short intervals, still remain. On the two sides bounded

---

[1] The Greek $\pi\acute{\epsilon}\rho\alpha = trans$, over or beyond.

[2] It is usually stated that Stamboul or Istamboul is a corruption of $\epsilon\dot{\iota}\varsigma\ \tau\dot{\eta}\nu$ $\pi\acute{o}\lambda\iota\nu$, though Dr. Koelle disputes this derivation and considers that it is a mere shortening of the name Constantinople by the Turks, analogous to Skender or Iskender from Alexander. Koelle's *Tartar and Turk.*

by the sea they were built close to the water's edge. In the course of centuries the Golden Horn had silted up a deposit of mud which even before 1453 formed a foreshore outside the north walls of a sufficient extent to have allowed Cantacuzenus to open a foss from Seraglio Point to Aivan Serai, formerly known as Cynegion. The side of the triangle most open to attack was that which faced the land and extended from the Horn to the Marmora. The walls on this landward side, constructed mainly during the reign of Theodosius the Second, had proved themselves during a period of a thousand years sufficiently strong to have enabled the citizens successfully to resist upwards of twenty sieges, and previous to the introduction of cannon were justly regarded as invulnerable.[1]

The landward walls are four miles long. From the Marmora to a point where the land has a steep slope for about half a mile down to the Golden Horn, they are triple. The inner and loftiest is about forty feet high and is strengthened by towers sixty feet high along its whole length and distant from each other usually about one hundred and eighty feet. Outside this wall is a second, about twenty-five feet high, with towers similar to though smaller than those along the inner wall. This wall alone is of a strength that in any other mediaeval city would have been considered efficient.

Between these two walls was the Peribolos or enclosure, which, though of varying width, is usually between fifty and sixty feet broad. Outside the second was yet another wall, which was a continuation in height of the scarp or inner wall of the ditch or foss and which may conveniently be called a breastwork. This breastwork, like the other two, was crenellated. Though, from the fact that it has been easier of access than either of the others, the summit has mostly perished, some portions of it are still complete. It is important, however, to note that the third wall or breast-

---

[1] In 1204 the Venetians and Crusaders under Dandolo and Monferra entered the ci ty by capturing the western portion of the walls on the side o the Horn.

work is disregarded by contemporary writers, and that they speak of the second as the Outer Wall. A second enclosure, called by the Greeks the Parateichion to distinguish it from the Peribolos, exists between the second and the third walls. The foss or ditch, which has withstood four and a half centuries of exposure since it last served as the first line of defence, is still in good condition. It has a width of about sixty feet.

The landward wall contained a number of gates which are conveniently described as Civil Gates and which during times of peace gave access to the city over bridges which were destroyed when it was besieged. The most important of these for our present purpose are the Chariseus, the modern Adrianople Gate; Top Capou or Cannon Gate, known in earlier times as the St. Romanus Gate, and the Pegè or Gate of the Springs, now called Silivria Gate. Besides these there were Military Gates leading from the city through the inner wall into the enclosures which were known in earlier times by their numbers (counting from the Marmora end of the walls) or from the division of the army stationed near them. The most noteworthy of these were the Third or Triton and the Fifth or Pempton. The latter is in the Lycus valley, about halfway between Top Capou and the Gate of Adrianople, and was spoken of during the siege as the St. Romanus Gate.[1]

As the most important military events in the history of the siege of Constantinople took place in the valley of the Lycus, between the Top Capou on the south and the Adrianople Gate on the north of the valley, it is desirable that the configuration of the locality should be noted carefully. Each of these gates is upon the summit of a hill, the Adrianople Gate indeed being the highest point in the city and, as such, having had near it, as is the almost invariable rule in lands occupied by Greeks, a church dedicated to St. George, who

---

[1] The position of the walls and gates is fully and admirably described in Professor Van Millingen's *Byzantine Constantinople*, who, however, does not suggest that the Pempton was the Romanus Gate of the chroniclers of the siege.

took the place of Apollo when the empire became Christian.[1]
Between the two gates exists a valley, about a hundred feet
below their level, which is drained by a small stream called
the Lycus. The distance between the two gates is seven
eighths of a mile. The double walls of Theodosius connect
them, while in front of the Outer Wall was an enclosure with
the usual breastwork forming the side of the foss. The
Lycus enters below these walls through a well-constructed
passage still in existence, and flows through the city until it
empties itself into the Marmora at Vlanga Bostan. The
tower beneath which it has been led is halfway between the
Adrianople Gate and Top Capou. About two hundred yards
to the north of this tower is the Fifth Military Gate or
Pempton, spoken of sometimes by the Byzantines as the Gate
of St. Kyriakè, from a church within the city which was close
to it, called the Romanus Gate by the writers on the siege,
and on old Turkish maps described as Hedjoum Capou or
the Gate of the Assault.[2] The foss has a number of dams
at irregular distances down each side of the valley. In its
lowest part no dams were necessary.[3]

The walls between Top Capou and the Adrianople Gate
were known as the Mesoteichion, and the name seems to
have been applied also to the whole of the valley. The portion of the walls on either side of the Adrianople Gate, or
perhaps those only on the high ground to the north of it,
was known as the Myriandrion—a name which was applied
occasionally to the Gate itself. From a tower to which
Leonard gives the name Bactatinian, near where the Lycus
entered the city, to Top Capou, the walls were described as
the Bachaturean.

Though the two magnificent Theodosian walls were as

[1] This was destroyed in the time of Suliman and replaced by a mosque
which is called after his daughter Miramah, though the Greeks were allowed
to build a church of St. George almost alongside it.

[2] Dr. Mordtmann is my authority for this statement. See note in the
Appendix on the position of the Romanus Gate.

[3] Paspates claims that there was always water in the foss during a siege,
though it was of no great depth. See p. 42 of his Πολιορκία τῆς Κωνσταντινουπόλεως. It is remarkable, however, that no mention is made of water by
the contemporary writers on the last siege.

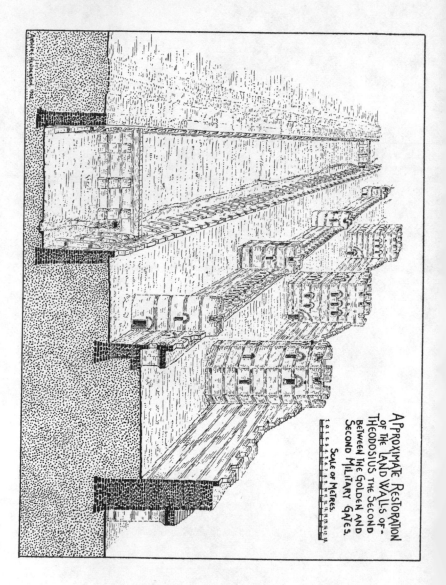

APPROXIMATE RESTORATION
OF THE LAND WALLS OF
THEODOSIUS THE SECOND
BETWEEN THE GOLDEN AND
SECOND MILITARY GATES.

SCALE OF METRES.

This photograph shows the present condition of a portion of the Landward Walls. They remain for the most part in an equally good state of preservation. The Inner and the Second, usually called the Outer, Wall and the Foss (now without water) are clearly shown. The Third Wall or Breastwork has lost its upper portion and its crenelations, except in a few places. The photograph is reproduced from one by M. Irenian, of Constantinople.

well constructed as elsewhere, and to the eye of an ordinary observer the city was as strongly protected in the Lycus valley as anywhere, yet this place appears to have been considered by many of the enemies of the city as its weakest point. Here, says Dethier, with whom Professor Van Millingen agrees, was the Heel of Achilles.[1] Many previous invaders, ending with Murad in 1422, had encamped in the Mesoteichion as the most suitable position for an attack upon the city.[2]

The accompanying sketch of the walls will show their general plan.

Under normal conditions a large detachment of the defenders of such high lines of walls ought to have been on the city side of the great Inner Wall. So few, however, were the besieged, that all had to pass into the enclosures to meet the enemy at the second or Outer Wall. Partly because of the small number of men, but partly also because it had been allowed to get out of repair,[3] the Inner Wall, which, as the highest and strongest, ought to have been the most serious obstacle, was hardly relied upon as a means of defence. Chalcondylas says [4] that the emperor and the leading Greeks deliberated as to where the enemy was to be resisted, and that they decided that they should defend the Outer Wall, which was strengthened by the foss in front of it, as had been done when Murad had attacked the city thirty-one years before. Leonard expressly states that the imperial troops were sufficient to guard only the Outer Wall, and the stockade which, at a late period of the siege, replaced a portion of it. As his own countrymen took part in this task, his testimony is entirely credible.[5] He adds, however, that in his opinion this plan of defence was a blunder; that he was

---

[1] *Byzantine Constantinople*, p. 86.

[2] Barbaro describes it as the place ' dove che sun la più debel porta de tuta la tera,' p. 21. The weakest gate he calls ' San Romano.'

[3] Quite a considerable number of towers in the Outer Wall bear inscriptions showing that they were repaired after the Turkish siege of 1422.

[4] P. 159.

[5] 'Antemurale solum urbis vallumque sat videbatur tutari posse,' p, 93.
' Operosa autem protegendi vallum et antemurale nostris fuit cura,' p. 95.

always persuaded that the lofty Inner Wall ought to have been kept ready as a refuge in case of retreat; that those walls which, through neglect or hard weather, had become broken or useless for operations against the enemy, might have been repaired even within the time which elapsed between the proposal for war and the commencement of the siege. Had they been repaired and guarded, they would have provided a reserve of safety to the city. It is when regretting that these repairs were not undertaken that, while excusing the emperor, Leonard breaks out into indignation, justifiable if his belief was well founded [1] against two persons in particular, Jagarus and a monk named Neophytus who had embezzled the moneys which had been bequeathed for the repair of the walls, and declares that the city was lost through the rascality of public robbers. Through their dishonesty, the besieged were driven to place all their hope in the Outer Wall and the foss. The Jews, he adds, were more prudent who when, at the siege of Jerusalem, they were defeated at the first wall, retreated to the second, and then to the third, by which they prolonged the siege of Vespasian and Titus for four years.

[1] Dethier argues that it was not. The Italians who were present in the city complain that the Greeks showed a want of patriotism in not being ready to give all their wealth for the defence of the empire. But the complaint is supported by very slight evidence. The Superior of the Franciscans (Dethier's *Siege of Constantinople*, p. 490) says that the city was lost through the avarice of the Greeks, because they would not consent to pay its defenders. He instances the case of a woman who had jewels and money of the value of 150,000 ducats, and of a man whose wealth in moveables amounted to 80,000 ducats. Jagarus and Neophytus, who are mentioned by Leonard, had been charged with the repairs of the walls, for which money had been given them, but, according to him, had misappropriated it. When the city was captured, 70,000 gold pieces were discovered by the Turks. But it is noteworthy that Phrantzes, who was in a better condition to know the truth in such a matter, has nothing but praise for Jagarus (p. 225). The statement of Leonard regarding them is examined by Dethier, who suggests that the sentence regarding the finding of the coin is due to the incorporation of a marginal note. Zorzo Dolfin, whose narrative is largely copied from Leonard, gives a somewhat different version.

As stated on the preceding page, the inscriptions on the Outer Wall still show that many towers had been repaired in the interval between Murad's siege and that of Mahomet, and two inscriptions at least, which may perhaps be taken as intended to apply to all the towers so repaired, bear the name of Jagarus himself. (Professor Van Millingen, p. 108, and Dethier's notes on Leonard, 593–5.)

Probably the opinion of the soldiers on such a question was worth more than that of the archbishop.[1]

Under these circumstances, the defenders of the city took up their position in the Peribolos or enclosure. The broken Inner Wall was behind them, the strong Outer Wall was in front. The Military Gates from the city into the enclosure were few and far between, there being only one usually in the long distance between the Civil Gates. The only other entrances into the enclosures were at the ends terminating at the Civil Gates.

With this explanation we may now understand the disposition of his troops and cannon made by Mahomet. He placed Zagan Pasha at the head of an army which was charged to guard the whole of Pera, to watch the Genoese in Galata and the whole of the northern shore of the Golden Horn, together with a part of the southern shore as far as the Woodgate or Xyloporta, which was at the extremity of the landward walls. He was ordered to build a bridge over the upper portion of the Horn, so that his troops might take part in the attack upon the city.

Disposition of Mahomet's army

The attack upon the landward walls between the Woodgate and up the hill in front of the palaces of Blachern and Porphyrogenitus, and as far as the Chariseus or Adrianople Gate, was entrusted to Caraja Pasha, the head of the European division. Certain of the guns were given to him in order that he might attack the wall at one of its weakest parts, probably where it runs at right angles to the end of the foss.

Isaac Pasha, the head of the Asiatic troops, and Mahmoud, both men who had had great experience in war, commanded the Asiatic division, which covered the ground between Top Capou and the Marmora.

The most important position, however, was that which existed between the Adrianople Gate and Top Capou known as the Mesoteichion. This was the place which Mahomet chose as the principal point of attack. There, he considered,

---

[1] Riccherio (often quoted as Sansovino, who was the editor of Riccherio and has written a bright account of the conquest) says, 'La speranza della difesa era tutta nel antimuro.' (Dethier's *Siege*, p. 955.)

was the Achilles' heel of the city. There, with Halil Pasha under him, were his head-quarters. His lofty tent of red and gold [1] was pitched about a quarter of a mile from the walls on a small knoll, which is described as opposite the Adrianople Gate and also as opposite that of Romanus. His tent was surrounded by those of the invincible Janissaries who, with other chosen troops, constituted his body-guard and occupied the same valley.

The Turkish army extended in front of the entire length of the landward walls. The Turks had dug a trench for their own defence in front of the whole of their line, and had placed a wooden palisade upon the earth thus dug out. This was quite near the edge of the foss itself and was pierced at intervals, so that, while it protected the besiegers, it also allowed them to keep up a constant fire on the besieged.[2]

On the Marmora the walls were to be watched by the fleet under Baltoglu from the southern end of the landward walls, round the present Seraglio Point as far as Neorion, which was near the end of the boom. The main object of the fleet was, however, to force an entry into the harbour, and for this purpose to capture or destroy the ships at the boom, an object which Baltoglu attempted to attain from the very commencement of the siege.[3]

The city was thus under attack on two sides, the third— namely, that looking over the Golden Horn—protected by the boom, was for the present inaccessible to the Turkish fleet.

The difficulty of determining the number and disposition of Mahomet's cannon opposite the landward walls arises from the fact that the position of several of them was changed and that their numbers possibly varied. Phrantzes mentions fourteen batteries along the length of the wall, each containing four guns. Barbaro speaks of nine batteries. Montaldo says that the Turks had in all two hundred guns or ' torments.'[4] Each of the nine batteries was strengthed by the addition of a heavy gun. Critobulus

[1] Chalcondylas, p. 95, Ven. edition.   [2] Ibid. p. 159.
[3] Crit. xxviii., and Barbaro.   [4] Ch. xxvii.

represents Mahomet as stating after his guns had done their work that he had opened a way into the city at three places, and this declaration affords a safe guide to the general disposition of the cannon. These were, first, between the present Tekfour Serai and the Adrianople Gate; second, opposite or near the Pempton or Gate of the Assault (usually spoken of by contemporaries as the Romanus Gate [1]) in the Lycus valley, and the last near the Third Military Gate between the Pegè or Silivria Gate, and the Rhegium Gate, now called Mevlevihana Capou. Here were the three principal stations of Mahomet's cannon. At these three places the ruined condition of the wall bears testimony to the vigorous attack of cannon. At them and nowhere else is it possible to pass over the foss, the breastwork and Outer Wall, and to see that the Inner Wall has been so broken down that a passage into the city was possible.[2]

Three cannon are especially remembered on account of their great size. According to Leonard, the largest—that, namely, cast by Urban, which threw a ball of twelve hundred pounds weight—was first placed at Caligaria [3] which then, as now, was 'protected neither by a foss nor by a front wall.' It was destroyed either by the besieged or through an accident by which Urban was killed, after it had done considerable damage to the walls.[4] It was, however, recast and transferred to the Lycus valley, where it demolished the Bactatinean tower.[5] The statement of Chalcondylas is that of these three large guns one was stationed opposite the Imperial Palace, probably at Caligaria, the second opposite the Romanus Gate, where the sultan had fixed his camp, and the third between them.[6]

The largest and most powerful gun remained during the siege at the Mesoteichion, in front of the imperial tent.[7]

---

[1] See Note in Appendix claiming that during the siege the Pempton was usually called the Gate of St. Romanus.

[2] Pusculus also gives these three places, but with the difference that he mistakes the Second Military Gate for the Third.

[3] Barb. p. 21.   [4] Phr. 242–47.   [5] Dolfin, p. 994.   [6] παρὰ τὰ πλάγια.

[7] See Prof. Van Millingen, 85–92. Barbaro states that the cannon were stationed at four places: opposite the Pegè Gate, by which he means the Third

These cannon are variously described as bombards, machines, skeves, helepoles (or 'takers of cities'), torments, heleboles, and teleboles. They threw stone balls of great size. The balls had been brought from the Black Sea. The largest, says Chalcondylas, was fired seven times a day and once each night. Archbishop Leonard states that he measured one which had been fired over the wall, and found it to be eleven spans (or eighty-eight inches) in circumference. Nor is such measurement exaggerated. Some of the stone balls have been preserved. They were probably fired over the wall, did not break, and remain nearly in the position where they fell. I have measured two of them, and they are exactly eighty-eight inches in circumference.[1] Tetaldi states that there were ten thousand culverins, and the same number is given by Montaldo. The number is possibly exaggerated. Yet Leonard speaks of 'innumerable machines' being advanced towards the wall, and afterwards of a great number of small guns being employed to batter the walls along all their lines. None of the cannon, I think, were mounted on wheels : the Great Cannon certainly was not, for Critobulus describes how it was first carefully pointed towards the object intended to be struck, and then embedded in its position with blocks of wood preparatory to firing.

Contemporaneously with the disposal of the large cannon, orders were given to fill up the ditch in front of them.

When we turn from the preparations made by Mahomet to besiege the city to those which the emperor and the citizens had made or were making, the first point which strikes us is the enormous disparity in numbers which the respective leaders had under them. To meet the mighty host of trained warriors under Mahomet, the emperor had

Constantine's army.

Military Gate (Triton) ; opposite the Palace, by which he probably means in the angle now occupied by the Greek cemetery opposite the Palace of Porphyrogenitus or Tekfour Serai ; opposite the Cresu Gate, probably the Chariseus or Adrianople Gate, and opposite the Romanus Gate. Philelphus also mentions the Pegè Gate as one of the chief places of attack (ii. 809).

[1] Pusculus gives fourteen palms as the circumference; Phrantzes and Critobulus, twelve ; while Barbaro gives thirteen to fourteen.

only about eight thousand men. This is the estimate in which nearly all writers concur. Phrantzes had exceptional means of forming a judgment on this point. He states[1] that Constantine ordered a census to be made of all men, including monks, capable of bearing arms, and that when the lists were sent in he was charged with making the summary. This showed that there were four thousand nine hundred and eighty-three available Greeks and scarcely two thousand foreigners. The result was so appalling that he was charged by the emperor not to let it be known. The estimate made by Phrantzes, though almost incredible, is substantially confirmed by other writers. Tetaldi says that there were between six thousand and seven thousand combatants within the city 'and not more.'[2] Leonard makes the number a little higher and gives as an estimate six thousand Greeks and three thousand foreigners. Dolfin, probably following Leonard, arrives at a like conclusion. Ducas says that 'there were not more than eight thousand.'

The powerful contingent of three thousand Italians is worthy of separate notice. Nearly all were of Venetian or Genoese origin. In them the city had the aid of men belonging to the most virile communities in the Mediterranean. The story of the trading establishments in the Levant, the Archipelago, and the Black Sea belonging to the citizens of Venice and Genoa is a brilliant record of daring, of adventure, and of energy. The expansion of the two states began about the time of the Latin conquest. Everywhere along these shores are the remains of castles built by Genoese or Venetians during the two centuries preceding the Moslem conquest. Dandolo had played the most important part in the capture of the city in 1204, and the capture gave Venice the sovereignty of the seas. The Genoese had aided the Greeks to recapture the city. Each republic had gained territory in Eastern lands. Each owned certain islands in the Aegean. The Genoese had succeeded in forming a large and important colony in Galata, which was now a fortified city. To check Turkish

---

[1] P. 241, κοσμικούς τε καὶ μοναχούς.   [2] See *ante*, p. 193.

progress was almost as important to the republics as to the Greeks. Venetians and Genoese recognised that once Constantinople was in the hands of the sultan, there would be an end of their development eastward of Cape Matapan. They were, therefore, both fighting for their own interests. They had much to lose and nothing to gain by the success of Mahomet. Nor were the soldiers of the republics destitute of chivalrous spirit. The rough sailor-surgeon, Barbaro, notes that other Venetians as well as Trevisano were willing to fight for the honour of God and the benefit of Christendom. Leonard and other writers testify to equally lofty sentiment on the part of the Genoese Justiniani. In their character and conduct, not less than in their mixed motives, derived from self-interest and chivalry, these foreign adventurers remind English readers of the Drakes, Frobishers, Raleighs, and other heroes of our own Elizabethan period. Unhappily for the city and for civilisation, Venice was unable to send more men before the final catastrophe. But to the eternal glory of the Venetians within the city, whose names are duly recorded by Barbaro 'for a perpetual memorial,' and of the Genoese who aided them, the conduct of the combatants from both republics was worthy of the compatriots of Marco Polo and of Columbus.

On the one side was an army of one hundred and fifty thousand men, containing at least twelve thousand of the best trained troops in the world; on the other, a miserable number of eight thousand fighting men to defend a length of between twelve and thirteen miles of walls.

The emperor, with Justiniani, completed the arrangements for the defence of the city. Justiniani with the seven hundred men he had brought with him to Constantinople, consisting of his crew and four hundred men in armour,[1] was at first placed in charge of the walls between the Blachern Palace and the Adrianople Gate, but was soon transferred with his men and some of the bravest Greeks to the Lycus valley as the position of greatest importance, honour,

[1] Crit. xxv.

and danger. The emperor himself fixed his headquarters in the same position. In this valley the choicest troops of the city and those of the sultan were thus face to face. Between the Adrianople Gate and Tekfour Serai was a contingent of Italians under three brothers, Paul, Antony, and Troilus Bocchiardo. They were stationed, says Phrantzes, at the Myriandrion, because there the city was in great jeopardy ; [1] Leonard says, ' in loco arduo Myriandri ; ' Dolfin, speaking of the same place under a somewhat different name, says ' in loco arduo Miliadro, dove pareva la cita piu debole.' [2] This contingent had been provided by the Bocchiardi at their own cost. The men were furnished with spingards and balistas for hurling stones at the enemy. The Caligaria—that is, the gate of that name, now called Egri Capou or Crooked Gate—and the walls thence as far as Tekfour Serai were defended by Caristo, an old Venetian, and by a German named John Grant, who had taken service with the emperor. Over the imperial palace at Blachern waved the flag of the Lion of St. Mark side by side with the banner of the emperor, to denote that Minotto, the Venetian bailey, was in command in that district. Archbishop Leonard and other Genoese, together with Hieronymus, were with him to assist in defending the walls as far as the Xyloporta on the edge of the Golden Horn.

On the emperor's left the walls were guarded by Cataneo and Theophilus Palaeologus at the Silivria Gate, while Contarini, the most renowned member of the Venetian colony, and Andronicus Cantacuzenus defended the walls around the Golden Gate and to the sea. [3] Under these leaders, along the whole length of the landward wall, Genoese, Venetians, and Greeks fought side by side.

Between a tower in the current off Seraglio Point and the Imperial Gate—that is, at the Acropolis, and thus

---

[1] ὅπου καὶ ἐν ἐκείνοις τοῖς μέρεσιν ἡ πόλις ἦν ἐπικίνδυνος. Phrantzes, p. 253.

[2] P. 1013. The *locus arduus* of the Myriandrion is the highest site of the city walls. Professor Van Millingen makes it identical with the Mesoteichion (p. 85), but Critobulus distinguishes between the two places (ch. xxvi.).

[3] Leonard ; but Phrantzes says, p. 253, that Manuel, a Genoese, was in command at the Golden Gate.

guarding the entrance to the harbour [1]—Gabriel Trevisano, already mentioned as the Venetian noble who was serving ' per honor de Dio et per honor di tuta la Christianitade ' was in command.[2] There, says Leonard, he did his duty as a shepherd and not as a hireling.

Near him for the present were the captains and the crews of the two Cretan ships who kept the Horaia Gate. Cardinal Isidore was at Seraglio Point with a body of two hundred men guarding the walls commencing at the Great Tower of St. Demetrius. James Contarini was stationed at Psamatia and guarded the western portion of the Marmora walls. The Caloyers or Greek monks were also in this part of the city, and near them was a small band of Turkish mercenaries under the command of Orchan.[3] The Grand Duke Notaras with a small reserve of men was near the church of the Apostles, now occupied by the Mahmoudieh Mosque, to render aid wherever it might be required.[4] Lastly, Diedo, who had been made admiral of the fleet, was stationed near the end of the boom.[5]

The cannon possessed by the besieged seem to have been few and of little value. Leonard relates that they were short of powder and of arms, and that it was impossible to use the cannon on account of the damage they were found to do to their own walls. Zorzo Dolfin confirms these statements and adds that the Venetians were short of saltpetre.[6]

---

[1] See Professor Van Millingen as to position of this gate, pp. 230-234. There were probably two Imperial Gates on the Golden Horn.

[2] According to Pusculus, Trevisano was from the first at Aivan Serai, the extreme west of the walls on the Horn and close to the Xyloporta.

[3] Barbaro, p. 19.

[4] Phrantzes states that the reserve was under Cantacuzenus and Nicephorus Palaeologus, and that the Grand Duke was in charge of the region from the Petrion to the Gate of St. Theodosia.

[5] Leonard's account hardly varies from that of Phrantzes and others, except that, with his strong religious prejudices, he prefers to name foreigners rather than Greeks. The distributions of the defenders of the city given by Zorzi Dolfin and Pusculus do vary, however, from those given by Phrantzes and Barbaro. These differences are set out in Dr. Mordtman's *Esquisse Topographique*, p. 23. See also Krause's *Eroberungen von Constantinopel*, p. 169.

[6] Dethier's *Siege*, p. 110. Chalcondylas says that it was found that the big gun of the Greeks did more damage to them by its recoil than to the enemy.

The emperor and Justiniani had collected arms and various kinds of missiles, shot and arrows, and all sorts of machines.[1]

Each army was equipped in much the same manner. Modern, mediaeval and ancient arms and equipment were employed side by side with each other. We read of dolabras, of wooden turrets, and of the Turks raising their shields above their heads and making a testudo.[2] Stone shot are thrown by the great slings, or catapults, known as mangonels or trebuchets, as well as by cannon. While each side relied largely on the bow, each side also discharged missiles at the other from arquebuses and culverins. Long-bows were so numerous in the Turkish army that the discharge of arrows from them is described by more than one author as darkening the sky. Cross-bows appear also in the description of the siege under the names of balistae and spingards. 'The archers,' says La Brocquière, 'were the best troops the Turks possessed.'[3] The ordinary soldier in the Turkish army was armed with a wooden shield and a scimitar. A few, among both the besiegers and the besieged, were armed with lances.

Uniformity in equipment or dress was not even attempted. Tetaldi says that in the Turkish army less than a fourth were armed with hauberks and wore jacques—that is, quilted tunics of cotton or leather, well padded;[4] that some were well armed in French, some in Hungarian, fashion, some in other modes; some had iron helmets, and others long-bows or cross-bows.

The Janissaries were trained to act eiuuci as cavalry or infantry. They carried bows and small wooden shields, and were further armed with a long lance or with a scimitar. The Anatolian division was composed mostly of cavalry.

[1] Crit. xvii. The word *machine* is usually used by contemporary writers to designate a cannon, though here, as elsewhere, it may be employed in a general sense. What is certain is that such cannon as the Greeks possessed were few in number and of small value.

[2] *Isidori Lamentatio*, p. 676 ; also Christoforo Riccherio, Sansovin, p. 957 : both in Dethier's *Siege*.

[3] P. 369.   [4] P. 145. Boutell's *Arms and Armour*.

Leonard, however, points out that though the cavalry were numerous they fought as infantry. Philelphus, who was a contemporary envoy at the Porte, states that the Anatolian troops were armed with scimitars, maces, and small shields.

The great superiority of the Turks as regards arms was in the cannon. While, as we have seen, the besieged could not use such cannon as they had for fear of destroying the walls from which they were fired, the Turk was under no such disadvantage, and was entirely up to date with the very latest improvements in heavy guns. The siege of Constantinople in fact marks an era in the employment of large cannon and gave to the world the first noteworthy intimation that the stone walls of the Middle Ages constituted no longer a secure defence. Cannon had, indeed, been known a century and a half earlier in Western Europe, and had been employed both by and against the Turks on the Danube; [1] but the astonishment which the introduction of large cannon caused at the siege of Constantinople shows that while the invention itself was new to the people of the East, its development was hardly less surprising to those of the West. / Critobulus remarks upon the siege that 'it was the cannon which did everything.' So novel was the invention that he gives a detailed account of the casting of one of the big guns, and explains how the powder was made, how the gun was mounted and loaded, and how it fired its stone ball. 'When fire is applied to the touch-hole, the powder lights quicker than thought. The discharge makes the earth around it to tremble, and sends forth an incredible roar. The stone ball passes out with irresistible force and energy, strikes the wall at which it has been aimed, overthrows it, and is itself dashed into a thousand pieces.' No wall was so hard or had such power of resistance that it could withstand the shock. Such is the incredible and unthinkable nature of the machine to which, as the ancient tongue had no name for it, he suggests that of helepolis or 'Taker of Cities.'

[1] La Brocquière, p. 361, where five forts on the Save are described as well furnished with artillery. He particularly notices three brass cannon.

In the early days of the siege, or possibly just before it began, Mahomet attacked all the Greek villages which had escaped the savagery of the troops in their march to the capital. Some kind of fortification existed at Therapia on the Bosporus. This was attacked by the Janissaries. Many of its defenders were slain, and the remainder, consisting of forty men, seeing that resistance was useless, surrendered. They were all impaled. Another fortification, known as Studium, was similarly attacked. Its thirty-six survivors were taken to a spot near the wall, so that they might be seen by the citizens, and were there impaled. At the island of Prinkipo the round tower still exists which had been a place of refuge for the protection of the inmates of the adjacent monastery. The monastery itself had been used as a place of retreat for the princely members of the imperial family, and had thus given its name to the Princes Islands. Baltoglu was sent with a portion of the fleet to attack it. Although he had cannon with him, he was unable to destroy its solid Byzantine masonry, and the thirty well-armed defenders refused to surrender. His crews thereupon cut down the neighbouring brushwood, and with this, with straw, and with sulphur, he smoked out the garrison. While some perished in the flames, others broke through the burning materials and surrendered. The admiral killed those who were armed, and sold into slavery the other inhabitants of the island.[1]

[1] There are still the remains of two towers in Prinkipo. I fix upon the one near the ruined monastery opposite the island of Antirobithos as the place of attack, with some hesitation. The account is given by Critobulus, xxxiii.

CHAPTER XII

THE SIEGE

INVESTMENT BY TURKS; FIRST ASSAULT FAILS; ATTEMPT
TO FORCE BOOM; ATTEMPT TO CAPTURE SHIPS BRING-
ING AID; GALLANT FIGHT AND DEFEAT OF TURKISH
FLEET; TURKISH ADMIRAL DEGRADED; TRANSPORT OF
TURKISH SHIPS ACROSS PERA INTO THE GOLDEN HORN.

WE have now arrived at the last act of the tragedy of
Constantinople. The Queen City is cut off from the outside
world. Its small fleet dare not attempt to pass outside the
boom which excludes the Turkish fleet. An overwhelming
force of ships had been collected to keep out supplies of
men or provisions. Before its landward walls is an army of
one hundred and fifty thousand fighting men and a crowd
perhaps equally numerous awaiting their chance of plundering the remnant of that wealth which had once been contained in the great storehouse of the Western world.

Mahomet's
army
before the
walls on
April 7,
1453.

On April 7 Mahomet's army had taken up its position
along the whole four miles length of the landward walls
from the Marmora to the Golden Horn, and with the aid of
the fleet prevented all access to or egress from the city. But
the men in it had made up their minds to hold it or to die.
They began on the first day of the siege to make the best show
they could. At the emperor's request, but also at their own
desire, the crews of the galleys under Trevisano and of two
others, numbering in all a thousand men, landed and marched
along the whole length of the landward walls in presence
of the enemy with the object of proving to the Turks that
they would have to fight Venetians as well as Greeks.
On the 9th the ships in the harbour were drawn up in

battle array, ten being at the boom and seventeen in reserve further within the harbour.

The Turkish army on the 11th placed its guns in position before the walls.

On the 12th the batteries began playing against the walls and, with ceaseless monotony, day and night the discharge of these new machines was heard throughout the city during the next six days. Their immediate effect soon showed that the walls, solid as they had proved themselves in a score of former sieges, were not sufficiently strong to resist the new invention. The huge balls, fired from a short distance amid a cloud of the blackest smoke, making a terrible roar and breaking into a thousand pieces as they struck the walls, so damaged them that they required daily and constant repair. The narratives of those present agree in representing the defenders from the very commencement of the bombardment as being constantly engaged in repairing the injury done by these 'takers of cities.' Large and unwieldy as they were, unmounted and half buried amid the stones and beams by which they were kept in position, they were yet engines of destruction such as the world had never seen. Planted on the very edge of the foss and requiring such management and care that the largest could only be fired seven times a day, they gave proof within a week of their employment that they could destroy slowly but surely the walls which had stood since the reign of the younger Theodosius. The defenders in vain suspended bales of wool and tried other means of lessening the damage. All they could accomplish was to repair and strengthen the damaged portions as rapidly as possible.

Cannonading commences April 12.

Already by April 18 a part of the Outer Wall and even two great towers of the Inner had been broken down in the Lycus valley.[1] Justiniani had been compelled to take in hand the construction of a stockade for their defence 'where the attack was the fiercest and the damage to the walls the greatest.' The walls of the foss, including the breastwork, had been broken down, the foss itself in this place

Damage done by cannon by April 18.

[1] Crit. xxxiv.

partly filled. The wonderful success already achieved by his great guns led Mahomet to believe that he could already capture the city. Accordingly, at two hours after sunset on April 18 he gave orders for the first time to attempt the city by assault.

Attempt to capture city by assault on April 18 fails.

Infantry, cuirassiers, archers, and lancers joined in this night attack. They crossed the foss and vigorously attempted to break through or destroy the Outer Wall. They had observed that in the repairs the besieged had been driven to employ beams, smaller timber, crates of vine cuttings, and other inflammable materials. These they attempted to set on fire ; but the attempt failed. The defenders extinguished the fires before they could get well hold. The Turks with hooks at the end of lances or poles then tried to pull down the barrels of earth which had been placed so as to form a crenellation and in this way to expose the defenders to the attacks of the archers and slingers. Others endeavoured to scale the hastily repaired and partially destroyed wall. During four hours Justiniani led his Italians and Greeks in the defence of the damaged part, and after a hard conflict the Turks were driven across the foss with a loss in killed and wounded estimated by Barbaro at two hundred.

The attack was local and not general, though Barbaro remarks that the emperor began to be in doubt whether general battle would not be given on this night, and ' we Christians were not yet ready for it.' The failure of this the first attack stimulated Greeks and Italians to press on the repairs to the Outer Wall. Every day, however, there were new assaults made at one place or another, but especially in the Lycus valley.

Attempt to force boom.

A few days after the return of Baltoglu with the fleet from Prinkipo, and probably contemporaneously with the attack in the Lycus valley on the 18th, the admiral was ordered to force a passage into the Golden Horn.

His fleet, counting vessels of all kinds, probably now numbered not less than three hundred and fifty ships. By their aid Mahomet hoped to gain possession of the harbour by destroying or forcing the boom. Accordingly, Baltoglu sailed down from the Double Columns, towards the ships stationed for its defence, and endeavoured to force an entry. The Turkish crews came on with the battle-cry of ' Allah, Allah!' and when within gun- and arrow-shot of their enemies closed bravely for the attack. The cuirassiers tried to burn the vessels at the boom with torches ; others discharged arrows bearing burning cotton, while others again endeavoured to cut the cables of some of the ships so that they might be free to destroy the boom. In other parts they sought to grapple with the defending vessels and if possible to capture them. Both sides fought fiercely, but the Greeks and Italians, under the leadership of the Grand Duke Notaras, had provided against all the Turkish means of attack. The defending ships were higher out of the water than those of the Turks, and this gave them an advantage in throwing stones and discharging darts and javelins. Stones tied to ropes had been taken aloft on the yards and bowsprits, and the dropping of these into vessels alongside caused great damage. Barrels and other vessels full of water were at hand to extinguish fire. After a short but fierce fight the assailants judged that for the present at least the attempt to capture the boom and thus obtain an entrance into the harbour was hopeless, and amid taunts and shouts of joy from the Christians withdrew to the Double Columns.

On April 20 we come to an incident at once interesting and suggestive.

In the midst of a story which is necessarily depressing from the consciousness that it is that of a lost cause, one incident is related by all Christian contemporary writers, whether eye-witnesses or not, with satisfaction or delight. This is the incident of a naval battle under the walls of the city itself. Spectators and writers dependent on the testimony of others who had seen the fight differ among themselves as to details but agree as to the main facts.

Three large Genoese ships on their way to Constantinople had been delayed at Chios [1] by northerly winds during the

Attempt to capture ships bringing aid.

[1] Ducas says four, but he is at variance with Leonard, Barbaro, and Phrantzes, and wrote his account from hearsay years afterwards.

month of March and part of April. Accounts differ as to
the object of their voyage. One would like to believe the
statement of Critobulus that they were sent by the pope to
bring provisions and help to the city and as an earnest of
the aid he was about to furnish, and that thirty triremes and
other great vessels were in preparation.[1] But Barbaro, who,
as a Venetian, seldom loses an opportunity of depreciating
the Genoese, says that they had been induced to sail for the
city by the imperial order allowing all Genoese ships
bringing provisions to enter their goods duty free. The
statement of Leonard, archbishop of Chios, that they had
on board soldiers, arms, and coin for Constantinople would
appear to confirm that of Critobulus.

The arrival of a fleet from Italy was expected and
anxiously looked for by all the inhabitants from the emperor
downwards. They had accepted, though they heartily
disliked, the Union, and they consoled themselves with the
belief that in return the pope and other Western rulers
would at once send a fleet with soldiers and munitions of
war. It was generally believed in the city that the ships
were sent by the pope. Even where it was doubted, all
agreed that the arrival of additional fighting men for the
defence of the walls was of supreme importance. Nor were
the Turks less interested. They, too, expected and feared
the arrival of ships from the West, and, in addition to their
objection to Italian ships, they had already learned the
value of Genoese and Venetian soldiers for the defence.

Ships
arrive at
mouth of
Bosporus.

When, about April 15, a south wind blew, the Genoese
weighed their anchors and made sail for the Dardanelles. On
their way they fell in with an imperial transport under
Flatanelas which had come from Sicily laden with corn.[2]
On the second day the wind became stronger and carried
the four ships through the straits and into the Marmora.
At about ten o'clock on the morning of April 20, their
crews saw in the distance the dome of Hagia Sophia.

When the Genoese ships were first seen, most of the
vessels of the Turkish fleet were anchored in the bay of

[1] Crit. xxxix.   [2] Phrantzes ; though Ducas says from Morea.

Dolmabagshe at the Double Columns. But the Turkish ships on the look-out at the entrance of the Bosporus appear to have observed the approaching vessels as soon as the watchmen in the city itself. They would also be seen by a portion of the Turkish army encamped outside the landward walls.

Upon the report of their coming the sultan himself galloped at once to his fleet, about two miles distant from his camp, and gave orders to the renegade Baltoglu to proceed with his vessels to meet the ships, to capture them if possible, but at any cost to prevent them passing the boom and entering the harbour of the Golden Horn. If he could not do that, he was told not to come back alive.[1]

The four ships desired to pass the boom ; the object of the Turkish fleet was to prevent them. Taking the lowest estimate of the number of the Turkish vessels sent against them, it was apparently hopeless that four ships dependent on the wind should be able to hold their own against a fleet of not less than a hundred and forty-five vessels so completely under control as that of Baltoglu, which contained triremes, biremes, and galleys. These Turkish ships, triremes, galleys, and even transports, were crowded with the best-equipped men of the army, including a body of archers and men heavily clad with helmets and breast-plates : in short, with as many of the sultan's best men as could be placed on board. Shields and bucklers were arranged around the larger galleys so as to form a breast-work of armour against arrows and javelins ; while on some of the boats the rude culverins of the period were ranged so as to bring them to bear against the four ships.

Then, after these hasty preparations, the Turkish fleet proceeded in battle array down the Bosporus to Seraglio Point and the Marmora. Captains and crews went out with confidence of an easy victory. The fight was to be against only four ships, and, with such overpowering superiority in numbers of skilled fighters, who could doubt of success ? The admiral, says Critobulus, believed that he had the

Turkish fleet resists.

[1] Ducas, p. 121, and Crit. xxxix.

Genoese already in his hand. Barbaro notes the shouts of delight with which the enemy came forward to the attack, the noise of their many oars, and the sound of their trumpets. 'They came on,' he says, 'like men who intended to win.'[1]

The archbishop, another spectator, notes also that the Turkish fleet advanced with every sign of joy, with the beating of drums, and the clanging of trumpets. Phrantzes, a third eye-witness, was specially impressed with the confidence with which the Turkish flotilla approached. They went on to meet the Genoese ships, he says, with drums and horns, believing that they could intercept them without difficulty. The wind being against them, sails were dispensed with, but as their progress was independent of wind the whole fleet advanced steadily to capture the foe.

Meantime the four ships kept on a direct course, steering for and striving to pass the tower of 'Megademetrius' at the Acropolis and to enter the Golden Horn.[2] As they sail along with a stiff south breeze behind them and keeping, as vessels usually keep on making for the Golden Horn with a southerly wind, well out from the land until they reach the Point, their progress is easily seen by the citizens. Many of them crowd the walls or climb the roofs of houses near the seashore, while others hasten to the Sphendone of the Hippodrome,[3] where they have a wide view of the Marmora and the entrance of the Bosporus.

Meantime the strong southerly wind has brought the four ships abreast of the city. Their short but sturdy hulls with high bows and loftier poops are driven steadily through the water by the big swelling mainsails o

---

[1] 'Come homini volonteroxi de aver victoria contra el suo inimigo (p. 23).

[2] Ducas, p. 121, says, to pass τὸν Μεγαδημήτριον τὸν ἀκρόπολιν. The tower stood near Seraglio Point; Dr. Mordtmann places it on the Golden Horn side, while Paspates, in Τὰ Βυζαντινὰ 'Ανάκτορα, p. 37, thought he had identified the foundations just beyond the bridge crossing the railway line to the Imperial Treasury. To have been a conspicuous landmark for ships steering from the Marmora to the harbour, as it is represented to have been, the church must have been very lofty if in the position adopted by Dr. Mordtmann.

[3] Pusculus, 385, Book iv.

the period. As they approach the Straits, when they are well in view from the Sphendone, they are met by the Turkish admiral who from the poop of his trireme commands them peremptorily to lower their sails. On their refusal he gives orders for attack. The leading boats pull for the ships, but both the advantages of wind and a considerable sea were with the larger vessels, while their greater height from the water made boarding under the circumstances extremely difficult. The Italians with axes and boathooks make short work of any who attempt it. The skirmish became a running fight in which the attackers shot their arrows and fire-bearing darts and threw their lances with little effect.

Fight commences.

The south wind continuing to blow, the ships held on their course until they entered the Bosporus and came near Seraglio Point. Then, all of a sudden, the wind fell,[1] and in a few minutes the sails flap idly under the very walls of the Acropolis.[2]

Wind drops.

The sudden fall of the wind had shifted the advantage of the position from the ships to the Turkish fleet. Then, indeed, says Pusculus, the real fight commenced. The Turkish admiral had apparently now complete justification for the belief that he would have an easy capture. The four ships were powerless to move, while Baltoglu could choose his own mode of attack by his hundred and fifty fighting vessels. When, while the ships were under the walls of the Acropolis, the wind fell, they would nevertheless drift over towards the Galata shore of the Bosporus by the current which after a south wind invariably sets in that direction. Probably they would be influenced also by the gust puffs which usually follow the sudden dropping of the south wind near Constantinople. The remainder of the combat is therefore to be fought at the mouth of the Golden Horn, between Seraglio Point and the shore east of Galata near Tophana, and just outside the walls of that city.

[1] Barbaro says, 'Quando queste quatro naves fo per mezo la zitade de nstantinopli subito el vento i bonazò' (p. 23).

[2] Pusculus iv. v. 415: 'Deserit illic ventus eas; cecidere sinus sub enibus arcis.'

Thousands of spectators had gathered to witness this second portion of the fight. The walls at Seraglio Point were crowded with soldiers and citizens fearing for the result but unable to render assistance. Nor could any aid be given by the crews of the ships of the imperial fleet which were near at hand on guard at the boom, though of course on the harbour side. At one time, says Phrantzes, the ships were within a stone's-throw of the land. On the opposite shore of the Golden Horn outside the walls of Galata, to which attackers and attacked were slowly drifting as they fought, the sultan and his suite watched the fight with interest not less keen than that of the Christians on the walls of Constantinople, but with the same confidence of success as was felt by the admiral.

Attack at mouth of Golden Horn.

A general attack was preceded by the order of Baltoglu to surround the becalmed ships. After the fleet had been disposed so as to act simultaneously, the order was given to begin the fight but, apparently, not to close in on the ships. Stone cannon-balls were discharged by the Turks and lances with lighted material were thrown so as to set fire to the sails or cordage. But the crews of the vessels attacked knew their business thoroughly. They easily extinguished the fire. From their turrets on the masts and their poops and lofty bows they threw their lances, shot their arrows. and hurled stones on the Turks unceasingly, and Baltoglu soon found that this method of attack was useless. Thereupon he shouted the order at the top of his voice for all the vessels to advance and board. The admiral himself selected for his special task the imperial transport as the largest of the four ships. He ran his trireme's bow against her poop and tried to board her. For between two and three hours— that is, so long as the fight endured—he stuck to her like the stubborn Bulgarian he was, and never let go. The crews of the other Turkish vessels hooked on to the anchors, seized on everything by which they could hold, and attempted on all sides to reach the decks of the ships. While some tried to climb on board, others endeavoured to cut the ropes with their axes, and set the ships on fire. Showers of arrows and

javelins were directed against the Christian crews. The
Genoese fighters were in armour and were proof against
the small missiles. Everything had been anticipated by
them. Their tuns of water extinguished the burning brands,
and their heavy stones and even small barrels of water
dropped from above sank or disabled the boats of their
assailants. The axe-men on board ' our ships ' chopped off
the hands or broke the heads of all men who succeeded in
getting near the deck. Meanwhile, as amid shouts and
yells and blasphemies one boat's crew after another was
defeated, others pressed near to replace them, and the
Genoese had to recommence their struggle against fresh and
vigorous men.

While the fight was going on, the vessels were always
drifting across to the Galata shore.[1] Five triremes attacked
one of the Genoese ships; thirty large caiques or fustae
tackled a second, and the remaining Genoese was surrounded
by forty transports or parandaria filled with well-armed
soldiers. The fight continued with great fury. The sea
seemed covered with struggling ships. An enormous
number of darts, arrows, and other missiles were thrown.
The quantity of the latter, says Ducas, with pardonable
exaggeration, was so great that after a while the oars could
not be properly worked. The sea, says Barbaro, could
hardly be seen, on account of the great number of the
Turkish boats.

All this time the imperial ship commanded by Flatanelas,
with the Turkish admiral's ship always holding on to her,
was defending herself bravely. Though Baltoglu would
not let go, the other attacking vessels which passed under
her bow were driven off with earthen pots full of Greek
fire and with stones.[2] The slaughter around her was great.
For a time, indeed, the aim of the admiral and the energy

---

[1] Barbaro, p. 24.

[2] I doubt whether Greek fire was so much used as it is usually asserted to
ave been. It was always dangerous to those who used it. When employed
y the Byzantine ships it caused great damage and still greater alarm. I agree
ith Krause that it was very rarely employed. See *Die Byzantiner des
Iittelalters*, by J. H. Krause; Halle, 1869.

of the attack seem to have been concentrated on the capture of the imperial ship. Chalcondylas declares that she would have been taken had it not been for the help which the Genoese were able to give her; and Leonard also says that she was protected by ' ours '—that is, by the Genoese ships. Probably it was in consequence of the risk which the imperial ship had run of being captured that presently the whole four lashed themselves together, so that, in the words of Pusculus, they appeared to move like four towers.[1] Each of the four ships, however, remained during the protracted battle a centre of attack in which the triremes took the most important positions, grappling them and being themselves supported by the smaller boats.

The fight was seen and every incident noted by the friends alike of attackers and attacked from the opposite sides of the Golden Horn. ' We, watching from the walls what passed, raised our prayers to God that He would have mercy upon us.' [2] Flatanelas, the captain of the imperial ship, was observed on his deck fighting like a lion and urging his men to follow his example. It was followed both by his officers and by those on board the Genoese ships. Nothing whatever occurred to show that they lost courage for an instant. The attack on the ships was apparently no nearer success than when it began. The spectators on both sides had seen ships and fleet drifting towards the Galata shore, and the citizens were aware that Mahomet with his staff was watching the fierce struggle. This shore contains a wide strip of level ground which has been silted up during the last few centuries and is now built upon, but which, like the corresponding low-lying ground outside the walls of Constantinople on the opposite side of the Golden Horn, either did not exist four centuries ago or was in part covered with shallow water.[3] Into the shallow water the

---

[1] Pusculus, iv. 340.   .[2] Phrantzes.

[3] Gyllius mentions this foreshore as existing in his time, gives its width and vividly describes how it was utilised and increased by the inhabitants of Galata (book iv. ch. 10). In digging for the foundations of the British post office in Galata in 1895, on a site that is now upwards of a hundred yards from the water, remains of an old wooden jetty were discovered. Indeed, I think

sultan urged his horse in his excitement until his long robe
trailed in it. He went out as far as was possible towards
his vessels, in order to make himself seen and heard. When
he saw his large fleet and thousands of chosen men unable
to capture the four ships and again and again repulsed, his
anger knew no bounds. Roused to fury, he shouted and
gnashed his teeth. He hurled curses at the admiral and
his crews at the top of his voice. He declared they were
women, were fools and cowards, and no doubt let loose a
number not only of curses and blasphemies, as the archbishop says, but of those opprobrious expressions in which
the Turkish language is exceptionally rich. The sultan's
followers were not less disappointed and indignant than
Mahomet. They, too, cursed those in the fleet, and many
of them followed him into the water and rode towards the
ships.[1]

Urged by the presence and reproaches of their great
leader, the Turkish captains made one more desperate effort.
For very shame, says Phrantzes, they turned their bows
against our ships and fought fiercely. Pusculus says that
Mahomet, watching from the shore, inflamed their fury.
But all was in vain. The Genoese and the imperial ship
held their own, repelled every attempt to board them, and
did such slaughter among the Turks that it was with difficulty the latter could withdraw some of their galleys.

Turkish ships defeated and retreat.

The later portion of the fight had lasted upwards of two
hours ; the sun was already setting, and the four ships had
been powerless to move on account of the calm. But the
fight was unequal, and they must have been destroyed, says
Critobulus, plausibly enough, if the battle had continued
under such conditions. In this extremity suddenly there
came a strong puff of wind. The sails filled, and the
ships once more had the advantage of being able to move.
They crashed triumphantly through the oars of the galleys
and the boats, shook off their assailants, and cleared them-

highly probable that in 1453 the whole of what is now the main street of
Galata from the bridge to Tophana was under water.

[1] Pusculus, 247.

selves a path. If at that time the whole fleet of the
barbarians, says Ducas, had barred the way, the Genoese
ships were capable of driving through and defeating it.
Thus, at the moment when the fight was the most critical,
they were able to sail away and take refuge under the walls
of the city. The wind had saved them. *Deus afflavit, et
dissipati sunt.*

The battle was lost, but the sultan once again shouted
out orders to the admiral. Ducas suggests that Baltoglu
pretended not to hear, because Mahomet, being ignorant of
ships and sailing, gave absurd orders. There was, however,
no longer any hope of success, and night coming on, the
command was again given, and this time heard by Baltoglu,
to withdraw to the Double Columns.

Barbaro, who was in the city, describes how he himself
took part in bringing the four gallant vessels inside the
boom. When it became dark, he accompanied Gabriel
Trevisano with the latter's two galleys, and Zacharia Grione
with his one, and with them went outside the boom. Fearing that they would be attacked, they did their utmost to
make it appear that their fleet was large. They had three
trumpets for each of the two galleys, and with these they
made as much noise as if they had at least twenty galleys.

In the darkness of the night the Turks thought their
fleet was about to be attacked, and remained at anchor on
the defensive. The four ships were safely towed within the
boom and into the port of Constantinople, to the indescribable
delight of Greeks and Italians alike.

The Turks were possibly hindered in the fight by their
numerical superiority. The oars of their galleys were broken
one boat got into the way of others, while in the confusion
every bolt or arrow shot from the ships told upon the crowded
masses of men in the enemy's vessels below them. Many
in the triremes were suffocated or trampled under foot
Every attempt to board either of the ships had failed. The
losses suffered by the Turks were undoubtedly severe, though
exaggerated by the victors. A few of their boats were captured or destroyed. The archbishop declares that he learned

from the spies that nearly ten thousand had been killed ;
Phrantzes, that he heard from the Turks themselves that
more than twelve thousand of these ' Sons of Hagar ' perished
in the sea alone. The version of Critobulus is the most
likely to be correct. He gives the killed as upwards of a
hundred, and the wounded as above three hundred.[1] The
losses on board the four ships were not altogether slight.
Phrantzes declares that no Christians were killed in the
battle, though two or three who were wounded ' departed
after some days to the Lord ; ' while Critobulus gives a much
more probable story of twenty-two killed, and half the crews
wounded.

All writers agree that the fight was manfully sustained
on both sides. The ships lay on the water without a breath
of wind, though there was probably a slight swell. It was
a small but brilliant sea fight of the old type between skilled
sailors and skilled soldiers, in which the latter were unable
to gain any advantage over their opponents fighting on their
own element, and had to withdraw humbled and defeated.

The disappointment and rage of the sultan were great and
not unnatural.

The unfortunate admiral was brought next day before
him and reproached as a traitor. Mahomet asked him how
he could expect to capture the fleet in the harbour since he
could not even take four ships, upbraided him for his inactivity and cowardice, and declared that he was ready himself
to behead him.[2] The admiral pleaded that from the beginning to the end of the fight his own ship had never quitted
its hold upon the poop of the largest vessel, and that he and
his crew had fought on uninterruptedly until recalled. The
Turkish officers also spoke on his behalf, testified to his
courage and tenacity, and called attention to the severe
wound on his eye accidentally inflicted by one of his men.
The sultan, after some hesitation, consented to spare his
life, but ordered him to be bastinadoed.[3] As a further

Turkish admiral degraded.

---

[1] Crit. xli.   [2] Barbaro, p. 24, and Phrantzes.
[3] According to Ducas, Mahomet himself inflicted the blows : an absurd
statement

punishment, he was deprived of all his honours, and whatever he possessed was given to the Janissaries.[1]

The success raised the hopes of the besieged, because they now firmly believed that these ships were only the forerunners of many others which were on their way to save the city. They had not yielded to Rome for nothing, and aid would come, and the city would yet be saved. In truth, a new crusade was not necessary to secure its deliverance. A few more vessels sent by the Christian states, with an army one tenth or even one twentieth of the number of the soldiers of the cross who had passed by Constantinople under Godfrey, would have been enough to prevent the conquest of the city by Mahomet. No further aid, however, came. All the hopes based upon re-union proved illusory, and Hungarians as well as Italians failed to render the assistance which might have been of first importance to their own interests.[2]

The fight with the four ships was on April 20. During that day the great bombards had been hard at work along the landward walls, and especially near the Romanus Gate. The sultan himself was absent on the following day at the Double Columns, superintending one of the most interesting operations connected with the siege, but the bombardment went on as if he had been present. An important tower known as the Bactatinian, near the Romanus Gate,[3] was destroyed on the 21st, with a portion of the adjacent Outer Wall, and, says Barbaro, it was only through the mercy of Jesus Christ that the Turks did not give general battle, or they would have got into the city. He adds that if they had attacked

Attack contemporaneously made in Lycus valley.

[1] Ducas, 121; Leonard, Phrantzes, and Nicolo Barbaro.

[2] Hunyadi, according to Phrantzes (p. 327), asked that Silivria or Mesembria, on the bay of Bourgas, should be given to him as the price of his aid, and Phrantzes declares that the emperor ceded the latter place, he himself having written the Golden Bull making the cession. He adds also that the king of Catalonia stipulated for Lemnos as the price of his aid. But no aid came from either.

[3] Barbaro, under April 21; Phrantzes, 246. The tower is called by Leonard Bactatanea. He afterwards writes of the breach near it as being in the Muru Bacchatureus. See, as to its situation, Professor van Millingen's *Byzantine Constantinople*, pp. 86, 87.

with even ten thousand men, no one could have hindered their entry. The Moscovite, speaking of the same incident, states that the Turks were so infuriated by a successful shot from the small cannon of Justiniani that Mahomet gave the order for an assault, raised the cry of '*Jagma, jagma!*' 'Pillage, pillage!' but they were repulsed. One of the balls, according to the same author, knocked away five of the battlements and buried itself in the walls of a church.[1] The defenders, among whom, notes Barbaro, were some 'of our Venetian gentlemen,' set themselves at once to make stout repairs where the wall had been broken down. Barrels full of stones, beams, logs, anything that would help to make a barricade, were hastily got together and worked with clay and earth, so as to form a substitute for the Outer Wall. When completed, the new work formed a stockade, made largely of wood and built up with earth and stones.[2] The 'accursed Turk,' says Barbaro, did not cease day and night to fire his greatest bombard against the walls near which the repairs were being made. Arrows and stones innumerable were thrown, and there were discharges also from firelocks or fusils[3] which threw leaden balls. He adds that during these days the enemy were in such numbers that it was hardly possible to see the ground or anything else except the white head dress of the Janissaries, and the red fezes of the rest of the Turks.[4]

Meantime the sultan was bent upon carrying into execution a plan for obtaining access to the harbour.

All accounts agree that the defeat of the Turkish fleet on April 20 had roused Mahomet to fury. More than one contemporary states that it was the immediate cause of Mahomet's decision to attempt to gain possession of the Golden Horn by the transport of his ships over land across

Transport of Turkish ships overland.

---

[1] As the only church in the neighbourhood of the place defended by Justiniani was that of St Kyriakè near the Pempton, the information is valuable as helping to fix the locality where the great gun was stationed. The Moscovite, ch. vii.

[2] The Moscovite, ch. vii., in Dethier's *Siege*; Barbaro, p. 27; Crit.

[3] *Zarabotane.*

[4] Barbaro, p. 27. The account of the fight given by Pusculus is very full and spirited. See note in Appendix as to the question where the naval fight took place.

the peninsula of Galata. The statement may well be doubted, but the failure to capture the four ships probably hastened the execution of a project already formed, and, like all his plans, carefully concealed until the moment for action.

Reasons
for such
project.
The reasons which urged Mahomet ·to try to gain entrance to the Golden Horn were principally three : to weaken the defence at the landward walls, to exercise control over the Genoese of Galata, and to facilitate the communications with his base at Roumelia-Hissar. So long as he was excluded, the enemy had only two sides of the triangular-shaped city to defend ; whereas if the Turkish ships could range up alongside the walls on the side of the Horn the army within the city, already wretchedly inadequate for the defence on the landward and Marmora sides, would have to be weakened by the withdrawal of men necessary to guard the newly attacked position.

The possession of the Horn would enable Mahomet to exercise a dominant influence over Galata. This was a matter of great importance, because at any time the hostility of the Genoese might have enormously increased the difficulties of the siege and probably have compelled him to raise it. There were, indeed, already signs that Genoese sentiment was unfriendly to him.

The position of the Genoese in Galata was a singular one. The city was entirely theirs and under their government. It was surrounded by strong walls which were built on the slope of the steep hill and with those on the side of the Golden Horn formed a large but irregular triangle. The highest position in the city was crowned by the noble tower still existing, and then known as the Tower of Christ. Constantinople and Galata were each interested in keeping the splendid natural harbour closed. Behind Galata—that is, immediately behind the walls of the city—the heights and all the back country were held by the Turks.

Like most neutrals, the people of Galata were accused by each of the combatants of giving aid to the other side The archbishop, himself a Genoese by origin, is loud in his complaints against his countrymen for having preferred their interests to their duty as Christians.   But it is abundantly clear that the Genoese continued to trade with their neighbours across the Golden Horn.   Whether the balance of services rendered to the combatants was in favour of the Greeks or of Mahomet may be doubtful, but there was no doubt in Mahomet's mind, or probably in that of any one else, that the sympathy of the Genoese, as shown by their conduct, was with their fellow Christians.   The Genoese ships with which the fight had just taken place were safe once they had passed the boom and had come under the protection of the Genoese on one side and the Greeks on the other.   The Golden Horn was thus a refuge for all ships hostile to the Turks.

It was necessary to give the Podestà and the Council of Galata a lesson.   But Mahomet had tried and failed to force the boom.   Nor could he obtain possession of the end which was within boundaries of Galata.[1]   To have made the attempt would have been to make war on the Genoese. But their walls were strong, their defenders brave, and the first rumour of an attack upon the city would be the signal for the despatch of the whole Genoese fleet and of all the forces that the suzerain lord of Galata, the duke of Milan, could muster for their aid.   Moreover, within the harbour there were between twenty and thirty large fighting ships, and the sea fight had now shown clearly how very much his difficulties would be increased if he forced the Genoese into open hostilities against him.

The third reason why Mahomet wanted command of the harbour was to secure his own communications.   His important division of troops under Zagan Pasha occupied the northern shore of the Golden Horn beyond Galata, together with the heights above the city.   While it was necessary to hold this position so as to keep in touch with

[1] In 1203 the Crusaders and Venetians had forced the boom tower on the Galata side and loosed the chain; but it was then outside the city walls.   In the time of Cantacuzenus, Galata had been enlarged so that the end of the chain was quite safe unless Galata were taken.   The walls terminated, as may still be seen by the remaining towers, near Tophana.

his fleet at the Double Columns and his fortresses at Roumelia-Hissar, the only means of communication between the main body of his troops encamped before the walls and those under Zagan was the distant and dangerous ford over the upper portion of the Golden Horn at Kiat-Hana, then called Cydaris. Once Mahomet obtained possession of the harbour he could without interruption build a bridge over the upper end of the Golden Horn by which communications between the two divisions of his army would be greatly facilitated.

To accomplish these three objects Mahomet judged that his wisest course was to let the Genoese severely alone and to attempt to obtain possession of the harbour by a method which should not force the neutrals to become open enemies. He resolved to accomplish the difficult feat of transporting a fleet overland from the Bosporus to the Horn. This feat may have been suggested to him by a Venetian who, fourteen years earlier, had seen one of a similar kind performed, in which his fellow citizens had transported a number of ships from the Adige to Lake Garda.[1]

The sultan's entire command of the country behind Galata would enable him to make his preparations possibly without even the knowledge of the Genoese. The ridge of hills now occupied by Pera was covered partly with vineyards and partly with bushes. The western slope, from the ridge along which runs the Grande Rue de Péra, down to the ' Valley of the Springs,' now known as Cassim Pasha, was used as a Genoese graveyard, and is still covered by the cypress trees that mark the Turkish cemetery which took its place. There existed a path from a place on the Bosporus near the present Tophana to The Springs at right angles to the road on the ridge of Pera Hill, the two roads forming a

---

[1] Leonard, and Sauli's *Colonia dei Genovesi in Galata*, p. 158. Other similar instances are cited by contemporaries, but it is not necessary to suppose that Mahomet had ever heard either of the fable of Caesar's attack upon Antony and Cleopatra or of a like feat performed by Xerxes. The Avars had made a crossing similar to that contemplated by Mahomet. The transport of the imperial fleet into Lake Ascanius in order to take possession of Nicaea in 1097 might possibly have been known to him.

cross and thus giving to Pera its modern Greek name of
Stavrodromion. This path followed the natural valley, now
forming the street by the side of which is erected the church
which is a memorial to British soldiers and sailors who
perished in the Crimean war, and then crossing the ridge
on a flat tableland over a few hundred yards descended in
almost a straight line by another valley which is also
preserved by a street to The Springs and the waters of the
Golden Horn. It was probably along this route that the
sultan had determined to haul his ships.

It is impossible to believe that Mahomet had arrived
hastily at his decision to accomplish this serious engineering
feat. In accordance with his usual habit, he would guard
his design with the utmost secrecy. At the same time, he
would push on his preparations with his customary energy.
The timber needed for making a species of tramway, for
rollers and for ship cradles, had been carefully and secretly
amassed and everything was ready for execution when the
leader gave the word. The plan and execution was a great
surprise, not only to the Greeks, but even to the people
of Galata. That the plan and preparations were conceived
and completed in a single day or night is incredible.[1]

Project not formed hastily.

If this conjecture is correct, Zagan, who was in command
of the Turks behind Galata and at the head of the Golden
Horn, would have been able to prevent the preparations from
becoming known. Possibly it was in order to conceal the
final arrangements that the sultan, a few days previously,
had brought his guns or bombards to bear on the ships
which were moored to the boom, while Baltoglu, as we have
seen, was attacking them from the sea. These guns were
stationed on the hill of St. Theodore, northward of the
eastern wall of Galata.[2] At daylight on April 21, one of

Mahomet diverts attention from project.

[1] Λοιπὸν ὁ ἀμερᾶς τὰς τριήρεις φέρας ἐν μίᾳ νυκτί, ἐν τῷ λιμένι τῷ πρωῒ
ηὑρέθησαν : Prantzes, 251.

[2] Dethier places them on a small plateau now occupied by the English
Memorial Church. [*Note on* Pusculus, book iv. line 482. Professor van
Millingen (p. 231), in discussing the question of the position of St. Theodore,
suggests that the sultan's battery stood nearer the Bosporus than the present
Italian Hospital. This suggestion is not necessarily at variance with the
position indicated by Dethier.]

them opened fire. The discharge of cannon was continued and would divert attention from what was going on behind the Galata walls. The first shot caused great alarm. The ball, followed by dense black smoke, went over the houses of the Genoese and made them fear that the city itself was about to be attacked. The second shot rose to a great distance, fell upon one of the ships at the boom, smashed a hole in it and sank it, killing some of the crew. The effect upon the crews of the other ships was for the moment to cause consternation. They, however, soon placed themselves out of range. The Turks continued to fire, though the balls fell short, and, according to Leonard, this fire was continued during the day. A hundred cannon-balls were discharged; many houses in Galata were struck and a woman was killed. The Genoese were thus decoyed into paying no attention to what was going on behind their city. During all the same day, Barbaro records that the bombardment against the San Romano walls was exceptionally heavy, and even during the night, according to Michael the Janissary, all the batteries directed against the Constantinople landward walls were kept hard at work. This, too, was probably intended to divert attention from the preparations for the immediate transport of the fleet.

These measures for diverting attention account for the passage of the ships not being generally known, if, indeed, it was known at all by any of the enemy, until it was accomplished.[1] For this reason no attempt was made to destroy them either before they were placed on land or as they reached the water. At the same time, Mahomet, who seldom neglected a precaution, had made preparations to repel any attempt made to oppose the transit.[2]

In the evening of the 21st or on the morning of the 22nd everything appears to have been prepared for the remarkable

---

[1] Philelphus, book ii. line 976: ' Genuae tunc clara juventus obstupuit.' Ducas, however, states that the Genoese claimed to have known of the proposed transport and to have allowed it out of friendship to Mahomet.

[2] ' Et hic quidem in superiori parte per montem navigia transportavit . . . . in litore stabant milites parati propulsare hostes bombardis, si accederent prohibituri deducere naves.' Chalcondylas, book viii.

overland voyage of the sultan's fleet.   Between seventy and
eighty vessels had been selected from those anchored in the
Bosporus.[1]

A road had been carefully levelled, probably following
the route already indicated, from a spot near the present
Tophana to the valley of The Springs.   Stout planks or logs
had been laid upon it.   A great number of rollers had been
prepared of six pikes, or about thirteen or fourteen feet, long.[2]
Logs and rollers were thoroughly greased and made ready
for their burdens.   The ships' cradles, to the side of which
poles were fixed so as to enable the ships to be securely
fastened, were lowered into the water to receive the vessels
which were then floated upon them, and by means of long
cables were pulled ashore and started on their voyage.

A preliminary trial was made with a small fusta, and this
having been successfully handled, the Turks began to transport others.   Some were hauled by mere hand power, others
required the assistance of pulleys, while buffaloes served to
haul the remainder.   The multitude of men at the sultan's
disposal enabled the ships to start on their voyage in rapid
succession.

Transport of eighty ships overland.

The strangeness and the oddity of the spectacle, the
paradox of ships journeying over land, seems to have impressed the Turks, who always have a keen relish for fun, as
much as did the ingenuity of the plan.   The whole business
had indeed its ludicrous aspect.   The men took their
accustomed places in the vessel.   The sails were unfurled as
if the ships were putting out to sea.   The oarsmen got out
their oars and pulled as if they were on the water.   The
leaders ran backwards and forwards on the central gangway or
histodokè, where the mast when not hoisted usually rested,
to see that they all kept stroke together.   The helms-
men were at their posts, while fifes and drums sounded as
if the boats were in the water.   The display thus made,

---

[1] Crit. says 68; Barbaro, 72 ; Tetaldi, between 70 and 80 ; Chalcondylas,
70; and Ducas, 80 ; Heirullah says there were only 20 ; the Janissary
Michael, 30 ; the *Anon. Expugnatio*, edited by Thyselius, sect. 12, says not less
than 80.

[2] 'Lacertus' is the word Leonard ingeniously uses for the Greek πῆχυς.

accompanied as it was by cheering and music, may probably be attributed rather to the desire of keeping every one in good humour than to the belief that such a disposal of the men could facilitate the transport of the vessels.[1]

The vessels followed each other up the hill in rapid succession, and amid shouting and singing and martial music were hauled up the steep ridge to the level portion which is now the Grande Rue de Pera, a height of two hundred and fifty feet from the level of the Bosporus. A short haul of about a furlong upon level ground enabled them to begin the descent to the Golden Horn, and so rapidly was this performed that before the last ship had reached the ridge the first was afloat in the harbour. The distance is described by Critobulus as not less than eight stadia. Taking the stadium as a furlong or slightly less, this is a correct estimate of the distance over which these ships travelled, if the ships started, as I have suggested, from the present Tophana. Nor is there reason to doubt the statement that the traject was made, as many contemporaries assert, in one night.[2]

[1] Crit. book iv. ch. 42. It is difficult to determine the size of the boat selected for this overland transit. Barbaro says, ' le qual fusti si iera de banchi quindexe fina banchi vinti et anchi vintido ' (page 28). This would agree fairly well with the statement of Chalcondylas, that some had thirty and some fifty oars. Mr. Cecil Torr calculates that a thirty-oared ship would be about seventy feet long, a statement which appears probable (*Ancient Ships*, p. 21). The mediaeval galleys and other large vessels propelled by oars differed essentially from those of the sixteenth century, which were worked with long oars. See note on p. 234. I am myself not entirely satisfied that among the boats were not biremes and possibly triremes in the sense of boats which had two or three tiers of oars, one above the other. Fashions change slowly in Turkey, and I have seen a bireme with two such tiers of oars on the Bosporus. No writer mentions the length of the vessels which were carried across Pera Hill. A large modern fishing caique in the Marmora, probably not differing much in shape from the fustae then transported, and containing twelve oars, measures about fifty feet long. When the boats are longer, two men take one oar, but this is very unusual. Leonard speaks of the seventy vessels as biremes. Barbaro calls them fustae. The former was probably the best Latin word to signify the new form of vessel. Many of the ships were large, though it may be taken as certain that none were of the length of the two galleys recently raised in lake Nemi, near Rome, which belonged to Caligula, each of which is 225 feet long and 60 feet beam.

[2] See note in Appendix on transport of Mahomet's ships.

CHAPTER XIII

CONSTANTINE ALLEGED TO HAVE SUED FOR PEACE ; ATTEMPT
TO DESTROY TURKISH SHIPS IN THE GOLDEN HORN ;
POSTPONED ; MADE AND FAILS ; MURDER OF CAPTIVES ;
REPRISALS ; OPERATIONS IN LYCUS VALLEY ; BRIDGE
BUILT OVER GOLDEN HORN ; SENDING TO SEEK VENE-
TIAN FLEET ; PROPOSAL THAT EMPEROR SHOULD LEAVE
CITY ; ATTACKS ON BOOM ; JEALOUSY BETWEEN VENE-
TIANS AND GENOESE ; NEW ASSAULTS FAIL BOTH AT
WALLS AND BOOM ; ATTEMPTS TO UNDERMINE WALLS ;
CONSTRUCTION OF A TURRET ; DESTROYED BY BESIEGED ;
FAILURE OF VESSEL SENT TO FIND VENETIAN FLEET ;
UNLUCKY OMENS.

DUCAS relates that about this time, when the emperor found Constan-
that the walls which had resisted the Arabs and other in- tine
alleged to
vaders were not strong enough to support the attack of have asked
for peace.
Mahomet's cannon, he sent an offer to pay any amount of
tribute which might be imposed on condition that the siege
should be abandoned.

His narrative would imply that the offer was made
immediately after the transport of the fleet overland.[1]

Mahomet replied to the emperor that it was too late : that
he meant to obtain the city or die in the attempt. He,
however, made a counter proposal. If the emperor would
leave it, he would give him the Morea, would appoint his
brother to rule over other provinces, and thus sultan and
emperor might live at peace with each other. If this
counter proposal were rejected, he declared his intention of
putting the emperor and all his nobles to the sword, of

[1] Ducas, xxviii.

allowing his soldiers to take captive the people and to pillage their houses. He himself would be content with the deserted city. Ducas adds that of course the offer of Mahomet was refused, because in what place could the emperor have appeared without meeting the scorn, not only of all Christians, but of Jews and even of the Turks themselves? This proposal is not mentioned by Phrantzes. Gibbon suggests that he is silent regarding it because he wished to spare his prince even the thought of a surrender. Ducas, however, is constantly inaccurate, and it may well be that he was merely relating an unfounded report which was current after the capture of the city, when he himself was but a boy. It is difficult to believe that if any proposal of the kind had been made at the time indicated it would not have been known to Leonard, Barbaro, Pusculus, Tetaldi, or others who were present at the siege, and if known that it would not have been mentioned. Phrantzes, writing in defence of the emperor, says that it is certain that he could have fled from the city if he had so desired and that he deliberately preferred the fate of the Good Shepherd who is ready to lay down his life for his sheep.[1] The same testimony is borne by Critobulus,[2] who says that although Constantine realised the peril which threatened the city, and although he could have saved his own life as many counselled him to do, yet he refused, and preferred to die rather than see the city captured.

The sudden appearance of the seventy or eighty ships in the inner harbour of the Golden Horn caused consternation in the city. Every one could understand that if this fleet were not destroyed, the number of men available for the defence of the landward walls must be very greatly lessened. Moreover, the walls now for the first time requiring defence were low and required constant watching. A bridge or pontoon was already in course of construction in the upper part of the Horn beyond the city walls, the use

---

[1] Phrantzes, p. 327.   [2] Crit. lxxii.

of which was now evident as a means of attacking the harbour walls.

A meeting was hastily called with the consent of the Venetian bailey, and perhaps by him, at which twelve men who had trust in each other were present. Among them was John Justiniani, who had already acquired the confidence not merely of his countrymen and of the emperor but of the Venetians. They met in the church of St. Mary, probably in the Venetian quarter near the present Rustem Pasha mosque, to decide upon the best measures for the destruction of the Turkish ships which had been so strangely carried over Pera Hill.[1] Various proposals were made. It was suggested that the Christian ships in the harbour should make a combined attack upon the Turkish vessels. It was objected that the consent of the Genoese at Galata would be required, and they were known to be unwilling to declare open war against Mahomet. In any case, precious time would be lost in obtaining their consent. The second proposal was to destroy the Turkish guns which had been placed on the western side of Galata to protect the ships, and then to attempt to burn the vessels. This was evidently a dangerous operation, because Zagan Pasha had a detachment of troops in the neighbourhood and the Venetians and Greeks were not sufficiently numerous to risk the loss of a body of men upon such an expedition. The third proposal was the one which finally commended itself to the meeting. If not made it was at least strongly supported by James Coco, the captain of a Trebizond galley, a man whom Phrantzes describes as more capable of action than of speech.[2] His project was, without delay, without consulting the Genoese, to make a dash and burn the Turkish ships in Cassim Pasha Bay. He himself offered to undertake the task.

Plan decided upon.

The meeting had been quietly called, and no time had been lost in arriving at a decision. It was of the very essence of Coco's proposal that it should be executed

---

[1] Barbaro says that the meeting was in St. Mary's ; but Pusculus (iv. 578) says, in St. Peter Claviger, which Dethier places near St. Sophia.

[2] Phrantzes, 256.

immediately and that it should be kept secret. His preparations were forthwith put in hand. He chose two transports of five hundred tons each and placed bales of cotton
and of wool upon them as armour to prevent damage from
cannon-balls. Two large galleys and two of the lighter and
swifter kinds of biremes or fustae were to accompany them.
Each fusta had twenty-four banks or thwarts and contained
seventy-two oarsmen, forty-eight abaft the mast and twenty-
four ahead of it. Accompanying each ship was a large
boat.[1] Coco's plan was to employ the two large ships as a
screen for the galleys and fustae, so that at the last moment
these swift vessels might pull rapidly forward and cut out
or burn the Turkish ships.

It was agreed that the vessels should be brought together
that same night of April 24, at an hour after sunset, the
Eastern method of computing the hours making this a fixed
and precise time, and the attack was to be made at midnight. The Genoese heard of the proposed attack and pressed
the Venetians hard to postpone the execution of the project,
in order that they might take part in it. Unluckily, they
consented. The preparations of the Genoese took four days.
During that period the sultan became aware of what was
proposed, added two big guns to those already stationed on
the shore at Cassim Pasha to cover his ships, and waited in
confidence for the attack.

Execution
postponed
till
April 28.

Contemporary writers charge the Genoese with having
betrayed the project to the sultan. Even Leonard evidently
believed in the existence of this treachery and hints that he
knows more than he cares to tell. Ducas states bluntly
that the Genoese told the sultan. Critobulus and Pusculus
each affirm that Mahomet had information from Galata.
Barbaro adds the further detail that the Podestà, as the
mayor of Galata was called, on learning what was proposed
to be done, immediately sent word to the sultan at St
Romanus Gate, and speaks of the 'accursed Genoese' a
'enemies of the faith and treacherous dogs' for so doing.

While it is difficult to reject all these statements, i

---

[1] Barbaro, under April 24 and 25.   [2] Pusculus, lines 585 et seq.

must be remembered that the cry of treachery is usually raised in similar cases when things go wrong, and, as the preparations must have been known to a great many people, it would have been wonderful indeed if Mahomet had not learned what so many knew.

In whatever manner the information was acquired, it cannot be doubted that the Turks had knowledge of the project, and that the Greeks and Venetians were not aware that it was known to the common enemy. ·

By April 28 everything was ready. Two hours before dawn the two ships with their bales of cotton and wool left the harbour of Galata—that is, the north-eastern portion of the Golden Horn. They were accompanied by the galleys, one under Trevisano and the other under Zacharia Grione. Both captains were experienced and brave men. Trevisano was the captain who had placed himself at the service of the emperor 'per honor de Dio et per honor di tuta la Christianitade.' Three swift fustae, each with well-armed and picked men and materials for burning the Turkish fleet, accompanied them. The leading one was commanded by Coco, who had chosen the crew from his own galley. A number of small boats carrying gunpowder and combustibles were to follow. The order was given, as previously arranged, that the ships should go first and the galleys and biremes follow under their shelter. When the expedition started, some at least were surprised to see a bright light flare up from the top of Galata Tower, which was probably rightly judged to be a signal to the Turks that the ships were leaving.[1] Everything was still in profound darkness and no sign or sound came from the Turkish ships to indicate that they were on the alert. While the Christian ships were pulled slowly and silently along, Coco, in his swift fusta, grew impatient at their slow progress. Naturally, says Barbaro, the ships with only forty rowers could not go so fast as did his fusta, which had seventy-two ; and, greedy of glory, he drew ahead of them in order that he might have the satisfaction of being first to attack and of being the destroyer of

Attempt made to destroy Turkish ships.

[1] Pusculus, iv. 610.

the Turkish fleet. Then suddenly the silence was broken
and the Turks showed they were prepared. Their cannon
opened fire and Coco's fusta was struck, but without being
much damaged. A minute or two afterwards, however, a
better aimed shot hit his vessel, going in at one side, and
out at the other.

Before you could have said ten paternosters she had sunk.[1]
The survivors of his crew were swimming with their light
armour and in the darkness for their lives. Many perished,
and among them Coco himself. Meantime the guns were
directed against the ships. The enemy fired from a short
distance and Barbaro tells us that though they could hear
the mocking laughter of their foes, they were unable, on
account of the darkness and the smoke arising from the
cannon and the smouldering cotton and wool of their own
ships, to render any assistance. By the time, indeed, the
other vessels had come up, the Turks had all their guns
in full play and the vessels had enough to do to look
after their own safety. Trevisano's ship, as probably the
largest of the galleys, was signalled for attack. Two shots
struck and went through her. She half filled with water
and had to be deserted, Trevisano and most of his men
taking to the water to save their lives.

Attempt
fails.

Then the whole Turkish fleet of seventy or eighty
vessels put out to attack the other two ships. The Italians
and Greeks fought valiantly, probably expecting to be supported by the rest of the Christian fleet, which, however, did
not arrive in time to give any aid. The fight was ' terrible
et forte : ' there was, says Barbaro, 'a veritable hell ; ' missile
and blows were countless, cannonading continual. The contest
raged furiously for a full hour and a half and neither of the
combatants could overcome the other. Thereupon both
retired. The two ships were not captured, and their crews
had once more maintained the superiority of the Christian
ships over a more numerous foe in smaller vessels.[2]

[1] Barbaro, 31.

[2] The account of this attempt to destroy the Turkish ships in the harbour
is best given by Barbaro, but Phrantzes and Pusculus are in substantial
agreement with him.

But the expedition had nevertheless failed. Eighty or
ninety of the best men, including many Venetians, had been
lost. Only one Turkish vessel had been destroyed. The
misfortune caused bitter grief to the Greeks and Latins.
The success of the Christian ships when attacked by the
Turks a few days earlier had led to the belief that on the
water at least they were invincible. The consternation and
even panic caused in the fleet by the failure was such that
if the Turks on that day had joined battle and taken the
offensive 'we should all,' says Barbaro, 'without a doubt
have been captured, and even those who were on shore.'
The depression in the city was increased and turned to rage
by the conduct of Mahomet. Some of the sailors had swum
to the northern shore and were captured by the Turks.
Forty of them were ostentatiously killed so that those
who a short while before had been their companions
witnessed their execution. Though one may blame the
inhumanity of reprisals, one cannot, in the event which
followed, be surprised at them. A large number of Turkish
prisoners in the city were brought bound from prison and
were hanged on the highest part of the city walls opposite
Cassim Pasha, where the Christian prisoners had suffered.[1]

Murder of captives.

Reprisals.

During these days the city walls on the landward side
had been the scene of constant attacks. The failure of the
first attempt, on the 18th, to pass the walls was followed by
steady firing day and night to destroy them. Probably on
April 23 the great cannon was removed to a position
opposite the Romanus Military gate, the place where
Justiniani was stationed, 'because there the walls were the
least solid and very low.'[2] From this time it commenced
and never ceased to batter them.

Operations in Lycus valley.

The disadvantages resulting from the transport of the
Turkish ships into the harbour were at once felt. While
continual pounding from the great cannon and other

---

[1] Phrantzes (p. 248) says 260 Turkish prisoners were executed.
[2] The Moscovite, ch. vii.

machines was going on at the landward walls and while
feints were being made which kept the defenders always on
the alert, to resist attacks or effect repairs, a portion of
their forces had to be told off to defend the north-western
walls facing the Golden Horn.   Many attempts were made
from these walls on the Horn, and from the Christian ships
to destroy the Turkish vessels.   Nearly every day as long as
the siege lasted, some of the Greek or Venetian ships were
told off to watch or attack them.   Sometimes the Turks
were chased to the shore : at other times the pursuers became
the pursued.[1]

Building
of bridge
over Upper
Horn.
To enable his troops to pass readily across the Golden
Horn, Mahomet commenced and carried through with his
usual energy the construction of a bridge over the upper
part of it, near the place where the landward walls join
those on the side of the Horn.   This district was then known
as Cynegion, and now as Aivan Serai.[2]   The bridge was
formed of upwards of a thousand wine barrels, all securely
fastened together with ropes.   Two of the barrels placed
lengthways made the width of the bridge.   Upon them
beams were fixed, and over the beams a planking sufficiently
wide to enable five soldiers to walk abreast with ease.[3]   The
object in placing the bridge so near the walls was, not
merely to facilitate communications between the troops
behind Pera and the army before the walls, but to attach to
it pontoons upon which cannon could be placed for attacking the harbour walls.

The paucity of the number of the defenders greatly alarmed

---

[1] Crit. xliv.

[2] Dr. Mordtmann places the bridge between Cumberhana and Defterdar
Scala.

[3] Ducas gives the above dimensions. Assuming the width from centre of
each barrel, including a space between them, to be four feet, this would give the
length of the bridge as 2,000 feet, which is about the width of the Horn at the
place mentioned. Phrantzes gives its length at a hundred fathoms and the
breadth fifty fathoms. These dimensions are clearly wrong if applied to the
bridge, since the length falls far short of the width of the gulf. Leonard says
it was thirty stadia long. Here, as elsewhere, I suspect that he uses stadium
for some measure about one ninth of a furlong in length. If this conjecture
is right, his estimate of the length of the bridge is about 2,000 feet.

the emperor and those around him who had gathered in council to meet the new dangers. They were compelled to recognise that this new point of attack, in the very place where, and where alone, the city had formerly been captured, required especial care, and accordingly they decided to send a strong detachment of Greeks and Italians to the north-west corner of the walls at Aivan Serai.[1]

From the moment the Turks had gained entrance into the inner harbour they never ceased to harass the city on every side.

During the next few days the cannonading against the walls was constant and the efforts to repair the damage equally persistent.

Barbaro mentions that on May 1 or 2 it was found that provisions were running short. The organisation for the supply of food to the soldiers was defective, and many complained that they had to leave the walls in order to earn bread for their wives and families. This led to the formation of what we may call a relief committee charged with the distribution of provisions.

Provisions running short at commencement of May.

On May 3, the besieged placed two of their largest guns on the walls opposite the Turkish ships in the harbour. The Turks replied by placing the two large cannons with which Coco's bireme had been attacked on the opposite shore to attack the walls. The besieged persisted in their endeavours to destroy the fleet. For a time they did more damage than the Turks were able to effect, but the latter brought other cannon and kept up their firing night and day. For ten days, says Barbaro, Greeks and Turks fired at each other, but without much result, 'because our cannons were inside the walls and theirs were well protected, and moreover the distance between them was half an Italian mile, and beyond the range of guns on either side.'

Skirmishes between ships and besieged.

Now that the siege had run into May the emperor and the leaders were becoming alarmed at the non-arrival of the Venetian fleet. The agreement with the Venetian bailey, in conformity with which a fleet was to be sent at once to

May 3: sending out of brigantine to find Venetian fleet.

[1] Phrantzes, 252.

the aid of the city, had been concluded on January 26, and no tidings had yet been heard of it. Its admiral, Loredano, was known to be a brave man 'who held strongly to the Christian cause,' but the fear was that he had not been informed of the agreement. Accordingly, on May 3, the emperor called together the notables of the Venetian colony and his chief officers, and suggested that one of their swiftest ships should be sent into the Archipelago and, if need be, as far as Euboea to seek for the fleet and to press Loredano to hasten to the relief of the city. Every one approved of the suggestion, and the same day a swift-sailing brigantine, manned only with twelve men, was made ready to sail. The crew were disguised to make them look as much as possible like Turks. At midnight the boom was opened. The ship hoisted the Turkish flag and sailed away, passing safely through the Marmora and the Dardanelles into the Archipelago.

Proposal that Constantine should leave the city. The author of the Moscovite chronicle, who was probably present at the siege, declares that Constantine during these days was urged by the patriarch and the nobles to leave the city, that Justiniani himself recommended this course and placed his ships at the emperor's disposal for such purpose. It was probably urged that he would be more likely to defeat the Turks from outside than within the city ; that, though the number of men for the defence of the walls was insufficient, the withdrawal of the emperor and a small retinue would be of little consequence, but that, once outside, his brother and other subjects would flock to his banner and he could arrange with Iskender Bey for the despatch of an Albanian army. In this manner time would be gained during which the long looked-for ships and soldiers from the West which the Venetians and the pope had promised, and to which other princes were ready to contribute, could arrive at Constantinople. Probably the presence of the emperor, with even a small band, elsewhere threatening the Turkish position would cause Mahomet to raise the siege.

The emperor, says the same writer, listened quietly, was

touched by the proposal and shed tears; thanked the chiefs for their advice, but declared that, while he recognised that his departure might be of advantage to himself, he would never consent to abandon the people, the clergy, the churches, and his throne in such a moment of danger. 'What,' he adds, 'would the world say of me? Ask me to remain with you. I am ready to die with you.' It was probably on this occasion that the emperor declared, as already mentioned, that he preferred ' to follow the example of the Good Shepherd who lays down his life for his sheep.'

Determined if possible to destroy the Christian fleet and apparently caring very little about resistance from Galata, the Turks placed two of their guns on the slope of Pera Hill and on May 5 commenced once more to fire over the corner of Galata at the ships lying at the boom. They took care, however, according to Barbaro, to aim at the Venetian vessels. Firing went on all day. A ball of two hundred pounds weight struck a Genoese merchant ship of three hundred tons burden, which was laden with a valuable cargo of silk and other merchandise, and sank her. The Turks continued firing all day long, and in consequence ships left the boom and retired to the shelter of the Galata walls.[1] The Genoese went to complain to the Turkish vizier of the unfriendly act of firing on and sinking one of their vessels. They reminded him that they were neutrals and were most anxious to preserve peace. According to Ducas, they declared that if they had not been friendly, the Turks would never have succeeded in transporting their ships overland, as they, the Genoese, could have burnt them. There are two versions of the reply given by the Turkish leaders. According to Ducas, they pleaded that they did not know that the owner of the sunken ship was a Genoese, and believed it to belong to the enemy. They urged the Genoese to wish them success in their efforts to capture the city and promised, in such case, full compensation to the owner of the sunken ship and cargo. According to Phrantzes, the sultan himself answered that the ships were

Marginal note: New attack on ships at boom, May 5.

[1] Barbaro, 36 ; Phrantzes, 250.

not merchant vessels but pirates. They had come to help
the enemy and must be treated as enemies. It is difficult
to decide which answer was given, but that recorded by
Ducas appears more in accord with the young sultan's
crafty policy. Whichever is the correct version, the Genoese
had to profess their satisfaction with it.

/ The failure to destroy the Turkish ships, the increased
labour thrown on the Venetians within the city, and the
doubtful conduct of the Genoese, led to ill-feeling between
the citizens of the two republics which caused a disturbance
amounting to a serious riot within the city itself.

Jealousy
between
Venetians
and
Genoese.

The traditional jealousy between Venetians and Genoese
was still formidable. In the present instance each accused
the other of not loyally defending Constantinople and of
being ready to send away their ships whenever they could
do so in safety. The Venetians replied to this accusation by
pointing out that they had unshipped the rudders from
many of their vessels and had deposited both them and the
sails within the city. The Genoese retorted that, though
they kept their rudders and sails on board ready for use at
any moment, they had their wives and children in Galata
and had not the slightest intention of abandoning so
excellent a situation. If they had advocated peace with the
Turks, it was at the desire of the emperor, with whom they
had a common interest. The reply was difficult to answer,
but carried no conviction to their rivals, because the
Venetians believed that, in spite of it, the Genoese were
acting solely to further their own interests. To the most
serious charge—that of giving notice to the Turks of the
attempt to burn their ships—the Genoese answered that the
plan had failed through the bad management of Coco, who,
with the object of gaining for himself alone the credit of
having destroyed the hostile fleet, had neglected necessary
precautions. Recrimination ran high and led to blows.
Phrantzes gives us a pathetic picture of the emperor appearing among the rioters and imploring them to make friends.
War against the enemy was surely bad enough ; he begged
them for the sake of God not to make war on each other.

His influence was sufficient to restore order, but while the hostile feeling was so far temporarily allayed as to make Genoese and Venetians content during the siege to lay aside their differences, it endured until the end.

On May 7, an assault was commenced which the besieged believed would be general by land and sea. On the previous days the monotonous firing against the walls had been constantly going on, and preparations had been noted as being made in the fleet for some new movement. Four hours after sunset thirty thousand Turks with scaling ladders and everything necessary endeavoured to force an entrance over the walls. The attempt lasted for three hours, but the besieged resisted bravely and the Turks had to retreat, having suffered, says Barbaro, much damage and, ' I should say, with a great many killed.' The sailors on their side were ready : the ships left the protection of the Galata walls and moved once more to take up their positions in defence of the boom, but the Turks did not come to the attack, possibly, as Barbaro suggests, because they were afraid of the Venetian ships.

Attempt to capture city by assault on May 7 fails,

The Moscovite mentions an encounter during this attack between a Greek strategos or general named Rangebè and a Turk named Amer Bey, the standard-bearer of the sultan. The Greek made a sortie, put the followers of Amer to flight, and then attacked Amer himself, whom he cut in two. The Turks, fúrious at the loss, surrounded Rangebè and killed him.[1]

The next day the Venetian Council of Twelve decided that Trevisano with his four hundred men should leave the entrance to the harbour and take up the defence of the newly threatened walls at Aivan Serai. There appears, however, to have been considerable opposition on the part of his crews, who preferred to remain afloat. Finally

---

[1] The Moscovite, xv. While there are useful hints in this anonymous author, he is generally untrustworthy. This fight, for example, is represented as being outside the walls. It is incredible that the Greeks should have made a sortie at this period of the siege. As an illustration of the untrustworthy character of the writer, it may be noted that the number of Turks killed during the siege totals up to 130,000 !

this was overcome, and on the 13th they went to their positions at the place mentioned, where the defenders had been occupied in constantly repairing the breaches made by the guns. Trevisano's galleys were left in the imperial harbour of Neorion near the end of the chain. His place was taken by Diedo, captain of the Tana galleys, who was now appointed to the chief command of the fleet.

A new assault on May 12. At midnight of the 12th fifty thousand Turks made an attack near Tekfour Serai, the Palace of the Porphyrogenitus, between Adrianople Gate and Caligaria, where a battery of guns had been planted from the commencement of the siege and had greatly damaged the breastwork and the Outer Wall. The attack was made with such force, and the shouting of the invaders was so loud, that Barbaro says ' most of us believed that they would capture the city.' Once more the attack failed. On the 14th, Mahomet removed the guns which he had placed on the slope of Pera Hill and had them taken to Aivan Serai and placed so as to attack the gate of the imperial palace of Blachern. It was found, however, that the guns in this position did no great harm, and they were once more removed, taken to the Lycus valley, and placed near the others to batter the walls near the Romanus Gate. From this time onward this was the principal place against which Mahomet concentrated his attack.

The entries in the diaries of the siege, showing that, while other parts of the wall were often attacked, the bombardment in the Lycus valley was unceasing day and night, occur during many days with monotonous regularity. Equally constant were the efforts for the defence : ' We, on our side, were working day and night to repair the walls with logs and earth and other materials.'

New attempts to force the boom, on May 16 and 17. On the 16th, Mahomet, probably because he had learnt of the landing of Trevisano's men from the fleet, ordered his ships at the Double Columns to make another attack upon the boom. One would have expected that the seventy or eighty ships that were in the Inner Horn would have co-operated in this attack but they did not move. Neither

Turk nor Genoese cared to risk open war with the other.
The Turkish fleet came down the Bosporus, and the Greek
and Venetian ships prepared to receive them. As the
Turkish ships came up to the attack, Diedo brought his
vessels from the shelter of the walls of Galata to the
boom. Thereupon the Turks retired, and using their oars
returned to the Columns. A similar incident occurred on
the 17th, but the Turks, again finding that the ships at the
boom were prepared for a fight, went back.

Mahomet, however unwilling to break with the Genoese,
was not content to have communication between the two
divisions of his fleet interrupted. Accordingly, once more he
renewed his attempt to destroy the boom. Barbaro appears Renewed
attempt on
May 21.
to have been on one of the ships defending it. On May 21
at two hours before daylight, the whole fleet moved out
from the Double Columns and with great noise of drums
and trumpets came down the Bosporus. All on board the
Christian vessels were greatly alarmed, but dispositions for
the defence were taken, and, as it was feared that contemporaneously a general attack upon the city was about to
be made, the alarm bells rang out and every one took his
allotted station either on shore or on the ships. Once more
the Turks decided that it was hopeless to attempt the
destruction of the boom, and therefore returned to their
moorings. It is impossible to say whether the Turks really
believed that they might destroy it or whether the three
attempts just mentioned were merely feints to tire out
the besieged and alarm them by a display of overwhelming
force. It is certain, however, that the Venetian and Greek
sailors were always ready to resist, and that, after this attempt
on May 21, Mahomet's fleet made no further attempt to
force its way into the harbour.

Already, on May 16, the besieged had discovered that Attempts
to under-
mine the
walls.
the Turks were attempting to undermine the walls and thus
enter into the city. Zagan Pasha, the renegade Albanian, in
command of Mahomet's army in Pera and opposite the walls
from Caligaria to the Horn, had under him a number of miners,
who had been brought from Novo Brodo in Serbia and who

possibly were Saxons brought to that country to work in the silver mines. These men took in hand the task of undermining. They commenced their work at a distance sufficiently far removed not to be observed by the besieged. Probably the first place attacked was between the Adrianople Gate and Tekfour Serai. They endeavoured to undermine the foss and the Outer Wall.[1] When this failed a second attempt was made against the walls of the quarter called Caligaria, and this, says Barbaro, because in that place there were no enclosures or, as he calls them, 'barbicans,' the wall being single and unprotected even by a ditch. This description enables us to identify the place as the wall running at right angles to the northern end of the foss. An Austrian named John Grant, who acted under the Grand Duke, took charge of the counterminers and succeeded in finding and entering the Turkish mine, where he and his men burnt the props. The works fell in and suffocated a number of Turkish workmen. The incident greatly alarmed the citizens, who feared that on future occasions Grant might not be fortunate enough to discover the mine before the Turks had entered by it or had blown up a part of the walls. Fortunately, the rocky character of the ground prevented the miners from meeting with any notable success. Phrantzes states that the only damage done by the Turks in mining was to destroy part of an old tower, which was soon repaired by the defenders.[2]

Construction of a turret, May 18.

At daylight on May 18, the citizens were astonished to see a wooden turret or 'bastion,' which had been built during the night.[3] The turret had been constructed with th

---

[1] Leonard, the *Vallum* and the *Antemurale*.   [2] Phrantzes, p. 244.

[3] 'Bastion' is the word used for a wooden tower or castle by Barbaro and k the translator of the Moscovite. Chalcondylas calls it *helepolis*, distinguishir it from the cannon which he names *teleboles*. Ducas speaks of cannon usual by the word χωνείαν, sometimes as τὰς πετροβολιμαίους χώνας or σκευ πετροβόλοι or simply as τὸ σκεῦος; Phrantzes employs the word *helepolis* for wooden turret (pp. 237, 244). The latter word is used by Critobulus for a canno It was an epithet applied to Helen, 'the Taker of Cities.' In the Bonn editi of Phrantzes it is also employed, both in the text and the Latin translation, f cannon; but a reference to the readings of the Paris MS. suggests that it is a error. Phrantzes's words for cannons are *teleboles* and *petroboles*.

same secrecy and celerity that Mahomet invariably adopted
in the execution of his plans.   Barbaro declares that all the
Christians in the city could not have made it under a month.
It was a huge structure.   It was only in the morning, when
they saw it complete in a place where no preparations had
been observed on the previous evening, that they realised
what had been done.   This ancient form of the 'Taker of
Cities' was stationed near the Romanus Gate.   It consisted
of a strong framework of long beams so high as to overlook
the Outer Wall.[1]   It had been partly filled with earth,
faced with a threefold covering of camels' or bullocks' hides,
and was built on wheels or rollers.   Steps led to its upper
platform.   These and the road which led to the camp, which
was sufficiently distant to be out of range, were also covered
for protection.   Scaling-ladders could be raised and thrown
from the summit of the turret to that of the wall.   If the
huge machine was, as Barbaro states, within ten paces of the
wall, it must have been built in the foss itself.   It dominated
the outer barbican or enclosure and would have allowed the
enemy under cover of its protection to fill the ditch from
three openings which were in the side presented to the walls
and to undermine them in safety.   The latter probably was
the principal object for which it was intended.   It would
also have enabled the Turks to prevent the besieged
from repairing the damages to the Outer Wall caused
by the cannon.   For this reason we can understand the
statement of Barbaro, that while it gave increased hope
to the Turks, it filled the besieged with alarm.   It was
built, according to Tetaldi, opposite the place defended
by Justiniani.[2]   Its dangerous character was soon shown.
The cannon having destroyed one of the towers near the

---

[1] The 'Chastel de bois' was 'si haut, si grand et si fort qu'il maistrisoit le
mur et dominait par-dessus' (Tetaldi, p. 25).

[2] Barbaro states that it occupied a place called the 'Cresca,' possibly a copyist's
error for Cressus (= Chariseus), the name which I believe he gave indifferently
with San Romano to the Pempton.   Elsewhere he uses Cresca for the Golden
Gate (e.g. p. 18).   Possibly, however, he is referring to another turret, which was
at the Golden Gate.   Barbaro's knowledge of places and names is not accurate.
Barbaro's 'bastion' is the 'helepole' of which Phrantzes speaks (p. 245), then
the three writers agree that the principal turret was at the Romanus Gate.

Romanus Gate, the turret was moved and stood overhanging the ditch. A fierce fight took place between the Turks inside it and the Greeks and Italians under Justiniani. The Turks flung earth, wood, and all kinds of material available into the foss, employing mainly the stone from the ruined tower, so as to form a level pathway across. The besieged fought hard from daylight till after sunset to prevent the Turks from making use of the turret, and the emperor and Justiniani assisted all the night at the repair of the tower.

It was probably the fact that the ditch had been largely filled with brushwood which brought about the destruction of the machine. The besieged managed to place barrels of powder in the ditch, set fire to the brushwood, and blew up the whole structure. Several of its occupants perished in the explosion. At daylight the sultan found that his huge turret was reduced to ashes, that the foss had been cleared out, and that the ruined tower had been in great part repaired. He swore that the thirty-seven thousand prophets could not have persuaded him that the besieged could have compassed its destruction in so short a time.[1]

A similar turret was erected opposite the Pegè Gate, or what is more probable, opposite the Third Military Gate and possibly there were others near the Golden Gate and elsewhere.[2]

Further attempts to undermine.

Undeterred by the discovery and failure of the attempt to undermine the walls at Caligaria, the Turks made other trials in the same neighbourhood. But Grant was always ready, countermined and destroyed the enemies' work before they could use it. On three successive days mines were found in this place, 'where there were no barbicans,' but they also were destroyed, and a number of Turks, who could not escape in time, either lost their lives or were captured.

On the 24th, a mine was found which had apparently been more carefully concealed. A wooden turret had been

---

[1] The Moscovite, 1087; Phrantzes, 247.

[2] Leonard, p. 93 : 'Mauritius Cataneus . . . inter portam Pighi, id est fonti usque ad Auream contra ligneum castrum, pellibus boum contectum, oppositu accurate decertat.' Cardinal Isidore, in the *Lamentatio*, says, p. 676 : 'Adm ventur urbi ligneae turres.'

built near the walls, which was intended to serve the double purpose of deceiving the besieged into supposing that its object was to facilitate the actual scaling of the walls, while at the same time it rested on a bridge of logs beneath which excavation was being made. It contained the earth and stones which were taken out. The ruse was, however, suspected, and the counterminers found and destroyed the mine. The last mine dug by the Turks was found on May 25. This, says Barbaro, was the most dangerous of all, because the miners got under the wall, and if powder had been employed, it would have brought down a portion, and have made an opening into the city.[1]

Altogether, says Tetaldi, the Turks had made fourteen attempts to undermine the walls, but the Christians had listened, had heard and detected them, and had either smoked out the Turks, destroyed them with stink pots, let in water on them, or had fought them hand to hand underground.[2] In all cases they had succeeded in preventing any dangerous explosion. The attempt to gain an entrance by mining had failed. In the words of Critobulus, Mahomet was now convinced that mining was vain and useless labour and expense, and that it was the cannon which would do everything.[3]

On the 23rd bad news reached the city. The small brigantine which had been sent out on May 3 returned. Once more, flying the Turkish flag, she ran the blockade of the Dardanelles and the entry of the Bosporus, her crew disguised as Turkish sailors. The Turks, however, near the city recognised and tried to catch her, but before they could bring their vessels to the boom, it was opened, and the brave little ship was once more safely in the Golden Horn.

Unfortunately, her crew had to report their failure to find the Venetian fleet. They had, nevertheless, done their work gallantly. Like the men, forty years later, under

Return of brigantine. Failure to find Venetian fleet.

[1] Barbaro, under dates of May 21, 22, 23, 24, and 25.
[2] As to the question whether there was water in the foss, see Professor Van Millingen's *Byz. Constantinople*, pp. 57-8.
[3] Crit. xxxi. Ἀλλὰ τοῦτο μὲν ὕστερον περιττὸν ἔδοξε, καὶ ματαία δαπάνη, τῶν μηχανῶν τὸ πᾶν κατεργασαμένων

Columbus, the sailors appear to have had a voice in determining what their ship should do. Having completed their task and decided that it was useless to search any longer for Loredano, a proposal was made to return to Constantinople. To this some of the crew objected. They professed to believe, perhaps did believe, that the city, if not already captured, would be taken to a certainty before they could reach it. They had done their best ; why should they run the gauntlet again and return to the doomed city, since they could do no good ? The greater number, however, were true to their engagement, and their answer has the best quality of seamanlike loyalty about it : 'Whether the city be taken or not ; whether it is to life or to death, our duty is to return,' and in consequence the brigantine made sail once more for the Golden Horn.[1]

Super-
natural
omens. During these days—that is, somewhere between May 22 and 26—certain events occurred of which mention is made by several writers.

Though we may regard the narrative of these events mainly as evidence of the superstition of the age, they have to be taken into account, inasmuch as they affected the spirit both of besiegers and besieged. The narratives are vague and not altogether reconcilable, but Critobulus, a man writing with exemplary carefulness long after the siege, probably gives the most accurate summary of what happened, though his account, like all others, is tinctured by the superstition of the time. He states that three or four days before the general assault, when all available citizens, men and women, were going in solemn procession through the city carrying with them a statue of the Virgin, the image fell from the hands of the bearers. It fell as if it had been lead. It was nearly impossible to raise it, and the task was only accomplished by the aid of the fervent prayers of priests and of all present. The fall itself created fear, and was taken to be an omen of the fall of the city. But this impression was deepened when,

---

[1] The return, as mentioned, was on May 23, but is given by Barbaro under the 3rd. This is one of the passages which show that his diary was revised and added to after the siege.

as the procession continued on its way, there happened a violent storm of thunder and lightning, followed by torrential rain. The priests could not make headway against the flood. The incident was manifestly supernatural. On the following day the impression was still further accentuated by the very unusual occurrence in Constantinople at the end of May of a thick fog, which lasted till evening. The cloud of fog gave complete confirmation of the impression that God had abandoned the city, because, as Critobulus remarks, the Divinity hides His presence in the clouds when He descends upon the earth.[1]

But the phenomenon of a light which appeared to settle over Hagia Sophia alarmed both sides. The sultan himself appears to have considered it an unfavourable omen, until the braver or more sceptical of his followers, without denying the evident fact that it was a heaven-sent omen, turned the difficulty by declaring that it was unfavourable to the Greeks. Within the city the besieged were even more alarmed than the Turks.

It is difficult to say what the phenomenon was. Men in that age expected omens and signs in the heavens and expressed their disappointment if none were vouchsafed to them. Writing, as all the narrators did, after the siege, they would look back to recall what were the signs of the divine displeasure, and they did not fail to find them. Around the story of some atmospheric phenomenon there grew a large myth, until we find The Moscovite recording that the light of heaven illuminated all the city; that the inhabitants, believing it to be the reflection of a fire caused by the Turks,

---

[1] Crit. xlvi.; Pusculus, iv. 889, says:

> Candida completo cum Phoebe surgeret orbe
> Moesta prodit, fati miseri cladisque propinquae
> Nuntia; nam tristis faciem velamine nubis
> Tecta atrae, mediaque latens plus parte sereno
> Incedit coelo.

Barbaro seems to describe an eclipse of the moon on May 22. The elder Dr. Mordtmann states that there was no full moon and consequently no eclipse on the 22nd, but that there was on the 24th. Dethier's note on The Moscovite, p. 1100. Phrantzes, p. 264, speaks of a light flashing from the sky settling over the city, and remaining during the whole night. See note, post p. 316.

ran towards Hagia Sophia and found flames bursting out of
its upper windows. These flames englobed the dome and
met in a single blaze which rose towards heaven and there
disappeared. The patriarch and the chief dignitaries of the
Church and members of the senate were so impressed with
the tidings of these wonderful signs that they went next day
in a body to the emperor to advise him to leave with the
empress. The patriarch reminded Constantine of well-known
and ancient predictions regarding the fall of the empire,
and named witnesses of the miracle. This new and terrible
augury meant that the grace and goodness of God had abandoned the city, and that it was decreed to be delivered to
the enemy. When the emperor learned the terrible news
he fell to the ground in a faint. He was revived with
aromatic water, and when he was pressed to leave the city
gave the answer, 'If it is the will of God, whither can we
fly before His anger?' He would die with his people.

The growth of the myth is evident. An imaginary empress [1] is brought in and a light is introduced, which, if it had
been visible as described, would have been recorded by every
contemporary writer. The unfortunate part of the story is
that it is difficult to say which parts are mythical and which
are true.[2]

Up to May 24, the city had been besieged for upwards
of six weeks. The failure of the brigantine to find the
Venetian fleet was a terrible disappointment to all within
the walls. If aid were coming from Western Europe, it
must be speedy. The besieged could do nothing but fight
on. During the whole six weeks the guns had been pounding against the walls day and night with ceaseless monotony,
and Greeks and Italians alike, while worn out by frequent
attacks and alarms, were continually occupied in the repair
of the damaged walls. Men and women, girls, old men and
priests, all, says Barbaro, were engaged in this wearisome

[1] Constantine was a widower, his wife, Catherine, having died in 1442, a year
after her marriage. Phrantzes, 195–8.

[2] The same remark applies to The Moscovite generally. There are so many
manifest fringes to what ought to have been the correct narrative of an eye
witness that it is impossible to distinguish truth from falsehood.

work. The breaching of the walls was steadily going on at three places, but the damages were greatest in the Lycus valley. There, indeed, all the force of the enemy seemed now to have been concentrated. There, especially, was the big bombard, throwing its ball of twelve hundred pounds weight which, when it struck the wall, shook it and sent a tremor through the whole city, so that even on the ships in the harbour it could be felt.[1]

[1] Barbaro, under May 20.

CHAPTER XIV

DISSENSIONS IN CITY: BETWEEN GREEKS THEMSELVES;
BETWEEN GREEKS AND ITALIANS; BETWEEN GENOESE
AND VENETIANS; CHARGE OF TREACHERY AGAINST
GENOESE EXAMINED; FAILURE OF SERBIA AND HUN-
GARY TO RENDER AID; PREPARATIONS FOR A GENERAL
ASSAULT; DAMAGES DONE TO THE LANDWARD WALLS;
CONSTRUCTION OF STOCKADE.

Dissen-
sions
among the
besieged.

IT is convenient to halt here in the narrative of the siege in order to call attention to certain dissensions within the city. These dissensions are made much of by the Latin writers and are probably exaggerated. They arose in great measure from a traditional ill-feeling, due to history, to difference of race and language, diversity of interest, and to the hostility between the Eastern and Western Churches. It is especially to the differences on the religious question that the Western writers call attention. In reference to the dissensions among the Greeks themselves, it must be remembered that the majority of them, priests and laity, either openly repudiated the arrangement made at Florence or conformed under something very near compulsion. The Greeks, says Leonard the Catholic archbishop, celebrate the Union with their voice but deny it in fact.[1] He points out that the emperor, fo whose orthodoxy he has nothing but praise, accepted it with heart and soul. But he was an exception. The majority still followed the lead of Gennadius and the Grand Duke Notaras. If it be true that the Grand Duke declared that he would prefer to see the head-dress of the Turk rather than that of the Latin priests, his prejudice furnished

[1] Leonard, *Opere*, p. 94.

evidence of the intensity of his dislike for the Latins, and is confirmatory of other statements made by Leonard. When the pope's name was pronounced in the liturgy, the congregation shouted their disapprobation. Most of the citizens had shunned the Great Church since the reconciliation service of December 12 as if it were a Jewish synagogue. Many who were present on a feast day when Mass was celebrated left the church as soon as the consecration commenced.

But in addition to the dissensions between the Greeks themselves was the hostility of both the Latin and Greek parties towards the Italians. Underlying the animosity arising from the difference on religious questions was a traditional sentiment of hostility. They were rivals in trade. Genoese and Venetians alike were interlopers, who were taking the bread out of the mouths of the citizens. The old bitterness arising from the occupation of the city by the Latins had never been forgotten. The largest colony, the Genoese, had taken advantage of the weakness of the empire they had helped to restore, in order to fortify and enlarge their city of Galata. The Venetians, who had taken the leading part in the conquest of 1204, had been allowed to settle within Constantinople, not because they were liked but because they were the rivals and the enemies of the Genoese. The exigencies of the situation which led to their having to be tolerated rankled among the Greeks as sorely as did the memory of the Latin occupation in which the Constantinopolitans felt the bitterness of a conquered people towards masters who held what to them was a hostile creed.

At the commencement of the siege, doubts had arisen among the citizens regarding the loyalty of the Venetians. Five of their ships which had been paid to remain for the defence of the city were discharging cargo, and the rumour spread that such cargo was for the use of the Turks. An imperial order stopped the discharge, and the Venetians saw in it a violation of their privileges under the capitulations. The emperor, however, convinced them that he had no such

design, and they promised, and faithfully kept their promise,
to defend the city until the end of the war.[1]

But although ultimately these various differences were
sufficiently overcome to prevent any considerable number of
men withdrawing from the defence of the city, discord always
smouldered and occasionally burst into flame. Leonard mentions an incident which illustrates the bitterness of feeling
which existed between the leaders respectively of Latins and
Greeks. In the very last days of the siege, when a general
attack was daily expected, Justiniani asked from Notaras the
Grand Duke, who was the noble highest in rank, that such
cannon as the city possessed should be given to him for use
in the Lycus valley. The demand was haughtily refused.
'You traitor!' said Justiniani ; 'why should I not cut you
down?' The quarrel went no further, but Notaras is said
to have been less zealous in his work for the defence of the
city. The Greeks, according to Leonard, resented the insult
and became sullen at the treatment of the Grand Duke,
because they believed that the glory of saving the city would
be gained by the Latins alone.[2]

On the day preceding the final assault the old jealousy
again showed itself. Barbaro relates that he and the other
Venetians made ' mantles '—some kind of wooden contrivance
for giving cover to the soldiers on the wall. They were
made at the Plateia, possibly near the end of the present
Inner Bridge. The Venetian bailey gave orders to the
Greeks to carry them to the landward walls. The Greeks
refused unless they were paid. Ultimately the difficulty of
payment was got over, but when the mantles reached the
wall it was already night ; and thus, says Barbaro, on account
of the greediness of the Greeks we had to stand at the defence
without them.[3]

The dissensions were further increased by discord between the Italian colonists themselves. We have already
seen that the emperor had been compelled to intervene to
prevent dangerous recriminations between the Venetians
and the Genoese. The former affected to despise the Genoese,

[1] Leonard, p. 92.   [2] Ibid. p. 95.   [3] Barbaro, under May 28.

while the latter, as the possessors of a walled city on
the opposite side of the Golden Horn and as the more
numerous, considered themselves the superiors of their rivals.
The Venetians, on account of their position within the city,
were compelled in their own interest either to help the
Greeks or to get away. The Genoese claimed to be in an
independent position. Each accused the other of the wish
to desert the city.

The most common charge, and one persisted in by the
Venetians, was that the Genoese were traitors to the city
and to Christianity, and it is difficult to say whether the
charge is well founded or not. Barbaro, himself a Venetian,
seldom loses an opportunity of speaking ill of the Genoese;
but the coarseness and recklessness of his attacks lessen
their value. If the charges of treachery depended on his
evidence alone, they might be dismissed. But other evidence
is at hand. We have seen that the Genoese are alleged to
have claimed that they could have burnt the sultan's ships
when they made their passage overland and would have done
so if they had not been his friends. Leonard, who was a
Genoese, evidently believed that they were traitors to
Christianity and were playing a double game. 'They ought
to have prevented the building of the fortress at Roumelia-
Hissar. But,' he concludes, ' I will keep silence, lest I should
speak ill of my own people, whom foreigners may justly
condemn.' They are nevertheless condemned by him because
they ' did not lend help to the Lord against the mighty.'

Charge of
treachery
against th
Genoese.

The evidence in their favour is, however, not weak.
First and foremost, John Justiniani was a Genoese. His
loyalty and the bravery and labours day and night of the
Genoese soldiers were beyond cavil. Ducas himself states
that the Genoese sent men from Galata who fought
valiantly under Justiniani; that many of them acted as spies,
sold provisions to the Turks, and secretly during the night
brought to the Greeks the news they had gathered. The
Podestà of Galata, writing shortly after the capture of the
city, declares that every available man had been sent across
the Horn to the defence of the walls. He protests that he

had done his best, because he knew that if Constantinople were lost, the loss of Pera would follow.[1]

The truth appears to be that the sympathy of the Podestà and the leading men was with their fellow Christians, but that the hostility of the Greeks and trade rivalry caused many of the Genoese too often to regard them as enemies. The Podestà is probably correctly expressing his own opinion and that of the better Genoese in stating that he foresaw that if Mahomet captured Constantinople, Galata would become an easy prey. But the certainty of making a good profit by dealing with the enemy was too great a temptation to be resisted by the ordinary merchant. Under cover of night he passed safely across the harbour and sold his goods to the citizens. He was equally ready during the day to deal with the Turks. The statement of Pusculus that the Genoese informed Mahomet by signal of the departure of the ships upon their night attack to burn the Turkish vessels which had been transported overland may be accepted as true, but the signal was probably the act of a private individual, for which the colony ought not to be held responsible. The boast reported by Ducas as having been made by the notables to Mahomet that they could have prevented the transport of the ships showed at least that they endeavoured to persuade him that they were neutral. It is by no means certain that had the Genoese desired to destroy the ships during the transit they could have made the attempt with a reasonable hope of success. They were far too few to meet the Turks outside the walls. However this may have been, they remained faithful to the conditions of the treaty which had existed before the time of Mahomet and which had been confirmed while he was at Adrianople on the express condition that they should not give aid to Constantinople. Even the complaint of Leonard that they could have saved the city if they had endeavoured to prevent Mahomet from securing a base of operations by building the fortifications at Hissar is a complaint against

<hr/>

[1] *Ep. Ang. Johannis Zacchariae Potestatis Perae*, Sec. 2, edition revised by Edward Hopf and Dethier.

the policy of neutrality. It would no doubt have been not only more in accordance with the crusading spirit but possibly wiser and better in the interest of Europe and of civilisation if the Genoese, as Leonard suggests that they ought to have done, had violated their treaty and had made common cause openly with the emperor from the first ; but to have done so would have been to risk the capture of Galata. Their policy was not a lofty one. Looked at by the light of subsequent events, it was not merely selfish but fatal ; but it was no more treacherous than the policy of neutrals generally is.

It is not improbable that the various dissensions between the citizens and the foreigners and between the latter themselves tended to make some of the Greeks lukewarm in their defence of the city. They were not going to fight for papists and heretics, or even for an emperor who had gone over to the papists. Leonard asserts that there were many defections ; that during the siege men who ought to have been at the walls tried to desert the city, pretended that they could not fight, that they wanted to attend to their fields and vineyards ; that others with whom he spoke urged that they must earn their bread, and that, in answer to his urging them to fight not only because of their duty to aid all Christians but because their own fate was at stake, they replied, ' What does the capture of the city matter to us if our families die of starvation ? ' [1] His statement that many men left the city is not sufficiently supported by other evidence to cause it to be accepted without hesitation.

In reading the charges brought against the Greek citizens by Leonard, it must be noted that he himself was a Genoese and a Latin archbishop. Unfortunately, almost all our accounts of the siege come either from Western writers or from Greek converts who are imbued with the usual bitterness against the professors of the faith which they have abandoned. Barbaro and Pusculus were Latins. Phrantzes and Ducas belonged to the Catholic party. The reports of the Podestà of Galata, of Cardinal Isidore, and other documents emanating from Latin sources all help to give a version unfavourable to

Witnesses against Greeks are nearly all Latins.

[1] Leonard, p. 94, and also Italian version given by Dethier, p. 644.

the Greeks. Indeed Critobulus almost stands alone as the representative of the larger party in the Orthodox Church. When, however, we get the account of an independent Western soldier, as in the case of Tetaldi, the charges against the Greek population disappear. In the whole of his clear and concise narrative, as well as in his estimate of how Europe might defeat the Turks, he has not a word to say against the conduct of the besieged. While praising the courage of the Turks highly as that of men who in the perils and hazards of war attach hardly any value to their lives, he yet judges that the Greeks with European help could defeat them.[1] These and other facts are at least sufficient to cause us to regard with suspicion attacks upon the loyalty towards the city and the emperor of the members of the Orthodox Church. Gibbon, influenced by the writers of the Latin Church— the only ones available to him—remarks ' that the Greeks were animated only by the spirit of religion, and that spirit was productive only of animosity and discord.' The observation or charge would hardly have been made if he had remembered the *ex parte* character of all the evidence before him. While there is truth in the statement that the spirit of religion produced animosity and discord, it is far from true either that it was the only spirit which actuated the Greeks or that it was productive only of animosity and discord. The Greeks were actuated by their own worldly interest, by their desire to preserve their own lives and property, their own city and their own government. Nor in admitting that they were even deeply animated with the religious spirit, can it successfully be maintained that this spirit only produced animosity. It was the religious spirit which animated Greeks as well as Italians to fight for the honour of God and the benefit of Christianity and thus tended to suppress discord and animosity. Even theological differences did not make the Greeks less eager to prevent a Moslem from taking the place of a Christian emperor. The Greeks differed from and even quarrelled with the Italians and their Romanised fellow citizens, but they regarded

[1] Tetaldi, pp. 32–35.

Genoese and Italians not merely as fighting for the interests
of Venice and Genoa, but as helping them to keep their
own, and the evidence is certainly insufficient to show that
such animosity and discord as existed prevented Greeks and
Italians alike from doing their utmost to keep the common
enemy of Christendom out of the city.

My reading of the contemporary narratives leads me to
conclude that, in spite of the isolated examples of dissensions
mentioned by Leonard, of deep differences of opinion on the
great religious question, and of constant jealousies between
Greeks and Italians and between Venetians and Genoese,
the unity of sentiment among the besieged for the defence
of the city was well maintained. They might quarrel on
minor questions, but on the duty and the desirability of
keeping Mahomet out they were united. I doubt the
statement as to many defections and, remembering how
many and grave the reasons for dissensions were, consider
that if they could be shown to have taken place in any
considerable numbers it would not be a matter for wonder.

We have seen that during the seven weeks in which *Prepara-*
Mahomet's army had been encamped before the triple walls *tions for a general*
of the Queen City he had attempted to capture it by attacks *assault.*
directed almost exclusively against the landward walls.
He was now preparing to make one directed upon all parts
of the city together. Hitherto, notwithstanding his balistas,
mangonels, and spingards, his turrets, his cannon and his
mining operations, he had failed. But his preparations had
all rendered the general assault which he contemplated more
formidable in character and easier of accomplishment. He
had collected together all the various appliances known to
mediaeval engineers for attacking a walled city; two
thousand scaling-ladders were ready for the assault, hooks
for pulling down stones, destroying the walls, and forcing
an entry. But the amassing of all his paraphernalia, and
even all his mining operations, sink into insignificance as
preparations for a general attack when compared with
the work done by his great cannon. Primitive as they

were in construction when measured with the guns of our own days, the Turks had employed them effectively.

Breaches made by Turks in three places.

They had concentrated their fire mainly in three places. Five cannon had discharged their balls against the walls between the Palace of Porphyrogenitus and the Adrianople Gate; four, among which was the largest, against those in the Lycus valley near the Romanus Gate, and three against the walls near the Third Military Gate.

The evidence presented to-day by the ruined condition of the walls in these places corroborates the statements made by contemporaries, that these were the principal places bombarded. Mahomet was already able to claim with some justice that he had opened three entrances for his army into the city.[1] Several of the towers between the Adrianople Gate and Caligaria had been destroyed. The Anatolian division had greatly weakened those in the neighbourhood of the Third Military Gate. But the most extensive destruction had been wrought by the Janissaries with the aid of the great cannon of Urban. While in each of the three places mentioned the Outer Wall is even now in an exceptionally dilapidated condition, the ruins in the valley of the Lycus show that this was the place where the cannon

Lycus valley chief point of attack.

had been steadily pounding day and night. Along almost the whole length of the foss, extending for upwards of three miles, its side walls and a great portion of the breastwork still remain, mostly, to all appearances, as solid as when they were new. But in the lower part of the Lycus valley hardly more than a trace of either is to be distinguished. The breastwork had been entirely destroyed and had helped to raise the foss to the level of the adjoining ground. A large portion of the Outer Wall and some of its towers had been broken down. The ruins of the Bactatinean tower had helped to fill the ditch; two towers of the great Inner Wall had fallen. A breach of twelve hundred feet long according to Tetaldi had been made opposite the place where Mahomet had his tent.[2] Here, where the largest cannon was placed, the struggles had been keenest. Here was the station of

---

[1] Crit. xlviii.   [2] See also the Moscovite, xx.

John Justiniani with his two thousand men, among whom were his own four hundred Genoese cuirassiers with their arms glittering in the sun to the delight, says Leonard, of their Greek fellow fighters. While the cannon had greatly damaged the walls in the other two places mentioned, here, says Critobulus, they had entirely destroyed them. There was a wall no longer, nor did there in this part exist any longer a ditch, for it had been filled up by the Turkish troops.

Hence it was that in this part Justiniani and those under him had been constantly occupied in repairs. Day after day the diarists recount that the principal occupation of the besieged was to repair during the night the part of the walls destroyed during the day by the cannon. Without experience of the power of great guns even in their then early stage of development, the besieged tried to lessen the force of the balls by suspending from the summit of the walls a sheathing of bales of wool. This and other expedients had failed.

As the best substitute for the broken-down Outer Wall Justiniani had gradually, as it was destroyed, constructed a Stockade, called by the Latin writers a Vallum and by the Greeks a *Stauroma*. On the ruined wall a new one was thus built almost as rapidly as the old one was destroyed. It was made with such materials as were at hand, of stones from the broken wall, of baulks of timber, of trees and branches, and even of crates filled with straw and vine cuttings, of ladders and fascines, all cemented hastily together with earth and clay. The whole was faced with hides and skins so as to prevent the materials being burnt by ' fire-bearing arrows.' In employing earth and clay the defenders intended that the stone cannon-balls should bury themselves in the yielding mass and thus do less damage than when striking against stone. Within the stockade was a second ditch from which probably the clay had been removed to cement the materials of the stockade, while above it were placed barrels or vats filled with earth so as to form a crenellation and a defence to the fighters against the missiles of the Turks.

Construction of stockade.

[1] Crit. lx.

The stockade was probably about four hundred yards long and occupied only the lower part of the valley, shutting in the portion of the Inner Enclosure and being thus a substitute for the Outer Wall. The usual entrance to this enclosure or Peribolos was by the Military Gate of St. Romanus—formerly known as the Pempton—which, indeed, had been constructed solely for this purpose, and by two small gates or posterns at its respective ends, one at the Adrianople Gate, the other at Top Capou. Another postern had, however, says Critobulus, been opened by Justiniani to give easier access to the stockade from the city.

The construction of the stockade had been commenced immediately after the destruction of the tower near the Romanus Gate, on April 21.[1] As the attention of the enemy had been principally directed to the attack on the walls in this part of the city, so the stockade which replaced the Outer Wall continued to the end to be the focus on which was concentrated nearly the entire strength of his attack. No one could say what would be Mahomet's plan of battle, but no one doubted that the stockade covering the St. Romanus Gate—or, as it is called in old Turkish maps, the 'Gate of the Assault'—would at least be one of the chief places against which he would direct an assault. Behind it and between it and the great Inner Wall was the flower of the defending army. The emperor himself had his camp quite near, though within the city, while Justiniani, standing for all time as the most conspicuous figure on the Christian side, was in command within the stockade. His energy and his courage had called forth the unqualified admiration of friend and foe. The jealousy of the Venetians at his appointment had long since been overcome. While Barbaro launches his recriminations against the Genoese generally, and even sometimes against Justiniani himself, even he is constrained to repeat that the presence of the great Genoese captain was *per benefitio de la Christianitade et per honor de lo mundo.* His example communicated itself to his troops, and he

---

[1] Barbaro, Pusculus, and Leonard agree with Critobulus in their description of the stockade.

thus became the hero of all who were fighting. All the city, says the Florentine soldier Tetaldi, had great hopes in him and in his valour. Mahomet himself was reported to have expressed admiration of the courage and ability, the fertility of resource and the activity of Justiniani, and to have regretted that he was not in the Turkish army. In front of the stockade was the sultan, surrounded by his white-capped Janissaries and the red-fezzed other members of his chosen bodyguard. Everything indeed pointed to a great fight at the stockade, where the great leaders and the flower of each army stood opposite each other.

About the beginning of the last week in May the Turks were alarmed by the rumour of an approaching fleet and of an army of Hungarians under John Hunyadi, both of which were reported to be on their way to the relief of the city.[1] The alarm, however, proved to be false. As Phrantzes laments, no Christian prince sent a man or a penny to the aid of the city.[2] At first sight it is somewhat surprising that no aid came either from the Serbians or Hungarians. During the early days of the siege assistance had been hoped for from both of these peoples. Phrantzes states that the despot of Serbia, George Brancovich, treated the sultan in such a manner as to make Mahomet taunt the Christians with his hostility to Constantine.[3] With the recollection of the Turkish victories at Varna and at Cossovo-pol, and especially of the fact that he had himself been attacked because he would not join in violating the peace between Ladislaus and Murad, it is probable enough that Brancovich was not unfriendly towards Mahomet. Indeed, at the request of the young sultan, he had used his influence to bring about a three years' armistice between the Turks and the Hungarians. It is not, therefore, surprising that no aid came from him.

[1] Phrantzes, 263.
[2] Ibid. 326. M. Mijatovich, in his pleasant and valuable Constantine, last Emperor of the Greeks, states that Mahomet received an ambassador from Ladislaus on May 26 (p. 198) ; but I do not know on what authority.
[3] Phrantzes, 325.

More success might have been anticipated from negotiations with Hungary. Here, however, the three years' agreement (made eighteen months before the siege) for an armistice stood in the way. The Hungarians had received a terrible lesson—at Varna—on the breaking of treaties, and they hesitated before violating the new arrangement. Ducas and Phrantzes agree in stating that the agents of Hunyadi had come to the city in the early days of the siege and had requested the sultan, on behalf of their principal, to give back the copy of the armistice signed by him in return for that signed by Mahomet. They gave as a pretext that Hunyadi was no longer viceroy of the king of Hungary. The design was too transparent to be accepted by the Turks.[1] The idea was to suggest to the sultan that the Hungarians were coming to the aid of the city ; that they had compunctions about breaking the treaty, but that, as it was not signed by the prince, they had a valid excuse for so doing. To this extent what was done indicated a spirit friendly to the besieged. The sultan and his council promised to consider the proposition, and put the agents of Hunyadi off with a civil and banal reply.[2]

Ducas tells a story regarding the visits of the agents of Hunyadi which may be noticed, though he is careful to give it as hearsay. He says that the officers in their suite showed the gunners how they might use their great bombard more effectually to destroy the walls by directing their fire in succession against two points instead of one, so as to form a triangle, and that the device succeeded to such an extent that the tower near the Romanus Gate and a part of the wall on each side of it was so broken down that the besiegers and besieged could see each other.[3]

[1] M. Mitjatovich's suggestion that the negotiations had probably emanated from the wily cardinal who had been the evil spirit of Ladislaus, or possibly from the crafty, but unpractical, mind of George Brancovich, appears plausible.
[2] Phrantzes, 326 ; Ducas, xxxviii.
[3] Ducas, xxxviii.

CHAPTER XV

LAST DAYS OF EMPIRE : SULTAN AGAIN HESITATES ; MES-
SAGE INVITING SURRENDER ; TURKISH COUNCIL CALLED ;
DECIDES AGAINST RAISING SIEGE ; PROCLAMATION
GRANTING THREE DAYS' PLUNDER ; SULTAN'S FINAL
PREPARATIONS ; HIS ADDRESS TO THE PASHAS AND
LAST ORDERS TO GENERALS. PREPARATIONS IN CITY :
RELIGIOUS PROCESSIONS : CONSTANTINE'S ADDRESS TO
LEADERS AND TO VENETIANS AND GENOESE ; LAST
CHRISTIAN SERVICE IN ST. SOPHIA : DEFENDERS TAKE
UP THEIR FINAL STATIONS AT WALLS, AND CLOSE GATES
BEHIND THEM : EMPEROR'S LAST INSPECTION OF HIS
FORCES.

BY May 25 it was well understood both by besiegers and Last days.
besieged that the crisis of the struggle had come and that a
general attack by land and sea and by all the forces which
the sultan possessed was at hand and would result in a contest which would probably decide the fate of the city.
Mahomet was able to choose his own time and make
characteristic preparations. The differences in the final
preparations of besiegers and besieged arose from two
causes : first, from the disparity in numbers between the
huge host of the besiegers and the small army defending
the city ; second, from the fact that the Turkish army consisted exclusively of men, while the population of the city
was largely composed of women and children, of priests,
monks, and nuns. On one side was a large host without
non-combatants ; on the other a small but valiant army
worn out by wearisome work, unrelieved, and encumbered
with a great number of useless non-combatants. While the

descriptions of what was done during the last days by the besiegers give us mainly military preparations with a day devoted to fasting and rest, those of the besieged are crowded with accounts of religious processions, of sensuous ceremonies, of penitents, of churches filled with people endeavouring to appease the wrath of an offended God and beseeching the aid of the Virgin and saints. But notwithstanding this colouring of the conduct of the defenders—and it must always be remembered that the descriptions are written by Churchmen—the soldiers were not unmindful of their duty. Constantine and the leaders neglected no precautions for defence, carefully noted that their orders were obeyed, and were now engaged in making a final disposition of their small force. All had their allotted task : even the women and children were called upon day and night to aid in repairing the damage done by the guns ; natives and foreigners vied with each other in zeal for the defence.

Whether the leaders realised that their struggles were hopeless may be doubted, though it is difficult to believe that they could feel confidence in the result. It is certain that they all recognised that the final struggle would be for life or death. The population generally were buoyed up with the knowledge of the failure of the Turks to capture the city in 1422, within the recollection of many of the citizens, and possibly—though not, I think, to any great extent—by the hope of miraculous intervention on their behalf. The faith which accepted the legend of an advance being permitted as far as St. Sophia and of an angel who would then descend and hand over the government of the city to the emperor may have existed among the women and monks, but it is not of the kind which soldiers, and still less even religious military commanders, possess. The leaders, from the emperor downwards, knew the weakness of the city, the insufficiency of men to defend fourteen miles of walls, and the overwhelming superiority in numbers of the Turkish army. The bad news brought on the 23rd by the brigantine sent to search for the Venetian fleet had almost dispelled hope of timely aid from the West, though many still clung

to the belief that they might welcome a few more Italians
who were reported to have been seen at Chios on their way
to the capital.[1]

On Thursday, May 24, Barbaro notes that there were
music and feasting and other signs of rejoicing among the
Turks because they had learned that they were about to
make a general attack.[2]

On the 25th and the 26th the great guns were constantly at work in the Lycus valley and at the two other
places already described. On the evening, however, of the
26th, at one hour after sunset, the Turks made a great
illumination along the whole length of their line. Every
tent in the enemy's camp could be seen. The fires were so
great as to show everything as clearly as if it were day.
They lasted till midnight. The shouts from the Turks rent
the heavens. The archbishop states that a Turkish edict or
Iradè had given notice that for three days praise should be
offered to God, but that on one day there should be fasting.
The illuminations in which the Turks indulged and the
nightly feasting are what take place usually during the
month of Ramazan. But as this was not Ramazan, every
one rightly conjectured that they indicated that the Turks
had received the welcome news of a general and immediate
attack.

Even, however, in these last days of the siege the sultan
appears to have seriously hesitated whether to make the
attack or abandon the attempt to capture the city. Many
of the Turks really appear to have lost heart. They had
been seven weeks before the city and had accomplished
nothing. The pashas themselves were divided in opinion.
Various rumours were current in the camp which increased
their hesitation. Western Europe would not allow Con-

Sultan hesitates to attack.

---

[1] Tetaldi says : ' Se l'armée de Venise que menoit et conduisoit Messire Jean
le Rendoul [Loredano] fut arrivé à Constantinople ung seul jour avant que
cette cité fust prinse, certes il n'y avoit aucun doute qu'ils eussent fort secouru
et fussent venus bien à point ' (p. 30).

[2] ' Per el campo del Turco in questo zorno se fexe asai feste, de soni, e de
altra condition de alegreze, e questo perche i sentiva che tosto i volea dare la
bataia zeneral ' (p. 48, under May 24).

stantinople to be captured. The princes of the West were
leagued together to drive the Turks out of Europe. John
Hunyadi, with a large force of infantry and cavalry, was on
his way to relieve the city.[1] A great fleet prepared at the
request and with the aid of the pope, the head of Christendom, was on its way out, and its van had already been
heard of at Chios.[2] There were not wanting many in
Mahomet's camp who were opposed to a continuation of
the siege and who urged him to abandon it. The sultan,
according to Phrantzes, was influenced and depressed by the
rumours of the interference of Western Europe, especially
by the news of the arrival of a fleet at Chios,[3] by the want
of success which had so far attended his efforts to enter the
city, by the stubbornness of the defence and the strength of
the walls, and, lastly, by omens deduced from flashes of
lightning which had played over the city, or from some
atmospheric effect which had lighted up the dome of St.
Sophia—omens which, at first interpreted as a sign of God's
vengeance on the Constantinopolitans, were a little later construed by some of the Turks to be a token that it was taken
under Divine protection.[4]

[1] Phrantzes, 263.

[2] Leonard, p. 95; Phrantzes, 263; Crit. xlvi.

[3] Crit. xlvii.

[4] The accounts of this light (or darkness), which alarmed both sides, are
somewhat conflicting. Perhaps here also Critobulus is the safest guide. In
chapter xlvi. he mentions the religious procession already described, where the
statue of the Virgin falls, and says it was 'three or four days before the attack.'
Immediately after came torrential rains with vivid flashes of lightning. Then,
'the next day,' there was a thick fog lasting till evening. Barbaro speaks of a
darkness, due, judging from his description, to an eclipse of the moon, lasting
from the first to the sixth hour after sunset, as being on the 22nd. This
alarmed the Greeks, he says, because of an ancient prophecy which declared
that Constantinople should not be lost until the moon should give a sign in the
heavens. Phrantzes (page 264) says: φῶς ἀστράπτον καταβαῖνον ἐξ οὐρανῶν καὶ
δι' ὅλης τῆς νυκτὸς ἄνωθεν τῆς πόλεως ἐστὸς διέσκεπεν αὐτήν. Possibly both
Phrantzes and Barbaro have the same atmospheric night effects in view: that
is, that there were frequent flashes of lightning during the night so long as the
eclipse lasted. The statement of Pusculus, who was in the city at the time, has
already been quoted. See p. 297, ante. The account of Critobulus appears
clear, but it does not eliminate the miraculous, for he declares that many
persons, both Romans and foreigners, declared that they had seen the Divinity
hiding Himself in the clouds.

It was probably in consequence of this depression that Sends Ismail to inquire as to possibility of surrender. even at this late stage Mahomet made one more effort to induce the Greeks to surrender the city. A certain Ismail, the son of Alexander who had obtained the rule over Sinope by accepting the suzerainty of the Turks, came into the city at the request of the sultan and endeavoured to persuade the Greeks to make terms. He spoke of his own influence with Mahomet and promised, if they would appoint a messenger, to use it to procure for him a favourable hearing. He declared that unless terms were made the city would certainly be captured, the men killed, and their wives and daughters sold as slaves.

Upon Ismail's suggestion a messenger, but a man of no particular name or family, went with Ismail to Mahomet. According to Chalcondylas, the answer sent to the Greeks was that they should pay an annual tribute of ten myriads or one hundred thousand gold bezants, and if this condition were not accepted Mahomet would permit as an alternative that all the inhabitants should leave the city, taking with them their own property, with leave to go whither they wished. He would be content to receive the deserted city. The Greeks, though with some difference of opinion, decided that they could not and would not accept either of the conditions offered. Possibly not a few of them were of the opinion of Chalcondylas, that the offer was not serious on the sultan's part—that is, that he did not believe that there was any chance of its being accepted—but that it was rather an attempt to learn what the feeling was among the Greeks in regard to their chance of success. Mahomet had nothing to lose by his offer. He knew that the inhabitants could not pay the amount of tribute demanded. If, on the other hand, they had been willing to desert the city in order to save their lives, he would have gained an easy victory without bloodshed—a victory which he was by no means certain he could gain after a general assault. If the story of Chalcondylas is to be believed, then additional doubt is thrown on the statement of Ducas that the emperor on a previous occasion had voluntarily offered to pay any tribute which might be demanded. I am disposed to give credence to Chalcondylas.[1] Ismail was a very likely man to be employed by Mahomet. The sultan rightly judged that the besieged would be willing to accept conditions, and would desire to learn what his conditions were. The answer convinced him, however, that his only chance of gaining the city was by fighting for it.[2]

On Friday, May 25, and Saturday the Turks continued their cannonading against ' our poor walls ' even harder than ever. Greeks and Italians busied themselves in repairing the damages as fast as they were made, and this in such good fashion, says Barbaro, that even after all that the great guns could do ' we made them as strong as they were at first.'

Sultan calls council to consider desirability of raising siege.Meantime it was necessary for the sultan to put an end to all hesitation as to the commencement of the general attack. A council was held for this purpose on Saturday the 26th or Sunday the 27th, in which the arguments in favour of and against the siege were fully discussed. Halil Pasha, the grand vizier and the man of greatest reputation, declared himself in favour of abandoning it. He reminded his master that he had always been opposed to it and had foretold failure from the outset. The strong position of the city made it invincible, now that the Latins were aiding the citizens. He urged that sooner or later Christian kings and people would be provoked by its capture and would intervene. The Genoese and Venetians, against their wish, would become enemies of the Turks if the war went on. He therefore advised retreat while this could be done in safety.[3] Halil Pasha's rival and enemy was the Albanian Zagan Pasha, who was next him in rank. While Halil was always

---

[1] Ducas also mentions the attempt recorded by Chalcondylas, but without mentioning the name of Ismail. Ducas thus mentions two negotiations for peace, the first (if it ever existed) being towards the end of April and the second nearly a month after.

[2] The Turkish historian Sad-ud-din, (p. 20) represents the emperor as offering to surrender everything except Constantinople ; to which Mahomet's reply was, ' Either the city, the sword, or El-Islam.'

[3] Leonard.

favourable to the Christians,[1] Zagan was their enemy.
Zagan, seeing the Sultan downcast at having to raise the
siege, boldly advocated an attack. He urged that the
appearance of the light over Hagia Sophia, which had been
taken by some of the Turks to indicate that the city was
under divine protection, really meant that it would be
delivered into the sultan's hands. He reminded his young
master that Alexander the Great had conquered the world
with a much smaller army than was now before the city.
As to the coming of fleets from the West, he neither believed
nor feared it. The division among its princes would bring
anarchy into any fleet they might get together. There was
and could be no concert among them. Besides, even if such
a fleet arrived, there were three or four times as many Turks
as any fleet could bring. He recommended, therefore, that
the attack should be pushed on vigorously : that the cannons
should be kept constantly going, so as to make new breaches
or widen those already made in the walls, and that all thought
of retreat should be abandoned. The younger members of
the council agreed with him, as did also the leader of the
Thracian troops—that is, the Bashi-bazouks—and strongly
urged an attack. This advice stiffened the sultan's own
determination. Mahomet ordered Zagan Pasha to go
himself that very night among the troops and learn what
was their mind on the subject.[2] Zagan obeyed the order,
returned, and reported that he had visited the army, which
desired orders for an immediate attack. He assured the
sultan that he could fight with confidence and be certain of
victory.[3]

Upon this report the sultan announced his intention to
make a general assault forthwith, and from this time devoted

Decides
upon
attack.

---

[1] Leonard, Phrantzes, and Tetaldi all speak of him as friendly to the
Christians. He was, however, disliked by Mahomet, because he had persuaded
Murad to send his son to Magnesia. Tetaldi says that the Christians in the
Turkish army shot letters into the city to let the besieged know all that went
on in the council.

[2] According to Leonard, the sultan ordered Zagan to fix a day for a general
assault.

[3] Phrantzes, 623-8, and also Leonard.

himself solely to completing his final preparations.[1] He
ordered that during the following nights fires should be
lighted and torches burned, that the soldiers should fast
during the following day, should go through their ceremonial
ablutions seven times and ask God's aid in capturing the
city.

Makes
final
arrange-
ments for
general
attack.

The sultan rose early on the morning of Sunday the
27th. He called those in charge of the guns and ordered
them to concentrate the fire of their cannon against the
walls of the stockade. He disposed his bodyguard, according to the arms they carried, into regiments—some of which
contained upwards of a thousand men—and directed that
when the order was given they should be sent forward in
succession; that after one division had fought it should
retire and rest while another took its place. In so doing he
intended that the general attack should continue until it
ended in victory without giving the besieged any time for
rest. It was perhaps the best way to take advantage of
his enormous superiority in numbers.

Then he visited the other troops from sea to sea, repeat-
ing his orders to the leaders, encouraging all by his presence,
and seeing that all arrangements had been made as he had
directed.

Mahomet sent a message to Galata insisting that the
Genoese should prevent help being sent clandestinely to the
city.

Proclaims
three days
of plunder.

He caused his heralds to proclaim through the camp
that his soldiers would be allowed to sack the city during

---

[1] The narrative of Phrantzes relating the decision of the meeting of the
Turkish council concludes by stating that this was on the 27th—that is, Sunday
(p. 269). It may have been, but it is difficult to believe that the council
meeting, the sending of Zagan to learn the opinion of the soldiers, his return
and the decision, together with the subsequent proclamation, were all crowded
into one day. Barbaro gives the proclamation as being made on Monday the
28th. Leonard says that, as a result of the meeting, a proclamation was issued
for the attack to be on Tuesday and for the three preceding days to be devoted
to prayer and one of them to fasting. If he is correct, the council could not
have been on the 27th. Tetaldi states that the council lasted during four days.
The statement appears possible, and perhaps gives the explanation of the
apparent discrepancies in the narratives.

three days : to announce that the sultan swore by the ever-
lasting God, by the four thousand prophets, by Mahomet,
by the soul of his father, and by his children, that the whole
population, men, women, and children, all the treasure and
whatever was found in the city should be given up freely by
him to his warriors. The proclamation was received with
tumultous expressions of triumph.[1]   'If you had heard the
shouts raised to heaven with the cry, 'There is one God, and
Mahomet is his prophet,' you would indeed have marvelled,
adds Leonard.

No attempt was made on the Saturday, Sunday, or
Monday to capture the city, but the guns were steadily
pounding away during all these three days.

On Sunday the great cannon fired three times at the
stockade, and at the third shot a portion of it came down.
According to the Muscovite, Justiniani was wounded by a
splinter from the ball and had to be led or carried into the city.
He, however, recovered during the night and superintended
once more the repairs of the walls.[2]

On the Sunday also every Turk was busy in completing
preparations for the final attack.[3]   Every man had been
ordered under pain of death to be at his post.

The Turks were observed to be fetching earth, crates of
vine-cuttings and other materials to level a passage across
the foss, making scaling-ladders, and generally to be bringing
forward all the engines for assault.   When the sun set,
fires and torches were lighted as on the previous night.
The illuminations were accompanied by such terrible shouts
that Barbaro, with not unnatural exaggeration, asserts that
they were heard across the Bosporus.   The soldiers, in high
spirits at the thought of the coming attack, were once more

---

[1] Leonard, 96, Phrant. 269 ; Barbaro adds that the Turks believed that on
the morrow they would have so many Christians in hand that two slaves could
be bought for a ducat : such riches that everything would be of gold, and
they could have enough hair from the heads of Christian priests to make ropes
with which to tie up their dogs.
[2] The Moscovite, xxii. This first wound is only mentioned by the
Moscovite.
[3] Phrantzes, 269.

feasting, after their day's fast. The besieged, hearing the shouts, the sound of the trumpets and guitars, of pipes, fifes, and drums, and the usual din, ran to the walls, for the illumination was so great that they were in hopes that the fires were devouring tents and provisions; but, says Ducas, when they recognised that there was no alarm among their enemies, they could only pray to be delivered from the imminent danger. The illuminations continued until midnight, and then, more suddenly than they had appeared, the fires were extinguished and the camp was left in complete obscurity.

The leaders on both sides had now but few final arrangements to make for attack or for defence. The sultan, as usual, personally superintended the making of those on the Turkish side.

On Monday morning Mahomet accompanied by a large following of horsemen, which Barbaro estimates at about ten thousand, rode over to the Double Columns and arranged for the co-operation of the fleet while the general bombardment and attack were being made by the rest of his forces.[1]   Admiral Hamoud, the successor of Baltoglu, was to spread out his ships on the Marmora side from St. Eugenius Gate to that of Psamatia, to prepare to enter the city by scaling-ladders from the ships, if entrance were possible, and at all events by his preparations and feigned attacks to draw off as many men as possible from the defence of the landward walls.[2]

Mahomet returned in the afternoon from the Double Columns. On the same day, and possibly on his return, the sultan summoned to him the heads of the Genoese community in Galata and confirmed the strict injunction he had already given them that on no account were they to render aid to the Greeks.[3]

After crossing the Golden Horn he once more rode along the whole line of the walls from the Horn to the Marmora,

---

[1] Barbaro, p. 50.

[2] Barbaro. Ducas says, from St. Eugenius to Hodegetria and as far as Vlanga (p. 282-3), which is substantially the same position as that given by Critobulus.

[3] Zorso Dolfin, p. 78.

to inspect his troops and see that all was ready. He passed before his three great divisions : Europeans, under Caraja ; the select troops, including the Janissaries, before the Myriandrion and the Mesoteichion, and the Asiatic division, between Top Capou and the sea, each of about fifty thousand men, and saw that all was ready. After having thus inspected his fleet and his army, he summoned the pashas and chief military and naval officers once more to his tent. Critobulus gives us an account of what was said which probably represents fairly what passed. The decision was taken. The city was to be attacked. Before the assault began it was necessary for Mahomet to explain his plan of assault, give his final orders, and hold out to his followers every possible inducement to fight bravely.

Mahomet addresses the pashas,

The sultan began by recalling to his hearers that in the city there was an infinite amount and variety of wealth of all kinds—treasure in the palaces and private houses, churches abounding in furniture of silver, gold, and precious stones. All were to be theirs. There were men of high rank and in great numbers who could be captured and sold as slaves ; there were great numbers of ladies of noble families, young and beautiful, and a host of other women, who could either be sold or taken into their harems. There were boys of good family. There were houses and beautiful gardens. 'I give you to-day,' said Mahomet, 'a grand and populous city, the capital of the ancient Romans, the very summit of splendour and of glory, which has become, so to say, the centre of the world. I give it over for you to pillage, to seize its incalculable treasures of men, women, and boys, and everything that adorns it. You will henceforward live in great happiness and leave great wealth to your children.' The chief gain for all the sons of Othman would be the conquest of a city whose fame was great throughout the whole world. The greater its renown, the greater would be the glory of taking it by assault. A great city which had always been their enemy, which had always looked upon them with a hostile eye, which in every way had sought to destroy the Turkish power, would come into their possession.

The door would be open to them by its capture to conquer
the whole of the Greek empire.

To this promise recorded by Critobulus may be added
what is said by the Turkish historian, that Mahomet urged
that the capture would be an augmentation of the glory of
their faith, and that it was clearly predicted in the 'Sacred
Traditions.' [1]

The sultan further urged them not to believe that capture
was impossible. You see, he remarked, that the foss is filled
and that the walls have been so destroyed by the guns in
three places that they may be crossed not only by infantry,
but even by cavalry. They form no longer an impregnable
barrier, for the way has been made almost as level as a race-
course.

He declared that he knew the defenders to be so weak
that he believed the reports of deserters who stated that
there were only two or three men to garrison each tower, so
that a single man would have to defend three or four crenellations ; and the men themselves were ill-armed and unskilled
in warfare. They had been harassed day and night and
were worn out, were short of provisions, and could not maintain resistance against a continuous attack. He had decided
to employ the great number of his followers in making a
continuous assault, day and night, sending up fresh detach-
ments one after the other, until the enemy from sheer
weariness would be forced to yield or be incapable of further
resistance.

Mahomet pretended once more to be uncertain what the
conduct of the Italians would be during the coming assault.
The cause was not theirs. They would not sacrifice their lives
where there was nothing to gain. The mixed crowd, gathered
from many places, had no intention of dying for the city, and
when they saw the waves of his men succeeding each other at
the attack they would throw down their arms and turn their
backs. Even if, from any cause, they did not run away, they
were too few to resist his army. The city, both by land and
sea, was surrounded as in a net and could not escape.

[1] Sad-ud-din, p. 16. Translation by E. J. W. Gibb.

Mahomet concluded by urging all to fight valiantly, assuring his hearers that he would be at their head and would see all that passed. He finished his address by charging his hearers to return to their posts, to order all under their commands to take food, and then to lie down for a few hours' rest. Silence was everywhere to be observed. They were enjoined to draw up their men in battle array at an early hour in the morning, and when they heard the sound of the trumpet summoning them to battle and saw the standard unfurled, then ' to the work in hand.'

The leaders of divisions remained, after the departure of the larger assembly, in order to receive their final orders. *and the leaders of divisions.* Hamoud, with his fleet, was to keep near the seaward walls and the archers and fusiliers [1] should be so ready to shoot, that no man dare show his head at the battlements. Zagan was to cross the bridge, and with the ships in the harbour to attack the walls on the Golden Horn. Caraja was to cross the foss—probably between Tekfour Serai and the Adrianople Gate, where was one of the three roads that Mahomet had opened into the city—and to try to capture the wall. Isaac and Mahmoud, at the head of the Asiatic division, were charged to attempt the walls near the Third Military Gate. Halil and Saraja, who were in command of the troops encamped around the sultan, opposite the third and most important breach—that, namely, at the Romanus Gate, defended by Justiniani—were to follow the lead which the sultan would himself give them.

Having thus made his final dispositions, Mahomet dismissed his inner council, and each leader went away to his own tent to sleep and await the signal for attack.

The speech to his leaders, which I have summarised in the preceding paragraphs from the report given by Critobulus,[2] is also recorded by Phrantzes, though at much less length. He describes it as having been made at sunset of

---

[1] τούφακας; in modern Greek the name for sporting guns is τουφέκια. The Turks call them *Toufeng*. Ducas uses the word μολυβδοβόλοι.

[2] Crit. xlvii. to lii.

the 28th,[1] and makes the sultan remind his leaders, with the
usual voluptuous details, of the glories of paradise promised
to the true believer who dies in battle.[2]

Meanwhile, within the city preparation of a different
kind had been made. After the meeting of the council of
Turkish nobles, the besieged, who seem always to have been
well informed of what went on in the enemy's camp, learned
at once that it had been decided to make a general assault
forthwith. All day long during the last day of agony the
alarm bell was ringing to call men, women, and children to
their posts. Each man had his duty allotted to him for the
morrow, while even women and children were employed to
carry up stones to the walls to be hurled down upon the
Turks.[3] The bailey of the Venetian colony issued a final
appeal, calling upon all his people to aid in the defence,
and urging them to fight and be ready to die for the love
of God, the defence of the country, and 'per honor de tuta
la Christianitade.' All honest men, says the Venetian
diarist, obeyed the bailey's command, and the Venetians,
besides aiding in the defence of the walls, took charge of the
ships in the harbour and were guardians of the boom.
Barbaro and his fellow citizens occupied the day in making
mantles for the protection of the soldiers upon the walls.

The silence during the Monday before the landward
walls was more impressive than the noise of previous warlike preparations. The Turks were keeping their fast
Probably during the afternoon they were allowed to sleep ir

---

[1] According to Critobulus, the meeting of the Council was on the 27th.

[2] Phrantzes, 269–70. Was the speech as recorded by Critobulus eve
delivered? The answer I am disposed to give is that a speech was delivere
which was substantially that reported by Phrantzes and Critobulus. Th
fashion followed by the Byzantine writers, and their desire to imitate classica
models, by putting all speeches in the first person, made it necessary to invent
speech if the substance of what was said were known. Critobulus, writing som
years after the capture and having had many opportunities of meeting with th
Turkish leaders, was in a position to learn what was said and done by then
and hence his report, wherever it can be tested, almost invariably proves trus
worthy.

[3] Barbaro, May 28.

order that they might be fresh for the attack on the following morning, for, says Critobulus, the Romans were surprised at the quietness in the camp. Various conclusions were drawn from the silence. Some thought that the enemy was getting ready to go away ; others that preparations were being completed which were less noisy than usual.[1]

The reader of the original narratives gets weary of the constant lament of their authors over the sins of the people, the principal one, if the writer is a Catholic, being the refusal to be sincerely reconciled with Rome ; if Orthodox, it is the neglect to give due honour to the saints. The deprecation of 'the just anger' of God was on every one's lips, and priests of both Churches speak confidently as to the cause of this anger. But assuredly, if the invocation of the celestial hierarchy were ever desirable, it was so on this last evening of the existence of the city as the Christian capital of the East.

A special solemn procession took place in the afternoon through the streets of the city. Orthodox and Catholics, bishops and priests, ordinary laymen, monks, women, children, and indeed every person whose presence was not required at the walls, took part in it, joined in every *Kyrie Eleeson,* and responded with the sincerity of despair to prayers imploring God not to allow them to fall into the hands of the enemy. The sacred eikons and relics were brought from the churches, were taken to the neighbourhoods where the walls were most injured, and paraded with the procession in the hope—to people of Northern climes and the present century inexplicable and almost unthinkable—that their display would avert the threatening danger.

Last religious procession in city.

It would be a mistake, however, to think that, because these processions and the veneration of the sacred relics are alien to modern modes of thought, they were not marked with true religious sentiment, or even that they were useless. They encouraged the fighters to go more bravely forth to battle against tremendous odds, and they comforted both them and non-combatants with the assurance that God was

[1] Crit. liv.

on their side. The archbishop concludes his account of this last religious procession in the Christian city, on the eve of the great struggle, by declaring that 'we prayed that the Lord would not allow His inheritance to be destroyed, that He would deign in this contest to stretch forth His right hand to deliver His faithful people, that He would show that He alone is God and that there is none else beside Him [no Allah of the Moslems] and that He would fight for the Christians. And thus, placing our sole hope in Him, comforted regarding what should happen on the day appointed for battle, we waited for it with good courage.'

When the procession had completed its journey, the emperor addressed a gathering of the nobles and military leaders, Greeks and foreigners. Phrantzes gives at considerable length the speech delivered by Constantine. Gibbon, while describing it as 'the funeral oration of the Roman empire,' suggests that the fullest version which exists of it, that namely of Phrantzes, ' smells so grossly of the sermon and the convent' as to make him doubt whether it was pronounced by the emperor. We have, however, the other summary given by Archbishop Leonard, who also was probably present. Each account is given in the pedantic form which is characteristic of mediaeval churchmen, Greeks or Latins. The reporter always seems to think it necessary to introduce classical allusions, to enlarge on the religious aspect of the coming struggle, and to report in the first person. But, bearing in mind this fashion of the time, and recalling the fact that the accounts of Phrantzes and the archbishop are independent, their records of the funeral oration are substantially identical and do not vary more than would do two independent reports written some months after the delivery of a speech in our own time.

The emperor called attention to the impending assault, reminded his hearers that it had always been held the duty of a citizen to be ready to die either for his faith, his country, his sovereign, or his wife and children, and pleaded that all these incentives to heroic sacrifice were now combined. He dwelt upon the importance of the city and their attachment

Funeral oration of empire.

to it. It was the city of refuge for all Christians, the pride
and joy of every Greek and of all who lived in Eastern
lands. It was the Queen of Cities, the city which in happier
times had subdued nearly all the lands under the sun. The
enemy coveted it as his chief prize. He had provoked the
war. He had violated all his engagements in order to obtain
it. He wished to put the citizens under his yoke, to take
them as slaves, to convert the holy churches, where the
divine Trinity was adored and the most holy Godhead
worshipped, into shrines for his blasphemy, and to put the
false prophet in the place of Christ. He urged them as
brothers and fellow soldiers to fight bravely in the defence
of all that was dear to them, to remember that they were
the descendants of the heroes of ancient Greece and Rome,
and so to conduct themselves that their memory should be
as fragrant in the future as that of their ancestors. He
entrusted the city with confidence to their care. For himself he was determined to die in its defence. He recalled to
them that he and they put their trust in God and not, as
did their enemy, in the multitude of his horsemen and his
hordes.

Both the reporters of this speech state that Constantine
concluded by addressing the Venetians and Genoese separately, and, indeed, give the substance of what he said. He
recalled to each group their valiant services and the aid
they had rendered in times past and expressed his confidence
in their assistance on the morrow.

The emperor endeavoured to infuse hope and confidence
into all the leaders by pointing out that hitherto the
defenders had been able to hold the walls, that the invaders
were like wild animals and fought without intelligence, that
the shouts, the fires, and the great noise were a barbarous
attempt to frighten them, but that, protected by the walls,
he and his people with their brave Italian allies would be
more than a match for the invaders. ' Do not lose heart,'
said he, ' but comfort yourselves with bright hopes, because,
though few in number, you are skilled in warfare ; strong,
brave and noble, and proved in valour.' He concluded by

urging them once more to be daring and steadfast, and
promised that in such a cause, by the grace of God, they
would win.[1]

We have nothing to enable us to judge whether the
emperor possessed the power of utterance which at various
periods in the world's history has enabled great soldiers to
kindle the enthusiasm of their followers. If ever occasion
demanded such power, beyond doubt it was the present
One advantage at least the orator possessed : he had an
audience entirely in sympathy with him. Whether he
succeeded or not in inspiring them with a confidence which
he can hardly have himself felt may be doubted. But that
all were determined to follow the emperor and to sacrifice
' wives and children and their own lives ' in defence of him
and their ancient city is attested by both reporters. The
leaders, after the fashion still prevalent in Eastern Europe
embraced and asked forgiveness of each other, as men who
were ready to die, and, solemnly devoting themselves to the
cause of the emperor, repaired to the great church of Hagi
Sophia, 'to strengthen themselves by prayer and the reception
of the Holy Mysteries, to confirm their vows to fight, and
if need be, unmindful of all worldly interests, to die for the
honour of God and of Christianity.'

Last
Christian
service in
Hagia
Sophia.

The great ceremony of the evening and one that mu
always stand out among the world's historic spectacles w
the last Christian service held in the church of Holy Wisdom
The great church had not been regularly used since the
meeting of December 12, which had led to so much heat
burning and ill-will. Now, at the moment of suprem
danger for Constantinople, the fairest monument of Easter
Christendom was again opened. The emperor and such
the leaders as could be spared were present and the buildi
was once more and for the last time crowded with Christi
worshippers. It requires no great effort of imagination
picture the scene. The interior of the church was the m
beautiful which Christian art had produced, and its bea
was enhanced by its still gorgeous fittings. Patriarch

[1] Phrantzes, 271-8 ; Leonard, 97.

ardinal, the crowd of ecclesiastics representing both the
Eastern and Western Churches ; emperor and nobles, the
ast remnant of the once gorgeous and brave Byzantine
aristocracy ; priests and soldiers intermingled, Constantinopolitans, Venetians and Genoese, all were present, all
realising the peril before them, and feeling that in view of
the impending danger the rivalries which had occupied them
for years were too small to be worthy of thought.   The
emperor and his followers partook together of ' the undefiled
and divine mysteries,' and said farewell to the patriarch.
The ceremony was in reality a liturgy of death.   The
mpire was in its agony and it was fitting that the service
or its departing spirit should be thus publicly said in its
most beautiful church and before its last brave emperor.
f the scene so vividly described by Mr. Bryce of the coro-
ation of Charles the Great and the birth of an empire is
among the most picturesque in history, that of the last Chris-
an service in St. Sophia is surely among the most tragic.[1]

The solemn ceremony concluded, all went to take up
their respective stations.   The Greeks, says Leonard, who is
by no means a witness partial to them, went to their posts
rengthened in their manly resolve to put aside all private
terests and acted together for the common safety steadily
nd cheerfully.

Italians and Greeks returned to their stations at the
ndward walls for the defence of the Outer Wall and with the
ner Wall behind them.   In order to prevent any of their
mber withdrawing from the fight the gates leading from
e city into the Peribolos, where they stood, were closed and
cked.   They thus voluntarily cut themselves off from all
ance of retreat.   It was done, says Cambini the Florentine,
iting while the siege was within the memory of persons
ll living, so that in taking from the defenders any means
retreat they should resolve to conquer or die.[2]

Defenders close gates behind them.

----

[1] Phrantzes, 279 ; The Moscovite, p. 1113. The ceremony is also mentioned
he Georgian Chronicle.

[2] *Libro d'Andrea Cambini Florentino della Origine de Turchi et imperio
i Ottomanni.* Edition of 1529, p. 25.

During the night the defenders, and especially those between the stockade and the Inner Wall, heard the noise of great preparations among the enemy.

The emperor rode from Hagia Sophia to the palace of Blachern, which he had occupied during all the time of the siege. Phrantzes, who was in company with him, asks who could remain unmoved while the emperor during his last and short stay in the palace demanded pardon of all there present. 'If a man had been made of wood or stone he must have wept over the scene.'

Depression is naturally the constant note of all the narratives of those present in the city during May 28. The Venetian closes the day's entry by recording in a quaint passage that the fasting and rejoicing among the Turkish army went on until midnight, and that then the fires were extinguished but that these pagans all day and night continued to beseech Mahomet that he would grant them victory and help them to capture this city of Constantinople; 'while we Christians all day and night prayed God and St. Mary and all the saints in heaven and with many tears devoutly besought them that they would not grant such victory that the besieged should not become victims of this accursed pagan,' and thus 'each side having prayed to its God, we to ours and they to theirs, the Lord Almighty with his mother in heaven decided that they must be avenged in this battle of the morrow for all the sins committed.'

Emperor's last inspection of defenders.

Shortly after midnight of the 28th–29th the emperor accompanied by Phrantzes, left the palace of Blachern on horseback to inspect the various stations and to see that all were on the watch. The walls and towers were occupied the gates from the city into the Peribolos were safely closed so that none might enter or leave.[1]

When they came to Caligaria,[2] probably on their return

---

[1] Phrantzes, p. 280. The closing of the gates behind the soldiers is mentioned also by other writers.

[2] The Caligaria Gate was the present Egri Capou. For a description Caligaria and the neighbouring palace of Blachern see Professor van Millingen Byzantine Constantinople, p. 128. Caligaria was the name of a district which was in the corner made by the wall running at right angles to the foss, which

they dismounted. They went up together into a tower from which, assuming it to be the one at the corner where the wall begins to descend towards the Golden Horn, which would be that most suitable for their purpose, they would have an uninterrupted view of the road and a considerable stretch of ground on both sides of it leading to the Adrianople or Chariseus Gate, while, looking in the other direction, they could see the outside of a large portion of the walls towards the Golden Horn and of the hill in front where the Crusaders had encamped in 1203 and near or upon which Caraja was at the head of the Bashi-bazouks. They heard the murmur of many voices and the noise of many preparations and were told by the guards that these sounds had continued during all the night and were caused by the transport of guns and other machines nearer to the ditch.[1] It was probably between one and two of the morning of the 29th when Phrantzes and his imperial master separated; and in all likelihood they never met again.

it terminates on the north just beyond Tekfour Serai, and that which leads down the steep slope to the Golden Horn.

[1] Phrantzes, p. 280.

CHAPTER XVI

GENERAL ASSAULT : COMMENCED BY BASHI-BAZOUKS ; THEY
ARE DEFEATED ; ANATOLIANS ATTACK—ARE ALSO DRIVEN
BACK ; ATTACKS IN OTHER PLACES FAIL ; JANISSARIES
ATTACK ; KERKOPORTA INCIDENT ; JUSTINIANI WOUNDED
AND RETIRES ; EMPEROR'S ALARM ; STOCKADE CAPTURED ;
DEATH OF CONSTANTINE : HIS CHARACTER ; CAPTURE OF
CONSTANTINOPLE.

General
assault
com-
mences
early
morning,
May 29,
1453.

THE general assault commenced between one and two hours
after midnight on the morning of Tuesday May 29.[1]

When the signal was given, the city was attacked simultaneously on all three sides. The orders given by Mahomet
on the previous day had been strictly obeyed. The ships

[1] The question when the general attack began is very much one of appreciation. According to Ducas, Mahomet commenced on the Sunday evening to make
a general attack and during the night the besieged were not permitted to sleep
but were harassed all night and, though in a less active manner, until between
four and five of the afternoon of Monday. Phrantzes declares the capture to
have been made on the third day of the attack and would thus make it begin
on Sunday, but his narrative shows that the general attack began after midnight of the 28-9th. Barbaro's statement substantially agrees with that of
Phrantzes and is that during the whole of the 27th the cannons were discharging their stone balls : *tuto el zorno non feze mai altro che bombardar in le
puovere mure ;* but on p. 51 he says that Mahomet came before the walls to
begin the general attack at three hours before day on the 29th. Critobulus
makes the general attack begin on the afternoon of the 28th, when the sultan
raised his great standard (Crit. lii and lv.). Karl Müller, in his excellent notes to
Critobulus, justly remarks that as Barbaro and Phrantzes were in the city their
evidence ought to be preferred to that of Critobulus. They both represent the
final assault as beginning very early in the morning of the 29th. The statements are reconcilable by supposing that the dispositions for a general attack
began on the Sunday, but that the actual general assault did not take place
until the Tuesday morning. Sad-ud-din says, on the authority of two Turkish
contemporaries, that ' the great victory was on Tuesday, the fifty-first day from
the commencement of the war ' (p. 34).

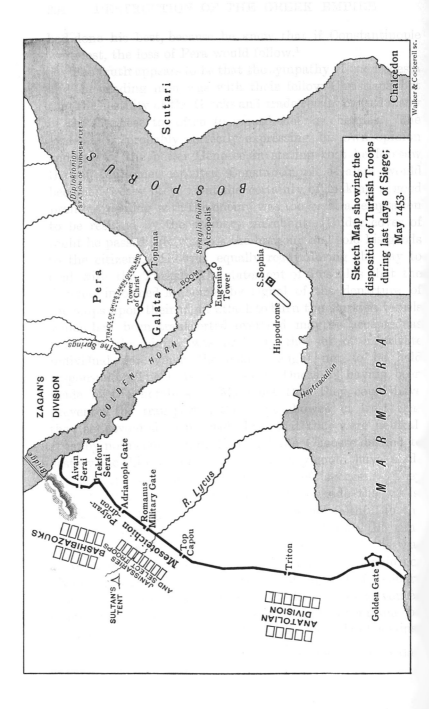

Sketch Map showing the disposition of Turkish Troops during last days of Siege; May 1453.

during the night had taken up the positions assigned to them on the sides of the Marmora and on the Golden Horn. The armies on the landward side began simultaneously to attempt the walls at several points.[1]

The principal assault was in the Lycus valley and against the stockade : where, says Tetaldi, twelve hundred feet of barbican had been destroyed by the cannon ; where, adds Chalcondylas,[2] four of the strongest towers had been destroyed ; where, says Ducas, the Outer Wall had been so completely broken down that the besiegers and besieged could see each other, and where, explains Critobulus, the Outer Wall had been so entirely overthrown by the cannon that it was no longer a wall but only a stockade built up with beams, fascines, branches and the like, and barrels of earth.[3]

The defenders were between the stockade and the Inner Wall. Here they had to defeat the enemy, in front of them or die. Mahomet's intention was to concentrate his attack on the stockade and on the walls between the Adrianople Gate and Tekfour Serai and to deal blow after blow against them with the whole of his available force while making sufficient show of attack elsewhere to draw away the defenders.

The assault was commenced by the Bashi-bazouks, the most worthless portion of Mahomet's army, who came up for this purpose from the northern end of the landward walls. Many among them were Moslems, but there were so many Christians and foreigners that Barbaro calls them all Christians.[4] Leonard declares that among them were Germans, Hungarians, and other foreigners of various kinds.[5] Mahomet's object in sending forward these men to make the first attack was mainly that they might exhaust the strength and the ammunition of the besieged. This, indeed, was his method of utilising his superiority in numbers.[6]

Assault begun by Bashi-bazouks.

---

[1] Cambini, 24. [2] P. 160. [3] Ch. lv. [4] P. 52.

[5] Leonard, p. 86 : ' Testis sum quod Graeci, quod Latini, quod Germani, Panones, Boetes, ex omnium christianorum regionibus Teucris commixti opera eorum fidemque didicerunt.'

[6] Riccherio, 958 : ' Percioche Maometh pensava, ricreando gli stracchi col rimetter nuove genti nella zuffa, verrebbe a non dar punto di spatio per riposarsi a Greci, di maniera che, non potendo sostener tanta fatica per lo continuo combattimento, si sarebbono agevolmente potuti vincere.'

Moreover, says Barbaro, he preferred that these Christians should be killed rather than his Mussulmans. The Bashi-bazouks advanced bearing all the scaling-ladders within shooting distance of the walls and probably extended themselves from Tekfour Serai to the stockade and beyond to Top Capou. They began the fight with a general discharge of arrows, of stones from slings, and iron and leaden balls. Then, with a wild disorderly dash, they rushed across the ditch and endeavoured to capture the Outer Wall and especially the stockade. They were armed in ways as numerous and varied as the races and creeds to which they belonged: some with bows, others with slings, with arquebuses or with muskets,[1] but most of them simply with scimitars and shields. Hundreds of ladders were placed against the walls and the bravest hastened to climb them. Others, mounted on the shoulders of their comrades, endeavoured to reach the summit or to strike at the defenders. In the darkness of this night attack, made by fifty thousand men, there was soon wild confusion everywhere, but especially in the valley to which for the present the action in my story is confined. At every point the invaders met with a brave resistance. While among the attacking party there were many who had no heart for the fight,[2] there were others who were not deficient in courage, but they had to meet the best soldiers in the emperor's army, a band of two thousand Greeks and Italians all under the leadership of Justiniani, 'the incomparable captain, the mighty man and genuine soldier.'

The defenders threw the ladders down, discharged their arrows, fired their muskets and culverins,[3] and hurled down a prodigious quantity of stones. The assailants were so numerous and so crowded together that the missiles of the besieged told heavily against them. The bravest who succeeded in climbing within striking distance were struck

---

[1] Crit. liv.

[2] Michael Constantinovich, a Servian who was with a contingent of his countrymen in the Turkish army, says, 'As far as our help went, the Turks would never have taken the city' (quoted by Mijatovich, p. 234).

[3] τούφακας, Crit. li.

down. The resistance was so stubborn that many began to
give way. But they had not yet sufficiently served their
purpose. Until their strength was exhausted, Mahomet
would not consent that they should cease to exhaust that of
the defenders. Those who attempted to withdraw found
themselves between the devil and the deep sea. A body of
Turkish chaouses had been told off with iron maces and
loaded whips to drive back any endeavouring to retreat, and
behind them again were stationed Janissaries ready with
their scimitars to cut down any who should succeed in
escaping through the line of chaouses. In this manner
the fight was prolonged for between one and two hours.

But in spite of all that could be done, in spite of
numbers and of courage, Mahomet's first division was
beaten back with many killed and wounded. Having
served its purpose in exhausting the strength of the small
body of the defenders, it was allowed to withdraw. Some
of the besieged appear to have considered the attack rather
as an attempt to surprise the city by a night alarm than as
part of the expected general assault. They were indeed weary
with hard fighting and hard work. For forty days they had
hardly known a single hour of rest,[1] and they hoped for it, at
least until the morning. They were soon undeceived.

Amid the darkness of the early summer morning a
division of Anatolian Turks could be distinguished pouring
over the ridge on which stands Top Capou. It was the
advance of disciplined men, distinguishable by their breast-
plates, and their arrival made the situation much more
serious. Here, indeed, was the general assault which all
expected at daylight. The bells throughout the city again
sounded everywhere an alarm; all the inhabitants were at
their posts. As the Anatolians came across the ditch up to
the stockade the struggle began once more in deadly earnest.
Trumpets, fifes, and drums sounded their loudest to encourage the assailants. Besiegers and besieged shouted and
roared at each other. Prayers for help, imprecations, clang
of bells within the city, roar of guns and small cannon

They are beaten back.

Anatolian division next attack.

[1] Chalc. p. 160.

within and without made up the pandemonium of a storming party. Ladders were once more placed against the walls and were hurled back; men scrambled on each other's shoulders trying hard to reach the summit of the stockade. ' Our men ' are continually throwing down stones and are resisting hand to hand all who attempt to scale or destroy it. ' More Turks were killed,' says Barbaro, 'than you would have thought possible.'

Now the great cannon, which during the night had been advanced as near the wall as possible, is brought into play. An hour before daylight a well-directed shot from the monster was aimed at the stockade, struck it and brought a portion of it down. Under cover of the dust from the falling stones and barrels of earth, but especially of the dense black smoke of the powder, a band of Turks rushed forward and, before they could be prevented, three hundred had entered the enclosure. The Greeks and Italians resisted manfully, fought fiercely to expel them, killed many and drove the remainder out.[1] The besieged raised shouts of triumph. The emperor was with his soldiers, always showing himself in the thick of the fighting, urging men by voice and cheering them by his example. This second attack was more systematic, fiercer, more desperate than the first. The Turks had no need of men behind them to prevent their retreat or to urge them forward. Shouting their wild battle-cry of Allah ! Allah ! they rushed on in the darkness as men who, if they do not court death, at least do not fear it; as men who believe they are fighting for God, and that in case of death they will be at once transported to a combined heavenly and earthly paradise.

They, too, are driven back. In spite of the discipline and daring of the Anatolian troops, of the stimulus derived from their fanatical creed and from the special promise of reward here and hereafter to those who should succeed in entering the Queen City or should perish in the attempt, the assault by them failed as completely as had that of the Bashi-bazouks. The

[1] Barbaro (54) says, Greeks and Venetians, omitting all mention of the Genoese.

stubborn bravery of a comparatively small number of Greeks and Italians behind the hastily formed stockade and the battered, thousand-year-old walls were so far more than a match for the invaders.

The success of the attackers was up to the present not more complete in other parts of the city. Zagan Pasha had made desperate attempts to scale the walls near the west end of the Horn under cover of showers of arrows and other missiles from the ships and from large pontoons drawn up as near as possible to the walls, but had been defeated by Trevisano. Caraja Pasha, north of the Adrianople Gate, had crossed the foss and made a vigorous attempt against the walls broken down by the cannon between that Gate and the Palace of Porphyrogenitus, now known as Tekfour Serai.[1] But that district, 'the high part of the Myriandrion,' [2] was held by the three brothers Bocchiardi, who had borne the cost of their men at their own charge, and who covered themselves, says Leonard, with eternal glory, fighting like Horatius Cocles and his companions who kept the bridge of old. Their neighbours at Tekfour Serai and around the southern portion of Caligaria under the Venetian bailey Minotto,[3] had been equally successful. All the invaders' attempts had been defeated. Critobulus is justified in commenting with pride on the defeat of this second attack. 'The Romans, indeed, proved themselves very valiant; for nothing could shake them, neither hunger nor want of rest, nor weariness from continuous fighting, nor wounds, nor the thought of the slaughter of their families which menaced them. Nothing could alter their determination to be faithful to their trust.'

There remained but one more chance—on May 29 at least—of capturing the city by general assault. Two divisions had failed. But Mahomet noted that his plan of attack by successive divisions had greatly weakened the defenders at the stockade. He therefore decided to put forth all his strength and to send forward his reserves.

Assaults in other places also fail

---

[1] Crit. lvi.   [2] Leonard : ' in loco arduo Myriandri.'
[3] Pusculus, iv. 173, and Zorzo Dolfin, 55.

These consisted of the *élite* of his army, the veteran warriors of his bodyguard, infantry bearing shields and pikes, a body of archers, another of lancers, and, more skilled and more trustworthy than all, his body of twelve thousand Janissaries.[1] These reserves were now to attempt the assault at the stockade under the immediate leadership of their great commander, while the remainder of the army made a simultaneous attack against other portions of the landward walls.

Mahomet began the new assault with the utmost care. Dawn was now supplying sufficient light [2] to enable him to superintend a more elaborate plan. The assault was not to be a mere wild rush and scramble. Having urged his guards to show their valour, Mahomet put himself at their head and led them as far as the foss.[3]

At the moment, says Barbaro, when the defenders were rejoicing at having driven out the three hundred from the barbicans, the pagans again fired their big gun and under cover of the smoke and dust the besiegers advanced. A huge but orderly crowd of archers, slingers, and musketeers discharged their arrows and other missiles. Successive volleys were steadily fired upon the Greeks and Italians defending the whole length of the stockade, so that they could hardly show a head over the battlements without being struck. The missiles fell in numbers, says Critobulus, like rain. They darkened the sky, says Leonard. When the defenders had been thrown into some confusion by this long hail of missiles, Mahomet gave the signal for advance to his 'fresh, vigorous, and invincible' Janissaries. They rushed across the foss and attempted as their predecessors had done, to carry the stockade by storm.

Ten thousand of these 'grand masters and valiant men,' says Barbaro, with admiration for a brave enemy, 'ran to the walls, not like Turks, but like lions.' Fighting in

Assault by Janissaries.

---

[1] Crit. lvii.

[2] Leonard, p. 98: 'Tenebrosa nox in lucem trahitur, nostris vincentibus. Et dum astra cedunt, dum Phoebi praecedit Lucifer ortum, Illalla, Illalla in martem conclamans, conglobatus in gyrum consurgit exercitus.'

[3] Crit. lvii.

presence of their sovereign, says Critobulus, they never lost
their dash, but fought like men possessed and as if life were
of no value. They tried to tear down the stockade; to
break or pull down the great barrels of earth which crowned it;
to drag out the beams and thus break down or make a passage
through into the Enclosure; to climb over it on the scaling-
ladders which once placed against the wall were immediately
crowded with assailants. Their shouts and yells, their calls
upon Allah, the noise of their drums, fifes, and trumpets,
the roar of the culverins and cannon once more struck
terror into the affrighted citizens and were heard, says
Barbaro, across the Bosporus. For a while all was mad
confusion.

We do not need the confirmation of Barbaro and Critobulus of the statement that the Greeks and Italians were
worn out with their long defence before the attack by the
Janissaries commenced. They had been hewing and hacking,
throwing down stones and hurling back ladders for nearly,
or perhaps quite, three hours and were unequal to contend
with many times their numbers of men ardent and fresh
for battle. But they knew, as indeed did every one within
the city, that the crisis of the attack was at hand, and they
manfully fought on. The church bells added to the din :
the alarm bells on the walls were calling for every available
help. Women and children, monks and nuns, were either
assisting to bring stones to their friends on the walls or were
on their knees praying that their great city should not fall
into the hands of the pagans. Justiniani and his little band
met the attack with lances, axes, pikes, and swords, and cut
down the foremost of their assailants. For a short time the
fight became a hard hand-to-hand encounter, neither party
gaining any advantage over the other.

Contemporaneously with this latter portion of the The
struggle in the Lycus valley, an incident, possibly of Kerko-
supreme importance, was taking place about half a mile to porta
the northward. incident.

Of the three ways into the city which Mahomet declared

he had opened for his troops, one was to the north of the
Adrianople Gate. The walls between this gate and the
Palace of Porphyrogenitus were, in construction, like those
in the Lycus valley, but the inner Theodosian wall, instead
of extending as far as that palace (now known as Tekfour
Serai), stopped short about a hundred yards from it. There
a short wall at right angles connected it with the second
or Outer Wall. In this transverse wall was a postern giving
access from the city to the Inner Enclosure or Peribolos. The
short Outer Wall north of the transverse wall, having to do
duty for the two city walls, had been made exceptionally
strong. A small postern gate, partly below the level of the
ground and underneath the extremity of the palace,[1] led
directly from the city to the Outer Enclosure. This gate
was known as the Kerkoporta or Circus Gate.[2] It had been
built up and almost forgotten for many years previous to
the siege, but when easy access to the Outer Enclosure was
deemed necessary, certain old men recalled its existence and
it was reopened. As its position caused it to be concealed from persons who were not close to the tower, it
may easily have been left undefended for a while during
the night under the impression that it would not be
noticed.[3]

[1] Παραπόρτιον ἐν πρὸ πολλῶν χρόνων ἀσφαλῶς πεφραγμένον, ὑπόγαιον, πρὸς τὸ
κάτωθεν μέρος τοῦ παλατίου.

[2] Its complete name was Porta Xylokerkou, because it led to a wooden circus
outside the city. See the subject fully discussed by Professor van Millingen,
Byzantine Constantinople, pp. 89-94.

[3] I am not satisfied that the Kerkoporta was the one indicated by Professor
van Millingen. On the map published by the Greek Syllogos, as well as in
Canon Curtis's Broken Bits of Byzantium, a small postern is shown in the
wall immediately south of the tower adjoining Tekfour Serai, and my own
recollection is that I saw this walled-up postern with Dr. Paspates in 1875. The
wall itself was pulled down on the outbreak of the last Turko-Russian war
and replaced by a slighter one. Whichever view be correct, the statement in
the text is not affected.

Professor van Millingen contends that the Kerkoporta strictly so called was
the small gate in the corner between Tekfour Serai and the adjoining tower on
the south. But he maintains also that the postern to which Ducas refers was
in the transverse wall, giving access from the city to the Inner Enclosure. He
remarks that if the Turks entered by the Kerkoporta they could have mounted
the great Inner Wall from the city. As to the latter objection, it must be

The Outer Wall between the Kerkoporta and the Adrianople Gate had been largely damaged and a breach made which had been stormed unsuccessfully during the night. The Turks had here also, as well as near the Romanus Gate, been able to pass the ditch and take possession of the Outer Enclosure.

As daylight approached, some of the enemy noticed that the Kerkoporta had been left open. A number of Janissaries (stated by Ducas to be fifty) hastened through and took possession of it. They were soon followed by others, who gained access to the Inner Enclosure first through the Kerkoporta and then through the neighbouring postern already mentioned in the transverse wall, the distance between the two posterns being about thirty yards. They surprised and attacked those who were occupied in resisting the attempts of Caraja's main division to storm the breach or scale the Outer Wall. Every foot they captured allowed their numbers to be increased by comrades who could now climb the Outer Wall without opposition or who crowded in through the Kerkoporta and the postern in the transverse wall. The besieged, overwhelmed by numbers, and having their retreat into the city through the postern cut off, fled towards the Adrianople Gate, the postern of which was soon blocked by the crowd, the stronger trampling upon the weaker, so that presently all egress from the Enclosure was impossible. A slaughter took place and a few Turks entered the city, while others mounted the walls, pulled down the emperor's flags and those of St. Mark and replaced them by the Turkish standards.

The entry of the Turks by the Kerkoporta is only related by Ducas, but it is incidentally confirmed by the fact mentioned by Phrantzes and other writers, that while the struggle in the Lycus valley was going on, the Turkish standards were raised on the towers to the north of the Adrianople Gate

remembered that the fighters were within the Enclosure defending the Outer Wall, and if the Turks entered through the postern in the transverse wall they would take the fighters in the rear. It would have been a better position for attack than on the Inner Wall.

before an entry had been effected elsewhere.[1] Critobulus's statement that Caraja's men crossed the foss, made a vigorous assault, and sought to pass within the broken-down (Outer) wall, but were repulsed, probably refers to the same incident.[2] Ducas is careful to state that the emperor and the Romans did not know what had happened, because they were at some distance and were too much occupied in defending themselves in a different place, which he explains to be where the wall had been broken down : that is, at the stockade in the Lycus valley. While they were thus fighting, he says, to resist the entry through the ruined wall, God willed that the enemy should enter the city by this other way. Leonard mentions that the arrangements for sending messengers from one part of the wall to another were defective. The emperor, however, was probably informed of the entry by the Kerkoporta and of the capture of at least part of the enclosure between that postern and the Adrianople Gate, and hastened thither before his army under Justiniani learned that the Turkish standards had been hoisted on the towers near the Adrianople Gate.[3] The few Turks who had entered the city, bent upon plunder, made for the rich monasteries of Choras and St. John in Petra and the Blachern palace; but it would appear that the brothers Bocchiardi were able to regain possession of the Enclosure and to prevent any considerable number of the enemy from following those who had entered the Kerkoporta. Possibly even they were strong enough to close it. The fact that the entry at the Kerkoporta is not mentioned by Critobulus may be taken to confirm the view that, if he knew of it at all, he only regarded it as a somewhat unimportant incident.

---

[1] Phrantzes, p. 285.   [2] Crit. lvi.

[3] Sad-ud-din gives an interesting variant of the story of Ducas. He states that while 'the blind-hearted emperor' was busy resisting the besiegers of the city at his palace to the north of the Adrianople Gate,' 'suddenly he became aware that the upraisers of the most glorious standard of "The Word of God" had found a path to within the walls' (Sad-ud-din, p. 30). The statement that the emperor was present at Tekfour Serai agrees with that of Ducas; but the latter's account of the events immediately following the entry by the Kerkoporta varies so much from that given by others that I suspect some sentences have dropped out of his narrative.

Meantime in the Enclosure in the Lycus valley the
truggle was being bravely fought out with pikes, axes,
avelins, long lances and swords, for now, as Critobulus is
:areful to inform us, 'the fight was hand-to-hand.' [1] The
obstinate resistance of the little band of Greeks and Italians
appears to have met with some success. The attack by the
Janissaries and the rest of the sultan's own division had so
far failed and was weakening.

It was at this moment that one of those fateful accidents
occurred which have at times decided the destiny of nations.
John Justiniani, who under the emperor was in supreme
command, was severely wounded. He bled profusely,
and determined to leave his command in order to obtain
medical aid. The wound was so severe that it proved mortal
within a few days. But those present did not recognise its
gravity. Some of his contemporaries deny that it was
sufficiently grave to justify his leaving the field, but Critobulus, writing some years afterwards, states that he had to
be carried away. [2] Leonard and Phrantzes say that when
the emperor was informed of his determination to enter
the city, Constantine besought and implored him not to
do so but to return to his post, endeavouring to persuade
him that the wound was slight and pointing out that his
departure would demoralise not only his own men but the
Greeks, and strongly urged that the fate of the city depended
on his remaining. Justiniani, however, pleaded the pain of
his wound, demanded that the key of the gate leading into
the city should be given to his men, [3] and insisted upon
leaving the Peribolos or Enclosure, promising to return when
his wound had been attended to. The keys of a small gate
which Justiniani had caused to be opened in the Inner Wall
to give easier access to the Enclosure behind the stockade
were brought and he entered the city. [4]

John Justiniani wounded.

---

[1] Crit. lviii.   [2] *Ibid.*   [3] Leonard, p. 37.

[4] It is difficult to identify the gate described as having been opened on to
the stockade. Critobulus gives no further indication of its position than that
here mentioned (ch. lx). Paspates thinks it was a temporary postern, walled up
after the siege when the Inner Wall was repaired to prevent smuggling, but
would place it not far from Top Capou, a position which cannot be accepted if

The story told by Chalcondylas is that in reply to the emperor's question whither he was going, Justiniani said that he was going where God Himself had opened a way for the Turks. It may well be doubted. He was accompanied, say Critobulus and others, by his own men, a statement, however, which can hardly apply to the whole four hundred. The unlocking of the gate proved at once to be a dangerous temptation to soldiers who had been fighting continuously for hours and who had seen the departure of their leader. Justiniani made his way to his ship, which was stationed at the boom, and escaped to Chios, where he died within a few days—or possibly on the way thither.[1]

His departure was calamitous and at once created a panic. He was a commander who had the full confidence of those under him, and his absence struck dismay into their hearts. Barbaro says that it was through his flight that the shout was then raised, 'The Turks have got in;' that everybody then cried in alarm to God for mercy, and that men wept like women. It was through him, and ' he lied in his throat, because they had not yet got in.' [2]   Leonard, himself a

Justiniani's departure creates a panic.

---

the stockade were, as I have placed it, near the Military Gate of St. Romanus. The Podestà of Pera, however, says that Justiniani went ' per ipsam portam per quam Teucri intraverunt ' (p. 648), which would indicate St. Romanus. Andrea Cambini, the Florentine already quoted, in his *Libro della Origine de Turchi*, published by the sons of the writer, says that Justiniani, who had behaved so well that the salvation of the city was largely attributed to him, was seriously wounded, and, seeing that the blood flowed 'in great quantity' and being unwilling that they should fetch a doctor, withdrew secretly from the fight . . . all the gates which led from the Antimuro [i.e. the Outer Wall] being closed, because thus the fighters had to conquer or die (p. 25).

[1] His monument still exists in the church of S. Domenico at Chios with an epitaph which contains the phrase ' lethale vulnere ictus interiit.' Phrantzes says that Justiniani was wounded in the right foot by an arrow ; Leonard, by an arrow in the armpit ; Chalcondylas, in the hand, by a ball ; Critobulus, by a ball in the chest or throat which pierced through his breastplate. The latter statement would be consistent with Tetaldi's which speaks of the wound inflicted by a culverin. Riccherio says Justiniani was wounded by one of his own men. Barbaro (who, it must always be remembered where he is speaking of the Genoese, was a Venetian and incapable of doing justice to a citizen of the rival republic) does not mention any wound, but states roundly that Justiniani decided to abandon his post and hasten to his ship, which was stationed at the boom.

[2] Barbaro, p. 55.

Genoese, who speaks of Justiniani with warm admiration, is hardly less severe upon him in regard to his manner of leaving the fight. He declares that, as he had at first shown courage, now he displayed cowardice. He ought to have borne the pain and remained, or at least to have appointed some one in his place. The spirit of his followers was broken by his desertion. The Podestà of Pera, also a Genoese, seems himself to have condemned his departure. He says the enemy was opposed right manfully, but Justiniani deserted his gate, and withdrew to the sea, and by that gate the Turks entered without resistance. Remembering that this is the testimony of the chief Genoese official against the great Genoese captain, it may be regarded as reflecting the general opinion of the time.[1] We, however, may well remember that Justiniani had remained in the city with his men, had worked day and night at the repairs of the walls, had, by the testimony of all, been the great organiser of the defence, and, knowing that he died of his wounds, may be charitable enough to believe that he did not desert his post except under the pressure of pain too great to be endured.

It is beyond doubt that his departure demoralised both the foreigners who remained and the brave little band of Greeks who had borne with them the brunt of the fighting. Leonard asserts that when his countrymen saw themselves without a leader, they began to abandon their posts.

Meanwhile the emperor, behind the stockade, was endeavouring to rally his men, and fighting with a courage

Emperor tries to rally defenders of stockade.

---

[1] Philip the Armenian, who was probably present in the city, states that Justiniani and his men deserted their stations and that thus the city was lost (pp. 675–6). Riccherio, while speaking of the wound as severe, declares that Justiniani promised to return, and attributes the departure of many of his followers to the fact that the postern gate, which he had required to be opened for his departure, suggested the idea of flight to his men. In other words it created a panic (p. 960). The contemporaries who excuse Justiniani are Cardinal Isidore (*Lamentatio*, p. 677: 'Ne caeteros deterreret, remedium quaerens clam sese pugnae subduxit') and Leonard, who both state that he went away secretly so as not to discourage his followers. Tetaldi further declares that he left his command to two Genoese. Leonard and the Podestà wrote while the impression of the fall and the sack of the city were too recent to enable them to give a cool judgment on Justiniani's conduct: the latter dating his letter June 23, and the archbishop August 16.

worthy of his great name. He himself took the post of Justiniani and led the defending party. He had no other men to replace those who had left, but he rallied the Greeks and the remainder of the Genoese and Venetians, and with his own small bodyguard rushed to the stockade.

Final charge of Janissaries.

Mahomet witnessed, from the opposite side of the foss, the demoralisation caused by the departure of Justiniani. He noted that the stockade and broken walls had fewer defenders, that many of them were secretly slipping away, and that those who remained were fighting less vigorously. He saw that the opportune moment for him had come and, calling out to his men, 'We have the city : it is ours already ; the wall is undefended,' urged his Janissaries to fear nothing, but follow him, and the city would be captured.[1] At his bidding and under his lead, the Janissaries hastened once more to rush the stockade and to climb upon the *débris* of the wall destroyed by the gun.[2]

The sultan had promised great rewards to the first who should gain a position on the wall. A stalwart Janissary named Hassan gained this honour. A man of gigantic stature, he was able, while holding his shield in his left hand, to fight his way to the top of the broken wall, and was followed by some thirty others. The Greeks resisted their entry and killed eighteen. But Hassan maintained his position long enough to enable some of his followers to climb up and get over the wall. A fierce skirmish took place, and many were killed on both sides. Hassan himself was wounded by a stone, slipped and fell, fought bravely on his knees, but was overpowered and killed.[3] But the discrepancy in numbers was too great. Once a few were able to maintain their position on the wall, the Turks mounted and got over to the inner side of the stockade in crowds. The remnant of the defending army stood their ground for a while, but the invaders drove a number of them back and into the deep ditch which had been dug between the great wall and the stockade and out of which it was difficult to

---

[1] Crit. lx.; also Leonard, 99. [2] Cambini, p. 25.
[3] Phrantzes, 285.

escape.[1] Many were thus killed within the Peribolos, of which for the first time the Turks were now the masters. Some of the invaders climbed the great wall behind the defenders to hurl down stones on them, and a fierce fight went on along the length of the stockade in the Lycus valley, and possibly indeed along the whole length of the walls in the Mesoteichion. Suddenly, in this the supreme moment of the struggle, shouts were heard both within and without the walls and from the direction of the harbour, shouts which were taken up by the Greeks, Ἑάλω ἡ πόλις : ' the city is taken ; the Turkish flags are flying on the towers.'

We have already seen what had happened to cause this cry to be raised. The detachment of Turks who had gained entrance through the Kerkoporta had captured some of the lofty towers between it and the Adrianople Gate, and had there raised the Turkish standards.

' " The city is captured ! " the cry sent dismay into the hearts of our men, but encouraged the enemy.' [2] It was not true, says Barbaro. The city was not then taken. But meantime the Turks were now up and over the walls in crowds. Within a quarter of an hour, says Barbaro, of their first obtaining possession of the stockade there must have been thirty thousand of them within the Peribolos.

The success of the Janissaries in overcoming the first serious line of defence [3] was followed up instantly by the other Turkish troops. The news of the entry across the stockade seems to have spread like wildfire, and though it is difficult to believe the statement of Barbaro that the Enclosure was filled from one end of the walls to the other with seventy thousand of the hostile army, it is possible that the vigour which follows success enabled the Janissaries and other portions of the army to obtain entry at once into the Enclosure at various other places. Some of the defenders fled in panic and made for the small gate through which Justiniani had retired, the only one behind them which was open. They rushed on in such haste as to trample each other down.

Stockade captured.

[1] Crit. lv.   [2] Phrantzes, p. 285.   [3] ' La prima sbara di barbacan,' p. 54.

At this moment the emperor, who had been called off to the northern end of the valley to learn the meaning of the display of the Turkish flags and to resist the inrush of the invaders who had entered by the Kerkoporta, returned. Spurring his horse, he galloped down the Enclosure to the stockade where the Turks were crowding in,[1] and tried to rally the remainder of the defenders. Calling upon his men to follow him, he threw off his imperial insignia, drew his sword, sprang into the thick of the fight, and attempted to drive the invaders back.[2] With Don Francisco of Toledo on his right, Theophilus Palaeologus and John Dalmata on his left, his own sword broken, he endeavoured to check the advancing crowd. Theophilus shouted that he would rather die than live. The four checked for a moment the inrush of the Turks, slew some of them, and cut their way to the wall where the Turks were pouring in. But they were hopelessly outnumbered. The emperor was lost sight of amid the crowd. He and his companions fell fighting, and the enemy continued to pour through the breaches.[3]

Once the enemy had obtained entrance into the Enclosure the defenders were in a trap. The only exit into the city open to them was by the small gate through which Justiniani had passed. The Military Gate of St. Romanus, the Gate of the Assault, remained locked. A heap of slain, Genoese and Greeks,[4] near it made escape impossible. The defeat of the survivors of the gallant band which Justiniani had led was forthwith completed by a body of the Janissaries who entered the Enclosure across the broken stockade, formed themselves in regular order, and swept everything before them.[5] Their overwhelming numbers soon enabled them to kill all opponents who had not escaped into the city. The great wall being partly broken down and without

Death of Constantine.

City captured May 29.

---

[1] Phrantzes, p. 285.   [2] Montaldo, xxiii. : ʻinsigniis positis.ʼ

[3] Montaldo (ch. xxiii.) incidentally confirms the version of Ducas. He states that the emperor determined on death only after he had learned that the enemy had entered the city and had occupied the palace and other places.

[4] Leonard, p. 99. In Dethier's edition a note states that one of the MSS. reads eighty Latins ʻ sine Graecis,ʼ p. 608.

[5] Leonard, 99, says that they formed a *cuneus* or *phalanx*.

defenders, and the Gate of St. Romanus being forced or
opened, access to the city was easy. A band made their way
to the Adrianople Gate, which they opened from the inside,
and the city was from that moment in the power of the
enemy.[1]
As the sun rose Mahomet saw that his great effort had
succeeded. Where Arabs, with even greater numbers than
he commanded, in the first flush of the victorious career of
Islam, with the presence of the great Eyoub, the companion
of the Prophet, to encourage them and to speak of the
wondrous rewards which Paradise had in store for the
believers who should enter New Rome or die in the attempt ;
where Murad thirty years before ; and where twenty
other besieging armies had been unable to capture the
world's capital, he had succeeded. Seated on horseback
beneath his great standard and insignia, he watched with
the legitimate pride of a conqueror the entry of his hordes
into the city.[2] The morning sun shed its rays upon him
and his standard as his soldiers thronged through the Gate
of the Assault or hastened towards that of Adrianople. The
entry was not long after sunrise and probably between five
and six o'clock.[3]

If credit is to be given to the story of the entry of the
Turks at the Kerkoporta as related by Ducas, then it may
be said that the capture of the city was due to two accidents :
the leaving open of that gate and the wound of Justiniani.
It is beyond doubt that the immediate cause of the capture
was the withdrawal of John Justiniani, followed by the flight
of a considerable number of his men.

In the words of Cambini, a contemporary of the siege,
but writing at a sufficiently remote period to look calmly

Capture of city due to two accidents.

---

[1] Crit. lxi.; Chalc. p. 164. Ahmed Muktar Pasha's *Conquest of Constantinople.*
[2] Crit. lxi.; Tetaldi, p. 23, speaks of ' deux banniers.'
[3] Crit. lxi.; Tetaldi, p. 29, ' à l'aube du jour ; ' Barbaro (p. 55) at sunrise.
Phrantzes says that possession of the city was obtained at half past two, which
by the then and present prevalent mode in the East of reckoning time would
correspond to about ten. Possession of the city would probably be about three
or four hours after the entry through the landward walls. Leonard says :
' Necdum Phoebus orbis perlustrat hemisphaerium et tota urbs a paganis in
praedam occupatur.'

upon the events he narrates, Justiniani had so conducted himself that, until he was wounded, every one looked to him for the salvation of the city, and upon his quitting the battle-field the courage of those whom he led failed them.

Whatever hypothesis as to the character of his wound be accepted, whether when urged by the emperor he could have remained or not, his departure was an irretrievable misfortune. Few as were the defenders when compared with the great host attacking, they had never altogether lost hope. The Podestà of Galata, writing within a month of the capture of the city, declares that he and the Genoese longed for the general attack, because victory for the Christians appeared certain.[1] On the other hand, there is reason to believe that the besiegers were far from confident of being able to capture it. There was, as we have seen, a strong peace party in Mahomet's camp headed by Halil Pasha. The reports were well founded of a fleet in the Archipelago on its way to the city. Thirty ships sent by the pope had arrived at Chios and were awaiting favourable winds at the time they heard of the success of Mahomet.[2]

There were rumours of a Hungarian army coming to attack them in the rear. The emperor had promised to give Selymbria to Hunyadi in return for his aid. Some inkling of the arrangement may have reached the sultan. The king of Catalonia had made an agreement with Constantine in return for the island of Lemnos.[3] It is in the highest degree

---

[1] P. 647; 'on the 29th of last month,' 'Qua die expectabamus cum desiderio quia videbatur nobis habere certam victoriam.'

[2] Crit. ch. lxx. Pusculus gives a somewhat different account (iv. 1025):

Auxilium Deus ipse negavit;
In Tenedi portu nam tempestatibus actae
Stabant bis denae naves, quas Gnosia tellus,
Quae Venetum imperium Rhadamanti legibus audit
Omissis, plenas frumento et frugibus, inde
Bis quinas Veneti mittebant Marte triremes
Instructas, urbi auxilio Danaisque; sed omnes
Mensem unum adverso tenuerunt sidere portum;
Nec prius inde datum est se de statione movere
Quam Teucri capiant urbem regemque trucident.

[3] Phrantzes, p. 327.

probable that Mahomet believed that if any of these forces should arrive before Constantinople either by land or by sea, he would have to abandon the siege. With these possible dangers threatening him, it is not unreasonable to conclude that if the besieged could have succeeded in repulsing the Turks in their greatest attack, and have held the city for even one day longer, Mahomet himself would have considered it necessary to withdraw his army, and Constantinople might possibly have been saved for Europe. Hence the withdrawal of Justiniani was an event of supreme importance. It led to the capture and decided the fate of the city, and gave the death-blow to the Eastern Empire. The ships bringing help, which were on their way, were too late. One is almost driven to the belief of Pusculus, ' Auxilium Deus ipse negavit.' [1]

In the struggle which took place, the emperor bore a part worthy of his name and of his position. He perished among his own subjects and the remnant of the Latins who were aiding him. Whether the story related by Ducas and Leonard, that the emperor asked if there was no Christian willing to kill him, be true or not, there can be no doubt that he met his death like a brave man. All accounts attest his courage. Critobulus states that when he saw that the enemy had succeeded and were pouring through the breaches in the walls, he shouted, ' The city is taken and I am still alive,' and thereupon dashed into the midst of the enemy and was killed. [2]

Death of Constantine.

The manner of his death is, however, doubtful. No contemporary writer was present. Phrantzes, who had attended him at and after midnight, expressly tells us that he had been sent on duty elsewhere. Critobulus states that the emperor fell near the postern which Justiniani had opened from the city to the stockade ; [3] Leonard, that he was struck down by a Janissary, recovered himself, was again struck down and killed. [4] Ducas declares that two Turks claimed to

Manner of his death.

---

[1] Pusc. iv. 1025.   [2] Crit. lxxii.   [3] Crit. lx.

[4] Leonard, p. 99 ; Polish Janissary, 332 ; Montaldo notes one report, that he was trampled down in the throng, and another, that his head was cut off Philelphus (book ii. v. 990) says, ' Enseque perstricto nunc hos, nunc eneca illos, Donec vita suo dispersa est alma cruore.'

have killed the emperor and to have taken his head, which
was recognised by Notaras, and that it was placed on a column
in the Augusteum, then stuffed and sent to be shown in
Persia, Arabia, and Asia Minor.[1] The story of Ducas is to
a certain extent confirmed by the Moscovite, who states that
a scribe brought the head of the emperor to Mahomet, who,
when he was assured that it was genuine, kissed it and then
sent it to the patriarch. It was then encased in a silver
vase and buried under the altar of St. Sophia. He adds
that the body was carried in the night to Galata and there
buried.[2] To some extent their story is confirmed by Pusculus, who says that in struggling with the Janissaries ' at the
mound,' where he killed three Turks, he was slain by the
mighty stroke of a sword ; that his head was cut off from his
shoulders by one who knew him, and taken to Mahomet,
who paid the promised reward.[3] None of these stories as to
the manner of death can be regarded as altogether trustworthy.   Barbaro, with the sailor-like bluntness which
usually characterises his matter-of-fact statements when not
attacking the Genoese, says, ' No news was received of his
fate, whether he was living or dead, but some say that his
body was seen among the number of the dead, while others
asserted that he was trampled to death at the entry which
the Turks made at the gate of St. Romanus.' Phrantzes
who, like Barbaro, was in the city at the time, records that
after the capture, the sultan caused diligent search to be
made to learn whether the emperor was alive or dead ; that
men were sent to seek among the heaps of the slain ; that many
heads were washed, but no one could recognise that of the
emperor ; but that a body was found which had the imperial
eagles embroidered on the socks and greaves, and that this
body was given over to the Christians to be buried with due

[1] See also ch. xxvii. of Montaldo, who adds that the head was sent to the
pasha of Babylon accompanied by forty youths and forty virgins, a procession
intended to make known the sultan's great victory.

[2] The Turks show a place in the bema of St. Sophia which they pretend to
be the tomb of Constantine.

[3] Sad-ud-din also makes a Turkish soldier strike off the emperor's head
(p. 31).

honours. Phrantzes [1] does not profess to have seen the body,
and makes no mention of the head having been brought to
the sultan and recognised by Notaras the Grand Duke, as
stated by Ducas. Tetaldi confirms the statement that the
emperor died at the time of the assault. He adds, ' Some
say that he had his head sliced off; others that he died at the
gate *en s'en cuidant yssir*. Either story may be true. He
died in the throng, and the Turks would have cut off his
head.'

Against the version of Phrantzes is to be placed the fact
that his tomb is unknown and that no contemporary—or,
indeed, subsequent—writer mentions where it was. Had it
existed, it is not likely to have been forgotten by the Greeks.
Had the body been purposely buried in a secret place, there
would probably have grown up a legend about it which
would have kept its memory green. [2]

Constantine Palaeologus Dragases in the fiftieth year
of his age disappears amid the final charge of the Turkish
Janissaries. Although there were rumours of his escape,
his death within the Inner Enclosure of the Lycus valley
cannot reasonably be doubted. His conduct during the
whole of the siege had earned respect. He had done his
best to encourage his subjects to fight bravely, had stimulated them by his speech and by his example. He had spared
no exertion day and night to organise the defence, had tried to
reconcile hostile parties and to unite all for the common safety.
When the long-standing jealousies and rivalries between
his own subjects and the citizens of the two republics
threatened to weaken the force available for the defence of

Character of Constantine.

---

[1] Phrantzes, p. 291.

[2] Until about ten years ago a tomb was shown by local guides to travellers
at Vefa Meidan as the burial-place of Constantine. It bore no inscription.
I. Mijatovich is mistaken in stating (in *Constantine, last Emperor of the
Greeks*, p. 229), on the authority of the elder Dr. Mordtman, that the Turkish
government provides oil for the lamp over his grave. Alongside the alleged
grave of Constantine is that of some one else, probably a dervish, and a lamp
was burnt there some years ago. Similar lamps are burnt nightly in many
other places in Constantinople. It is now entirely neglected. Dr. Paspates
suggests, and probably with truth, that the whole story grew out of the desire
or custom by the owner of a neighbouring coffee-house.

the city, it was he who by his personal influence and the respect and even affection which he had acquired and inspired persuaded them to postpone their quarrels. Fanatical Greeks and equally fanatical Catholics had almost forgotten for the time their animosities and had joined forces for the honour of God and for the defence of Christianity. At his instigation, Roman cardinal and Orthodox bishops had thrown themselves energetically into the common labour of resisting the Moslem hordes. At his entreaty the task of completing the Union of the Churches was by common accord allowed to stand over. The example of the religious chiefs was followed by their flocks. Whenever we are able to get a glimpse of the emperor's personality we see him as a man without conspicuous ability but whose devotion to his country was complete, whose sympathy made friends of all who were brought into contact with him, and won for him the admiration of his own troops and of the brave Italians who fought under him. His refusal to leave the city when urged to do so by the patriarch and other leaders both of the Church ánd people was the more praiseworthy when it is remembered that the arguments in favour of departure were at least plausible, and that he had apparently come to the conclusion that, in spite of all his exertions, Mahomet would succeed in capturing it.

He was holding the last great stronghold of Eastern Christianity against the attempt of Islam to capture that which in the eyes of all Moslems represented the capital of Christendom. The steadfastness and tenacity with which the imperial city had maintained its lordship for upwards of a thousand years and had during the whole of that period served as a bulwark against the invasion of Europe by Asiatic hordes were worthily represented in its last emperor. Various causes, for which he can in no way be held responsible, had sapped the strength of the city and made its capture possible, but with a Roman obstinacy that would have done honour to the best of his predecessors he deliberately chose not to abandon it but to die in its defence. To his eternal honour it must be said that, despairing of o not considering the question of ultimate success, he never wavered, never omitted any precaution to deserve victory, but fought on heroically to the end and finally sacrificed his life for his people, his country and Christendom. The exact spot where he lies buried is unknown, but, in the bold metaphor, quoted as already old by the great consort of Justinian, he judged that 'the empire was an excellent winding-sheet.'[1] His death was a fitting and honourable end of the Eastern Roman Empire.

[1] ὡς καλὸν ἐντάφιον ἡ βασιλεία ἐστί. The conclusion of Theodora's speech as recorded by Procopius.

CHAPTER XVII

ATTACKS IN OTHER PARTS OF THE CITY: BY ZAGAN
AND CARAJA ; BY FLEET ; THE BROTHERS BOCCHIARDI
HOLD THEIR OWN ; PANIC WHEN ENTRY OF TURKS
BECAME KNOWN ; INCIDENT OF SAINT THEODOSIA'S
CHURCH ; MASSACRE AND SUBSEQUENT PILLAGE ; CROWD
IN SAINT SOPHIA CAPTURED ; HORRORS OF SACK ;
NUMBERS KILLED OR CAPTURED ; ENDEAVOURS TO
ESCAPE FROM CITY ; PANIC IN GALATA ; MAHOMET'S
ENTRY ; SAINT SOPHIA BECOMES A MOSQUE ; FATE OF
LEADING PRISONERS : ATTEMPTS TO REPEOPLE CAPITAL.

Entry of
Turkish
army.

THE author of the Turkish Taj-ut-Tavarikh or ' Crown of
History,' written by Khodja Sad-ud-din, states that after the
sultan's troops had forced a way into the city—not, as he is
careful to explain, through any of the gates, but across the
broken wall between Top Capou and the Adrianople Gate—
they went round and opened the neighbouring gates from the
inside, and that the first so opened was the Adrianople Gate.
Then the army entered through these gates in regular order,
division by division.[1]

While the principal assault was that made under the
sultan's own eyes in the Lycus valley, the city had been elsewhere simultaneously attacked. Though all other attacks
sink into insignificance beside this, yet they are deserving of
notice. The most important were those made by Zagan Pasha

[1] My authority for this statement is on p. 228 of a remarkable book in
Turkish, published only in September 1902, describing the ' Conquest of Constantinople and the establishment of the Turks in Europe.' Its author is
Achmed Muktar Pasha. It is especially valuable as containing many quota-
tions from Turkish authors who are inaccessible to Europeans.

from one or more large and specially constructed pontoons
which had been brought as close as possible to the walls
at the western end of the Golden Horn and by Caraja
Pasha between the Adrianople Gate and Tekfour Serai.

Zagan had brought all his division across the bridge near
Aivan Serai, and his soldiers, during the early morning, had
made a continuous series of attempts to scale the walls from
the narrow strip of land between them and the water, while
his archers and fusiliers attempted to cover the attacking
parties from the pontoons. His efforts were aided by the
crews on board the seventy ships which had been transported across Pera Hill and which were now stationed at
intervals extending from the pontoons to the Phanar. They
were stoutly and successfully opposed by Gabriel Trevisano,
who had charge of the walls upon the Horn as far as the
Phanar.[1]

Caraja's vigorous assault, as has been already mentioned,
was at one of the three places where Mahomet boasted that
his cannon had made a way into the city. It was probably
a part of his division which had followed the discoverers of
the open Kerkoporta into the city. Zagan and Caraja were,
however, defeated.[2]

The Turkish fleet under Hamoud had done its part elsewhere. During the night it had come in force to the boom
and had taken up a position parallel to it. When, however,
the admiral saw that there were against him ten great and
other smaller ships, all ready for the defence, he carried out
the orders which had been given on the previous evening,
passed round Seraglio Point, and took up a position opposite
the walls on the side of the Marmora, where the caloyers
or monks were among the defenders. But all the efforts of
the Turks in the fleet on the side of the Marmora failed to
effect an entrance. Small as was the number of the men
dispersed along the walls, they held their own and repulsed
all attempts to scale them. It was only when they saw the
Turks in their rear that they recognised that their struggle
had been in vain. Then, indeed, some flung themselves in

Attacks by Zagan and Caraja fail.

By fleet also.

---

[1] Barbaro, p. 56.   [2] Crit. lvi.

despair from the walls ; others surrendered in hope of saving
their lives. The walls were abandoned.[1] Once the Turks
had succeeded in effecting their entry through the stockade
in the Lycus valley, followed as such entry was by the
marching in of the divisions through the ordinary gates, the
defence of the city was hopeless.

Probably among the earliest from the fleet to effect an
entry were men who appear to have landed at the Jews'
quarter, which was near the Horaia Gate on the side of the
Golden Horn.[2]

The two brothers Paul and Troilus Bocchiardi in the
highest part of the Myriandrion, near the Adrianople Gate,
maintained their resistance for some time after they had
observed that the Turks were pouring in on their left.
Seeing that further resistance was useless, they determined
to look after their own safety and to make for the ships. In
doing so they were surrounded, but fought their way through
the enemy and escaped to Galata.[3] Greeks and Latins alike,
who were defending the walls on the Marmora and Golden
Horn, judged that it was now impossible to hold them.
From the latter position they could see that the Venetian
and imperial flags which had waved over the towers from
the Adrianople Gate down to the sea had been replaced by
the Turkish ensigns. They were, indeed, soon attacked in
the rear. The crews of the Turkish ships, likewise learning
from the hoisting of the Turkish flags in lieu of those of St
Mark and the empire that their comrades were already
within the city, made more strenuous efforts than before to
scale the walls, and in doing so met with little resistance
when the defenders saw the Turks on their rear.[4]

The church of St. Theodosia—now known as Gul Jami, or
the Mosque of the Rose, still a prominent building a short distance to the west of the present inner bridge—was crowded

---

[1] Crit. lxiii.

[2] The Horaia Gate occupied the site of the present Stamboul Custom
House. The Validé Mosque, at the end of the present outer bridge, is built on
part of the Jewish quarter. See the subject fully discussed by Professor van
Millingen, p. 221 and elsewhere.

[3] Leonard, 99 ; Phrantzes, 287.   [4] Barbaro, pp. 55, 56.

with worshippers who had passed the night in prayers to the
Saint for the safety of the city. The 29th of May was her
feast, and a procession of worshippers was met and attacked
by a band of Turks, who had made their way to the
Plateia, probably the present Vefa. Those who took part
in the procession, mostly women, were apparently among
the first victims after the capture of the city.

The Greek and Italian ships had for some time, with the
aid of the defenders, prevented the men from the Turkish
vessels from scaling the walls. When, however, the
Turkish sailors succeeded in making their entry into the
city, the Christian ships began to take measures for their
own safety. The neighbouring gates had been thrown open,
and the Turkish sailors joined their countrymen in the
plunder and slaughter. Their ships both in the Horn and
on the side of the Marmora were, according to Barbaro,
absolutely deserted by their crews in their eagerness after
loot. The defenders fled to their homes, and Ducas regret- General
fully observes that in so doing some were captured ; others throughout
found neither wife, child, nor possessions, but were them- city.
selves made prisoners and marched off. The old men and
women who could not walk with the other captives were
killed and their babes thrown into the streets. From the
moment it was known that the Turkish troops had entered
there was a general and well-founded panic. The Moscovite
says that there was fighting in the streets, that the people
threw down upon the invaders tiles and any available
missiles, and that the opposition was so severe that the
pashas became afraid and persuaded the sultan to issue an
amnesty. But the story is improbable. There were few
men within the city capable of fighting except those who
had been at the walls. When there became a ' Sauve qui
peut ! ' these men hastened, as Ducas reports, to their homes.
That many of the fugitives, even old men and women,
knowing the fate before them and their children, may have
fought in desperation, willing to die rather than be captured
by an enemy who spared neither men in his cruelty nor
women in his lust, is likely enough, but that there was

anything like an organised resistance in the streets is incredible.[1]

The Turks seem, indeed, to have anticipated greater resistance than they met with. They could not believe that the city was without more defenders than those who had been at the walls. This, indeed, is their sole excuse for beginning what several writers describe as a general slaughter. From the entry of the army and camp-followers until midday this slaughter went on. The Turks, says Critobulus,[2] had been taunted by the besieged with their powerlessness to capture the city and were enraged at the sufferings they had undergone. During the forenoon all whom they encountered were put to the sword, women and men, old and young, of every condition.[3] The Turks slew all throughout the city whom they met in their first onslaught.[4]

The statements made by the spectators of such scenes as they themselves witnessed are apt to be exaggerations, but a Turkish massacre without elements of the grossest brutality has never taken place. The declaration of Phrantzes that in some places the earth could no longer be seen on account of the multitude of dead bodies is sufficiently rhetorical to convey its own corrective.[5] So, too, is the account by Barbaro of the numbers of heads of dead Christians and Turks in the Golden Horn and the Marmora being so great as to remind him of melons floating in his own Venetian canals, and of the waters being coloured with blood.[6] That many nuns and other women preferred to throw themselves into the wells rather than fall into the hands of the Turks may be true. Their glorious successors in the Greek War of Independence, and many Armenian women during the massacres in 1895-6, chose a similar fate in preference to surrendering to Turkish captors.

Probably the truth is that an indiscriminate slaughter went on only till midday. For the love of slaughter was

---

[1] The Moscovite, xxv. The whole chapter is full of improbable statements.
[2] Ch. lxi.   [3] Barbaro, p. 55.   [4] *Thyselii Expugnatio*, ch. xxvi.
[5] Phrantzes, p. 291.   [6] P. 57.

tempered by the desire for gain. The young of both sexes, and especially the strong and beautiful, could be held as slaves or sold or ransomed. The statement of Leonard is therefore probably correct, that all who resisted were killed, that the Turks slew the weak, the decrepit and sick persons generally, but that they spared the lives of others who surrendered.

The Turkish historian Sad-ud-din says, 'Having received permission to loot, they thronged into the city with joyous heart, and there, seizing their possessions and families, they made the wretched misbelievers weep. They acted in accordance with the precept, " Slaughter their aged and capture their youth." ' [1]

The brave Cretan sailors, who were defending the walls near the Horaia Gate, took refuge in certain towers named Basil, Leo, and Alexis. They could not be captured, and would not surrender. In the afternoon, however, their stubborn resistance being reported to the sultan, he consented to allow them to leave the city with all their belongings, an offer which they reluctantly accepted.[2] The Cretans seem to have been the last Christians who quitted their posts as defenders of the city.

The panic caused by the morning's massacre was general. Men, women, and children sought to get outside the city, to escape into the neighbouring country, or to reach the ships in the harbour. Some were struck down on their way; others were drowned before they could get on board. The foreigners naturally made for their own ships. Some of them have placed on record the manner of their escape. Tetaldi says that ' the great galleys of Romania remained [3] till midday trying to save what Christians they could, and receiving four hundred on board,' among whom was one

Flight towards ships.

[1] *The Capture of Constantinople*, from the Taj-ut-Tavarikh by Khodja Sad-ud-din. Translated by E. J. W. Gibb, p. 29.

[2] Phrantzes, 287. Professor van Millingen (p. 189) believes that these towers were a little to the south of the present Seraglio Lighthouse. One of them had an interesting inscription, stating that it was built by the emperor Basil in 1024.

[3] Another version of Tetaldi's *Informacion* calls the galleys in question Venetian (Dethier, p. 905).

named Tetaldi, who had been on guard very far from the place where the Turks entered.' He stripped himself and swam to one of these vessels, where he was taken on board. Barbaro relates that when the cry was raised that the Turks had entered the city everybody took to flight and ran to the sea in order to seek refuge in the Greek and foreign ships.

It was a pitiable sight, says Ducas, to see the shore outside the walls all full of men and women, monks and nuns, shouting to the ships and praying to be taken on board. The ships took as many as they could, but the greater number had to be left behind. The wretched inhabitants expected no mercy, nor was any shown to them. Happily, the Turks had now become keener after plunder than after blood. When they found that there was no organised force to resist them, they turned their attention solely to loot. They set about the pillage of the city with something like system. One body devoted its attention to the wealthy mansions, dividing themselves for this purpose into companies ; another undertook the plunder of the churches ; a third robbed the smaller houses and shops. These various bands overran the city, killing in case of resistance, and taking as slaves men, women and children, priests and laymen, regardless of age or condition. No tragedy, says Critobulus, could equal it in horror. Women, young and well educated ; beautiful maidens of noble family who had never been exposed to the eye of man, were torn from their chaste chambers with brutal violence and publicly treated in horrible fashion. Virgins consecrated to God were dragged by their hair from the churches and were ruthlessly stripped of every ornament they possessed. A horde of savage brutes committed unnameable atrocities, and hell was let loose.[1]

The conquering horde had spread themselves all over the city. For, while the regular troops had probably been kept in hand on the chance of resistance, there were others who could not be restrained from going in search of loot. Some even among the first who had entered by the Kerkoporta had

Plunder organised.

[1] Crit. ch. lxiii.

rushed to plunder the famous monastery of the Virgin, the
small chapel of which, known as the Kahriè mosque, still
attests by its exquisite mosaics the wealth and artistic
appreciation of its former occupants. The famous picture
attributed to St. Luke was cut into strips. Others among
them rushed off towards the many churches in Petra.
These were, however, only a small number. It was in the
afternoon of the day when the horde had entered across the
broken walls and through the gates that they swept like a
torrent over the city. Soon the organised bands, which had
divided the city among them in order to capture the population and to seize all the gold and silver ornaments which
they could lay hands on, began to amass their treasures.
Old men and women, children, young men and maidens were
tied together in order to mark to whom they belonged.

The loot from private houses and churches was put
ou one side for subsequent division and the partition was
made with considerable method. Small flags were hoisted
to indicate to other companies the houses plundered, and
everywhere throughout the city these signals were waving,
sometimes a single house having as many as ten.[1]

A body of troops more amenable to discipline than we
may suppose the Bashi-bazouks to have been hastened across
the city towards Saint Sophia. Many inhabitants took
refuge in the churches, some probably with the idea that
the Turks would recognise that the sacred buildings should
afford sanctuary; others in the hope or possible belief of
some kind of miraculous interference on their behalf. Ducas
relates that a crowd of affrighted citizens ran to the great
church of Holy Wisdom because they believed in a prophecy
that the Turks would be allowed to enter the city and
slaughter the Romans until they reached the column of
Constantine—the present Burnt Column—but that then an
angel would descend from heaven with a sword and place it
and the government of the city in the hands of one whom
he would select, calling upon him to avenge the people of
the Lord, and that thereupon the Turks would be driven from

St. Sophia
crowded
with
refugees.

—————
[1] Barbaro, p. 57.

the West. It was on this account, he declares, that the
Great Church was, within an hour from the tidings of the
entry of the Turks becoming known, filled with a great crowd
who believed themselves to be safe. By so doing they
had only rendered their capture more easy.

The first detachment of Turks who arrived and found
the doors closed soon succeeded in breaking in. The
great crowd were taken as in a drag-net, says Critobulus.
The miserable refugees thus made prisoners were tied or
chained together and any resistance offered was at once
overcome. Some were taken to the Turkish ships, others to
the camp, and the loot collected was dealt with in the same
manner. The scene was terrible, but, unhappily, one which
was destined to be reproduced with many even worse features
in Turkish history, because, while the chief object of the
Turkish hordes in 1453 was mainly to capture slaves and
other plunder, the attacks on many congregations in later
years, down to the time of the holocaust of Armenians at
Ourfa on December 28 and 29, 1895, were mainly for the
sake of slaughter. In the Great Church itself the Turks
struggled with each other for the possession of the most
beautiful women. Damsels who had been brought up
in luxury among the remnants of Byzantine nobility, nuns
who had been shut off from the world, became the subjects
of violence among their captors. Their garments were torn
from them by men who would not relinquish their prizes to
others. Masters and mistresses were tied to their servants;
dignitaries of the Church with the lowest menials. The
captors drove their flocks of victims before them in order to
lodge them in safety under charge of their comrades and to
return as quickly as possible to take a new batch. Ropes,
ribbons, handkerchiefs were requisitioned to bind them. The
sacred eikons were torn down and burnt, the altar cloths, chandeliers, chalices, carpets, ornaments—indeed everything that
was valuable and portable—were carried off. The greatest
misfortune of all, says Phrantzes, was to see the Temple
of the Holy Wisdom, the Earthly Heaven, the Throne of
the Glory of God, defiled by these miscreants. One would

hope that his story of its defilement and of the scenes of open profligacy is exaggerated.[1] The other churches were plundered in like manner. They furnished a plentiful harvest. The richly embroidered robes, chasubles woven with gold and ornamented with pearls and precious stones, and church furniture, were greedily seized, the ornaments being torn from many of the objects and the rest thrown aside. A crucifix was carried in mock solemnity in procession surmounted by a Janissary's cap.

While we can understand the indignation of the devout believers at the contemptuous destruction of sacred relics for the sake of the caskets in which they were contained, we can hardly regret the disappearance of the so-called sacred objects themselves. But it is otherwise with the destruction of books. The professors of Islam, whatever may have been their conduct in regard to particular libraries, have usually held the all-sufficiency of the Koran. That which contradicts its teaching ought to be destroyed; that which is in accordance with it is superfluous. The libraries of the churches, whatever Mahomet himself may have believed, were to the ignorant fanatical masses which followed him anti-Islamic. The only value of books was the amount for which they could be sold. Critobulus says that not only the holy and religious books, but also those treating of profane sciences and of philosophy, were either thrown into the fire or trampled irreverently under foot, but that the greater part were sold—not for the sake of the price but in mockery—for two or three pence or even farthings.[2]

Wanton destruction of books.

The ships of the Turkish fleet had among their cargo, says Ducas, an innumerable quantity of books.[3] In the booty collected by the Turks they were so plentiful and cheap, that for a nummus—probably worth sixpence—ten volumes were sold containing the works of Plato and Aristotle, treatises on theology and other sciences.

---

[1] οὗ ἔσοθεν τῶν ἀδύτων καὶ ἄνωθεν τῶν θυσιαστηρίων καὶ τραπέζων ἤσθιον καὶ πίνον καὶ τὰς ἀσελγεῖς γνώμας καὶ ὀρέξεις αὐτῶν μετὰ γυναικῶν καὶ παρθένων καὶ αἴδων ἐπάνωθεν ἐποίουν καὶ ἔπραττον. Phrantzes, p. 290.

[2] Crit. xlii.   [3] Ducas, xlii. : βιβλία ὑπὲρ ἀριθμόν.

Christian and Moslem writers agree in stating that the sack of the city continued, as Mahomet had promised, for three days. Khodja Sad-ud-din, after affirming that the soldiers of Islam ' acted in accordance with the precept, " Slaughter their aged and capture their youth," ' adds, with the Oriental imagery of Turkish historians : ' For three days and nights there was, with the imperial permission, a general sack, and the victorious troops, through the richness of the spoil, entwined the arm of possession round the neck of their desires, and by binding the lustre of their hearts to the locks of the damsels, beautiful as houris, and by the sight of the sweetly smiling fair ones, they made the eye of their hopes the participator in their good fortune.' [1]

It must, however, not be forgotten that although those who took the principal part in the sack were Mahometans, yet there were also no small numbers of Christian renegades.[2]

Numbers killed or captured.

As to the number of persons captured or killed, the estimates do not greatly differ.

Leonard states that sixty thousand captives were bound together preparatory to their final distribution. In such circumstances exaggeration is usual and almost unavoidable. But Critobulus, writing some years afterwards, estimates that the number of Greeks and Italians killed during the siege and after the capture was four thousand, that five hundred of the army and upwards of fifty thousand of the rest of the population were reduced to slavery.[3]

Such of the Genoese and Venetians as had succeeded in escaping from the city were preparing to get away to sea with all haste. Happily the Turkish ships had been deserted by their crews, who were busy looking after their share of plunder on shore.[4] In their absence a large number of

[1] P. 31. Khodja Sad-ud-din, translated by E. J. W. Gibb.

[2] Report of Superior of Franciscans. He was present at the siege and arrived at Bologna July 4, 1453.

[3] Crit. lxvii. The Superior of the Franciscans reported that three thousand men were killed on both sides on May 29. Probably we shall not be far wrong in saying that between three and four thousand were killed on May 29 on the Christian side and fifty thousand made prisoners.

[4] Barbaro and Ducas.

combatants, mostly foreigners, contrived to take refuge either on board some of the various ships in the harbour or in Galata. The Venetian Diedo, who had been appointed captain of the harbour, when he saw that the city was taken, went over to the podestà of Galata, says Barbaro, to consult whether he should get his ships away or give battle. The advice of the podestà was that he should remain until he received an answer from Mahomet by which they would learn whether the conqueror wanted war or peace with Venice and Genoa.

Meantime, the gates of Galata were closed, much to the disgust of Barbaro himself, who was one of the Venetians thus locked in.[1] When, however, the Genoese saw that the galleys were preparing to make sail, Diedo and his men were allowed to leave. They went on board the captain's galley and pulled out to the boom, which had not yet been opened. Two strong sailors leapt upon it with their axes and cut or broke the chain in two.

Panic among foreigners.

The boom was apparently very strong, for, according to Barbaro, the Turkish captains and crews, when they went ashore to plunder, believed that the Christian vessels within the harbour could not escape, because they would not be able to pass through it.[2] The ships passed outside and went to the Double Columns, where the Turkish fleet had been anchored, but which was now deserted. There they waited until noon to see whether the Venetian merchant vessels would join them. They had, however, been captured by the Turks.[3] Diedo, on learning this, left with his galleys. Other Venetians hastened to follow. Some of the vessels had lost a great part of their crews, and one regrets to read that the brave Trevisano was left a prisoner in the hands of the Turks. Happily for those who had reached

---

[1] Barbaro pretends, indeed, that they were the victims of a trick on the part of the Genoese, who wished to secure their own safety by seizing their ships and delivering them to Mahomet. His story, like everything else he says about the Genoese, may well be doubted.

[2] A portion of the chain which formed part of the boom is now in the narthex of St. Irene. Its links average about eighteen inches long.

[3] Tetaldi states that the Turks captured a Genoese ship and from thirteen to sixteen others.

the ships, there was a strong north wind blowing; for, says Barbaro, 'if there had been a head wind we should have all been made prisoners.' Seven Genoese galleys also got outside the boom and escaped.[1] The remaining fifteen ships, which belonged to Genoa, and four galleys of the emperor, were taken by the Turks.

In Galata.   The alarm had spread to Galata, and many of its inhabitants crowded to the shore, praying to be taken on board the Genoese ships. They were ready to barter all they possessed for a passage. Some were captured on their way to the ships : among them, mothers who had deserted their children, children who had been left behind by their parents. Household goods, and even jewels, were abandoned in the mad haste to escape from the terror. The number of fugitives was far in excess of the carrying capacity of the vessels which were hastily preparing to put to sea.

Mahomet, according to Ducas, knew of the preparations and flight of many, and ground his teeth with rage because he could do nothing to prevent their escape. Zagan Pasha, to whom the Genoese, when they saw that Constantinople was captured, opened the gates of Galata,[2] seeing the struggling crowd of men, women, and children attempting to get away, and probably fearing that their flight would bring war not only with Genoa but with other Western powers, went among the fugitives and begged them to remain. He swore by the head of the Prophet that they were safe, that Galata would not be attacked, and that they had nothing to fear, since they had been friendly to Mahomet. If they went away, he declared the sultan would be dangerous in his anger ; whereas if they remained their capitulations would be renewed on even more favourable conditions than they had received from the emperors.

In spite of these promises, as many left the city as could. They were hardly in time, because Hamoud, the Turkish admiral, had by this time got his sailors in hand again and, the boom being already opened, entered the harbour and destroyed the Greek ships which remained.[3]

[1] Ducas says five.   [2] Crit. lxvii.   [3] *Ibid.* lxiii.

The podestà and his council went to Mahomet and presented him with the keys of Galata. He received them graciously and gave them specious promises. The report of the podestà himself, written less than a month after the capture of the city, confirms in its essential features the accounts given by Ducas, Leonard, and others of the panic which seized the population under his rule. The Turks, he says, captured many of the burgesses who had been sent to fight at the stockade. A few managed to escape across the water and returned to their families, while others got on board the ships and left the country. He himself was disposed to sacrifice his life rather than abandon his charge. If he also had left, Galata would have been sacked, and he remained to secure its safety. ' I therefore sent ambassadors to my lord Mahomet, making submission and asking for the conditions of peace.' No answer was sent on the first day to this request, during which the ships were getting away as fast as possible. The podestà begged their captains for the love of God and their kindred to remain at least another day, as he felt confident that he would be able to make peace. They, however, refused, and sailed during the night. The statement regarding the sultan's anger was confirmed, for the podestà relates that Mahomet told his ambassadors, when he learned the news of the general flight, that he wanted to be rid of them all. Thereupon the podestà himself went to Mahomet, who either on the same day or shortly afterwards came into Galata and insisted that the fortifications should be so changed that the city would be at his mercy. The walls on the sea front were to be in great part destroyed: so also was the Tower of Galata—called sometimes the Tower of the Holy Cross—to which one end of the boom had been attached, and other strong portions of the defences.[1] All the cannon were taken away from Galata and the arms and ammunition belonging to the burgesses who had fled. Mahomet promised that these should be returned to those who came back. Accordingly, the podestà

---

[1] About three fourths of the sea-walls were taken down. The remaining fourth was spared, and a portion of them near Azap Capou still remain.

sent word to Chios to the merchants and other refugees that if they returned they would receive their property.[1] Mahomet, as a pledge of his sincerity and as the best means of convincing the Genoese of his desire to be at peace with them, granted ' capitulations ' by which they were to retain most of the customs and privileges which they had previously obtained from the empire. They were to retain the fortress of Galata and their own laws and government ; to elect their own podestà ; to have freedom of trade throughout the empire, and keep their own churches and accustomed worship—but subject to the prohibition of bells— and their private property and churches were to be respected.[2]

Mahomet's entry into Constantinople.

The massacre had been limited to the first day. The permission to pillage had been granted for three days. On the afternoon of the day of the capture, or possibly on the following day, Mahomet made his triumphal entry into the city. He was surrounded by his viziers and pashas and by a detachment of Janissaries. He came into the city through the gate now called Top Capou, rode on horseback to the Great Church, descended and entered. As he passed up the church he observed a Turk who was forcing out a morsel of marble from the pavement, and asked why he was

---

[1] *Angeli Johannis Zachariae Potestatis Perae Epistola.* Leonard, p. 100. Ducas says that Mahomet had an inventory made of the property of those who had fled, and gave the owners three months within which to return, failing which, it would be confiscated.

[2] Zorzo Dolfin, p. 1040. See also Sauli's *Colonia dei Genovesi in Galata,* vol. ii. p. 172, and Von Hammer, vol. ii., where the treaty is given in full in the appendix. Usually Dolfin's narrative is taken from Leonard, but the paragraphs relating to the capitulations are an exception. Dolfin uses the word *Privilegio.* The capitulations are called at different times by different names : grants, concessions, privileges, capitulations, or treaties. I have already pointed out, in the *Fall of Constantinople,* that the system of ex-territoriality, under which, in virtue of capitulations, foreigners resident in Turkey are always under the protection of their own laws, is the survival of the system once general in the Roman empire. Of course it is ridiculous to speak of the capitulations as having been wrongfully wrung from the Turks by Western nations, and equally absurd to claim that their grant shows the far-reaching policy of the Turks in their desire to attract foreign trade. The Turks found the system of ex-territoriality in full force and maintained it, being unwilling, as they still are, to allow Christians, whether their own subjects or foreigners, to rank on an equality with Moslems.

thus damaging the building. The Turk pleaded that it was only a building of the infidels and that he was a believer. Mahomet had a sufficiently high opinion of the value of St. Sophia to be angry with him. He drew his sword and struck the man, telling him at the same time that, while he had given the prisoners and the plunder of the city to his followers, he had reserved the buildings for himself.

Mahomet called for an imaum, who by his orders ascended the pulpit and made the declaration of Mahometan faith. From that time to the present, the Temple of the Holy Wisdom of the Incarnate Word has been a Mahometan mosque. Hagia Sophia becomes a mosque.

On the same day [1] Mahomet entered the Imperial Palace, and it is said that as he passed through the deserted rooms in all the desolation resulting from the plunder of a barbarous army, he quoted a Persian couplet on the vicissitudes of mortal greatness : ' The spider has become watchman in the imperial palace, and has woven a curtain before the doorway ; the owl makes the royal tombs of Efrasaib re-echo with its mournful song.' [2] The statement rests on the authority of Cantemir, and, whether historically correct or not, such a reflection under the circumstances is not in disaccord with what we know of the character of the young sovereign.

The fate of the men of most eminence among the defenders of Constantinople is illustrative of Mahomet's methods. The bailey of the Venetians, with his son and seven of his countrymen, was beheaded. Among them was Contarino, the most distinguished among the Venetian nobles, who had already been ransomed and who in breach of faith was killed because his friends were unable to find the enormous sum of seven thousand gold pieces for his second ransom. The consul of Spain or the Catalans, with five or six of his companions, met with the same fate. [3] Cardinal Isidore in Fate of defenders after capture. Venetian bailey and other leading Venetians beheaded. Cardinal Isidore.

---

[1] Ducas makes the entry to Hagia Sophia on the 30th. Phrantzes and Chalcondylas, on the 29th.

[2] Cantemir, vol. ii. p. 45 (ed. Paris, 1743). He gives the Persian text.

[3] Report of podestà ; Philip the Armenian, p. 680 ; also Leonard, 101.

his flight abandoned his clerical robes, and, after having been captured in the disguise of a beggar and sold into slavery, was ransomed for a few aspers.[1]

Phrantzes.

Phrantzes, the friend of the emperor and the historian of his reign, had an even less happy experience. He suffered the hard lot of slavery during a period of fifteen months. His wife and children were captured and sold to the Master of the Sultan's Horse, who had bought many other ladies belonging to the Greek nobility. A year later he was able to redeem his wife. But the sultan hearing of the beauty of his daughter Thamar took her into his seraglio. She was then but fourteen years old, and died in 1454, shortly after her captivity.[2]. In December of 1453 his son John, in the fifteenth year of his age, preferring death to infamy, was killed by the sultan's own hand.[3]

Notaras.

Most unhappy of all was the Grand Duke Notaras. He was the most illustrious prisoner, and was indeed next in rank to the emperor himself. He may be taken as a type of the old Byzantine nobility. We have seen that he had been the leader of the party which had resisted union with Rome. On account of this opposition Notaras had incurred the hostility of those who had accepted it, and as our sources of information come almost exclusively from men of the Roman faith or from those who had accepted the Union, he is not usually spoken of with favour. Phrantzes was his rival and enemy. Ducas gives two reports regarding his treatment by Mahomet. According to one, he was betrayed by a captive who purchased his own liberty by the betrayal of the Grand Duke and Orchan. At first the illustrious captive was looked upon favourably by the sultan, who condoled with him and ordered a search for his wife and daughters. When they were found, the sultan made them presents and sent them to their house, declaring to the Grand Duke that it was his intention to

---

[1] Riccherio (p. 967), whose narrative is singularly clear and readable. See also the report of the Superior of the Franciscans.

[2] Phrantzes, 385.

[3] *Ibid.* p. 383 : ἐν ᾧ δὴ χρόνῳ καὶ μηνὶ ἀνεῖλεν αὐτοχειρίᾳ τὸν φίλτατόν μου υἱὸν Ἰωάννην ὁ ἀσεβέστατος καὶ ἀπηνέστατος ἀμηρᾶς, ὃς δῆθεν ἐβούλετο τὴν ἀθέμιτον σοδομίαν πρᾶξαι κατὰ τοῦ παιδός.

make him governor of the city and allow him the same rank
that he had held under the emperor. This version is confirmed
by Critobulus,[1] who adds that Mahomet was dissuaded from
appointing him governor of the city by the remonstrances
of the leading Turks, who represented that it would be
dangerous. According to the other report, Mahomet charged
him with not having surrendered the city. Notaras is
represented as replying that it was neither in his power
nor in that of the emperor to do so, and to have made some
remark which increased the suspicion and hatred which the
sultan felt for his grand vizier, Halil Pasha. Whichever of
these reports is correct, no hesitation is expressed by Ducas
as to what followed. On the day following the interview, the
sultan, after a drinking bout, sent for the youngest of the
sons of the Grand Duke. Notaras replied that the Christian
religion forbade a father to comply with such a request.
When the answer was reported, Mahomet ordered the eunuch
to return, to take the executioner with him, and to bring the
youngest son together with the Grand Duke and his other
son. The order was obeyed and was followed by another to
put all three to death. The father asked the headsman to
allow the execution of his sons to precede his own. His reason
for this request, says Critobulus, was, lest his lads, being
perhaps afraid to die, might be tempted to save their lives by
renouncing their faith. Drawing himself up to his full height,
firmly and unflinchingly, with the stateliness of an ancient
aristocrat, the old noble witnessed the beheading of his two
sons without shedding a tear or moving a muscle. Then,
having given thanks to God that he had seen them die in the
faith of Christ, Notaras bent his head to the executioner's
sword and died like a worthy representative of the proud
Roman nobility. 'For this man,' says the same writer, 'was
pious and renowned for his knowledge of spiritual things,
for the loftiness of his soul and the nobility of his life.[2]

Including Notaras and his two sons, nine nobles of high
rank were put to death, all invincible in their faith. The
heads were taken by the executioner into the hall to show

---

[1] Crit. lxxiii.   [2] *Ibid.*

says Ducas, to the beast greedy of blood that his commands had been obeyed.[1]

Phrantzes tells the story somewhat differently. He begins his version by stating that the sultan, though elated with the great victory, nevertheless showed himself to be merciless. He makes the Grand Duke offer his wealth of pearls, precious stones, and other valuables to Mahomet, begging him to accept them and pretending that he had kept them to offer to his captor. In reply to the sultan's question, Who had given to Notaras his wealth and to the sultan the city ? the captive answered that each was the gift of God. To this the sultan retorted, ' Then, why do you pretend that you have kept your wealth for me ? Why did you not send it to me, so that I might have rewarded you ? Notaras was thrown into prison, but was sent for next day and reproached for not having persuaded the emperor to accept the conditions of peace which had been submitted. Thereupon, the sultan gave the order that on the following day he and his two sons should be put to death. They were taken to the forum of the Xerolophon and the order was carried out.[2] Gibbon justly remarks that neither time nor death nor his own retreat to a monastery could extort a feeling of sympathy or forgiveness from Phrantzes towards his personal enemy the Grand Duke.

The version given by Leonard is marked with the same personal hostility towards Notaras which characterises that of Phrantzes. Leonard accuses his old rival of having thrown blame both on Halil Pasha, who had always been friendly towards the emperor, and on the Genoese and Venetians. In the account given by both these writers they were reporting a version spread and probably believed by the Unionist party, as to which it is improbable that they could have had direct evidence. What is important in the narrative of Leonard is that he confirms the ghastly story of Ducas as to the demand for the youngest son by the sultan.[3] The fate of the Grand Duke and his family was that which

---

[1] Ducas, p. 137 : ἐμφάνισας αὐτὰς τῷ αἱμοβόρῳ θηρίῳ.   [2] Phrantzes, 291.

[3] Pusculus also is violently hostile to Notaras, and probably for the same reason : because he would not accept the Union.

befell all the nobles and the chief officers of the empire. Their wives and children were generally saved, Mahomet himself taking possession for his own harem of the fairest and distributing the rest among his followers.[1]

The end of Orchan was attended by fewer circumstances of ignominy. He had defended a part of the walls near Seraglio Point. Orchan must always have anticipated death if he were captured. It was believed that the sultan had determined to kill him, as an elderly member of the reigning house, in accordance with the custom that was common in the governing family of the Turks, not only at the time in question but for at least three centuries later. Orchan, who was either the son or the grandson of Suliman the brother of Mahomet the First, had fled for safety to the emperor, who had refused to give him up and had treated him with kindness. When it was no longer possible to hold the towers which had been placed under his charge, he and the rest of their defenders surrendered. Among them was a monk, with whom Orchan changed clothes. He joined the Grand Duke, and the two lowered themselves outside the walls, but were caught by the Turks and taken on shipboard. Unfortunately, the rest of the defenders of the towers, who had been taken prisoners, were brought on board the same Turkish ship. A Greek offered to reveal Orchan and the Grand Duke if he were promised his liberty, and, having received the assurance, pointed to the man dressed as a monk and to Notaras. Orchan was at once beheaded and his head taken to Mahomet.[2]

Orchan.

The city was made a desolation. The followers of Mahomet, soldiers and sailors, left nothing of value except the buildings. Constantinople, says Critobulus, was as if it had been visited by a hurricane or had been burnt. It was as silent as a tomb. The sailors especially were active in

[1] Ducas, 137.
[2] Crit. (lxiii.) gives a different version. He states that he tried to pass as a Turk, in which his knowledge of the Turkish language aided him : but that he was recognised and flung himself from the walls. His head was cut off and carried to the sultan, who had offered a great reward for his capture dead or alive.

destruction. The churches, crypts, coffins, cellars, every place and every thing was ransacked or broken into in search of plunder.[1] Mahomet, according to the same writer, wept as he saw the ravages his soldiers had wrought, and expressed his amazement at the ruins of the city which had been given over to plunder and had been made a desert.[2]

All the Turks who first entered the city became rich, says the Superior of the Franciscans.[3] Captives were sent in great numbers to Asia Minor either for sale or to the homes of the armed population who had taken part in the siege. Only a miserable remnant remained in Constantinople.

Affection of Constantinopolitans for their city. The reader of the accounts of the siege, and indeed of its history generally before 1453, cannot but be struck with the attachment shown by its inhabitants towards their city. For them it is the Queen of Cities, the most beautiful, the most wealthy, the most orderly, and the most civilised in the world. There the merchant could find all the produce of the East, and could trade with buyers from all countries. There the student had access to the great libraries of philosophy, law, and theology, the rich storehouse of the writings of the Christian Fathers, and of the great classics of ancient Greece. In quietness and security, generations of monks had copied the manuscripts of earlier days free from the alarms which in Western and Eastern countries alike disturbed the scholar. The Church, the lawyers and scholars had kept alive a knowledge of the ancient language in a form in all its essential features like that which existed in the days of Pericles. Priests and laymen were proud to be inheritors and guardians of the writings of classical times and to consider themselves of the same blood as their authors. Though often almost as intolerant towards heretics as the great sister Church of the West, they did not and could not regard Aristotle and Plato, Leonidas and Pericles, and the rest of their glorious predecessors as eternally lost because they had not known Christ, and their sense of

---

[1] Crit. lxiii and lxvii.   [2] *Ibid.* lxvii.
[3] Report, p. 940. The houses were empty and bore the marks of the reckless ravages of a savage horde.

relationship with them helped to develop a conviction of the
continuity of their history, not only with Constantine and the
Roman empire, but with the more remote peoples who had
given them their language.   The New Rome had for a
thousand years been towards all Eastern Christians all that
the Elder Rome was to those in the West, and their pride
in its stability and security was great.   Once, and once
alone, had it been captured.   But the unfortunate attack
made by the West in 1204, the results of which had
been so correctly foreseen and foretold by Innocent the
Third, had been in part overcome.   This new capture was
infinitely more serious.   The essential difference between
the two is commented on by Critobulus.   By the first the
city sustained a foreign domination for sixty years and lost
much of its wealth.   A great number of beautiful statues
and other works of art, coveted by the whole world, were
taken away and many more destroyed.   But there the
mischief stopped.   The city did not lose all its inhabitants.
Wives and children were not taken away.   When the
tyranny was past, the city recovered and once more it
figured as the renowned capital of an empire, though only a
simulacrum of what it had once been.   It was still in the
eyes of all Greek-speaking people the leader and example of
all that was good, the home of philosophy and of every kind
of learning, of science, of virtue, and in truth of all that is
best.[1]   Now, all was changed : the new conquerors were
Asiatics.   A false religion replaced Christianity.   The
capital was a desert.

The city's situation of picturesque beauty, as well as its
Christian and historical associations, increased the love for it
of its inhabitants and made them as proud of Constantinople
as ever were the Italian citizens of Florence or Venice.   It
is therefore not surprising to find that, on its conquest, the
grief and the rage of those who had lived in it are almost
too great for words.   She, says Critobulus, who had
formerly reigned over many people with honour, glory,
and renown, is now ruled by others and has sunk into

[1] Crit. lxix.

poverty, ignominy, dishonour, and shameful slavery. The lamentations of Ducas are as sincere as those of Jeremiah. Its inhabitants gone; its womanhood destined to dishonourable servitude; its nobles massacred; the very babes at the breast butchered; the temples of God defiled: all present a spectacle on which he enlarges with the expression of a hope that the anger of God will be appeased and that His people will yet find favour. Unhappily, the Greek race had entered upon the darkness of the blackest night, and nearly four centuries had to pass before the dawn of their new day was at hand.

Mahomet's attempts to repeople the capital.

At a later date Mahomet himself recognised that it was necessary to do something towards the repeopling of Constantinople. He gave orders that five thousand families should be sent from the provinces to the capital, and commanded the repair of the walls.[1] It does not appear, however, that they were repaired in an efficient manner. It is generally easy to distinguish between Turkish repairs and those effected at an earlier date. Critobulus states that Mahomet ordered the renewal of those parts which had been overthrown by the cannon and of both the sea and the landward walls, which had suffered by time and weather.[2] The sea walls were probably thoroughly repaired; of those on the landward side probably only the Inner Wall. Experience had shown that more than one strong wall was a disadvantage rather than otherwise. Ducas states that the five thousand families sent to Constantinople by Mahomet from Trebizond, Sinope, and Asprocastron under pain of death included masons and lime-burners for repairing the walls.[3]

---

[1] Ducas, 142.   [2] Crit. bk. ii. ch. i.

[3] Von Hammer states that the walls were completely repaired in 1477, but gives no authority (*Histoire de l'empire ottoman*, iii. 209). A valuable hint is obtained from Knolles, who, writing his history of the Turks in 1610, says that ' the two utter walls with the whole space between them are now but slenderly maintained by the Turks, lying full of earth and other rubbish ' (Knolles's *History*, p. 341, 3rd ed. 1621). The lowest of the three walls has almost entirely disappeared except as to the lower portion, which forms one of the sides of the foss. In the Lycus valley, and even throughout the whole length of the landward walls, I think it is manifest to an observer that only the Inner Wall has been repaired.

In order to attract population to the capital, Mahomet recognised that it was necessary to conciliate the Greeks. It may be, as Critobulus asserts, that he felt a genuine pity for the sufferings of the captives. As a young man, with, for a Turk, quite exceptional knowledge of the literary possessions of the old world, it is easy to believe that he was desirous of satisfying the Christians, while his general intelligence must have convinced him that trade and commerce, from which a revenue was to be derived, would be much more likely to flourish with them than with men of his own race. Critobulus insists that his first intention was to employ Notaras and others of the leading Greeks in the public service, and that he recognised when it was too late that he had been misled into the blunder of putting them to death, and sent away from his court some of those who had counselled their executions, and even condemned some others to death.[1] A few days after the conquest, he ordered the captives who formed part of his own share in the booty to be established in houses on the slope towards the Golden Horn. From among the noble families he selected the young men for himself. Some of these he placed in the corps of Janissaries ; others, who were distinguished by their education, he kept near him as pages.[2]

It was during these days that Critobulus the historian sent envoys to the city, who took with them the submission of the islands of Imbros, where he was living, of Lemnos and Thasos. The archons had learned of the capture of the city. Most of them fled, fearing that admiral Hamoud, who had returned with the fleet to Gallipoli, would attack the inhabitants of the islands and treat them as he had done those of Prinkipo. Critobulus, however, sent a large bakshish to Hamoud and arranged that if the inhabitants submitted there should be no attack. Thereupon Critobulus had sent the envoys to Constantinople, with rich presents for the sultan, to make submission. The islanders were ordered to pay the same taxes to the sultan as they had formerly paid to the emperor, and thus, says the historian,

[1] Crit. lxxiii.   [2] *Ibid.* lxxiv.

were preserved from the great danger which threatened them.[1]

Mahomet published an edict within a few weeks of the capture of the city, that all of the former inhabitants who had paid ransom, or who were ready to enter into an agreement with their masters to pay it within a fixed period, should be considered free, be allowed to live in the city, and should for a time be exempt from taxes. Phrantzes states[2] that even on the third day after the capture an order was issued allowing those to return who had fled from the city and who were in hiding, promising that they should not be molested. Upon the question whether on such return they would, as Critobulus relates, have to pay ransom Phrantzes is silent. A few weeks later, after his visit to Adrianople, Mahomet sent orders to various parts of his empire to despatch families of Christians, Jews, and Turks to repeople the city. He endeavoured to allure Greeks and other workmen by employing them on public works, notably in the construction of a palace—for which, Critobulus rightly says, he had chosen the most beautiful site in the city, namely, at Seraglio Point—on the construction of the fortress of the Seven Towers around the Golden Gate, and at the repairs of the Inner Wall. He ordered the Turks to allow their slaves to take part in this work, so that they might earn money not only to live but to save enough for their ransom.[3]

Toleration of Christianity decreed.

Mahomet's most important step towards conciliation was to decree the toleration of Christian worship and to allow the Church to retain its organisation. As George Scholarius had been the favourite of the Greeks who had refused to accept the Union with Rome, Mahomet ordered search for him. After much difficulty, he was found at Adrianople, a slave in the house of a pasha, kept under confinement as a prisoner, but treated with distinction. His master had recognised, or had learned, that his captive was a man of exceptional talent. He was sent to the sultan, who was already well disposed towards him on account of his renown

[1] Crit. lxxv.   [2] Phrantzes, 304.   [3] Crit. bk. ii. ch. i.

in philosophy. Scholarius made a favourable impression in the interview by his intelligence and manners. Mahomet ordered that he should have access to the palace when he wished, begged him always to speak freely in their intercourse, and sent him away with valuable presents.[1]

A Record of the ecclesiastical affairs of the Orthodox Church, written within ten years after the capture, states that Mahomet, desiring to increase the number of the inhabitants of Constantinople, gave to the Christians permission to follow the customs of their Churches, and, having learned that they had no patriarch, ordered them to choose whom they would. He promised to accept their choice and that the patriarch should enjoy very nearly the same privileges as his predecessors. A local synod having been called, George Scholarius was elected, and became known as Gennadius. The sultan received him at his seraglio, and with his own hands presented him with a valuable pastoral cross of silver and gold, saying to him, 'Be patriarch and be at peace. Count upon our friendship as long as thou desirest it, and thou shalt enjoy all the privileges of thy predecessors.'

After the interview the sultan caused him to be mounted upon a richly caparisoned horse and conducted to the Church of the Holy Apostles, which he presented to him as the church of the patriarchate as it had formerly been.[2]

After the election of Gennadius, the sultan, according to Critobulus, continued his intercourse with the new patriarch and discussed with him questions relating to Christianity, urging him to speak his mind freely. Mahomet even paid him visits and took with him the most learned men whom he had persuaded to be present at his court.[3]

---

[1] Crit. bk. ii. ch. ii.

[2] *Ecclesiastical and Civil Affairs after the Conquest*, by Athanasius Comnenos Hypsilantes, pp. 1, 2. The version of Phrantzes agrees with that given above. He gives a full account of the usual procedure on the appointment of a patriarch and confirms the statement that the Church of the Apostles was assigned to Gennadius as an official residence. Subsequently it was taken from the Greeks, was destroyed and replaced by a mosque built in honour of the conqueror and known as the Mahmoudieh. The former patriarch, says Phrantzes, was dead.

[3] Crit. bk. iii. ch. v

During the long reign of Mahomet his attention was again and again directed to the repeopling of his capital. In addition to the attempts already mentioned, Critobulus recounts many other efforts made with the same object. But the sultan's inducements mostly failed. The Christians mistrusted his promises, and experience showed that they were justified in so doing. Mahomet addressed himself to the Greek noble families and endeavoured to persuade them to return to the city. He publicly promised that all who came back and could prove their nobility and descent should be treated with even more distinction than had been shown to them under the emperor and should continue to enjoy the same rank as before. Relying on this promise, a number of them returned, on the feast of St. Peter. They, however, paid dearly for their credulity. Either the promise which had been given was of the hasty, spasmodic kind which has often characterised the orders of most of the Ottoman sultans and was repented of, or it had been given treacherously with no idea of its being kept. The heads of the nobles soon sullied the steps of Mahomet's court.[1] The repeopling which could not be done by persuasion was attempted more successfully by force.

In 1458, while Mahomet was attacking Corinth his army made a raid in the neighbouring country and brought in more than three thousand prisoners, men, women and children. These were sent to settle outside the walls of Constantinople, on the lands which had been devastated before the siege. In the following year the sultan returned from the Peloponnesus. The artisans whom he had captured were settled in the capital ; the remainder in the neighbourhood. In the same year he ordered that the most well-to-do inhabitants of Amastris on the Black Sea, including all the Armenian merchants, should be sent to the capital. It was partly to employ the workmen thus brought together that he ordered the construction of the mosque which bears his name.

---

[1] *Commentari di Theo. Spandugino Cantacusino.*

In 1460 he published an Iradè inviting all who had ever lived in the capital to return. There were many fugitives, says Critobulus, at Adrianople, Philippopolis, Brousa, and elsewhere, who had been sold as slaves or had left the city before the siege : learned, noble, and industrious men who by their ability had already gained positions of comfort and even of wealth. All these, therefore, he transported to the capital, giving some of them honour, others permission to build where they liked, and to others again all that was needed to establish themselves. He transported to the capital all the inhabitants of the two Phocaeas. He sent his admiral in chief with forty ships into the Archipelago for the same purpose. The people of Thasos and of Samothracia were carried *en masse* to the capital.[1]

[1] All these illustrations are from book ii. of Critobulus.

CHAPTER XVIII

CAPTURE OF CONSTANTINOPLE A SURPRISE TO EUROPE;
CONQUEST OF TREBIZOND ; SUMMARY OF ITS HISTORY.
CHARACTER AND CONDUCT OF MAHOMET: AS CON-
QUEROR ; HE INCREASES TURKISH FLEET ; AS ADMINIS-
TRATOR ; AS LEGISLATOR ; HIS RECKLESSNESS OF
HUMAN LIFE ; AS STUDENT ; WAS HE A RELIGIOUS
FANATIC ? SUMMARY.

THE capture of Constantinople sent an electric shock
throughout Europe. The great achievement of the young
sultan came as an almost incredible surprise. During the
whole subsequent course of his reign the greatest question
of interest in the West was, What progress is Mahomet
making? Menaces of what he intended to do, reports of
what he had done, occupied the attention of all. As with
the capture of the Queen City the Greek empire came to an
end, it is not my purpose to endeavour to tell the story of
his subsequent life and conquests. But as he figured so
largely on the European stage, and as his exploits and
administration firmly established the Turks in Europe, it is
desirable to indicate some of the principal events of his
reign and to sketch the leading features of his character.

Conquest
of Trebi-
zond.

His successes as a soldier were many and important
One of the first of his conquests was to put an end to the
empire of Trebizond. As its history and decay played an
unimportant part in the destruction of the Greek empire, i
has been unnecessary to give an account of this pretentiousl:
named State. It had occupied a narrow strip of land along
the southern shore of the Black Sea, of varying length, from
a point near Batoum towards the west, on one occasion

stretching to within sight of the Bosporus, but never including either Amassus or Sinope. Its population, though Greek-speaking, was mostly composed of Lazes.

When the Latin invaders were on the point of capturing Constantinople, two young Greek princes had escaped to Trebizond, defeated the Byzantine governor, and one of them, named Alexis, was acclaimed emperor. He took the title of Grand Comnenus and Emperor of the Faithful Romans. It seemed for a short while as if he, instead of Theodore Lascaris at Nicaea, might take the lead of the Greek peoples, and indeed Theodore had to arrange with the sultan of Konia—or, as he called himself, of Roum, that is, of the Romans—to prevent Alexis from attempting to extend his territory to Nicaea. But the power of the Trebizond empire did not increase, although the city from which it took its name became large, wealthy, and populous. Even before 1228 it had become tributary to the Seljuk sultan and so continued till 1280. A series of more or less uninteresting and incompetent emperors and empresses continued to hold a semi-independent position, amid alternate intrigues and struggles with Turkoman and Turkish tribes, and fierce fights with the Genoese, until the advent of Timour. The emperor of Trebizond, as in later years he called himself, consented to become the vassal of this great leader, and agreed to send twenty ships to join a like number which the Greek emperor was to prepare at Constantinople to attack Bajazed. The defeat of the Ilderim at Angora rendered such joint action unnecessary. When Timour retired, Trebizond languished until its territory was little more than a small district around the capital. It was first attacked by the Ottoman Turks in 1442, and made a successful defence. After the capture of Constantinople, the emperor John consented to become a tributary prince of Mahomet, but shortly afterwards attempted to unite the emirs of Sinope and Caramania and the Christian kings of Georgia and Lesser Armenia in a league to attack his suzerain. Before anything could be done, John died, and when Mahomet, in 1461, having subjugated the Greeks in Morea, turned his attention to Trebizond,

Summary of its history

no allies were ready to aid David, the new emperor. A great expedition of sixty thousand cavalry and eighty thousand infantry was led by Mahomet himself to David's capital, while a large fleet co-operated with the army. The alternative was given of massacre or submission. The emperor surrendered and Trebizond became part of the Ottoman empire. A large party of the population was subsequently sent to repeople Constantinople.[1]

Mahomet as con-queror.   Mahomet's biographers claim that he conquered two empires and seven kingdoms : those of Serbia, Bosnia, Albania, Moldavia, Morea, Caramania, and Kastemouni. The two empires may be admitted ; the seven kingdoms can only be said—even where they are entitled to take rank as kingdoms—to have been conquered by Mahomet, with the reserve that he reaped where his ancestors had sown. But with this proviso the statement is sufficiently near the truth to be accepted.

If his successes had been equal to his ambition or to his designs he might fairly be classed with the world's great military leaders. He fought, however, with far less success than Alexander, who was his great exemplar, and almost always with the advantage of overwhelming numbers. His progress was checked by the courage of John Hunyadi and the Hungarians. Scanderbeg continued for twenty years, with comparatively few followers and small resources, to wage guerilla warfare against him, and the knights of St. John triumphantly repelled his attacks upon Rhodes. Nor was he able to defeat the power of Persia.

Mahomet's wars were essentially those of conquest. He required no pretext for making war. It was sufficient that he wished to extend his own territory. His warlike nation

---

[1] Fallmerayer's *Geschichte des Kaiserthums von Trapezunt.* Not only is this work the great authority for the history of Trebizond, but Fallmerayer himself brought to light the most valuable materials for its history. He was the discoverer in Venice of the chronicles of Panaretos in the library of Cardinal Bessarion. Since Fallmerayer wrote, the MS. of Critobulus has been discovered. In book iv. a full account is given of the capture of Trebizond and the treatment of its emperors. Finlay's *History of Trebizond* is very good, but he wrote without seeing the account of Critobulus.

MAHOMET THE CONQUEROR.

From a painting formerly in the Sultan's palace at Top Capou at Constantinople, and attributed to Gentile Bellini. I am unaware by whom the photograph
was taken or where the original picture now is.

MAHOMET II.

From a medallion in the British Museum, which, according to Sir A. H. Layard, was probably executed by Gentile Bellini from the portrait painted in 1480 by Bellini himself.   The portrait is in the possession of Lady Layard, and an engraving of it is given in Sir A. H. Layard's edition of Kugler's 'Italian Schools of Painting' (vol. i. p. 304).

Though the two portraits are surrounded with very similar and beautiful arabesque arches and evidently are of the same person, that of Sir Henry Layard differs from the one reproduced on the opposite page in showing a more receding chin and a thinner beard than even the medallion.   The name of Gentile Bellini appears on both paintings.

during the first years after the conquest of the city was
always ready to aid in the execution of his designs against
other states. His energy and ambition allowed him little
time for rest and as the years went by wore out the strength
and even the patience of his followers. He kept his army—
which included almost every available man of the Turkish
race under his sway—occupied almost continually for nearly
twelve years after 1453, until at length, worn out with long
marches, weakened by constant labour, and having sacrificed
their goods, their horses, and their health for their master,
his soldiers, including the very Janissaries themselves, became discontented and clamoured for rest. Critobulus, who
makes this statement, records that an expedition into Illyria
was reluctantly postponed because Mahomet was compelled
to recognise at last that rest was absolutely necessary for
troops who had not known it for years.

From the moment of his conquest of the city he saw the
importance of keeping up a strong fleet. He maintained
and enlarged that which he had prepared for the blockade
of the city, and was at all times able, upon any sign of revolt,
to send a sufficient force by sea to maintain his rule. Indeed,
it may be said that once he had imposed his peace upon all
the districts round the Marmora and the Aegean, his fleet
enabled him to preserve it. With its aid, too, he succeeded
in exacting tribute from Egypt and Syria. Critobulus notes
that his master, having observed that the Venetians and
Genoese had gained their success in the Mediterranean by
means of large ships, constructed a number of new vessels
which were able to cope with them, and raised a sufficient
number of oarsmen to resist their attacks on the Turkish
coasts.

*He im-
proves
Turkish
fleet.*

Nor was Mahomet less active in improving the civil
organisation of his government. We have already seen that
before his conquest of the city, he commenced reforms in the
collection of the taxes. He dismissed incompetent pashas
and replaced them by others distinguished by their intelligence, their honesty, and their military capacity, for it
must always be remembered that militarism was and is the

*Mahomet
as re-
former of
the ad-
ministra-
tion.*

vital part of Turkish administration. Critobulus claims that the aim he had most completely at heart was to secure the best and the most just administration possible. The finances of the country he found in the utmost disorder. One third of the revenue was wasted, and this in a short time he made available for his own purposes. He continued his reform in the system of tax-collecting and, while thus increasing the revenue, took care to strike terror into the farmers of the taxes and all those whose duty it was to see that money entered the public treasury and that it was not plundered when it got there. Both in the government of the army and in the civil administration Mahomet bestowed the utmost care upon details, and trusted nothing to his subordinates until he had seen every preparation made for a satisfactory control.

Mahomet as law-giver.

The Turks speak of Mahomet as the Canouni or Law-giver, and the epithet is deserved. But while his edicts in aid of better organisation and less corrupt administration are deservedly praised by them, it is as the lawgiver that we come upon one of the darkest sides of his character. Von Hammer points out that the Turkish histories of many centuries furnish examples of political fratricides, but that it was reserved to the law of Mahomet the Second to legitimise the slaughter of younger brothers by the Ottoman sultans.[1] His predecessors had practised the crime. Mahomet not only followed their example but made the practice legal.

His reck-lessness of human life.

Connected with all his achievements there is the stain of blood. Many contemporary writers speak of him as a monster of cruelty. We may discredit the statement that he caused Christians to be put to death while he feasted, as insufficiently proved. But even Critobulus, who is usually an apologist, has, as a faithful historian, to speak of his cruel deeds. When Castrion surrendered, he killed every man in the garrison and sent the women and children into slavery. When Gardikion submitted, its defenders were treated in a similar manner.[2] Von Hammer dismisses as unfounded the story of Mahomet having the bodies of fourteen pages ripped open to find who had eaten a poor woman's cucumbers,

---

[1] iii. 302.   [2] Crit. bk. iii. ch. xxi. and xxii.

and the singularly dramatic story of the slaughter of Irene in order to demonstrate to his troops that though he loved the most beautiful woman in the world he was yet master of himself, justly remarking that the massacre of garrisons faithful to their trust, the execution of the members of the imperial family of Trebizond and of the king of Bosnia, cry sufficiently aloud without need of exaggeration. Resistance to his lusts or even to his lawful desires was punished relentlessly by death.[1] He executed his grand vizier Mahmoud because of his independence. He tortured and then put to death his old tutor and vizier Halil Pasha. He sawed five hundred prisoners in halves whom he had captured in Achaia. 'He was more cruel than Nero, and delighted in bloodshed,' says Tetaldi. Probably it would be impossible to find a contemporary writer who does not employ similar language. Many of his acts are without the shadow of excuse. They are the result of wild impulse which had never been under control, and deserve to be classed as wanton cruelties inflicted by a man who was reckless of human suffering. There are others which may be put down to what he probably regarded as the exigencies of his position. If in his opinion the assassination of a brother, the slaughter of a great number of his enemies in war, and the murder of those of his subjects who opposed him were necessary to the accomplishment of his objects, he never hesitated. Like other great military rulers, Caesar yesterday, Napoleon to-day, Mahomet regarded men as so many counters, to be kept so long as they were useful in his game, to be cast aside when no longer wanted. Belonging to a family accustomed to absolute rule of the Eastern type, to a race which has never valued life as against military success, and having been reared amid dangers where his struggle for power and even for life was almost daily, he swept away every man who opposed him. His enemies would have dealt hardly with him, and he never appeared to doubt that he was justified in dealing hardly with or getting rid of them. It was part of the game of war. *Vae victis!* And yet this

---

[1] Von Hammer, iii. 232.

man seems occasionally to have sympathised with the
suffering he had caused, and even to have exercised rigorous
justice. Critobulus, after recounting many cruel deeds, adds
that Mahomet showed special kindness towards prisoners of
war, and whenever in his rides through the city he encountered
them would stop his horse and give generously to all.
According to Cantemir and other Turkish historians, this
monster of cruelty and legaliser of fratricide bowstrung his
eldest son for having violated the wife of another.

Mahomet
as student.

It is a welcome change to turn from Mahomet the blood-
drinker, the lawgiver who first made the horrible practice
legal which was to shock Europe during nearly four
centuries, to Mahomet the student, the patron and
companion of scholars and artists, and the man who was
interested in questions of religion. He was a linguist and
knew, says Phrantzes,[1] five languages besides his own—
Greek, Latin, Arabic, Chaldean, and Persian. His favourite
study was history. The achievements of Alexander the
Great had filled the world from India westward with his
fame, had been the subject of romance, and had caused his
name to be regarded throughout the East as that of an
almost supernatural hero. Alexander figures constantly in
the lives of the Turkish sultans as a fascinating historical
figure. As late as 1621 a French writer notes that the then
reigning sultan while at dinner had the history of his predecessors read over to him or the Life of Alexander the Great.[2]
But upon none had the memory of the Macedonian made so
great an impression as upon Mahomet. Alexander was the
leader whose career was to be imitated and whose conquests
were to be rivalled. His contemporaries frequently compare
the two men. 'It was,' says Critobulus, 'the Alexanders
and the Pompeys, Caesar and the like rulers, whom
Mahomet proposed to himself as models.' 'This young
Alexander,' says Ducas, referring to the transport of part of
Mahomet's fleet over land, 'has surpassed the former one,
and has led his ships over the hills as over the waves.' 'He
wished,' says Tetaldi, 'to conquer the whole world, to see

[1] i. 32.   [2] *Voyage au Levant par ordre du roy*, 1630.

more than Alexander and Caesar or any other valiant man
who has ever lived.' Phrantzes describes him as a careful
reader of the Lives of Alexander, of Octavius Caesar, of the
Great Constantine, and of Theodosius.

Mahomet had continued from his boyhood to show his
interest in studies, not only by his own reading but by
welcoming other students, 'for he was constantly striving
to acquire those arts by which he should excel his predecessors and extend the bounds of his kingdom as far as
possible.' 'He gathered to himself virtuous and learned
men,' says Phrantzes. He was, says Lonicerus,[1] an
admirer of intellect and of the arts. He caused learned
men and skilled artists to be brought to him at great
expense. He employed Bellini,[2] a Venetian, and other
artists, and loaded them with gifts. Virtue strove with vice
within him. He had read all the history, says Critobulus,
that was accessible to him in Arabic and Persian, and such
Greek literature as had been translated into either of these
languages, including Aristotle and the writings of the Stoics,
and was skilled in astrology and in mathematics. A few
years after he became sultan a certain George Ameroukes is
found attached to his suite, a man described by Critobulus[3]
as learned in philosophy, natural science, and mathematics.
Mahomet made much of him, and called him often to
discuss philosophical questions. Not a day passed without
interviews with him or with other learned men attached to
the court. In matters relating to foreign countries he was
especially curious. Having met with the geographical
writings of Ptolemy, he not only had them translated into
Arabic, but charged George to make a map of the world
with all the indications that he could give of the various
countries, rivers, lakes, mountains, cities, and distances ; for,
says Critobulus, ' the science of geography appeared to him
necessary and most useful.' [4] In the course of his expedition

---

[1] *Turcorum Origo*, p. 22.

[2] This was Gentile Bellini, who arrived in Constantinople in 1479 and left at
the end of 1480. He was sent, at the request of the sultan, by the Doge of
Venice.

[3] Crit. bk. iv. ch. ix.   [4] *Ibid*. bk. v. ch. x.

to reduce Mitylene and Lemnos he visited the ruins of Troy and the traditional tombs of Achilles and Ajax and admired the good fortune of the heroes who had a poet like Homer to commemorate their deeds. 'It is said,' cautiously remarks his biographer, 'that he believed that God had charged him to be the avenger of the ancient city.' [1] He frequently called the patriarch, the learned Gennadius, and discussed with him questions of theology.

Was Mahomet a religious fanatic?

Mahomet cannot justly be represented as a religious fanatic. He of course conformed to the practices of Islam, built many mosques, and did nothing to show irreverence for the teaching of the Prophet. He was possibly in his youth a devout believer in the tenets of Islam. But it is difficult to believe that a man who conversed freely with Gennadius on the difference between Christianity and his own religion, and who had paid as much attention as he had paid to Greek and Arabian philosophy, should be a fanatic. Mahomet's most recent Turkish biographer claims that he was tolerant and alleges as a reason for this statement that he did not follow the example of the Arab conquerors and put all to the sword who did not accept Islam. The more fanatical Mahometans probably urged him to take this course. [2] The hope of plunder and the value of captives as slaves probably furnished a more effective argument against general extermination.

Moreover, Mahomet had need of an industrious population, not only for the repeopling of the capital but to furnish a revenue.

His subjects, even of both religions, regarded him as a Gallio, or as a man of no religion. [3] The statements that in private he branded the Prophet as a robber and impostor, or that he was half converted to Christianity by Gennadius and that shortly before his death he became a great worshipper of relics and burned candles before them,

---

[1] Crit. bk. v. ch. xi. It is possible that as some of the Latin writers spoke of the Turks as Teucri, in the belief that they were the descendants of the Trojans, Mahomet may have been under the same illusion.

[2] Les Sultans Ottomans, par Halil Ganem, p. 129 (Paris, 1901).

[3] Chalcondylas.

may be dismissed as not supported by trustworthy evidence.[1] The sovereign's readiness even to discuss Christianity and speak with unbelievers upon questions of philosophy and religion would be certain to obtain for him the reputation of atheist from the ignorant among his own people ; for to the faithful Mahometan no other religions need be discussed : they exist only for condemnation ; to study them is to express a doubt upon the all-sufficiency of the teaching of the Koran, and a doubt on such a subject is treason to the faith. But at least such accusations do not point towards fanaticism. The man who by one party is claimed as almost persuaded to be a Christian and is regarded by the other as an atheist or at least a disloyal believer in Islam can hardly have been a religious persecutor. It may be true that after conversing with the patriarch or with any other unbeliever he went through the prescribed forms of washing, but if he wished to preserve the loyalty of his subjects it was necessary for him to observe such formalities of purification. He was at the head of the Turkish nation, that is, of an armed camp, a nation in the field whose chief if not sole bond of unity was, as it still remains, the belief in the prophet-hood of the founder of Islam. Nearly all his soldiers held the one great creed and went into battle with shouts of ' Allah ! ' and ' Mahomet ! ' They believed, as the followers of the Prophet have always fervently believed, that death on the battle-field fighting for Islam is the shortest road to Paradise and the Houris. The Turks were ready to obey and endure unto death for the sake of the sovereign whom Allah had placed at their head. Some of them were as full of religious enthusiasm as crusaders, as confident that they were working for God as Cromwell's Ironsides, and as fanatic as a grossly ignorant army can be which believes itself to be immeasurably superior to the enemy because, on the one hand, it possesses the true faith, while, on the other, the enemy, more learned in the world's despicable science and philosophy falsely so called, is in the

[1] These and many other fictions of the like kind come from Spandugino and Sansovino.

abysmal darkness of unbelief. The support of such men was not to be risked by any nonconformity with the rites which are the outward signs of Islam. Mahomet would have been of all rulers the most blind to his own interest if he had derided their beliefs.

But though Mahomet was the leader of a nation containing many fanatics, there is nothing to show that he shared their fanaticism. If he appealed to it, it was because it gave force to his army. He was no more inclined to be a fanatic himself than was Napoleon to be a democrat when he called upon his troops to fulfil their mission of carrying democratic principles to England and other countries assumed to be suffering under despotic rule. In a different age and under different circumstances Mahomet might have been a thoughtful student, or an excellent civil administrator, but it is difficult to conceive that he could ever have been a religious persecutor.

He remained all his life a student, desirous of learning, but he was at the same time a man of energy, a successful general, and a good administrator. He was without high ideals of life, but capable of spasmodic kindness, a man not given to sensual pleasures—in his later years at least—sober, intolerant of drunkenness, seeking his pleasure in glory.[1] He appears to me essentially a lonely man; one who took each man's censure but reserved his judgment; one who, in his own phrase, would pluck out a hair from his beard if he believed that it knew his designs. He was too suspicious and too highly placed to have friends. He was supremely selfish and only considered himself bound to respect his promise when it suited his purpose to do so. Circumstances compelled him to be a soldier, and his great natural abilities

---

[1] Zorzo Dolfin (p. 985) says: 'E homo non dedito a libidine, sobrio, in tempo del ramadan non vol aldir sobrieta; a nulla volupta, a nulla piacea e dedito saluo a gloria.' This is in striking contradiction with Barbaro's account, which in describing Mahomet says, 'Che a un momento importantissimo alla vigilia della gran bataglia s'inebriò col capedan pascia secondo la sua usanza.' Barbaro's narrative is written immediately after the capture of the city, and, as usual, he is careless of the accusations which he brings against the Turks or Genoese.

made him a successful one, but his ambition, which was spasmodically great—which meditated the conquest of Naples, an expedition against Rome, and other conquests, as stages in his great design of conquering the world [1]—wanted pertinacity and was joined to an emotional, almost a sentimental, nature. He relieved his loneliness and friendlessness by hard work, study, and the companionship of artists and learned men.

Cantemir calls him the most glorious prince who ever occupied the Ottoman throne, but adds that he did not listen to the voice of conscience, and that he broke his word without any hesitation when it seemed politic so to do. Chalcondylas speaks of him as great in intellect, in conquest, and in cruelty. Halil Ganem says, with truth, that by his military exploits Mahomet occupies the first place in the Ottoman annals. He impartially states also that he shed abundance of blood to secure peaceful possession of the throne, and for his pleasure. 'To shed blood became for this grand monarch a function which he exercised with an incredible *maestria.*' [2] His long series of victorious conquests and especially his success in the capture of the city have caused him to be known in Ottoman history as the Fetieh or Conqueror.

In forming a judgment upon the character of a ruler whose reign marks an epoch of importance in the world's history, it is needful to take account of his life and his acts in their entirety : to ask what the man accomplished and with what means ; what were his ideals and how far he realised them. We may recognise that Cromwell was a great ruler notwithstanding Drogheda, and that William the Third was a great statesman in spite of Glencoe, even supposing that he fully approved of that massacre. Taking a broad view of the character of Mahomet, we may observe that his conquests were made by means of overwhelming numbers, that his army from its composition was the most mobile in existence, and that its greatest success was but the final act in a series which had been

---

[1] Zorzo Dolfin, p. 936.   [2] *Les Sultans Ottomans*, pp. 150 and 125.

gained by his predecessors. But while giving due importance to these considerations, it yet remains true that his
reign marks an epoch, not only of Turkish history, where its
influence is the most conspicuous, but in that of Europe
generally. To him more than to any other ruler the organisation of the Turks as a governing power is due. To him
must also be credited the creation of Turkey as a European
State. Subsequent sultans built on the foundations which
he had laid. It is also not too much to say that none of his
successors have done so much to give orderly government to
the Turkish race as Mahomet. But for the fact that the
influence of Moslemism strangles the moral and intellectual
growth of the Turkish people, the rule of a few more sultans
possessed of the like capacity and determination to secure
strong, orderly, and even just government might possibly
have placed Turkey among the civilised nations.

CHAPTER XIX

DISPERSION OF GREEK SCHOLARS, AND THEIR INFLUENCE
UPON REVIVAL OF LEARNING ; GREEK A BOND OF UNION
AMONG PEOPLES OF EMPIRE ; DISAPPEARANCE OF BOOKS
AFTER LATIN CONQUEST ; DEPARTURE OF SCHOLARS TO ITALY
BEGINS AFTER 1204 ; THEIR PRESENCE STIMULATES REVIVAL
OF LEARNING ; ENTHUSIASM AROUSED IN ITALY FOR STUDY
OF GREEK ; STUDENTS FROM CONSTANTINOPLE EVERYWHERE
WELCOMED ; INCREASED NUMBERS LEAVE AFTER MOSLEM
CONQUEST ; RENAISSANCE LARGELY AIDED BY GREEK
STUDIES ; MOVEMENT PASSES INTO NORTHERN EUROPE ;
MSS. TAKEN FROM CONSTANTINOPLE.

AGAINST the manifold evils resulting from the destruction of
the empire by the Turks must be set off the dispersion of
Greek scholars throughout Italy and the consequent spread
of a knowledge of Greek literature throughout Europe.

The Greeks of Athens and others belonging to the *Influence of Hellenism upon empire.* Hellenic race continued during the whole period of the existence of the empire to exercise a powerful influence upon the thought of the empire, upon its government, and upon the Church. At all times there were two influences striving against each other for leadership, one Asiatic and the other Hellenic. Without entering upon the interesting question how far these different and often hostile tendencies left their trace upon the Church and government, it is sufficient for my present purpose to note that the Greek influence prevailed for centuries and, aided by the commercial spirit of the Greek race, which had given them the leading part in the trade of the empire and hellenised every port on the Aegean and the Marmora, succeeded in causing Greek speech to become the general language of the Church and empire.

The Greeks who were of Hellenic blood had never forgotten their own language or their classical writers. Others who had adopted their language came in time to consider themselves of Greek descent and gloried in the writings of ancient Greece, as if they were the works of their ancestors. Language and literature led to the belief in a common origin. Just as Shakespeare and the English Bible are a bond of union among English-speaking people, so the possession of the Greek classics, of the New Testament, and the Liturgies of the Church knit together the various Greek-speaking peoples under the empire. The common people learned to love the old Greek stories, to treasure the beautiful half religious, half mythical tales, the exploits recorded by Homer, no less than the simple mixture of inspiriting and patriotic historical narrative with the garrulous and ever pleasant stories of Herodotus. A long series of successive generations were nursed upon them, as they have indeed continued to be down to the present day.[1]

Greek, a bond of union.

There thus arose a traditional, historic, and patriotic feeling which bound together all Greek-speaking peoples, whether actually descendants from the Hellenic race or not. It existed in all sections of the community and led to a pride of race which has rarely been equalled. One curious illustration of the affection which existed for their reputed ancestors is noted by Dean Stanley and other writers. In mediaeval pictures still remaining in the monasteries of

---

[1] The fascination of the old Greek stories still continues even among the poorest Greeks, and it is astonishing how generally they are known. I have often heard old Greek women, unable to read or write, tell children Greek *paramythia* which have evidently been handed down by oral tradition. A few years ago, in travelling among the mountains of Bithynia, I came on Easter Monday to a Greek village, far remote from any other, and away from all lines of communication, where they were performing a miracle-play. The villagers, dressed in their best, were all present as actors or spectators. The play itself was a curious mixture of incidents in the life of Christ and of others—and these formed the largest part—from Greek mythology. No one knew anything of its origin, and all the information obtainable was that the play had always been performed on Easter Monday.

Mount Athos and elsewhere, the originals of which were painted many centuries ago, Pericles and Leonidas and other great men of their race are introduced among the occupants of heaven.

The wealthier classes, the scholars, the nobles and their wives, down to the last period of the existence of the empire aimed at speaking and writing Greek with elegance and purity. They recognised that they were the heirs of literary treasures which were greater than those possessed by any other European people. They realised that in the long series of Greek authors from classical times down through nearly two thousand years to the period in which they were living they had an historical literature longer and more complete than any race known to them.

There had been indeed dark periods in the literary history of the empire as in that of other countries. In Constantinople during the four centuries which preceded the Turkish conquest, though to a less extent than in Western Europe, learning and literature had been largely neglected. After the time of the great scholar Photius (patriarch of Constantinople between 877 and 885) few works of importance had been produced. The students of Constantinople had come to take but small interest in any study which did not concern theology, law, or history. Possibly they ceased even to guard the treasures they possessed with the like care which their predecessors had shown. Many valuable manuscripts disappeared. The Latin conquerors are admittedly responsible for the destruction of a large number of books. In the *Myriobiblion* of Photius, an abridgment of two hundred and eighty authors which is rich in extracts from historians, he gives us all we possess of certain writers. But two thirds of the works he enumerates have been lost since the time of the Fourth Crusade and will probably never be recovered.[1] No writer quotes any of the lost authors after 1204.[2]

Disappearance of books after 1204.

[1] See Aristarchi's (the Grand Logothete) papers on Photius in the *Transactions of the Greek Syllogos of Constantinople*, and two volumes edited by him of that patriarch's sermons and homilies, published 1901.

[2] Heeren, in his *Essai sur les Croisades*, p. 413, quoted in Hallam's *Middle*

D D

Service
rendered
by empire
in pre-
serving
Greek lan-
guage and
literature.

But beneath the cloud of ignorance which had descended during the Middle Ages not only upon the empire but upon all Europe, there were always in Constantinople a considerable number of scholars and students. These men kept alive the love of Greek learning. While none of them produced any work which deserves to be classed as literature of a high order, they rendered immense service by preserving that which existed. The lawyers and clergy had greatly assisted in maintaining the vigour and clearness of Greek speech. The knowledge and practice of law in a form not materially different from that in which it had been left by the great jurists of the sixth and seventh centuries furnished a field for the exercise of the most acute intellects, and trained men in precision of thought and exactitude of expression. The legal maxims of the lawyers of the New Rome in their Latin form had given a set of principles of law for all Europe, and still claim the admiration of those who take pleasure in lucidity and epigram. The dissensions and heresies in the Church in like manner contributed to the use of Greek in a correct form. Exact definition in matters of dogma was a necessity, and incidentally helped to preserve Greek in its ancient form. The writings of theologians were judged by a well-educated caste which required that they should approximate to the language which to them was accepted as a model.

The Histories of Nicetas, of Anna Comnena, of George Acropolitas, of Pachymer, and of others down to Critobulus, which help to fill up the period between the eleventh and sixteenth centuries, are all written in respectable Greek and show a feeling for literary effect which recalls, though it too often seeks to imitate, the writings of the Greek classical historians. The education of the higher clergy was in Greek philosophy and theology ; and schools for the study of these subjects continued in existence down to the final conquest. The remark of Gibbon is probably true that 'more books and more knowledge were included within the

Ages, ascribes the loss of all the authors missing from the library of Photius to the Latin capture. Probably the statement is too sweeping.

walls of Constantinople than could be found dispersed over the extensive countries of the West.' [1]

While not losing sight of the fact that the Greek Church from the time of Justinian had exercised influence in Venice and Calabria, it may yet be stated that the departure of Greek scholars from Constantinople for the West began with the Latin conquest. Italy, on account of her commerce with the East and the intimate relations which had existed between Venice and other cities and the New Rome before the Latin occupation, was the country to which most of the fugitives turned their steps. Venice, owing to the part she took in the Latin conquest of the city, had become Queen of the Seas, and naturally received at first the largest contingent. But the supremacy of Venice was now shared by various rivals, and Greek students found their way to other cities. *Departure of Greek scholars for Italy*

Greek was still spoken in Calabria, where the liturgy was said in that language and where, indeed, the language is still spoken,[2] but with this exception nowhere else in Italy had any knowledge of Greek been preserved. Boccaccio asserts that even the Greek characters were unknown.[3] In the troubles which existed during the century and a half preceding the Moslem conquest the number of exiles increased. Many priests and monks were glad to escape from the disorders in their native land by seeking refuge in Italy.

While these voluntary exiles contributed largely to awaken an interest in the study of Greek, it must be noted that their arrival in Italy was at an opportune period. Gibbon remarks that in 'the resurrection of science Italy was the first that cast away her shroud.' The study of the Latin classical authors had already been recommenced. There had been a gradual awakening from the stupor, the indifference, and, in spite of a few individual exceptions, the *aids revival of learning in Italy.*

[1] Gibbon, vol. vii. 116.

[2] See H. F. Tozer's article on 'The Greek-speaking Population of Southern Italy,' in *Journal of Hellenic Studies*, x. p. 99.

[3] 'Nemo est qui Graecas literas novit.' Quoted in Hodius, *De Graecis illustribus*, p. 3.

deep contented ignorance of the Middle Ages. Antiquity as represented by its architecture, its sculpture, and its literature, was now to furnish the ideal of the Renaissance. A great movement arose for the reproduction of classical architecture. But contemporary with it came the study of Latin classics. Virgil had never been altogether neglected and had, indeed, been regarded with a superstitious reverence. He was now glorified and 'imitated. Other Latin authors were diligently studied, and then the natural result followed. The students of Cicero and Virgil began to look for their models to the authors whom the Romans had admired and had imitated. The study of the great Latin classics inevitably called for a knowledge of those written in Greek. The leaders in the revival of the study of the Latin authors were those who led the way also in the study of Greek. Petrarch and Boccaccio shared with Dante not merely the honour of forming Italian as a modern language but that also of leading the way to the appreciation of Greek learning by the scholars of Western Europe. Greek scholars were welcomed. We have seen that Barlaam, a Calabrian by birth, the short, eager, stammering controversialist, whose bitter tongue, learning, and subtilty made him the leader in the angry controversy in Constantinople regarding the Inner Light in the time of Cantacuzenus, was sent on an embassy to Italy by the emperor. Cantacuzenus, though favouring the other side, attests the learning and ability of Barlaam and his acquaintance with Plato and Aristotle. At Avignon, he was persuaded by Petrarch to act as instructor in Greek, and with him the poet [1] read the works of Plato. Petrarch, though his acquaintance with Greek did not enable him to read the manuscript of Homer with which he had been presented, yet speaks of the gift in terms which show his admiration of Greek literature to have been profound and enthusiastic. It is recorded of him that he was able to select the greatest of the Greek poets by listening to the reading of their works although he was unacquainted with their language.

[1] Hodius, *De Graecis illust.*

A few years afterwards, in 1360, Boccaccio, for twenty years the friend of Petrarch, persuaded a certain Leontius of Salonica, a pupil of Barlaam, to give public lectures upon Homer at Florence. Leontius lodged in the house of Boccaccio, was paid by the republic of Florence, and was probably the first professor of Greek in Italy or any Western country. His appearance was against him, for he was ill clad, had an ugly face, with long unkempt hair and beard, and a sullen manner. But all was excused on account of his knowledge of the Greek language and his delight in its literature. His public reading of Homer pleased the Florentines, and Boccaccio obtained a prose translation of the Iliad and Odyssey made by his *protégé*. At the end of three years the lecturer resigned his post and went to Constantinople. Boccaccio himself not only learned Greek but became a lecturer throughout Italy upon its literature and helped to create an enthusiasm for its study.

Manuel Chrysoloras, about 1366 or the following year, after he had failed in his mission from the Emperor Manuel to France and England to obtain aid against the Turks, returned to Florence, the centre of the new intellectual movement in Italy, to teach the Greek language and explain its literature. His lectures were followed with delight. Boys and old men were among his audience. The study of Greek became the fashion. One of his pupils, Leonard Aretinus, who subsequently became the secretary of four successive Popes, tells how his soul was inflamed with the love of letters and how on hearing Chrysoloras it was a hard struggle to decide whether he should continue the study of law or be introduced to Homer, Plato, Demosthenes, and those poets, philosophers, and orators who are celebrated by every age as the great masters of human science. He gave himself up to Chrysoloras, and so strong, he declares, was his passion for the new studies that the lessons he imbibed during the day were the constant subject of his nightly dreams.[1]

The school of Chrysoloras was transferred from Florence

Enthusiasm in Italy for study of Greek.

[1] Hodius, p. 28.

to Pavia, thence to Venice, and finally to Rome, and everywhere was well attended. Aroused by his teaching, some of
his pupils went to Constantinople to increase their knowledge
of Greek and to acquire books and manuscripts. In that city,
between 1400 and 1453, the libraries and monasteries were
freely opened to the Italian students. The libraries were still
stocked with the treasures of Greek learning and literature,
and every effort was made by Italian scholars to draw upon
their stores. The trading agents of the Medici and other great
Florentine houses were instructed to buy manuscripts without regard to cost and to send them to Florence. The best
credentials that a young Greek could bring from Constantinople was a manuscript. The discovery of an unknown
manuscript, says Tiraboschi, was regarded almost as the
conquest of a kingdom. Aurispa, one of the pupils of Chrysoloras, returned to Venice in 1423, with two hundred and
thirty-eight volumes.

The Florentines had led the way in the acquisition of
Greek and the collection of manuscripts. The chiefs of
the political factions were also the leaders of intellectual
progress and vied with each other in the noble rivalry of
encouraging the new studies as much as they did in building
libraries. Cosimo, the head of the Medici, carried out a well-
organised plan for encouraging the revived learning. The
leaders of his school in Florence were Niccolo di Nicolo
and Lionardo Bruni, the latter of whom died in 1443. The
chief ecclesiastics were hardly less eager than other scholars.
The popes themselves threw their influence into the new
movement. In 1434 Eugenius the Fourth took up his
residence in Florence when he was expelled from Rome.
Amid his own serious troubles, with refractory Councils, a
hostile capital, the Bogomil and Hussian heresies, and the
ever vexed question of the reunion of the Churches, Eugenius
found time to encourage the study of Greek and to give a
welcome to all Greek priests and students who brought with
them their precious manuscripts. He appreciated the profound learning of Bessarion, archbishop of Nicaea, who had
come to take part in the council at Ferrara and afterwards,

in 1438, at Florence, retained him, as we have seen, after the Council, and made him in the following year cardinal. His patronage of Bessarion is the more remarkable since the Greek was an adherent and exponent of the philosophy of Plato as opposed to that of Aristotle. The other Greek Church dignitaries who were present at the Council, and who were hardly less distinguished, were welcomed as scholars even by those who treated them with scant courtesy as priests of the Orthodox Church. George Gemistos, who adopted the name of Plethon, the founder of a school of Neoplatonism, was one of them, and was popular generally except with the priests. George Scholarius, whom we have seen as the leader of the anti-unionist party in Constantinople, and afterwards as patriarch, Theodore Gaza, Andronicus, Philelphus, and others of repute, were also present. Cosimo de' Medici, through the influence of Gemistos, undertook the task of translating Plato. When Gemistos died, in 1450, in the Morea, his body was taken to Florence as a mark of respect for his services in teaching Greek. The patronage of Eugenius was continued by his successor Nicholas the Fifth, the first ' humanist ' who was made pope and the founder of the Vatican library.

The succession of scholars was kept up by constant new arrivals from Constantinople. Philelphus (or, in its Italianised form, Filelfo), who had married a daughter of Chrysoloras, was for a while secretary to the Venetian bailey in Constantinople, and had gone thither in 1420 mainly in order to study Greek. He was sent as envoy to Murad. He states that, though when in Constantinople he found the Greek of the common people much corrupted, yet that the persons attached to the imperial court spoke the language of Aristophanes and Euripides and of the historians and philosophers of Athens, and that the style of their writing continued to be elaborate and correct. It is especially interesting to note that the most elegant and purest Greek was spoken by the noble matrons.[1] He gained, upon his return to Italy, by his knowledge of Greek and his great

[1] *Philelphi Epis.* in 1451.

learning, a wide reputation and came to be regarded as the most universal scholar of the age. On his visit to Naples, in 1453, he was treated as an equal by princes.[1]   Many other distinguished teachers also during the same period visited Constantinople in pursuit of learning or manuscripts.

But while I have mentioned some of the leading Greeks who contributed before the Moslem conquest to the revival of the study of Greek literature in Italy, it should be noted that there were a host of others less known to fame who sought refuge from the disorders of the empire and found profitable employment in their new homes. Between the death of Petrarch, in 1374, and the conquest of Constantinople, in 1453, Italy had recovered the Greek classics. The intellectual movement caused a great increase in the reproduction of manuscripts. Among the professional copyists, those who could write Greek were specially esteemed and received very large pay.[2]   They did their work so admirably that the new invention of printing with moveable types which came in just about the time of the Moslem conquest of Constantinople was regarded as unsuitable for, or unworthy of, important books. The envoys of Cardinal Bessarion when they saw for the first time a printed book in the house of Constantine Lascaris laughed at the discovery ' made among the barbarians in some German city,' and Ferdinand of Urbino declared that he would have been ashamed to own a printed book.[3]   Notwithstanding this prejudice, Greek books were soon printed in Italy—though, for several years, only in Italy.

Increased number of fugitives after 1453.

The impulse given to the study of Greek by exiles during the half-century, preceding the conquest of Constantinople and by the enthusiasm of a series of scholars from Petrarch and Boccaccio down to 1453, was greatly stimulated by the increase of fugitives consequent on the capture of the city. Among the scholars who made their way westward the best

[1] Filelfo died in 1481. Dethier gives the letter which he wrote to Mahomet praying for the release of his mother-in-law, a prayer which was granted.

[2] *Das Schriftwesen im Mittelalter* (Leipzig, 1875), pp. 392 etc.

[3] Burckhardt's *Renaissance in Italy*, p. 192.

known are Lascaris, who rose to high distinction as a statesman, Callistos, Argyropulos, Gaza, and Chalcondylas. Between 1453 and the end of the century, Greek was studied with avidity. Youths learned to speak as well as to write it.

The arrival of numbers of scholars in Italy shortly before and shortly after 1453 is contemporaneous with the full springtime of the great revival of learning. A series of remarkable efforts had been made to restore ancient Roman and Greek glory as seen in literature and architecture. Learning was regarded as a new and improved evangel. The learning of the ancients was compared with the ignorance of the Churchmen. The new movement marked a great reaction and went to unjustifiable extremes. Some of the advocates for classical influence went to the extent of discarding Christian in favour of Pagan morality. A curious passionate enthusiasm for the classic and venerated past took possession of the most enlightened men in Italy. Paganism, because it was contemporaneous with the classical period, invaded the Church itself. All the architecture, art, and literature of Christianity was bad except in so far as it approximated to Pagan models. The late J. A. Symonds gives a striking illustration of the distance this enthusiasm carried men, in suggesting that Faust may be taken as the symbol of the desire during the Renaissance for classical learning. Faust is content to sell his soul to the devil, but in return he sees Homer and Alexander and obtains Helen as his bride and is satisfied.[1] The careful study of the Latin classics, the marvellous development of painting, architecture, and sculpture, but, above all, the keen interest felt in the newly developed study of Greek with its Platonic

Renaissance in excelsis.

---

[1] Gibbon selects some examples to show the anti-christian character of the classical enthusiasm. (1) At the Council of Florence, Gemistos Pletho said in familiar conversation to George of Trebizond that in a short time mankind would unanimously renounce the Gospel and the Koran for a religion similar to that of the Gentiles (Leo Allatius). (2) Paul II. accused the principal members of the Roman Academy of heresy, impiety, and paganism (Tiraboschi). I suspect the first charge of being grossly exaggerated or invented, but the fact that such a statement could be credited shows to what extent the classical reaction had gone.

philosophy and its new vision of life, were all to produce wonderful fruit within a generation after 1453 and to culminate in Italy in an age of singular intellectual brilliancy.

The study of Greek, at first almost confined to Florence, gradually spread over the whole of the peninsula and finally passed north of the Alps into Germany, where it was taken up with great earnestness. Opposed by the ignorant monks everywhere, and by others who feared that the authority and repute of Latin authors would be terminated, it gradually won its way. In 1458 a Greek professor was appointed in Paris, and one in Rome. Similar professorships were established in most of the Italian universities, following in this respect the example of Florence. In the reign of Henry the Seventh, Oxford consented to receive Grocyn and Linacre as teachers of Greek.[1]

As the zeal for a knowledge of Greek died out in Italy it took deeper root in Germany. Chrysoloras and George of Trebizond were followed by a succession of students, until we meet with the names of Germans and Dutchmen who had gone to Italy to make themselves acquainted with the recovered language and literature. Among them that of Erasmus holds the foremost place.

The movement known as 'The Revival of Learning' was accomplished before the end of the fifteenth century, and all investigators are agreed that it had been very largely contributed to by Greek exiles during the half-century preceding and following the Moslem conquest.

Its paganisation of Christianity proved temporary. But the critical examination of the text of the Greek New Testament and of the Greek Fathers had more durable results. It called attention to the contents of a book which had hitherto been taken as outside controversy. When the study of Greek passed north of the Alps, the examination of the sacred writings was no longer in the hands of *dilettanti*

---

[1] It is curious that the non-progressive party in Oxford, who violently opposed the introduction of the new studies, called themselves Trojans. Roper's *Life of Sir T. More* (ed. Hearne), p. 75. The archbishops of Chios and Pusculus invariably describe the Turks as Teucri.

who looked upon the text with the contempt of scholars disposed to accept paganism as the complement of a higher form of civilisation, and who had no patience with what they regarded as trivialities, but in those of religious and earnest German students, with results, in Erasmus, Luther, Melanchthon, Calvin, and others, the end of which is not yet visible.

The manuscripts which were taken to Italy were the seed destined to yield a rich literary harvest, and their removal from Constantinople was an advantage. It is otherwise with the manuscripts which perished. In 1204 the rude Venetians and Crusaders destroyed great numbers for the sake of their covers.[1] A manuscript which had cost many months of labour, which was written and perhaps illuminated with great skill, was worthy of a costly covering. Some of the bindings were enriched with jewels or with silver or gold clasps and other decorations. The covers rather than the interior were the objects then coveted. There is reason to believe that in the two subsequent centuries thousands of manuscripts disappeared, many possibly stolen or sold for their bindings. But as learning in Constantinople made little progress after the Latin occupation, it is probably to the ignorance of the monks that the disappearance of many of them ought to be attributed. Yet all the evidence which exists shows that an enormous number of manuscripts remained in Constantinople until 1453. We have seen that Ducas declares that during the days following the sack of the city ten volumes on theology and other studies, including Aristotle and Plato, were sold for a small silver coin, and that an incredible number of manuscripts of the Gospels after they had been stripped of their gold and silver bindings were either sold or given away.[2] Critobulus adds that while a very great number of books were burnt or ignominiously trampled to pieces, the larger number were sold at ridiculous sums, not for the sake of their price, but in contemptuous wantonness.[3]

MSS. destroyed or carried away.

---

[1] *Exuviae sacrae Constantinopolitanae.*
[2] Ducas, xliii.
[3] αἱ πλείους δὲ αὐτῶν, οὐ πρὸς ἀπόδοσιν μᾶλλον ἢ ὕβριν &c. Crit. ch. lxii.

I am unaware what authority Hody has for stating[1] that
after the capture of the city a hundred and twenty thousand
books were destroyed, but that the destruction was great
cannot reasonably be doubted.[2]

After the conquest the treasures guarded by the Greek
monks rapidly began to disappear, and especially from the
capital. The octagonal libraries, one of which formed
usually an adjunct to every church, were taken from the
Christians by the victorious Turk and applied to other uses,[3]
and the contents were for the most part dispersed or destroyed. Successive travellers for two centuries found rich
gleanings among them, and the number of manuscripts taken
or sent away suggests that the original stores in Constantinople had been enormous. Janus Lascaris returned to Italy
with two hundred books, eighty of which were as yet unknown in the libraries of Europe. Even as late as the time
of Busbeck, who was ambassador of the Holy Roman
Emperor to Suliman in 1555, he was able to conclude the
announcement of his return home by saying: 'I have whole
wagon-loads, if not ship-loads, of Greek manuscripts, and
about two hundred and forty books which I sent by sea to
Venice. I intend them for Caesar's library. I rummaged
every corner to provide such kind of merchandise as my
final gleaning.'[4]

While it is beyond doubt that the dispersion of students
from Constantinople aided the intellectual movement in

---

[1] Hodius, *De Graecis illustribus*.

[2] Aeneas Sylvius, in 1454, before the diet of Frankfort says : ' Quid de libris
dicam, qui illic erant innumerabiles, nondum Latinis cogniti ? . . . Nunc ergo et
Homero et Pindaro et omnibus illustrioribus poetis secunda mors erit.'

[3] One such at least still remains at Zeirek Jami.

[4] Probably more manuscripts existing as rolls (the original *volumen*) than in
book form have disappeared. The Turks, for example, when they occupied Mount
Athos during the Greek revolution, found the rolls very convenient for making
haversacks. The books have perished mostly from neglect. The discovery by
the present bishop of Ismidt of the *Teaching of the Twelve Apostles* (Διδαχὴ τῶν
δώδεκα ἀποστόλων) in 1883, in the library of a monastery on the Golden Horn
bound up with other manuscripts, the first of which only was indexed, gives
hope that others of value may yet be found. The same remark applies to the
recovery, about six years ago, of the Purple MS. of the Gospels, known techni-
cally as Codex N, and now at St. Petersburg.

Western Europe by introducing new ideals of poetry, of history, and of philosophy, as well as by modifying the conceptions of classical art and architecture,[1] there is no ground for the belief that, if the city had not been captured, Greek. influence would not have made itself felt in the Renaissance. The dispersion hastened the development of a movement which had already begun, awakened a spirit of inquiry, and conducted scholars into new fields of thought earlier than they would have arrived if not thus aided. In this sense, and to this extent, it may be claimed as a beneficial result of the capture of Constantinople.

[1] The influence of Byzantine art upon the West does not fall within the limits of my task. But every one interested in the subject is aware that during some centuries its influence was dominant. In the composition of pictures as well as in their drawing and treatment Western artists for a long time copied those of Constantinople. In painting, Byzantine influence prevailed throughout Italy from Justinian to the middle of the fourteenth century. Giotto, who died in 1336, was, says Kugler, the first to abandon the Byzantine style. In the intervening centuries the monasteries of Constantinople, Salonica, and Mount Athos were the central *ateliers* of painting, and furnished the models for artistic activity to all Europe. The mosaics in the church of San Vitale at Ravenna are magnificent illustrations of what Byzantine art was in the time of Justinian. Those in Hagia Sophia, as well as its general plan of colour-ornamentation, are still unsurpassed. Those of the Kahrié Mosque belonging to the fourteenth century are interesting and show a deep feeling for colour-combination as well as accuracy of drawing. Byzantine architecture in like manner greatly influenced the builders of churches in Western lands. The front view of St. Mark's in Venice in the thirteenth century placed side by side with that of the Kahrié Mosque at the present day shows that the plan of the earlier one was familiar to the architect of the other, and, as has been pointed out by an architect who has made a careful study of the two buildings, when St. Mark's differs from the Kahrié, the difference may be found in details reproduced from another church in Constantinople, that of the Pantocrator. The resemblance between St. Mark's and the Kahrié illustrates Mr. Fergusson's observations on the decoration of the exteriors of Byzantine churches. He points out that while the interior of Hagia Sophia is ' the most perfect and most beautiful church which has yet been erected by any Christian people,' the exterior was never finished (Fergusson's *History of Architecture*, ii. 321). The Kahrié of to-day resembles St. Mark's of the thirteenth century before the exterior casing was added to it.

The question of the influence of Byzantine art and architecture on the West has often been dealt with. For a list of books on the subject see Karl Krumbacher's *Geschichte der byzantinischen Litteratur*, pp. 1124–27.

CPAPTER XX

CONCLUSION : THE CAPTURE EPOCH-MARKING; ALARM IN
EUROPE; DISASTROUS RESULTS; UPON CHRISTIAN SUBJECTS
AND ON EASTERN CHURCHES; DEMORALISATION OF BOTH;
POVERTY THE PRINCIPAL RESULT ; DEGRADATION OF
CHURCHES : TWO GREAT SERVICES RENDERED BY THE
CHURCHES; RESULTS ON TURKS : POWERLESS TO ASSIMI-
LATE CONQUERED PEOPLES OR THEIR CIVILISATION.

THE capture of Constantinople marked an epoch in the
world's history. The dispersion of its scholars and its
treasures of learning leavened Western thought; the lessons
gained from Turkish warfare, from the discipline of the
Janissaries and the mobility of the army were learned by
European states. These results entitle the event to be
regarded as of importance, but another, the conviction,
namely, brought home to Europe of the significance of the
capture, helps still further to entitle it to be regarded as
epoch-marking. The Slavic and Teutonic as well as the
Greek and Latin races had been developing for centuries,
unchecked by any external influence, in the direction of
human progress which we understand by the word ' civilisation.' From Ireland to Constantinople and even to the
banks of the Euphrates all the peoples had accepted
Christianity, a religion which had not been substantially
changed either in dogma or discipline by any of the various
races included in the above area, a religion which had aided
them to develop the morality, the habits and customs, the
thoughts and ideals, which are comprehended in the
modern conception of civilisation. The capture of Constantinople was the intrusion into this Christian area of a foreign

force, with a different morality, and with a tendency hostile to the habits, customs, and aspirations which it encountered. The capture was the latest step in a series of successful efforts to detach a large mass of territory from the area of European civilisation. As large sections of the empire had during successive centuries been lost, Constantinople came to stand in her loneliness as the representative of European ideals of Christianity. When the city was taken, Western statesmen were compelled to recognise that the remaining European area of civilisation was face to face with an Asiatic, a non-Christian, and a necessarily hostile movement. The European peoples, for the first time during centuries, were awakened from their dream of security and saw the possibility of the advance of races professing the creed which had been held by those who in the early days of Islam had utterly rooted out the civilisation and Christianity of North Africa. The shock and alarm were universal.

The military reputation of the Turk was enormously increased by the capture of Constantinople. Hallam justly observes that though the fate of the city had been protracted beyond all reasonable expectation, the actual intelligence operated like that of a sudden calamity. 'A sentiment of consternation, perhaps of self-reproach, thrilled to the heart of Christendom.' [1] Those who knew what the progress of the Turks had been and how numerous and mobile were the hordes at the disposal of the sultan were the most anxious regarding their further progress. The podestà of Pera, writing within a month after the capture, declares that Mahomet intended to become lord of the whole earth and that before two years were over he would go to Rome and 'By God, unless the Christians take care, or there are miracles worked, the destruction of Constantinople will be repeated in Rome.' [2] Other contemporary writers express the like dismay. Aeneas Sylvius, in the presence of the diet of Frankfort, pointed out that by the capture of Constantinople Hungary lay open to the conqueror, and

Alarm created in Europe.

---

[1] Hallam's *Middle Ages*, ch. vi.
[2] *Angeli Johannis Epistola*, p. 62.

declared that if that country were subdued Italy and Germany would be open to invasion.

The rapid extension of their power by sea as well as by land was soon a constant source of anxiety to the nations whose territory bordered on the Mediterranean. Piratical expeditions upon their shores with the object of carrying off slaves kept them in perpetual alarm. When Don John of Austria, in 1571, defeated the Turkish fleet at Lepanto, the dread of the victorious Turk was so acute and the relief at the completeness of his victory so great that the Venetians congratulated each other with the cry that the Devil was dead, and the pope commemorated the great triumph by preaching from the text 'There was a man sent from God whose name was John.'

From the capture in 1453 until John Sobieski relieved Vienna, upwards of two centuries later, the universal topic of European politics, quiescent for a few years but constantly becoming paramount, was the progress made by the Grand Turk. During the whole of this period he had continued to be the terror of Europe.

La Brocquière, who had noted the traffic in Christian slaves by the Turks and the oppression of their Christian subjects, remarked that it was a shame and scandal to Europe to allow herself to be terrorised by such a race. A succession of travellers from the West, who, one after another, observed the sufferings of the Christians, the misgovernment of the Turkish empire, its rapid increase, and the widespread terror of the Turkish name, vainly endeavoured to show how the Turks might be defeated ; but their victorious progress was unchecked until 1683.[1]

The results of the destruction of the empire were of a uniformly disastrous character. Constantinople, which had been the heart of the empire and for centuries the great

---

[1] See, for example, Cuspinianus, *De Turcorum Origine* ; the author was in the employ of the emperor Maximilian I. and insists again and again on the necessity of resisting the Turk and the certainty of being able to do so with success. Almost every European traveller in Turkey during two centuries, beginning with La Brocquière and Tetaldi, made similar representations.

bulwark of European civilisation, became the stronghold of
the professors of a hostile creed. After aiding Europe by
resisting the long encroachments of the Turks, it had first
become an isolated outpost of Christianity surrounded by
hostile hordes, and then, after a century of struggle, not
altogether inglorious, had been overwhelmed by them. By
its capture Europe lost all that its citizens might have contributed to civilisation. The philosophy, art, theology, and
jurisprudence which had emanated from its schools had,
happily, leavened Western lands—happily, because after the
conquest the city ceased to exercise any influence on
European thought. Under the rule of its new masters it
was destined to become the most degraded capital in Europe,
and became incapable of contributing anything whatever of
value to the progress of the human race. No art, no literature, no handicraft even, nothing that the world would gladly
keep, has come since 1453 from the Queen City. Its capture,
so far as human eyes can see, has been for the world a misfortune almost without any compensatory advantage.

The disastrous results of the conquest fell with greatest
force upon the conquered subjects of the empire. The great
cry which went up from the Christians who had fallen under
Turkish rule, and which has never ceased to be justified
among their descendants to the present hour, was that the
new rulers failed in the primary duty of government—to
render life and property secure. Tried by a higher standard
of good government, as an institution which should secure to
its subjects justice, the rule of the Turk fell immeasurably
short. The Christians became *rayahs* or cattle, and as such
were legally incapable of possessing the same rights as
Moslems. While an analogy to such inequality might be
found in other countries, in Turkey the Christians found
that the rights which even the law of the conquerors
accorded them were denied. Their property was arbitrarily seized. They were constantly harassed and pillaged
by their Mahometan neighbours and no redress could
be obtained in the law courts, for Christian testimony
was not admissible against the word of a Moslem. The

*Results
upon
Christian
subjects.*

effects of this legal inequality were soon apparent and have
continued to the present day.   The Christians were tillers of
the ground, artificers, or merchants.   Their earnings exposed
them to the envy of their Moslem neighbours, who, being
less experienced in agriculture or less skilful in trade, less
energetic and less intelligent, were unable, as they are still, to
compete with them successfully.   Their superior power of
creating wealth, rather than the fanaticism of a hostile creed,
has from the time of the conquest led to fierce outrages
upon the Christians and to raids upon their property, and
when combined with such fanaticism has produced the
periodical massacres which have occurred during nearly
every decade in Turkish history.

The difficulties of the Christian traders and agriculturists
were greatly increased by the conduct of the conquerors in
allowing the great roads and bridges to get out of repair.
Turkish ignorance, contempt for industry and commerce,
belief that such matters were only of interest to unbelievers,
led even the governing class to allow the public works
which they had found in the country to fall into ruin.
The traveller in Asia Minor and in European Turkey finds
everywhere the remains of roads once well constructed and
well preserved, which the Turks have made few or no efforts
to maintain, reconstruct, or replace.   The destruction or
decay of the means of communication coupled with the
want of security soon made it useless for the Christian tiller
of the soil to engage in agriculture or even increase his
flocks and herds.   The surplus over what was necessary to
supply his own wants could not be taken to market.
Abundance of evidence shows that the Christians in
almost every part of the empire had possessed large flocks
and herds of cattle.   These, indeed, formed a special
temptation to the Turks, who at all times since their entry
into Asia Minor and Europe were given to making raids on
neighbouring Christian lands.   After the conquest it soon
became useless for the Christians to attempt to keep a form
of property which was so easily carried off.   Those who in
spite of all obstacles contrived to save a few hundred aspers

became objects of envy to their Moslem neighbours and
carefully hid their little savings. The want of security and
the absence of roads were evils which the Christian shared,
though to a less extent, with the Turk. All inducements to
the accumulation of wealth, but especially for Christians,
were removed, till at length all alike ceased to save or do
more work than was necessary to keep body and soul together. Nor can it be said that the condition of the
population under Turkish rule has in this respect greatly
improved at the present day. In the interior of the empire
the man who has acquired a little wealth is careful not to
appear better off than his neighbours. In the capital and a
few seaports, Christians had a somewhat better chance, but
even there the practice of squeezing a wealthy Greek or Armenian merchant and stripping him of his property lingered
into the last century and is even yet not altogether extinct.

Poverty as the consequence of misgovernment is the
most conspicuous result of the conquest affecting the
population of the empire. Lands were allowed to go out of
cultivation. Industries were lost. Mines were forgotten.
Trade and commerce almost ceased to exist. Population
decreased. The wealthiest state in Europe became the
poorest ; the most civilised became the most barbarous. *Population impoverished,*

The demoralisation of the conquered people and of their
churches resulting from the conquest and especially from
the poverty it produced were not less disastrous than the
injury to their material interests. The Christians lost heart.
Their physical courage lessened. In remote districts, and
especially in mountainous regions, where the advantage of
natural position counterbalanced the enormously superior
numbers of the enemy, the Christians continued to resist.
The Greeks in Epirus gave a good account of themselves
during centuries, while the Armenians round about Zeitoun
and the inhabitants of Montenegro even continued to keep
something like independence. But the Greek, Bulgarian,
and Armenian populations, all of whom had fought well
in resisting the Turks, became less virile. Grinding poverty
and constant, though usually petty, oppression even more *and demoralised.*

than the periodical massacres took away from them much of their manliness.

The influence of the conquest upon the Orthodox Church was purely mischievous. The ecclesiastical revenues were seized. The priests had to eke out a living on the miserable pittances they could obtain from performing the services of the Church for an impoverished people, and soon came to be chosen from the peasant class. Poverty of the flock meant poverty throughout the hierarchy. Learning declined and disappeared. The parish priest knew his office by heart, but in course of time hundreds of priests were unable to understand the classic words and phrases with which the liturgy of Chrysostom and others employed in the Eastern Church abound. The most commodious churches were transformed into mosques. The libraries perished. Thousands of precious manuscripts were destroyed. The means of obtaining an educated clergy no longer existed. The voice of the preacher was regarded with suspicion, and the Orthodox Church as a power for the education of its congregations became almost valueless. There were no longer any heresies or dissensions which invited discussion, for people and clergy were alike sunk in ignorance. The art of preaching was forgotten. Religious teaching or expression of thought in or out of the Church almost ceased to exist. The Church of Chrysostom was condemned to silence. To all appearances, there was little or no consciousness of lofty ideals or aspirations towards them. Piety, as understood in the West, seemed for centuries to be unknown. A book like the 'Imitatio' or even the 'Pilgrim's Progress' would have been unintelligible. Churches as well as people had become sordid and destitute of aspiration. Ignorance and other causes, due to the conquest, reduced the Churches to a stagnant level of uniformity, superstition, and spiritual death.

With the substitution of an ignorant for a learned priesthood the influence of the Church upon Western Europe ceased. Down to the conquest it had not only claimed an equality with the Latin Church, but its learning was respected by popes, cardinals, and scholars, who recognised that it merited gratitude for its guardianship of Christian learning and for the succession of scholars who had expounded the treasures of its literature.

Yet amid all the meanness and debasement of the Christian Churches it should ever be remembered that they rendered to their people two inestimable services. They helped to preserve family life and to keep the great mass of their members from abandonment of the Christian profession. However abject the Church, however subservient at times its leaders became to the Ottoman rulers, and however we of the twentieth century may despise priestly pretensions and the claims of any body of men to have a supernatural commission, it is a duty to recognise that the service rendered by the Churches to the Christian subjects of the sultan, and indeed to humanity, in preserving the habits of family life was immeasurably great. One may fully admit that the priests were ignorant, and that the Church became more than ever saturated with pagan superstition; but it safeguarded the idea of Christian marriage based upon the union of the husband for life with one wife. Children were reared in the companionship of a father and mother to each of whom chastity and the necessity of forsaking all others was not merely a tradition and an ideal, but a duty enjoined by the universal teaching of the Church. The results of the education of children amid such teaching, tradition, and environment can only be appreciated when they are compared with those which are produced among their Moslem neighbours, where, under a system fatal to family life, the mother holds a position immeasurably inferior to that of the father.

Benefits conferred by Church.

The Church also helped to prevent the Christian population from abandoning their religious belief, and, to the philosophical student of religions hardly less than to Christians, this result should be regarded as pure gain. The Christians were permitted to have their own religious services, and the attempt was seldom made forcibly to convert them to Mahometanism. The teaching of Mahomet that the 'People of the Books' were not to be molested so long as they submitted and paid tribute, usually secured a contemptuous toleration of their worship. There was little formal interference with their religious practices. Their processions, rites, and ceremonies only encountered opposition from the fanatical brutality of individuals, though Christian worshippers were constantly exposed to petty persecutions from persons in authority who expressed their dislike and loathing of Christianity in a thousand different ways. But it must always be remembered to the credit of the Christians that abandonment of their faith would at any time have saved them from all persecution and have placed them on an equality with their conquerors. The singularly democratic creed and practice of Islam at once open every preferment to the convert. The negro, the Central Asiatic, no less than the Christian rayah, once he has pronounced the *Esh-had*, is on an equality in theory and in practice with the descendant of the Prophet. Turkish history abounds with instances of renegades or their sons rising to the highest positions in the state. A Christian who accepted Islam had every career open to him. The Christian subjects of the empire have always been aware of their own superiority in intellectual capacity to their Turkish neighbours. This superiority is manifest in every country where Moslems and Christians live side by side. It is mainly due to the inferior position assigned in practice in every Mahometan country to woman, a position illustrated by the custom of repudiation—which the husband may exercise in lieu of divorce—by the lack of family life in which children are nurtured in the companionship of both parents, and even by the absence of a family name.[1]

Inducements to renounce Christianity.

[1] One of the best illustrations of the degraded position assigned to woman in Mahometan countries is found in the fact that the popular belief is that she has no soul. The influence of such a belief is of course fatal to the progress of the race. I am well aware that Khaireddin Pasha and other progressive Mahometans have maintained that this belief is contrary to the teaching of the Koran, and that Mr. Hughes and other well-informed students of the sacred writings of Islam agree in this opinion. Still, my statement as to the popular belief is not affected by these researches into the original teaching. It is not alleged that the houris of Paradise are the representatives of earthly women.

It would indeed have been remarkable if with the unspeakable advantages of family life on their side the Christians had not been superior in capacity to their neighbours. But, in spite of their lively consciousness of such superiority and of the advantages to be gained by perversion, few Christians became renegades.

But, notwithstanding the fact that their refusal to abandon a higher for a lower form of religion must be accounted to them for righteousness, the Christians passed into a Slough of Despond. Disarmed and oppressed, they became demoralised and lost self-respect. Their progress and development, material, intellectual, and moral, was arrested. They fell back upon deceit and cunning and the other vices with which a subjugated people seeks to defend itself against its oppressors and which are the usual characteristics of a people held in bondage. The most disastrous result of the conquest upon the people was to create a low standard of morality, and, as in the course of time habits form character, this result endured and continues to the present day. Dishonesty, unfair dealing, bribery, and untruthfulness came to be regarded among all the Christian races of the Ottoman Empire as venial offences or as pardonable blunders. This deterioration of character was not, and is not, confined to laymen. The environment of all classes has

Degradation of people.

The sensual rewards promised to faithful men are clear and unmistakeable. The rewards to women in the Koran have to be searched for and are the result of interpretation. As a confirmation of the truth of my statement I may refer to the interesting interview given by Sir Edward Malet in *Shifting Scenes* (1901), p. 67. He describes a meeting which he had with Tewfik, the Khedive of Egypt, at a very critical moment, when indeed the latter's life was in hourly danger. He represents Tewfik as saying: 'Death does not signify to me personally. Our religion prevents us from having any fear of death; but it is different with our women. To them, you know, life is everything: their existence ends here; they cry and weep and implore me to save them.'

As to the custom of repudiating a wife, two learned Moslems, one Turkish and the other Indian, and both enlightened men, assure me that repudiation, though a general custom, is contrary to the teaching of Islam, which only recognises divorce. Both, however, admit that the practice is general, though they consider it irreligious or—what is the same thing in the Sacred Law of Islam—illegal.

been powerful for evil, and the standards in particular of commercial honesty generally prevalent in Christian nations have neither been preserved nor attained.

Under Turkish rule punishment often failed to follow detection. In some cases—notably, for example, bigamy—the conquering race recognises no offence and therefore awards no punishment. The Christians had and have so little confidence in their chance of obtaining justice that it is the exception to prosecute an offender. A man will rather suffer loss than waste his time in appealing to a court where he knows that he will certainly incur expense and inconvenience and that the offender, provided he can pay, can escape condemnation. It is to this impossibility of obtaining justice that must be ascribed more perhaps than to any other cause the lowering of the morals of Eastern Christians. Those who know them best, from Arab Christians in Syria to the Greeks and others in Constantinople and the Balkan Peninsula, and whose sympathies are entirely with them in the persecution they have undergone, and in their desire to shake off the oppressor's yoke, have regretfully to confess that the reputation which they have acquired in Western Europe for untrustworthiness and untruthfulness is not undeserved. Happily, in Greece and other countries which have been freed from Turkish misrule there are abundant signs of an awakening to the necessity of regarding offences from a loftier standpoint and of presenting in the Churches a higher ideal of morality ; signs, too, of the public opinion which is bringing these countries into line with Western states.[1]

---

[1] I may add here that the great value of Christian missions from the West in the Turkish Empire, those of the Latin Church and of the American Protestant Churches alike, lies not only in their educational work but still more in their holding up to the members of the Eastern Churches higher standards of truthfulness and morality. Their influence has been already very useful. They have kindled a desire for instruction, and have infused new life in many of the members of the ancient Churches. While Greeks, Bulgarians, and Armenians look with intense distrust on any attempts to proselytise, they have all been awakened by these missions to the necessity for education. Considering the means at their disposal, I think it may be fairly said that no other people during the last half-century has done so much for education as the Greeks. The

The conquest of Constantinople had but little effect on the mass of the Turkish population. The Turks ceased to be mainly a nomadic people, and great numbers of them took possession of the arable lands of the conquered races. But in other respects their habits and characteristics remained unchanged. They had and have their virtues. They are brave and hardy, and, except when under the influence of religious fanaticism, are hospitable and kindly. Their religion inculcates cleanliness and sobriety. While its teaching must stand condemned in regard to the treatment of non-Islamic peoples and, judging by the universal experience of Moslem countries, in regard to the position, fatal to all progress, which it assigns to woman, it has nevertheless helped to diffuse courtesy and self-respect among its adherents. Unhappily, the Turkish race has never had sufficient continuous energy to be industrious nor enough intelligence to desire knowledge.

Fortunately for the populations under the rule of the Turk, his religious intolerance has only become virulent at intervals; for when his fanaticism is awakened, corruption and cruelty in the administration of government show themselves at their worst. It is so in Morocco now, where the fiercest Moslem intolerance and perhaps the most cruel and corrupt government in the world co-exist. It has been so at various periods under Turkish rule. Sultans have alternated in their government between periods of lethargy, sloth, and sensuality and those of spasmodic activity. But

desire of every Greek who makes money seems to be to found a school in his native place. In Constantinople several large and excellent institutions, both for boys and girls, exist, all of course unaided by the Government, and in other cities of the Turkish empire like efforts have been made by patriotic Greeks. In Bulgaria one of the first acts of the newly enfranchised state was to establish an efficient system of education. The Armenians are not behind either, and their efforts, perhaps to a greater extent than those of the other two peoples mentioned, are directed to bringing their priests into line with those of the West. In 1896 the American missionaries in Turkey met in a 'summer school' on the island of Proti, near Constantinople; the late Armenian patriarch visited them, and, having spent a day in listening to their discussion on questions of teaching and Biblical scholarship, declared that he would be ready to sacrifice his life if his own priests could have the advantage of such gatherings.

the periods of fanaticism have been those not only of massacre and exceptional cruelty but of want of patriotism, and the worst corruption in the administration of government.

In Greece and Italy more vigorous physical races in earlier times had triumphed over peoples further advanced in civilisation. But the conquerors profited by the civilisation of the vanquished and the latter became more virile. The two races coalesced and formed a united people. No such results followed 1453. The Turkish nation was unable to assimilate the civilisation of the peoples it subdued, and its work has been simply to destroy what it could not take to itself. It has fallen so far short of reconciling the conquered races and welding them to itself so as to form one people that the assertion may safely be made that every century since 1453 has widened the gulf between it and the Christians.

In one respect only has the Turk been able to appreciate the progress made by his neighbours and, in part at least, to appropriate their development—namely, in the art of war. He knows and cares nothing about art, science, or literature. He has made a miserable failure of government. His civil administration is probably more corrupt than it was four centuries ago. He admits that, since his defeat at Lepanto in 1571, Allah has given the dominion of the seas to the Giaours. But as a soldier he has always been ready to learn from European nations.

That the heavy weight of misrule has hindered and still continues to hinder the progress of the Christian races is attested by all who are acquainted with Turkey. Condemned to constant persecution and a sordid poverty which leaves on travellers an overpowering sense of human misery, and living amid a hopeless and dispiriting environment, they passed into the blackest night which ever overshadowed a Christian people. It is true that they were not utterly destroyed, as other Christian nations have been, but,

except for the feeling of solidarity arising from community
of race and of religious belief and for the hope which
the Churches aided them to keep alive, their night was
without a single ray of light. They and their countrymen who had escaped into foreign lands looked in despair
and in vain for the signs that the night would pass. It is
barely a century ago since the keener-sighted watchmen
observed indications of dawn. The daylight has arisen
upon Roumania, Serbia, Greece, Bulgaria, and other
countries once under Turkish rule, and signs of dawn are
visible, though with indications of blood-red, in Macedonia
and Armenia. Sooner or later, but as surely as light over-
comes darkness, the Christian and progressive elements
in the Turkish empire will see the day and rejoice in it.

The friends of the liberated territories have often complained of the vagaries, the inconstancy, and the slow rate
of progress of the re-established states. They are apt to
forget that to shake off the effects of centuries of bondage
is a task which has never been accomplished in a single
generation. All historical precedents, from the time when
Moses led the children of Israel into the desert, teach the
same lesson. But it is satisfactory to note that while
each of the states that have obtained emancipation was, a
century ago, far behind the civilisation even of Constantinople, it is now far ahead of it. If the traveller who
eighty years ago spoke contemptuously of the collection of
mud huts which fanatics are pleased to call Athens, while
they refer to their barbarian occupants as Greeks, could
now be placed on the Acropolis, he would see the well-built
and prosperous capital of a country which, in spite of
financial difficulties, is flourishing in agriculture, trade, and
commerce ; the chief city of a people which has recovered
its self-respect, is full of patriotism, of zeal for education,
and of intellectual life, and whose Church has awakened to
the necessity of an educated priesthood and a higher
standard of morality. A like prosperity could be noted in
every other land which has escaped from Turkish bondage.

Wherever, indeed, the dead weight of Turkish misrule has been removed, the young Christian states have been fairly started on the path of civilisation and justify the reasonable expectations of the statesmen, historians, and scholars of the West who have sympathised with and aided them in their aspirations for freedom.

APPENDICES

APPENDIX I

NOTE ON ROMANUS GATE AND CHIEF PLACE OF
FINAL ASSAULT

SOME doubt exists as to the position of the Romanus Gate mentioned by the historians of the siege, and as this position determines those of the great gun, of the stockade, and of the principal place of the final assault, it is desirable to endeavour to set such doubt at rest.

What I desire to show may be summed up in the following propositions.

(1) That contemporary writers agree in stating that the principal place of attack and the final assault was at or near the Gate of St. Romanus.

(2) That the present Top Capou had long been known as the Gate of St. Romanus.

(3) That there is evidence to demonstrate that the final assault was not at or near Top Capou but in the Lycus valley.

(4) That the Pempton is the Gate referred to by contemporary writers as the Romanus Gate.

Among the evidence showing that the principal place of attack was at or near the Romanus Gate is the following :

Barbaro (p. 21) states that four great guns were 'alla porta de San Romano dove che sun la piu debel porta de tuta la tera. Una de queste quatro bombarde che sun a la porta da San Romano' was the big gun cast by Orban. On p. 16 he speaks of an attack as being against 'le mure da tera de la banda de San Romano.' On p. 26 he mentions the destruction of a tower, presumably the Bactatinean, spoken of by Leonard. This tower was 'de la banda de San Romano.' It was destroyed by the big gun with a portion also of the wall (' con parechi passa de muro '). On

p. 27 he describes the repair of the walls going on at the Gate
called San Romano. On p. 40 he again says that the weakest
place in the landward walls was at San Romano, 'dove che iera
roto le mure.' On p. 53 he adds that the Turks fought furiously
' da la banda da tera, da la banda de San Romano dove che iera
el pavion ' of the emperor. On the same page he describes them
again as still fighting ' da la banda de San Romano.' On p. 55
he describes the entry of the Turks into the city as being ' da la
banda de San Romano,' and on p. 57 he states that the emperor
was killed at the entry which the Turks had made ' a la porta de
San Romano.' According, therefore, to Barbaro, the Romanus
Gate is the central place of attack and of capture.

But Barbaro was a Venetian, and probably did not know the
city well. Phrantzes and Ducas, however, were citizens. The
first, on p. 254, says that Justiniani took charge of the defence ἐν
τοῖς μέρεσι τῆς πύλης τοῦ ἁγίου Ῥωμανοῦ, which the Bonn editor translates correctly by saying that he defended the 'regionem ad portam
Sancti Romani.' Phrantzes further identifies the place by saying
it was where the Turks had stationed their largest gun because
the walls were convenient for attack and because the sultan's tent
was pitched opposite. As to the position of the sultan's tent
Phrantzes and others say that it was opposite the Romanus Gate.
Ducas, however, states that it was opposite the Chariseus or
Adrianople Gate. Phrantzes, p. 287, says further that the emperor
and many soldiers fell ἐν τῷ τόπῳ ἐκείνῳ πλησίον τῆς πύλης τοῦ
ἁγίου Ῥωμανοῦ where the Turks had built their wooden tower and
stationed their largest gun. Ducas says that the Turks placed
this big gun near (πλησίον) the Romanus Gate. He further describes the destruction of the tower (presumably the Bactatinean
mentioned by Leonard) which was near the Romanus Gate.
Other authors could be cited who use similar expressions.

In fact, all the evidence is in favour of my first proposition,
that the principal place of attack was at or near the Romanus
Gate.

(2) It is undisputed that Top Capou (that is, Cannon Gate) was
known in early times as the Gate of St. Romanus. It is mentioned under that name, for example, in the 'Paschal Chronicle ' in
the time of Heraclius, and again in the reign of Andronicus the
First by Nicephorus Gregoras (ix. ch. 6), and as late as the middle
of the fourteenth century by Cantacuzenus (p. 142, Ven. ed.).

(3 & 4) The evidence to show that the final assault was not at
or near Top Capou is abundant.

Owing, however, to the constant mention of St. Romanus and

the undoubted association of that name with Top Capou, it has been naturally assumed that the chief place of attack was at or near the latter Gate. Even Paspates was driven to disregard the evidence of his own eyes and to fix the assault on the steep part of the slope near Top Capou (Πολιορκία, p. 186).

But all observers who have studied the question on the spot, with the exception of Paspates, are now agreed that the chief place of assault was in the Lycus valley. In such case it necessarily follows that the name Romanus was given during the siege to some other gate than Top Capou.

The late Dr. Dethier was the first to suggest that the Gate spoken of by the contemporaries of the siege as St. Romanus was the Pempton. Let us examine the evidence. It is worthy of note that Phrantzes places Justiniani in the 'region' or district of the Romanus Gate. The Italian writers, knowing less of the city, say 'at' such Gate.

Now what was the Pempton? Each of the two Civil Gates on the landward side which we need here regard—namely, Top Capou and the Adrianople Gate—crowned a hill on one side of the Lycus valley and was exceptionally strong. They formed, in fact, with their towers and barbicans two of the strongest positions in the landward walls. The bridges across the foss opposite these and the other Civil Gates were intended to be broken down during a siege, and in fact were broken down when Mahomet's siege commenced.[1] The Military Gates which led from the city to the Peribolos were then opened, though they were generally walled up in times of peace. The Pempton or Fifth Military Gate or Gate of the Fifth (for both forms of names are found) was the one which gave access to the Enclosure in the Lycus valley. It was known also in early times as the Gate of St. Kyriakè, from a neighbouring church, and as the Gate of Puseus from a Latin inscription still existing upon it, dating probably from the time of Leo the First, recording that Puseus had strengthened it.[2]

It is a remarkable fact that no writer who was either a witness of the siege or subsequently wrote upon it mentions the Pempton either under that name or by those of Kyriakè or Puseus. It is impossible to believe that it was not used. It was built for the express purpose of giving access to the troops into the Peribolos within which, beyond all doubt, the most important fighting took place. To admit that Justiniani and the soldiers under him were stationed between the Outer and the Inner Walls in this part and

---

[1] 'Pontes qui ad moenia ducunt dirumpunt.' Pusculus iv. 137.

[2] Professor van Millingen's *Byzantine Constantinople*, p. 96.

yet to suggest that the Pempton was not used is altogether unreasonable. Dethier's suggestion is, that when the Civil Gates
were closed people gave to the Military Gate the name of the
nearest Civil Gate. Probably the earlier names given on account
of their numbers were generally unknown. The latest instance I
have found of the use of Pempton is in the ' Paschal Chronicle.'

In support of this view it is important to note that many contemporaries speak of another place where the cannonading was
severe as at the Pegè Gate (as, for example, Barbaro and Philelphus), whereas no one doubts that the present condition of the
walls affords conclusive evidence that the writers intended to
indicate Triton—that is, the Third Military Gate between the Pegè
and the Rhegium Civil Gates.

The suggestion that the Pempton was commonly called the
Romanus Gate explains various statements which are otherwise
irreconcilable. We have seen that Ducas says that the sultan
was encamped opposite the Chariseus Gate, while Phrantzes
places him opposite the Romanus. Dr. Mordtmann urges [1] that
from the small knoll where, according to Ducas and Critobulus,
Mahomet's tent was pitched, an observer might fairly describe its
position as opposite either, but if the Pempton were called
Romanus, such a suggestion would be much more plausible.
Again, Barbaro, as already quoted, places the great gun opposite
the San Romano Gate because this was the weakest gate of all the
city. But on p. 18 he uses the same phrase in stating that the
' Cressu ' or Chariseus was the weakest gate in all the city, the
explanation being, I think, that as the Pempton was about midway between the Romanus and the Chariseus Civil Gates he heard
it called indifferently by either name. Tetaldi, the Florentine soldier
who was present at the siege, states that two hundred fathoms of
Outer Wall were broken down during the last days. Now, although
the Inner Wall was repaired by Mahomet [2] and continued fairly
complete, no attempt appears to have been made to rebuild the
Outer.[3] The spectator has little difficulty in distinguishing where
the twelve hundred feet of Outer Wall of which Tetaldi speaks
was destroyed. It was opposite the Pempton and, judging from
the condition of the walls, certainly not opposite the present Top
Capou. But the same writer says that it was ' à la porte de
Sainct Romain.' [4] The Moscovite or Slavic chronicler says that
the great cannon were placed opposite the station of Justiniani

[1] Esquisse Topographique, p. 25.   [2] Critobulus, Book II. ch. i.
[3] Knolles, History of the Turks, p. 341 (written in 1610, edition of 1621).
[4] P. 28.

'because the walls there were less solid and very low,'[1] a description which would not apply to those near Top Capou, but which, like all the descriptions given, does apply to the lower part of the Lycus valley. Here, in the phrase of Professor van Millingen, was the heel of Achilles, the Valley of Decision.[2] The weakness of this portion of the walls is illustrated by the fact that when Baldwin the Second expected an attack by Michael he walled up all the landward gates 'except the single one near the streamlet where one sees the church of St. Kyriakè'—that is, except the Pempton.[3] In other words, the walls being there the weakest, it was anticipated that there would be the attack, and the entry into the Peribolos must be kept open to defend the Outer Wall. In the 'Threnos' the siege is described as being at the ' Chariseus Gate,' now St. Romanus, which is called Top Capou.[4] Apparently the confusion in this description is hopeless, but if the Pempton were called indifferently, as by Barbaro, Romanus and Chariseus, it becomes intelligible.[5]

A statement by the ' Moscovite ' (ch. vii.) also points to the Pempton as the chief point of attack. He mentions that on April 24 a ball from the great cannon knocked away five of the battlements and buried itself in the walls of a church. The only church in the neighbourhood either of Top Capou or the Pempton was one dedicated to St. Kyriakè, which was in the Lycus valley near the Pempton. But the attack is always stated to be against the Romanus Gate.

Near the Pempton the Peribolos is now about twenty feet higher than the level of the ground on the city side of the Great Wall. Beyond doubt this is largely due to the accumulation of refuse and broken portions of the wall, but, allowing for this, an observer will probably conclude that the Peribolos was at the time of the siege several feet higher than the level on the city

---

[1] 1078, Dethier's edition.

[2] *Byzantine Constantinople*, p. 96. In the same manner Dethier, commenting on Pusculus, iv. line 169, says : ' Pseudoporta Charsaea vel Pempti omnium celeberrima et in fortificatione calx Achilles erat. Hic enim ab utra parte, nempe a Porta Polyandrii [Adrianople Gate] et a Porta Sancti Romani in vallem Lyci linea recta murús descendit, idque contra omnem legem artis fortificationum.'

[3] The *Anonymous Chronicle*, in verse, of the Latin Capture (edited by Joseph Mueller and Dethier), line 390.

[4] *Threnos*, 610-613.

[5] Dethier and the elder Mordtmann considered (in error, as the learned son of the latter and Professor van Millingen agree) that they had proved that the Pempton was the Chariseus. See, in addition to the sentence just quoted from the *Threnos*, the archaeological map of the Greek Syllogos and also Dethier's note on Pusculus, iv. line 172.

E F

side. This same discrepancy of level did not exist—if, indeed, any existed—at Top Capou. Hence when the small gate was opened from the city by Justiniani to give easier access to the stockade, men had to ascend to it. This is what Critobulus implies they had to do. The gate was opened to lead ἐπὶ τὸ σταύρωμα (lx. 2).

Critobulus states that Mahomet drew up his camp 'before the *Gates* of Romanus.'[1] The argument Dethier draws from the plural, 'gates,' is not perhaps worth much, but it is remarkable that in speaking of other gates Critobulus usually employs the singular : as, for example, in ch. xxvii. 3, 'The Wood-Gate, as far as the gate called Chariseus.' Gregoras also employs the plural : παρὰ τὰς πύλας τοῦ Ῥωμανοῦ (Book ix. ch. vi.).

The Turkish writers throw very valuable light on the question and show clearly that the assault was not at Top Capou, but rather nearer the Adrianople Gate.

The imaum Zade Essad-Effendi says that in the final assault Hassan mounted the broken wall where the Franks were defending it, 'which wall was to the south of Edirne Capou'—that is, of the Adrianople Gate. The Turkish writer Sad-ud-din, who died in 1599, gives similar testimony. He states that Constantine 'entrusted to the Frank soldiers the defence of those breaches which were on the south side of the Adrianople Gate.' And again : 'The Turks in the final assault did not rush to the gates but to the breaches that were made in the broken wall between Top Capou and the Adrianople Gate, and, after the capture, went round and opened the gates from the inside, the first to be opened being the Adrianople Gate.'[2] If the Venetian and Genoese soldiers had been near Top Capou the writer would not have described their position as he does. Probably he was ignorant of any name for the gate in the valley where the assault occurred, and therefore describes the breaches with sufficient accuracy as south of the Adrianople or Edirne Gate.

Lastly, Dr. Mordtmann calls attention to the fact that on old Turkish maps the Pempton is marked as Hedjoum Capou or Gate of the Assault.[3] If it were the Gate of the Assault, as I also believe, it was the gate spoken of by contemporaries as Saint Romanus, and all difficulties as to the place of the general assault the position of the stockade defended by Justiniani, and the station of the great guns vanish.

Thereupon the description of Critobulus makes the arrange-

---

[1] Ch. xxiii. : πρὸς ταῖς καλουμέναις πύλαις τοῦ Ῥωμανοῦ.

[2] Ahmed Muktar Pasha's *Siege of Constantinople* (1902).

[3] *Esquisse Topographique*, pp. 12, 21.

ment of Mahomet's army clear. His guards were encamped opposite the Mesoteichion and the Myriandrion—that is, opposite the whole length of walls between Top Capou and the Palace of Porphyrogenitus (ch. xxvi.). His three largest guns were stationed opposite the Pempton or Military Gate of Romanus, and his imperial tent was pitched in a place, and at a distance from the walls, where it could properly be described indifferently as opposite either the Chariseus or Romanus Gate.

In conclusion, I would suggest that the name Top Capou was given or transferred by the Turks, after the siege and when the Pempton was walled up, to the Civil Gate of St. Romanus. There was no need for a name among ordinary people for an unused gate, and the Turks, instead of using the name of a Christian saint, spoke of it as that near which the great cannon was placed, or shortly as Top Capou—that is, Cannon Gate. It is remarkable that Gyllius, though mentioning that there was a gate at the situation of Top Capou, calls it neither by that name nor by that of St. Romanus.[1]

[1] Book i. ch. 20.

APPENDIX II

WHERE DID THE SEA-FIGHT OF APRIL 20, 1453, TAKE PLACE?

THE late Dr. A. D. Mordtmann,[1] and Dr. Paspates,[2] followed by M. Mijatovich,[3] and M. E. A. Vlasto.[4] answer, that it was to the west of the Marmora end of the landward walls: that is, off Zeitin Bournou. In favour of this view they give the following reasons:

(1) Because during the fight the sultan rode into the water, and he could not have done so if the fight had been on the north shore of the Golden Horn, as the shore there is too steep. The answer to this is, that the Galata shore four centuries ago was like that of the Golden Horn outside the walls of Constantinople now, and consisted of a low flat of mud, now built upon. The present Grande Rue de Galata is really the 'Strand' of Galata, and is all land reclaimed from the sea. This is even now obvious; but Gyllius observed the growth of this flat land and gives a curious description of it.[5] This argument therefore fails.

(2) Because Barbaro mentions that the wind dropped when the ships were 'per mezo la citade,' which Dr. Mordtmann considered to mean halfway along the length of the city between the end of the landward walls and Seraglio Point, or, as he puts it definitely, at Vlanga Bostan. But 'per mezo' means here simply alongside or opposite or abreast of the city. It is used as meaning 'through the midst' in the same paragraph, when Barbaro states that he is going from the city on board certain galleys 'per mezo la citade.'

It is undisputed that a southerly wind had been blowing four days: a strong wind which had brought the ships from Chios. There would therefore be a current running northwards. Consequently if the wind had suddenly dropped opposite Vlanga

---

[1] *Belagerung und Eroberung Constantinopels im Jahre 1453.*
[2] Πολιορκία.   [3] *Constantine, the last Emperor of the Greeks.*
[4] *Les derniers Jours de Constantinople.*   [5] Book iii. ch. x.

Bostan the ships would have drifted toward the Bosporus and not backwards to Zeitin Bournou.

(3) Because Pusculus says that the townsfolk crowded to the Hippodrome to see the fight, and they would not have done so (because buildings intercepted the view) if the fight had been at the mouth of the Golden Horn.

The Hippodrome is four miles as the crow flies from the sea opposite Zeitin Bournou, and the spectators would not have crowded to such a place when they could have seen so much better from a hill behind Psamatia and elsewhere. If, however, the fight, or any part of it, took place opposite Seraglio Point, spectators on the Sphendone of the Hippodrome would have had an excellent view of the ships as they approached and as they passed, and of an attack made in the Bosporus before the ships passed the Acropolis. I have tested this on several occasions.

(4) Because Phrantzes says the fight took place about a stone's-throw from the land where the sultan was and that he and his friends watched it from the walls,[1] and that the only place where these two requirements can be satisfied is Zeitin Bournou.

The mouth of the Horn satisfies both requirements equally well. Dr. Paspates observes that ships coming to Constantinople with a south wind do not keep near the walls, but keep well out; and the remark is just. They take this course to avoid the eddy current, which if they kept near the walls would be against them. If the ships were about a stone's-throw distant from the land, they would not only be out of their usual course but taking another where their progress would be hindered.

(5) Because Ducas (who was not a witness of what he relates) says that the Turkish fleet set out to wait for the fleet off the harbour of the Golden Gate.[2]

There probably never was a harbour of the Aurea Porta. Paspates says there was a *scala* near the Golden Gate, whic indeed is shown in Bondelmonte's map, but the ships could not discharge at an open *scala* in the Marmora with a south wind blowing, even if there had been depth enough of water where it existed, which, at the present day at least, there is not.

The statement of Ducas is improbable, because, as the object of the ships was to get past the boom from St. Eugenius to Galata, the ships with the wind which was blowing would have simply passed the fleet or gone triumphantly through them, if they had been waiting off the Golden Gate, and have made for Seraglio Point and the harbour.

---

[1] 248-9.　　　[2] ἐκ τοῦ λιμένος τῆς χρύσης πύλης ἐκτός.

I suggest that the words of Ducas (Χρύση Πύλη) are either an error in the copying or are a mistake made by Ducas. They may be a transcriber's mistake for Horaia Porta—that is, the gate near Seraglio Point, on the Golden Horn. Horaia Porta and Aurea Porta are almost undistinguishable in sound, the aspirate being unpronounced. The similarity in sound had led at an early period to confusion.[1]

It may nevertheless be true that the fleet set out to await the ships off the end of the landward walls. There is not, however, the slightest evidence that it ever got there. On the contrary, as we shall see, the evidence shows that it did not. Once it is established that it never got so far, the contention that the fight was off Zeitin Bournou falls.

These are all the arguments which, so far as I know, have been urged in favour of the Zeitin Bournou position. Some of them are destructive of the others, and, with the exception of the statement of Ducas as to the Turkish fleet setting off for the Harbour of the Golden Gate, are all deductions from the evidence of the authorities rather than direct evidence. Moreover, as will be seen, important statements of witnesses testifying to what they themselves saw are either entirely overlooked or set aside without any sufficient reason.

My contention in the text is that the fight commenced at the mouth of the Bosporus off Seraglio Point; that the wind suddenly dropped while the ships were under the walls of the Acropolis at that Point; that the ships drifted towards the Galata or Pera shore, and that the most serious part of the fight took place off such shore, where it was watched by the sultan and into the waters of which shore the sultan rode. The evidence in support of this view is the following:

(1) It is agreed on all sides that the Turkish fleet was stationed at the Double Columns (Diplokionion).

(2) Leonard the archbishop says that he was a spectator from the city, and that the sultan was on the slope of the Pera hill. Leonard is a witness deserving of confidence. He was present during the whole siege. He had much to do with the people of Galata, who were, like himself, of the Latin Church. In describing this particular incident, he speaks of himself as a spectator

---

[1] *E.g.* in the ancient account of the regions of the city given in the *Notitia utriusque Imperii* the Aurea Porta is mentioned as in the 12th Regio—that is, near the Seven Towers. Upon this Pancirolus remarks ' The Greeks call it [i.e. the Aurea Porta] 'Ωραία.' Ducas might have been told that the fleet went to the 'Ωραία πόρτα and understood it to be the Aurea Porta or the Golden Gate.

of the fight.[1] His letter is an official report addressed to the pope
within three months after the event, and therefore while its details
were fresh in his memory and not like the account of Ducas, who
was not present at the siege and only wrote years afterwards. His
testimony, if he is to be believed—and I know no reason why he
should even be doubted—is decisive. 'The King of the Trojans '
(as he calls the Turks throughout) looked on from Pera hill.[2]

Le Beau, who took the view which I adopt, relied no doubt
upon Leonard's narrative in describing the battle. Dr. Mordtmann
remarks upon Le Beau's statement that no one standing upon the
hillside at Pera could see a fight at sea beyond Seraglio Point.
The observation is correct, and my deduction is that, when the
ships were first attacked, they were abreast of Seraglio Point and
not beyond or behind it. Dr. Mordtmann's is that the sultan
could not have been at Pera, and this notwithstanding that the
archbishop says that he was there and implies that he saw him
there. The archbishop further mentioned that when the sultan
' blasphemed,' as he rode into the water and witnessed the loss his
men were suffering, it was from a hill.[3] But the archbishop does
not leave his readers in doubt as to what hill he means. A few
sentences later in his narrative we are told that the sultan had
concluded that he would be able from the eastern shore of the
Galata hill either to sink the ships with his stone cannon-balls, or
at least drive them back from the chain.[4] The rest of the passage
shows unmistakably that the sultan, in Leonard's belief, was on
the shore outside the Galata walls : that is, exactly where a
spectator might be supposed to be who, having come from Diplokionion, wanted to see the most of a fight in or near the mouth
of the Horn. Unless, therefore, within a short period after the
capture of the city, the archbishop had become hopelessly muddled
as to what he himself saw, we must conclude that the fight did
not take place off Zeitin Bournou but in or near the mouth of the
Golden Horn.

Pusculus, another spectator, says the ships entered the
Bosporus and that the wind dropped while they were under the
walls of the Acropolis. The account given by this writer is clear
and precise. He was in the city and relates what he witnessed,
and although he wrote his poem some years afterwards, when safe

---

[1] ' Intuentibus nobis,' p. 90.

[2] ' Teucrorum rex ex colle Perensi proconspicit,' p. 90. It must be remembered
that all across the Horn was Pera, and that Galata is properly Galata of Pera.

[3] ' Rex qui ex colle circumspicit,' p. 90.

[4] ' Cogitavit itaque ex colle Galatae Orientali plaga vel eas lapidibus
machinarum (ᵇʳˉ ere vel a cathena repellere,' p. 91.

in his native city of Brescia, he had the broad outlines of the siege well in his recollection. His narrative is the following, and is in complete accord with that of every other eye-witness. The ships are seen approaching on the Marmora; some of the townsfolk flock to the Hippodrome where (from the Sphendone) they have a view far and wide over the sea, and can observe them taking the usual course for ships coming from the Dardanelles to the capital with a southerly wind. The Turkish admiral with his fleet has gone to meet them, and orders them to lower their sails. The south wind still blows full astern, and with belly-ing sails they hold on their course. The wind continues until they are carried to a position where the Bosporus strains against the shore of either land.[1] That is, as I understand the phrase, until they are at least well past the present lighthouse. 'There the wind fails them; the sails flap idly *under the walls of the citadel.*[2] Then, indeed, began the fight; the spirits of the Turks are aroused by the fall of the wind ; Mahomet, watching from the shore not far off, arouses their rage.' My only doubt as to this interpretation arises as to the question whether the writer did not mean that the wind dropped, not merely off Seraglio Point, but within the mouth of the Horn.

Ducas says the sultan, when the ships came in sight of the city, 'hastened' to his fleet, and gave orders to capture them or, failing that, to hinder them from getting inside the harbour. This hastening of the sultan meant a journey of between two and three miles from his camp in the Mesoteichion to Diplokionion. Once he was there, his natural course would be to follow on shore the movements of his fleet, until he reached the eastern walls of Galata, which is exactly the place where the archbishop stations him. If it should be objected that Mahomet's hastening to his triremes implies that they were stationed near Zeitin Bournou, the answer is twofold : first, that there would be no haste necessary, and secondly, that even Ducas implies that the fleet was in the Bosporus, as indeed Barbaro and others say that it was.

The two statements of Phrantzes—first, that the fight was about a stone's-throw from the land where the sultan was on horseback and rode into the sea to revile his men, and, second, that he (Phrantzes) and his friends watched the fight from the walls [3]—

'Nec flare quievit
Structa donec statuit super aequora, Bosporus arctat
Litora ubi geminae telluris.'

Book iv. 413.

[2] 'Deserit illic ventus eas ; cecidere sinus sub moenibus arcis,' iv. 415.

[3] ἡμεῖς δὲ ἐκ τῶν τειχῶν ἄνωθεν ταῦτα θεωροῦντες, p. 248.

are both reconcilable with the contention that the fight was where I have placed it. I conclude that the balance of evidence is in favour of the opinion that the fight commenced in the open Bosporus off Seraglio Point, and, the wind continuing, the ships rounded the Point, and that then the wind dropped, the general attack took place, and the ships drifted to the Galata shore.

When the question is considered ' What position accords with all the accounts of the eye-witnesses?' there can be only one answer. The people watch from the Hippodrome, says Pusculus, and would have a good view until the ships had rounded the point. The vessels were aiming for Megademetrius, says Ducas : which was the usual landmark for vessels to steer for when coming to the Golden Horn from the Marmora with a south wind. ' We being spectators ' from the walls and the sultan being on the Pera slope watching the fight, says Leonard ; and the vessels being about a stone's-throw from the shore, says Phrantzes. Pusculus answers the question ' Where were Leonard and the other spectators ? ' by telling us that the wind dropped under the walls of the citadel.

There is yet another test which may be applied and which ought almost of itself to settle the question. Upon considering the position without reference to authorities upon matters of detail and upon a priori grounds, an unbiassed local investigator would discard the Zeitin Bournou position and accept that of the Bosporus-Galata. Four large ships want to enter the Golden Horn, since there is no harbour on the Marmora side of the city sufficiently large into which they could enter. They are approaching with a southerly wind. The Turkish fleet consists of large and small sailing boats which are stationed nearly two miles from the Horn in the Bosporus. The object of the fleet is to capture or sink the ships, or at least to prevent them from entering the harbour. What, under these circumstances, would the commander of the fleet do ? He would keep his boats well together near the mouth of the Horn and attempt to bar the passage. He would recognise that he had little chance of capturing comparatively large sailing vessels on open sea so long as they were coming on with a wind. So long as the ships were sailing, they would be attacked at a great disadvantage. Wait for them near the Horaia Porta, when they would have to stop, and they could then be fought at an advantage. If the wind suddenly dropped, the Turkish admiral would naturally give orders to attack. This is what, as I contend, actually happened. The fight would then be seen by Greeks from the walls and by Mahomet and his suite from the Galata or Pera shore. What would happen when the wind became calm, would be that the vessels would drift. I repeat what I have said in the text, that it may be taken as beyond doubt that after a strong southerly wind has been blowing in the Marmora for four or five days—and it was such a wind which had brought the ships from Chios—there would be in the Marmora and the Bosporus near Seraglio Point a strong current setting in the same direction, and the ships would drift toward the Galata shore. It would then be quite possible to have got within a stone's-throw, as Phrantzes relates, and for their crews to have heard the reproaches of the sultan.

APPENDIX III

NOTE ON TRANSPORT OF MAHOMET'S SHIPS
WHAT WAS THE ROUTE ADOPTED?

IN commenting on the story of the transport of Mahomet's ships overland from the Bosporus into Cassim Pasha bay, Gibbon says ' I could wish to contract the distance of ten miles and to prolong the term of one night.' [1] I have sufficiently remarked in the text upon the time occupied in the transit. The distances given by the various authors who describe the incident are confusing, but ten miles is beyond a doubt wrong.

In order to learn what the distance was, it is necessary to determine what was the route adopted by Mahomet. Two routes have been suggested: the first is from Dolma Bagshe, across the ridge where the Taxim Public Gardens now exist and down the valley leading to Cassim Pasha; the second, from Tophana along the valley which the Rue Koumbaraji now occupies, across the Grande Rue, and down the valley commencing at the street between the Pera Palace Hotel and the Club to Cassim Pasha. It is convenient to speak of these routes as those of Dolma Bagshe and Tophana respectively. No writer who saw the transport of the ships has described the route. We may gather evidence, however, on several points which will aid us to determine it.

The evidence as to the distance traversed is the following. The archbishop speaks of it as being seventy stadia. I should agree with Karl Müller, the editor of Critobulus, that the *seventy* stadia of Leonard is a clerical error, the figure being intended to apply to the number of ships, but for the fact that a little later Leonard speaks of the bridge built over the upper Horn as thirty stadia long and gives the distance of the Turkish fleet from the Propontis to its anchorage at the Double Columns as a hundred stadia. As both these distances are about nine or ten times too long, it is evident that by ' stadium ' he means some other measure

[1] Vol. vii. p. 184.

than the ordinary stadium, which is 625 feet long, or rather less than a furlong.[1] I therefore suggest that when Leonard speaks of seventy stadia he makes the difference traversed about eight stadia as the word is understood by his contemporaries. Critobulus in describing the overland passage of the boats says they travelled ' certainly eight stadia ' (στάδιοι μάλιστα ὀκτώ). Probably Critobulus, writing a few years afterwards and mixing with Turks, Greeks, and Genoese in Pera itself, would have the best chance of learning the truth as to the actual road taken. ' Certainly eight stadia ' is what an observer who did not wish to exaggerate might estimate the distance between the present Tophana and Cassim Pasha to be, and if my suggestion as to Leonard's measure be accepted, then the two writers are substantially in accord. Barbaro gives the distance traversed as three Italian—equal to two English—miles. The evidence as to distance, therefore, is somewhere between eight stadia and two miles.

The evidence as to the place from which the ships started is important also. Barbaro states that they left the water at Diplokionion, a place which he describes as two miles from the city (say, one and a third English mile), and therefore not so far as the Double Columns ; Ducas, from a place ' below Diplokionion ; ' Pusculus :[2] 'Columnis haud longe a geminis ; ' Phrantzes, ἐκ τοῦ ὄπισθεν μέρους τοῦ Γάλατα : a phrase which certainly does not imply that the route travelled was so far from the walls of Galata as Dolma Bagshe is. Chalcondylas and Philelphus[3] say, ' behind the hill which overhangs Galata.'

It is interesting to determine where Diplokionion or the Double Column was. It has usually been considered to be Beshiktash, and Cantemir so translates it. Professor van Millingen places it rather in Dolma Bagshe bay—say, half a mile south of Beshiktash.[4] The late Dr. Dethier says[5] that the present Cabatash and Tophana were formerly called Diplokionion and that, as he expresses it, 'Columnae et incolae emigrarunt post

[1] Other contemporary authors give us distances which enable us to get an approximate length of a stadium : e.g. Chalcondylas says that the walls of Constantinople were 111 stadia, or a little over 13 English miles, in circuit. Critobulus gives the total length of walls as 126 stadia and the length of the landward walls as 48. Both his figures are somewhat too high, unless they are intended to give the measure of the sinuosities of the walls. But the statements both of Chalcondylas and Critobulus as well as that of Leonard, if his intention is to represent a measure about a ninth or tenth of a furlong, are all pretty nearly accurate.
[2] Book iv. line 550.   [3] Book ii. line 974.
[4] *Byzantine Constantinople*, p. 234.   [5] Note to Pusculus, p. 237.

adventum Turcorum in suburbium Beshiktash.' I am unaware of his authority for this statement. It appears to me certain that the Columns were at Dolma Bagshe, which may be called the southern extremity of Beshiktash. They are so marked in Bondelmonte's map made in 1422. It is worth nothing that none of the authors place the starting-point at the Columns except Barbaro, and that even he qualifies his statement by explaining that it was two Italian miles from the city.

Having thus seen the evidence (1) as to the distance travelled and (2) as to the starting-point, we may ask What was the probable route? Dr. Paspates in his 'Poliorkia'[1] discusses the question, and sensibly remarks that the shortest route would be preferred, unless there were exceptional difficulties. Now the difficulties by the Tophana route are decidedly less than by the other. The distance is less by half than that of the Dolma Bagshe route and the height to be surmounted is 250 feet against 350. Paspates suggests the route I have adopted—namely, from Tophana. Dr. Mordtmann adopts the Dolma Bagshe route and objects to that of Tophana because the Turkish ships could have been seen by the Christian ships at the chain and that these were strong enough to hinder the undertaking, especially as the sultan had no batteries on the eastern side to oppose the fleet.[2]

To this view—and anything suggested by so careful an observer as Dr. Mordtmann is deserving of attention—is to be opposed (1) that the point of departure adopted by him at Dolma Bagshe could also be seen from the chain, though of course not so distinctly as at Tophana; (2) that though there was no battery above Tophana, there was one above the eastern end of Galata walls, and probably, as Dethier suggests, very nearly on the site now occupied by the Crimean Memorial Church; (3) that the height to be surmounted is lower by nearly a hundred feet than by the Dolma Bagshe route; (4) that the distance to be traversed is less than half by the Tophana route than that from Dolma Bagshe; (5) that it is not by any means clear that the Christian ships could have hindered the execution of the project, since the Genoese were absolutely powerless on land outside their own walls. It may, however, be true, as Ducas asserts, that the Genoese alleged that they could have stopped the transit if they had wished. But the allegation, if true, at least implies that they knew what was going on, and, as mentioned in my text, Mahomet was ready for opposition.

[1] P. 138.
[2] 'Die letzten Tage von Byzanz,' in the *Mitteilungen des deutschen Exkursions-Klubs in Konstantinopel.*

The shortest distance ought to furnish one indication of the route. The evidence as to what that distance is stated to be should furnish another, and the starting-point of the expedition a third. I claim that the eight stadia of Critobulus and the eight or nine given by Leonard are not greatly at variance with the three Italian or two English miles of Barbaro, and that from the evidence of these three witnesses we may say that the distance travelled was about a mile or a little over. Now the actual distance by the Tophana route is a little over a mile and ' certainly eight stadia.'

The indication gathered from the starting-point is that the ships left the water well below the Double Columns. But I submit that there is no place suitable for such an undertaking as that under consideration between Dolma Bagshe and Tophana. The indications, therefore, drawn from the place of departure, if they do not point to the Tophana route, are not at variance with it.

As to the precise place at which the ships arrived on the Golden Horn Critobulus is probably again the safest guide. They came to the shore τῶν ψυχρῶν ὑδάτων—that is, to the Cool Waters, otherwise called the Springs and now known as Cassim Pasha. There they were launched into the Golden Horn. The statement is confirmed incidentally by several authors who mention that the fleet was opposite a portion of the walls where stands the Spigas Gate—that is, the gate leading to the passage across.[1] Cassim Pasha itself was sometimes spoken of as Spigae.[2] Andreossi (in 1828) suggests that the ships started from Baltaliman or rather the bay of Stenia, but the only evidence in favour of this route is the statement of Ducas—who more than any other contemporary is constantly inaccurate—that they started from the Sacred Mouth (a name usually employed to designate the north end of the Bosporus but used by Ducas for the part between Roumelia and Anatolia-Hissar) and that they reached the harbour opposite the monastery of St. Cosmas which was outside the landward walls.

Dr. Mordtmann and Professor van Millingen think that the balance of evidence is in favour of the route from Dolma Bagshe. The route which Dr. Paspates and Dr. Dethier approved is that which appears to me also not only the most probable but to have the balance of evidence in its favour. The tract along which the ships were hauled formed the short arm of a cross, the long one of which was the road along the ridge now known as the Grande Rue de Péra: the two giving the modern Greek name to the city, of Stavrodromion.

---

[1] εἰς πυγάς.   [2] *Esquisse de Constantinople*, by Dr. Mordtmann, sect. 71–75.

APPENDIX IV

THE INFLUENCE OF RELIGION ON GREEKS AND MOSLEMS RESPECTIVELY

In reading the contemporary authors of the period between the Latin and the Moslem conquests the following questions suggest themselves: What was the influence of the Orthodox Church upon the people of the capital and of the empire? What was its value as a national ethical force? and how did its influence as such a force compare with that of Islam?

Before attempting a reply to these questions certain facts must be noted. It must be remembered that the empire was composed of many races and languages. In the Balkan peninsula alone there were always at least half a dozen races with as many different forms of speech. In Asia Minor the component elements of the population were even still more numerous. The Church largely aided the State in the endeavour to keep these divergent elements under the rule of the empire. Her special task was to change the various races into Christians. But even when this task was completed to the extent of causing them all to profess Christianity they retained their racial characteristics and traditions. These characteristics, though widely various, may be classified in two categories. In other words, it may be said that among all the different populations of the empire there were two streams of tendency: the Hellenic and the Asiatic. The tendency and influence of each were markedly present in the church from the first days of the empire and continued until 1453. Greek influence left an indelible impress upon the Orthodox Church. But while it influenced the other races of the empire, the Greeks themselves fell to some extent under the Asiatic influence. Greek tendency was always to make of Christianity a philosophy rather than a religion. The opposite tendency, which I have called Asiatic and which corresponds fairly well to what Matthew Arnold called Hebraic, had less enduring results upon the population but was nevertheless constantly present. The two tendencies were constantly striving one against the other within the Church.

Greek influence (1) largely aided in the formation of a philosophical body of theology, (2) helped to perpetuate paganism and develop a paganistic tendency, and (3) deprived the Church of the religious enthusiasm which the Asiatic tendency might have provided and has often inspired. The service of the Greeks in reference to the formation of a body of theological philosophy is too completely recognised to require any notice. Greek influence helped to perpetuate paganism in various ways. It was naturally always most powerful in the Balkan peninsula, its chief centres being Athens and Salonica, but had great weight also in the western cities of Asia Minor. Greek polytheists in pre-Christian times were not opposed to the recognition of other gods than those worshipped by themselves. How this rational toleration, which was as utterly opposed to the exclusive spirit of Asiatic Christianity as to that of Islam itself, tended to perpetuate paganism will be best understood by recalling the early history of the later Roman empire. The population under the rule of New Rome had for the most part adopted the profession of Christianity because it was the religion of the State. Most people found little difficulty in conforming to the demands of the emperor and became Christians. Under such circumstances Christianity did not conquer paganism : it absorbed without destroying it. Just as in Central Asia many tribes who have come under the power of Russia have been ordered to elect whether they would declare themselves Christians or Moslems, so in the days of the early Christian emperors, and especially under the laws of Theodosius the choice was between a profession of the Court creed or remaining in some form of paganism where its professors would be subject to various disabilities and persecutions. The conformity which resulted was curious. The people became nominally Christians, but they brought with them into the Church most of their old superstitions. Their ancient deities were not discarded but were either secretly worshipped or came to be regarded as Christian saints : their festal days became the commemoration days of Christian events. I do not forget that something of the same kind went on in the Western Church and that the missionaries, finding themselves unable to persuade their converts to abandon their old observances, deftly adopted them into the Christian Church. But all that was done in this direction in the West was small in comparison with what went on in the East. St. George took the place of Apollo. St. Nicholas replaced Poseidon. The highest hill in every neighbourhood on the mainland and in every island of the Marmora and the Aegean had fittingly been crowned with a temple dedicated to the God of Day. The great dragon, Night, had been overcome by Helios. To this day it is almost universally true that all the peaks in question have an Orthodox church which has taken the place of the temple of Apollo and is dedicated to his successor, St. George.[1] In like manner the temples built in fishing villages to Poseidon have almost invariably been dedicated to St. Nicholas. The episcopal staff of a Greek bishop has the two serpents' heads associated with Aesculapius. The distribution of holy bread at funerals, the processions to shrines, to sacred groves, to Hagiasmas or holy wells, and numerous other customs of the Orthodox Church, are survivals or rudimentary forms of paganism.[2]

Asiatic influence was more powerful in Constantinople than in Greece. The explanation of this fact is to be found in the remoteness of Athens from the capital; in the greater intellectual life of Constantinople; in the presence of many leaders of thought from the cities in Asia Minor under Asiatic influence, and in the traditional Roman sentiment derived from the influence of Latin rulers, literature, and tradition. The iconoclastic movement towards the end of the eighth century was a genuine attempt to get rid of pagan practices. It failed because of the base character of some of its imperial supporters, because of the opposition of the less cultured western church, and because the Empress Irene, a native of Athens and brought up among the traditions of paganism which still lived on in what was then a remote part of the empire, placed herself at the head of the Hellenic party and with her strong will was able to prevent any reformation being accomplished.

But paganism in Greece and Asia Minor lived on long after the

---

[1] Mr. Theodore Bent, who had paid greater attention to the archæology of the Greek Islands and to their present condition than any other Englishman, called my attention to the fact that the churches on the highest peaks not dedicated to St. George were usually dedicated to St. Elias, or to the Transfiguration, and suggested that there may have been a confusion in the minds of the islanders between Elias and Helios, the aspirate in the latter word being silent in modern Greek.

[2] Valuable suggestions and information are given by Mr. Sathas in reference to the survival of paganism in *Documents inédits*, Athens, vol. i. Lord Beaconsfield in *Lothair* shows a true insight into the actual condition of Greek Christianity when he represents Mr. Phœbus as describing what he proposes to do with an island which he has leased in the Aegean. He will restore paganism, will set up the statue which he has sculptured of the American Theodora in a grove of laurel still much resorted to, and will have processions in the beautiful pagan fashion. The people are still 'performing unconsciously the religious ceremonies of their ancestors.' *Lothair*, ch. xxvii. and xxviii.

time of Irene. The Hellenistic influence struggled hard against the Asiatic or what was not unfitly called the Roman party. When we come to the last century of the empire's history, we find its influence triumphant, and this to such an extent that we see Plethon and his school, as the representatives of a phase of Greek thought, dreaming of the restoration of paganism. I conclude, therefore, that Greek influence helped to perpetuate paganism or at least a paganistic tendency.

Greek influence deprived the Church of the religious enthusiasm which the study of the Old Testament has often inspired. It must always be remembered that the Greeks had the New Testament in a language they could understand. Every one recognises that a large part of the intellectual movement in England during the sixteenth and seventeenth centuries was due to the translation of the sacred Scriptures into the vernacular. But there has been no period in the history of the Greek race since the compilation of the Christian record in which the Greeks have not had the advantage of a familiarity with the Gospels and the writings of St. Paul. They knew the New Testament well. Its Greek was colloquial. But they were less familiar with the Old Testament. Although frequent allusions are made to the stories in the older book by many writers during the later centuries of the Church's history, the Septuagint was written in a language less understood by the people. Indications that the Old Testament influenced men's conduct are lacking, and point either to a want of familiarity with it, or to some other cause which made its influence less than that which it has had on other peoples. The passionate zeal of our own Puritans, with their application of Jewish history to English politics ; the political principles of the defenders of civil liberty in America ; the fierce enthusiasm of the Scotch Covenanters, of the Dutch Protestants, and of the Boers, were all derived from the Old rather than from the New Testament. The influence of the more ancient book might have been great upon the Asiatic party if its writings had been as familiar as those of the New Testament. As it was, though its influence was undoubtedly felt, that derived from the New Testament became more powerful as the centuries went on, ultimately triumphed, and led to results which assist us to furnish an answer to the questions under examination.

What, then, was the general effect of the double stream of influence on the members of the Orthodox Church ? The familiarity of the subjects of the empire with the text of the New Testament combined with the intellectual genius of the Greek race led them to take a delight in the study of the philosophical questions which the New Testament, and especially the writings of St. Paul, suggest. To take a keen interest in any metaphysical study is for any people a gain, and it is none the less so when the subject is theology. Now the interest of the population in theological questions was at all times absorbing.

When these questions were settled by the Church, the Asiatic influence made itself felt and produced a conservatism, a stubborn refusal to change or abandon any position, which the more fickle-minded or philosophical Greek could never have displayed. Each of the two tendencies exerted its influence upon the conduct of the Orthodox Church. Speaking generally, we may say that all its members were devotedly attached to their faith—or perhaps it would be more exact to say, to their creeds. Of political questions in the modern sense they knew little. In their ignorance of foreign nations, questions of external policy hardly interested them, but the intellectual life of the country—mostly confined to the great cities, to Nicaea, Salonica, Smyrna, and above all the capital— was fully awake to theological questions. While ready to discuss, they maintained every dogma and every article with a persistence which increased as the years rolled on. They took a keen interest in any question whenever any heretic appeared who attempted to throw doubt on what the Church had decided. They were ready to die for their faith.

The writers of the Greek Church show by abundant examples that they and the people believed in the existence of a God who lives and rules the world and the conduct of individuals. Their very superstitions afford sufficient evidence of such a belief. He was an avenging God. Black Death and Plague are described as the instruments of His vengeance. Omens and signs in a variety of forms were the means by which He, or some of the Hierarchy of Heaven, intimated to the faithful what was about to happen. The absence of omens was a sign of His displeasure or His abandonment of their cause.

The men who discussed the religious questions which arose during the later as well as the earlier centuries of the empire regarded them as tremendous realities. The discussions were not mere exchange of opinions or formulating of phrases : not mere academical disputations, among the learned of the time, of meta-physical abstractions, but were often careful attempts to solve the insoluble. The results were of supreme importance. If you believed aright, you would be saved. If you disbelieved or believed wrongfully, you would be damned in the next world and, as far as the believers could accomplish it, in this also. Unless the eagerness, the passion, the deadly Asiatic earnestness of the religious discussions or wranglings be realised, no true conception can be formed of fourteenth and fifteenth century life in Constantinople.

Contemporary writers supply abundant and indisputable evidence that, from the patriarch downwards, the members of the Greek Church attached overwhelming importance to the correctness of their orthodoxy. The utmost care about correct definitions was taken by the Church to check paganism. The miscreant was a worse offender than the man who disregarded the ordinary laws of morality. Souls were to be saved by right belief. As in the Western Church, whosoever would be saved, it was necessary before all things that he should accept the right formulas. But the Eastern gave greater prominence to the formulas than even the Western. While the Roman Church attached most importance to its Catholicity and to the necessity of propagating the faith, the Greek Church always prided itself rather on its Orthodoxy. If the question were whether the empire was Christian, and if the test of being a Christian nation were the jealous guardianship of every dogma in the precise manner that it had been formulated by the Councils of the Church, then the Orthodox Church, to which the inhabitants of the capital and empire belonged, would take a very high rank among Christian nations.

It is not possible to doubt that the keen interest taken in the discussion of religious questions quickened the intellectual development of the population, and in this respect the influence of the Church was purely beneficial. To suggest, as did the historians of the eighteenth century, that the Greeks were at once profoundly theological and profoundly vile is not only to ask that an indictment should be framed against a whole people, but is contrary to general experience and to fact. In spite of the occasional conjunction of theology and immorality in the same individual, the nation which takes a lively interest in the former is not likely to be addicted to the latter.

A strong and, I think, an unanswerable case might be made out to show that the religion of the Orthodox Church beneficially influenced the conduct of men and women in their individual capacity and in their relations one with another. All believed in the doctrine of eternal punishment and in the divine gifts granted to the Church by which punishment might be avoided. In their constant efforts to take advantage of the graces at the disposal of the Church, and in their endeavours to attain the ideal of Christian philosophy, men and women were led by their religion to be more moral, more honest, and more kindly one to another, than they would otherwise have been.   The denunciations of those who had been guilty of unclean conduct, and the constant praise of almsgiving, lead to the conclusion that the Church had so far exercised influence for good.   It had given the citizens of the empire a higher standard of family and social life.   The very stubbornness which the Asiatic tendency supplied, and which led all to resist every attempt to change the formulas of the faith, came in itself to stand the population in good stead after 1453.   Their wranglings on religious questions helped to form a public opinion which prevented any considerable number of Christians from abandoning their religion.   We may safely conclude, therefore, that the Orthodox Church had aided in developing intellectual life, in raising and maintaining a high tone of morality, and in so attaching its members to their religion that when the time of trial came they remained faithful.   It had done more.   While accomplishing these objects it had raised a whole series of heterogeneous races to a higher level of civilisation and had largely contributed to make the empire the foremost and best educated state in Europe.   It had checked the Greek tendency to attachment merely to the city or province and had made patriotism and brotherhood words of wider signification than they possessed in Greece.

It is when we pass from the influence of the Church on the conduct of the individual, to ask what was the value of its ethical teaching in regard to national life, whether it ever set before the nation a lofty national ideal, or whether it ever caused a wave of religious enthusiasm which influenced the nation as a whole, that we find the Orthodox Church during the later centuries of its history greatly lacking.   Religion was to guide the conduct of the individual and to save him from eternal punishment. There was little or no conception of it as an aid to national righteousness.   There was no inspiration for national action, such as a study of the Old Testament has often supplied.   There was never any great religious fervour for the accomplishment of an object because it was believed to be the divine will.   I am not thinking of such religious enthusiasm as led to the abolition of the slave trade or of slavery, to the temperance movement or to that for the diminution of crime and the reform of criminals or for the bettering the condition of the labouring classes and the like. These are social developments belonging to later years, which may be credited, in part at least, to the account of Christianity. It is in the contemporary religious movements of other portions of the Christian world that the measure of the national religious life of the empire must be taken. The series of Crusades enables a comparison of this kind to be fairly made, though other standards of comparison suggest themselves. The empire under the rule of Constantinople had a greater interest in checking the progress of the Moslems in Syria, Egypt, and Asia Minor than had the Western nations. But in the whole course of Byzantine history, though the empire steadily resisted the Mahometan armies, there was no display of religious enthusiasm to lend its aid at any time comparable with that which was shown in the West. An Eastern Peter the Hermit could not have aroused the members of the Orthodox Church. No Godfrey de Bouillon could have found statesmen in the East to have espoused his cause. If leaders had been forthcoming, followers would have been wanting. Though the statesmen of the West were influenced by many motives to join in the Crusades, they, too, were largely under the sway of religious fervour. The nations of which they were the leaders did display such fervour for the accomplishment of objects which were believed to be in conformity with the divine will. As for the great mass of crusaders, it cannot be doubted that they took the cross mainly because they believed that they were doing the will of God. Absence of precaution, deficiency of organisation, unreasoning fanatical zeal, unreasonable and senseless haste to come into conflict with the infidel, the army of child crusaders, the sacrifices men made of their property, most of the incidents, indeed, which make up the narratives of the Crusades, show that the Soldiers of the Cross were steeped in religious fervour, and were in a condition of pious exaltation. They were, as they called themselves, an army of God. They were willing to face any danger, and to go to certain death for their Master's cause.

The Greek was always ready to defend a dogma. He entertained a profound dislike and contempt for Christian heretics who were usually less well informed than he and were generally fanatically in earnest, but he was more tolerant of heresy than the men of the West, who in the Middle Ages bestowed on heretics a fanatical hatred and contempt greater even than that felt towards the infidel, and like that entertained in the present day towards anarchists as enemies of the human race.

No cause ever presented itself to the Greek as capable of arousing such fervour as the soldiers of the West displayed. Religion having become a New Testament philosophy, and the Old Testament inspiration in national life having been lost, there was little care for its propagation. The missionary age of the

Orthodox Church in the empire, as soon as the Hellenic influence
triumphed over the Asiatic, had passed away. Since the days of
Cyril and Methodius, the great apostles of the ninth century, the
Church could show few conversions and few serious attempts at
conversion. That the Church should be orthodox was apparently
enough. There was no attempt to enlarge its area. Christianity
appeared to be regarded by one party as the best system of
philosophy, and by the other, much as the Jew regarded his
religion, as a sacred treasure to be kept for his own use and not to
be offered to outside unbelievers. His religion in the later centuries
never really moved the Greek to engage in missions. Except in
regard to personal conduct, to almsgiving, kindness to his fellow-
members of the Orthodox Church, and personal and commercial
morality, he was incapable of religious sentiment. Something due
to his race, something to his traditions, and something to his
theological training, made Christianity, except as a philosophical
system, sit lightly upon him and failed to make it a powerful
national force. Then, as now, the Greek members of the Orthodox
Church could not sympathise with or even comprehend the
religious sentiment which has led the men of the West, whether
acknowledging the jurisdiction of Rome or not, to undertake
great movements, or even war, in defence of an object whose only
recommendation was that it had right on its side.

In spite of the fact that in the empire and throughout Asia
Minor nationality and religion were, as indeed they are to this
day, always confounded or regarded as synonymous terms, Orthodox Christianity was unable to add a powerful religious sentiment
to the defence of the empire. As a force inducing them to resist
the encroachments of Islam, like that which influenced our
fathers against Spain or the Ironsides against Charles, I doubt
whether it was ever of much value. We have seen a patriarch
writing apparently with great satisfaction that the Church was
allowed to retain its liberty under Turkish rule. Throughout
the long centuries of struggle against Islam, there were many
Christians who transferred themselves to the jurisdiction of the
sultans in order that they might live in peace. The individual
aspect of Christianity was regarded, not the national.

It is when the influence of the Church upon the spirit of the
population of the empire is compared with that of Mahometanism
upon the Turkish hordes that its weakness as a dynamic force is
most plainly seen. Mahometanism, like Christianity in Western
lands and in Russia, is a missionary faith. Islam as a fighter's
religion, with its fatalism, its rewards of the most sensual pleasures

that a barbarian is capable of conceiving, and its ennobling teaching that fighting the battles of the faith is fighting for God, has produced the most terrible armies that have ever come out from among any of the races among which its converts have been made. Islam in the twentieth century has spent much of its original force, because doubt as to its divine origin has entered into the hearts of its ablest members. Those among them who have seen or have otherwise learned the results of Christian civilisation instinctively and almost unconsciously judge the two religions by their fruits. Such men either become entirely neglectful of the ceremonious duties which their religion imposes, or, if they profess to have become more intent in their religious convictions than before, perform their ceremonies with a sub-consciousness that their religion is not better than that of the unbelievers. In whichever category they fall they lose their belief in the exclusively divine character of their creed. Nor do the studies in astronomy, medicine, geology, and other modern sciences fail to implant a similar and even a greater amount of scepticism in the Mahometan than they have done in the Christian mind. While visits to foreign countries and scientific studies are undertaken by few, their influence as a leaven is great.

In the centuries preceding the Moslem conquest of Constantinople scepticism was absent among both the Christian and Mahometan masses. The Ottoman Turks in the fifteenth century, more perhaps than at any other time, were full of the zeal of new converts. They were in a period of conquest which stimulated them Many, perhaps most of them, believed in their divine mission. They were the chosen people, whose duty it was to give idolaters the choice of conversion to the one true faith or of death, to subdue all nations who accepted either the Old or the New Testament but refused to accept the prophethood of Mahomet, and to treat them as rayahs or cattle. Their spiritual pride caused them to think of those who professed any form of Christianity as being inferior and divinely predestined to occupy a hopelessly lower plane, as having only the privilege that their lives should be spared so long as they paid tribute and accepted subjection. Their central, overpowering belief was that they had a mission from God and the Prophet, and the result of such belief was fearlessness of danger. It was their duty to kill idolaters and subjugate Christians. Whatever happened to them in the fulfilment of this duty was not their business but God's. He would bring about the predestined victory or the temporary defeat; but in either case it was well with them. If they lived, the plunder of their enemies was their reward; if they died, then heaven and the houris.

When this attitude of mind is compared with that which existed among the members of the Orthodox Church, we see at once great divergences between the two forms of faith as national ethical forces. On the one hand, the student of comparative religions must give that Church credit for having aided the growth of the population in the Christian virtues; for having given them an inspiration enabling them to suffer and to hope, for having preserved learning, developed national intelligence, cultivated exact thought, for having promoted philosophical studies and in various ways guarded the treasures of classic times until the rest of Europe was ready to receive them. On the other hand, such student, while recognising that Mahometanism prevents progress by assigning an inferior position to woman, by inculcating a spirit of fatalism which mischievously affects almost every act of the believer's life and keeps the Turkish race in poverty, and by presenting a lower ideal of life, will have to admit that its influence as a religious force, with its ever-present sense of a Supreme Power, omnipotent to save or to destroy, was far greater than that of the Orthodox Church, and that the Church failed to supply the stimulus of a national inspiration comparable with that of the hostile creed, or with that furnished by Christianity to the men of the West.

INDEX

ABASSID dynasty used symbol of the Crescent, 141 n.

Achaia, principality of, 40

Acropolitas, George (historian), 16; at the Union ceremony at Lyons in 1274, 34

Agriculture: Turks have never taken kindly to, 58

Alans, Asiatic tribe, 43 sqq., 47, 61, 64

Alexander of Sinope, 317

Alexis, Emperor of Trebizond (1222), 9; called himself Grand Comnenus and Emperor of the Faithful Romans, 387

Ali, chief of a Turkish band : shared in Othman's raids on the empire, 61

Ali Pasha (grand vizier of Bajazed), 134, 136

Alphonse of Aragon, 129

Amadeo of Savoy, 91

Amer Bey, standard-bearer of Mahomet II., 289

Ameroukes, George (mathematician): at the court of Mahomet II., 393

Amogavares, Spanish mercenaries, 42

Amurath, son of Orchan. See Murad

Anatolia-Hissar, 120, 126, 164 n., 213, 215

Anatolians: defeat of their attack in the siege, 337 sqq.; their discipline and daring, 338

Andronicus II., Emperor (1282-1328 : son and successor of Michael VIII.): hostility to Unionist party, 37; question as to marriage of his son Michael, 37 sq.; Latin attempts against his empire, 38; calls to his aid Roger de Flor and the Catalan Grand Company, 39; their actions caused introduction of Turks into Europe, 49; loss of Imperial territory through Othman's attacks, 61; Turks cross Dardanelles, 61 sq.; Andronicus's son Michael co-emperor with his father, 65, 67; quarrels

between Andronicus II., and Andronicus his grandson, 67 sq.; Andronicus II. abdicates and ends his days as a monk, 68

Andronicus III. (Palaeologus), Emperor (1382-41 ; son of Michael IX.; successor to Andronicus II.): quarrels with his grandfather and causes him to abdicate, 67 sq; constant warfare with Turks, 68; the emperor seeks aid from the West, with little result, 69; his death (1341), 70

Andronicus, son of John V.: regent during his father's absence, 92; his boyish compact with Sultan Murad's son, and its punishment, 94; retaliation on his father, 94 sq.

Angora (1402), 112; details of the battle, 142 sqq.; result of Timour's victory, 147

Anjou, Charles of (King of Sicily): designs restoration of Latin empire, 34; his forces find other employment, 36

Apocaukus: his strife with John Cantacuzenus, 71 sq.; hired (1343) a Turkish fleet and army, 100

Arabs: their various attempts to capture New Rome, 230

Aragon, Frederic of, 38

Aragon, Peter of, 36 : his mercenary troops, 41

Archers, Turkish, 135; their excellence, 167, 251

Aretinus, Leonard: enthusiasm for Greek, 405

Armenia, king of, 38

Arquebusers : Anatolian, 167 ; German, 173

Arrows carrying flaming materials, used by Timour, 146

Arsenius, patriarch: excommunicated Michael VIII. for cruel treatment of the boy John Lascaris, 26;